Christian Reformed
Church Order
Commentary

Henry DeMoor

FAITH
ALIVE®
Christian Resources

Grand Rapids, Michigan

ISBN 978-1-59255-533-8

10 9 8 7 5 4 3 2 1

Mixed Sources
Product group from well-managed
forests and other controlled sources
www.fsc.org Cert no. SW-COC-002283
© 1996 Forest Stewardship Council
FSC

Dedication

When I completed my doctoral dissertation in 1986, I dedicated it to my wife, Ina, as it should be, and noted my gratitude to her and the remainder of our nuclear family, our four children, Renee, Tanya, Larissa, and Ryan.

Now that I have completed this commentary, I need to dedicate it to my other family, the people of the Christian Reformed Church in North America (hereafter: CRCNA). This church warmly received me when I arrived as an eleven-year-old Dutch immigrant kid in Strathroy, Ontario. It provided me with a challenging education based on a solid Christian worldview at the liberal arts college it owns and operates, Calvin College, in Grand Rapids, Michigan. It steered me and prodded me toward ministry while at its seminary, Calvin Theological Seminary, on the very same campus. It removed a lot of rough edges and taught me a great deal about preaching, pastoral ministry, church governance and a host of other things while I ministered in Duncan, British Columbia, and Edmonton, Alberta. And, as if that weren't enough, it placed its confidence in me and allowed me to serve as a seminary professor, administrator, and as an adviser to the church, its people, and its assemblies, for no less than twenty-four years. So this is the church that received me, nourished me, kicked me out of its snug nest to contribute what I could to its mission, and then just kept on encouraging and blessing. Warts and all, this is my family too, and to this family I dedicate this book.

I am grateful to the Administration and Board of Trustees of Calvin Theological Seminary for giving me a final sabbatical year to write this commentary. I thank my good friends and colleagues in ministry, Leonard Hofman and Kathleen Smith, for cheerfully offering critique as I wrote. And I am grateful, above all, to the Lord of the church who blesses and strengthens this family of mine on its pilgrimage through the ages.

Contents

Preface

It has been four decades since the last commentary on the Church Order of the CRCNA saw the light of day. Zondervan Publishing House published the final edition of Idzerd Van Dellen and Martin Monsma's *Revised Church Order Commentary* in 1967; that edition's fourth and last printing appeared in 1970. In the meantime, of course, there have been a few versions of what is known as a *Manual of Christian Reformed Church Government*: William Brink and Richard De Ridder's in 1979, 1980, and 1987; Richard De Ridder and Leonard Hofman's in 1994; David Engelhard and Leonard Hofman's in 2001; and Peter Borgdorff's in 2008. These manuals do have some brief commentary. Their primary purpose, however, is that of ordering materials: compiling various policy decisions of synod and listing them under appropriate Church Order articles, thus making them readily accessible for the church in one place. They aim to tell us what we are to do. Commentaries, however, have the opposite purpose. They also refer to various policy decisions, but their chief intent is to provide a context for the rules of the church. That context may be theological, historical, practical, or any combination thereof, whatever seems most helpful in illuminating why the CRCNA does what it does.

It is important to know the "why" behind the rules. If that's not clear to us, we are not truly privy to the wisdom of our tradition. How easy, then, to fall off one of two cliffs on the sides of the road. The cliff on the right is deadly legalism. We follow the rules for what they are, not why we have them. It's like parents answering their children's "Why?" with "because I said so." The cliff on the left is deadly anarchy. We don't like rules, period. It's the mission that counts and we'll do it our way. It's like parents saying to children: "Do whatever you feel is right." It's the so-called "freedom" that reminds us of a goldfish jumping out of its bowl to gain more "space." The church needs both manuals and commentaries. It needs to stay on the road between the cliffs and follow the rules, but also follow the precious principles they represent—principles that sometimes "fade in time" and need to live again. My hope is that this commentary will be that kind of vital contribution to our church's pilgrimage.

The articles of the Church Order that appear in this commentary are in the latest version: the one that has been updated by Synod 2010. The material that synods have decided to place in the Supplements to the articles of the Church Order does not appear. Instead, I have only cited what I considered to be relevant to the discussion at hand. For the latest version of the Church Order articles and a complete listing of the supplemental material, the reader is referred to the current Church Order booklet available in PDF format at www.crcna.org under "synodical resources."

For each article, I provide some exposition, a deductive sketch that crisply states our modus operandi. The sketch is followed by some questions and answers, an inductive section that also seeks to get at the "why" of our rules. These questions have come to me from different sources over many years of teaching the discipline of church polity at Calvin Theological Seminary: from students, of course, but also from churches, assemblies, and individuals. A few of these questions with my answers have been previously published in articles or presentations. None are "dreamed up" or fictional. They truly reflect the reality of church life in the last quarter-century.

All Scripture references are rendered in Today's New International Version (TNIV).

It is my hope that this book will be helpful for churches, assemblies, students, and ministry practitioners. May all our ways be fitting to who we are in Christ, by grace, as a people of Christian and Reformed persuasion in twenty-first century North America.

Introduction

Article 1

a. The Christian Reformed Church, confessing its complete subjection to the Word of God and the Reformed creeds as a true interpretation of this Word, acknowledging Christ as the only head of his church, and desiring to honor the apostolic injunction that in the churches "everything should be done in a fitting and orderly way" (1 Cor. 14:40), regulates its ecclesiastical organization and activities in the following articles.

b. The main subjects treated in this Church Order are: The Offices of the Church, The Assemblies of the Church, The Task and Activities of the Church, and The Admonition and Discipline of the Church.

In this introductory article of the Church Order, the CRCNA insists on three things: complete subjection to the Word of God and the Reformed creeds, the confession of Christ as the only head of the church, and the desire to have order, some kind of regulation in its affairs. This latter desire—and how it blends with the first two convictions—is not obvious to all Christians.

The Church: Spirit-Led, Yet Ordered

The church is the Spirit-led community of those chosen in Christ to be God's people in his world. But it is also a human institution fully embedded in all aspects of created reality. The tension between these two truths permeates church polity without ever finding complete resolution. On the one hand, the church must constantly be reminded that it is the Lord's. On the other, it must recognize that it must structure itself and order its affairs in appropriate ways. This is precisely what the apostle Paul held before the Corinthian church in New Testament days. When some found ways to divide that congregation as if it were merely a human organization with its accompanying divisions and power struggles, Paul insisted that the church was not of Apollos, nor of himself, but of Christ as the only Lord and Master. When others claimed that they were spiritual enough to be "above the law" for worship, Paul insisted that God is a God of order and proceeded to present his prescriptions for their gatherings.

Paul's utterance in 1 Corinthians 14:40—a favorite among church order specialists—that "everything should be done in a fitting and orderly way" is more than just a "proof text" for rules. In fact, it holds the above-mentioned tension within it. It speaks of orderliness but also of fittingness, of conduct that is becoming, appropriate to the church's true nature, namely, that in all its ways it point to Christ, its Lord. The same is true of Article 30 of the Belgic Confession. On the one hand, it suggests orderliness by stating that officebearers must be chosen according to the rules. On the other, it insists that the "true church ought to be governed according to the spiritual order that our Lord has taught us in his Word."

In the same way, John Calvin argues in his *Institutes of the Christian Religion* that "some form of organization is necessary in all human society to foster the common peace and maintain concord," and, accordingly, churches must have certain laws. Without them, he claims, "their very sinews disintegrate and they are wholly deformed and scattered" (4.10.27). But the point of such laws is "that the people who are governed become accustomed to obedience to God and to right discipline" (4.10.28) and that "ceremonies . . . ought to lead us straight to Christ" (4.10.29). The church, says Calvin, requires a kind of "order and decorum" that is not specifically taught in the Scriptures (because it is "not necessary to salvation"), but one that must be there nonetheless for "the upbuilding of the church." Such "order and decorum" can be "variously accommodated to the customs of each nation and age." There is no call for rigidity here. One may "change and abrogate traditional practices" and "establish new ones," and often "love will best judge what may hurt or edify." On the other hand, all such practices and rules must be "tested against" more "general rules" that can clearly be "drawn from Scripture" and are, therefore, "wholly divine." In this matter of its polity, the church may not be capricious about its rules, nor merely take its cue from society at large, but must be certain that its "human constitutions . . . are founded upon God's authority" (4.10.30). In Calvin's teaching, therefore, there is clearly a similar tension. He favors "useful observances" when they contribute to the "upbuilding of the church." He charges us not to require certain things "too fastidiously of others," not to elevate law to the level of "superstition," and not, as churches, to "despise another because of diversity of outward discipline." There is a measure of freedom in choosing laws, but, again, they must be "edifying" and in tune with principles clearly taught in God's Word (4.10.32). The challenge, apparently, in every age, is to know the "general rules" and be creative about specifics.

The Church: Human but Christ-Ruled

In some ways church law inevitably reflects the particular political flavor of the environment, whether that be monarchical, aristocratic, or democratic. On the other hand, in its focus and intent, church law must always be *christocratic*. It must reflect the fact that—whatever else it may be in any age—the church is always and ever a community of the King, a Christ-ruled fellowship.

From the beginning, there have been those in the Christian church who have insisted that order, regulation, and church law of any kind is out of place among God's people. Rudolf Sohm and Emil Brunner are good examples, claiming that church law is inevitably a "substitute" Christians invent when they have failed to experience the fullness of the Holy Spirit among them. So beginning with Constantine in the fourth century, if not earlier, they claim, the church has come to be fashioned after the ways of Roman government rather than the Scriptures. For these people, adopting regulations—whatever their character—is in and of itself the downfall of the spiritual church, the work of those who are weak in faith and wish to be led by rules rather than by God himself. This is, in effect, to resolve the tension by declaring it to be nonexistent. The church must be led by the Spirit alone. But that is not what Paul told the Corinthians.

At the same time, there have been some in the Christian church who insisted that order and church law must be drawn from that which governs human society in general. The notion, for example, that our assemblies are governed by Roberts' Rules of Order—though false—is frequently heard among us. When Article 37 insists that "the authority for making and carrying out final decisions remains with the council as the governing body of the church" people often complain, opting for democratic rather than christocratic principles. The very notion that Christ-representatives (members of council) have the final say rubs them the wrong way because culture has taught them otherwise. But again, this is in effect to resolve the tension by declaring it to be nonexistent. The church must be led by rules of ordered society. But that also is not what Paul taught the New Testament church. Order, yes, but then an order that is based on general rules clearly drawn from Scripture.

The Church: One, Holy, Catholic, Apostolic

One way to begin identifying the "general rules" that must hold in every age is to ensure that our church polity is in harmony with what the Nicene Creed confesses to be the four permanent attributes of the church of Christ: its unity, holiness, catholicity, and apostolicity. Reformed church orders, for example, have always spoken of officebearers as more than mere functionaries in congregational life: they are Christ-representatives who lead God's people in their mission as pilgrims sent to bring good news (apostolicity). These orders have always sought to build in a measure of accountability whereby local churches were placed within a larger framework of broader assemblies (catholicity). They have insisted on entire sections devoted to church discipline, upholding wherever possible the purity of the church's life and doctrine (holiness). And they have sought to give expression to the oneness in Christ that must be experienced in every age, whether that be within the local church, specific denomination, or on the larger front of ecumenical relationships (unity).

Beyond these, there are undoubtedly other "general rules" that are clearly drawn from Scripture and now lie at the foundation of the Christian Reformed Church Order. We hope, in what follows, to uncover them at the root of our regulations.

Church Order: Minimal, Flexible, and Biblical

One thing is clear: there must be a minimum of rules. This too is the heritage of the sixteenth-century Reformers. Martin Luther, for example, ceremoniously burned the entire *Codex Iurus Canonici*, the "church order" of his time, along with the papal bull that excommunicated him. From that day on, he insisted that there be few regulations in the church. They have too much potential for binding the conscience. The tragedy of Luther's life, of course, is that disorderliness in the German churches required re-introducing some of the very laws he had so liturgically rejected, and that he never developed a positive polity that would avoid that danger, yet recognize the need for order. This would be the unique contribution of John Calvin. As with Luther, Calvin envisioned a minimum of regulations, flexible ones at that, but these were also to be manifestly biblical. True, the Scriptures do not present a specific church polity good for every age. Nonetheless, they do present a number of guidelines for what is edifying and upbuilding in the church of Christ. As the Belgic Confession, Article 32, puts it,

> although it is useful and good for those who govern the churches to establish and set up a certain order among themselves for maintaining the body of the church, they ought always to guard against deviating from what Christ, our only Master, has ordained for us. Therefore we reject all human innovations and all laws imposed on us, in our worship of God, which bind and force our consciences in any way. So we accept only what is proper to maintain harmony and unity and to keep all in obedience to God.

The Christian Reformed Church Order is a "child" of the Reformation era, specifically, of the Church Order of Dort (1618-1619). Over the years it has changed dramatically, especially in 1965, when it was completely revised. And every year since, it seems, more changes are made. In itself this need not surprise nor concern us. The church is on a pilgrimage. It moves through different times, places, and circumstances. Yet as it does, it must continue to test all of its polity against the general rules drawn from the Word that abides unchanged. It is important, therefore, that church leaders distinguish between that which is transient and that which is permanent, adapting to the times without abandoning the wise experience of the centuries.

That is why grasping the fundamentals of Reformed church polity is so crucial for those who wish to lead wisely in the body of Christ. Sound leadership inspired by God's Word allows Christ truly to be "the only head of his church" and, as the Belgic Confession so poignantly adds, "the only universal bishop" of our souls (Article 31).

Has our denomination always been called the Christian Reformed Church?

No. Here's the history of the name, in its most often used English version, complete with old Dutch nomenclature where applicable, since that was the predominant language during the first few decades of its beginnings in 1857:

1857-1859: None

1859-1861: Holland Reformed Church
(*Hollandsche Gereformeerde Kerk*)

1861-1863: Free Dutch Reformed Church

1863-1880: True Dutch Reformed Church
(*Ware Hollandsche Gereformeerde Kerk*)

1880-1894: Holland Christian Reformed Church
(*Hollandsche Christelijke Gereformeerde Kerk*)

1894 (officially 1904)-present: Christian Reformed Church
(*Christelijke Gereformeerde Kerk*)

When it came time to be legally incorporated, we added the phrase "in North America." This occurred in 1974. All of this courtesy of Richard H. Harms, CRCNA archivist, in his excellent publication *Historical Directory of the Christian Reformed Church* (2004).

What has not changed is the singular word "Church." There have been many attempts to change the official name to the "Christian Reformed Churches in North America," but none has been successful. Those who sought the change wanted to give expression to the "relative autonomy" of individual congregations. Others responded by insisting that we recognize the "organic unity" as a gift of Christ and see ourselves as mutually accountable congregations in a single denomination.

To be quite frank, I am tired of elders who never want anyone to rock the boat. It is almost as if they just want to keep the ship afloat (to stick with the metaphor) and never dream the dreams of visionaries, the ones who want to raise the sails and catch the wind of the Spirit.

Am I wrong to believe that in the CRCNA order trumps vision and renewal and that this will ultimately lead to our demise?

Thanks for a terrific and thoughtful question.

You are certainly not wrong in your desire that our churches live by the Spirit's breath. The church is on a mission in the world, and people of the Reformation gladly acknowledge that a Reformed church (as institution) is to be defined as one that is constantly reforming—being transformed by God's leading.

My problem with your question, to be just as frank, is that it sets things up in such a way that maintaining order necessarily detracts from that exciting mission. But this is true only if that order lacks biblical roots and quenches the Spirit. In my view, a *properly functioning* church order does not dam up the rivers of ministry and outreach. It just sets up the banks of the flowing river so that the water does not move chaotically and without any direction at all. I will not accept an either-or, maintenance *or* mission. I truly believe that we need both, and that the one complements the other. Good, biblically based order keeps us from repeating history's mistakes, prevents us from being overwhelmed by controversies that paralyze us, and actually enhances the mission we're on.

My Th.D. mentor was fond of quoting John Calvin, who once said that we ought not to change from hour to hour. I'm always happy when the sun shines, my mentor would continue, and it's just fine with me when it comes up a little later and goes down a little earlier because of autumn breaking out. On the other hand, it must not go down at noon—that would be altogether too undependable. That's true of liturgy and—as far as I'm concerned—of all order in the church.

Oh, and let me end this by rendering this paraphrase of Mark Twain's famous observation after reading his own obituary; namely, that reports of the CRCNAs imminent demise are "greatly exaggerated."

I. The Offices
of the Church

This first section of the Church Order deals with the *who* of the institutional church: they are its leaders, given by Christ "to equip his people for works of service, so that the body of Christ may be built up until we all reach unity in the faith and in the knowledge of the Son of God and become mature, attaining to the whole measure of the fullness of Christ" (Eph. 4:12-13).

I. The Offices of the Church

Article 2

The church recognizes the offices of minister of the Word, elder, deacon, and ministry associate. These offices differ from each other only in mandate and task, not in dignity and honor.

Offices: Instruments of Christ

The offices are instruments of Christ's ministry and organs of his rule. They constitute his lordship and saving presence among his people as well as his continuing witness to his world. They are "tools of the great workman" (John Calvin) and "beams of light whose source lies elsewhere" (Abraham Kuyper). As ministers, ministry associates, elders, and deacons proclaim the Word, extend the claims of the gospel, nurture faith, bring healing, apply discipline, and show mercy, Christ's promise is fulfilled in their work: "I am with you always, to the very end of the age" (Matt. 28:20).

The authority of officebearers resides in the One they proclaim and exemplify. Though they provide leadership, they do not rule the church "since they are all servants of Jesus Christ, the only universal bishop, and the only head of the church" (Belgic Confession, Article 31). Nor are they mere "functionaries" set aside by the congregation for particular tasks. They are ordained or installed and held "in special esteem" (Belgic Confession, Article 31) precisely because they are the normal channels through which Christ is represented among us and his Word reaches our lives. We need to catch the biblical balance.

The spineless sons of Zebedee once persuaded their mother to pop the impertinent question they dared not ask themselves: "Lord, in your Father's kingdom, may we be at the top of the heap?" Their fellow disciples, Matthew reports with a wink of his eye, became indignant: after all, they wanted to be there themselves. Only somewhat amused by their lust for power, Jesus used the occasion to set them all straight:

> "You know that the rulers of the Gentiles lord it over them, and their high officials exercise authority over them. Not so with you. Instead, whoever wants to become great among you must be your servant, and whoever wants to be first must be your slave—just as the Son of Man did not come to be served, but to serve, and to give his life as a ransom for many" (Matt. 20:25-28).

Can Jesus be clearer? Even so, we liberally sprinkle our vocabulary with such terms as *ruling elders*, *spiritual supervision*, and *headship* without blinking an eyelash. At times, our thinking about church office has taken on a decidedly authoritarian character. Predictably, the opposite then also occurs. Guided by Jesus' words on "servant character," we go through times of anti-authoritarianism where everyone is said to be "equal and at the same level" and officebearers are nothing more than congregational servants appointed to certain tasks.

We have Jesus present, the Lord of the church. Officebearers are not "bishops," as if he is absent from the scene, nor are they "mere agents of the congregation," as if they have no word of authority from the Lord. They are channels of Christ's Word, of the Spirit's leading, of the Father's care. The authority is not absent. It is also not so much "in their person" but rather in the Word, their "ministering work." As Louis Berkhof wrote some seventy years ago:

> But while it is true that Christ exercises His authority in the Church through the officers, this is not to be understood in the sense that He *transfers* His authority to His servants.

21

He Himself rules the Church through all the ages, but in doing this, He uses the officers of the Church as His organs. They have no absolute or independent, but only a derived and ministerial power (*Systematic Theology*, p. 583).

Offices: How Many?

The Scriptures do not provide us with a precise list and number of offices for all time. Some have claimed that references to early church structures in the book of Acts and the Pauline epistles are prescriptive and limit us, for example, to preaching elders, teaching elders, and deacons. Others claim that there is a multiplicity of offices in the New Testament, indicating that the Spirit will provide as needed in every age—and the possibilities are therefore boundless. Still others find that the threefold office of Christ— prophet, priest, and king—must be replicated in the offices of the church: ministers, deacons, and elders. Those three: no more, no less. Most agree that one can discern in Scripture and church history a threefold *pattern* of proclamation, oversight, and service that allows for the number of offices appropriate to the needs of the church, in its judgment, at any particular time of its pilgrimage. There are three dimensions of officebearing, not necessarily three and only three offices.

The earliest provision in the CRCNA, in fact, lists four offices: those of the ministers of the Word, the "doctors," the elders, and the deacons.

As originally conceived by John Calvin, the office of "doctor" was an ecclesiastical office to be held by those called to teach the church and guard it from heresy. This office never quite materialized in the Reformed tradition beyond Calvin's day. By the time the CRCNA began, it was already being defined more precisely as the service of theologians called to train students for the ministry of the Word. Subsequently, the conviction grew that the training of ministers must not be left to the academy or university, but that the church must have its own seminary for that purpose. As a result, the 1965 Church Order dropped the reference to "doctors," insisting that theological professors are nothing other than ministers of the Word with a specialized calling.

For much of its history, the CRCNA struggled to find an "official place" for what was commonly referred to as "lay workers in mission and evangelism," difficult to do if one is committed to "threefold office" as a biblical given. Indeed, the 1965 Church Order asserted resolutely that "the offices *instituted by Christ* in His Church are those of the minister of the

Word, the elder, and the deacon" (italics mine). As pressures mounted to provide official status, the church considered two options: ordaining the lay worker as an elder "with an extraordinary task of evangelism" or as a "minister of the Word-evangelist." Synod 1978 blended these options as it moved to establish a fourth office of evangelist, who shall be "acknowledged as an elder" of the calling church. Synod 1979 then drew the logical conclusion and weakened the 1965 statement by rephrasing it to read: "The church *recognizes* the offices of minister of the Word, elder, deacon, and evangelist" (italics mine). Synods 2003 and 2004 proposed and adopted changing the nomenclature from "evangelist" to "ministry associate," an umbrella term covering the office of evangelist and any others that might yet be adopted.

Parity of the Offices

The second sentence of Article 2 finds its roots in two earlier provisions that read as follows:

> Equality shall be maintained among the ministers of the Word with respect to the duties of their office and in all other matters as far as possible, according to the judgment of the consistory and, if necessary, of the classis. Likewise equality shall be maintained among the elders and deacons.

> There shall be no lordship in God's church, whether of one church over another church, of one minister over other ministers, or of one elder or deacon over other elders or deacons.

In both cases there was room for the interpretation that the principle of "equality" applies only *within* the office of minister of the Word and also only *within* the offices of elder and deacon, not to all officebearers. While notions of *essential* hierarchy are clearly inconsistent with the Reformed tradition, it may be that these earlier provisions reflect the idea of a *functional* hierarchy whereby the ministry of the Word is considered to be more significant to the life of the church than the services of elders and deacons. In any case, Synod 1965 ended all ambiguity in earlier formulations by adopting the current statement that clearly acknowledges a parity of all offices.

Why ordain officebearers at all? Isn't all of this just a leftover of Roman Catholic hierarchy in the life of a Reformed church? Isn't an unordained church school teacher as significant in the faith maturation of our children as their ordained ministers and elders? And don't all members participate in what our 1973 report on ecclesiastical office called "universal office-sharing"?

Your concern is valid. As children of the Reformation, we do not believe that a small professional elite acts as "priests" that stand between God and God's people—so that access to God's grace and his access to our praise is possible only through them. At the same time, we have learned from the error of the sixteenth century Anabaptists who denied any office in the church. The Pauline epistles leave little doubt that the apostle wanted officebearers appointed in every place, and that such people must meet certain qualifications. They must not "rule over God's people" in the way Christ alone may do that, but they most surely represent the only Mediator as he leads his people through life. They speak and act with his authority. The clarity of that Pauline message, however, is easily lost on us who spend most of our days in democratic environments.

The Scriptures speak of the need for the church to "have confidence in your leaders and submit to their authority" (Heb. 13:17), to name just one passage. As John Calvin put it, it is precisely because Christ "does not dwell among us in visible presence" that he "uses the ministry of men to declare openly his will to us by mouth, as a sort of delegated work." True, he does this "not by transferring to them his right and honor," but most assuredly so that "through their mouths he may do his own work—just as a workman uses a tool to do his work" (*Institutes*, 4.3.1). Take away the tools, and you have effectively removed the normal channels of the work and ministry of Christ himself.

There is a sense in which all Christian believers are called to be "ministers of the gospel." But not all are called to be "ministers of the Word." We all have responsibility in witnessing Christ's grace to the world. But not all have the added mandate to equip God's people to carry out that responsibility. As for church school teachers—perhaps we ought to ordain them as well. After all, they are ministering to our people, equipping them, young and old. Their service is also to equip and train others in the Christian faith and life. And that fits our definition of office: equippers of God's people. To recognize this, however, is not the same as suggesting that all should be ordained or that none should be ordained. The Scriptures implicitly recognize set-apart leaders, for example when Hebrews urges us to "have confidence in your leaders, and submit to their authority" (Heb. 13:17).

You mention our 1973 report on Ecclesiastical Office and Ordination. It is also necessary to read our 2001 report on Ordination and "Official Acts of Ministry," because it offers a much-needed corrective to the "functionalistic" tone of the earlier one:

> Ordination is not a way of recognizing a person's academic credentials, elevating the prestige of religious professionals, or granting of tenure in the church. It is a recognition and enactment of a pastoral relationship between Christ and the church, mediated in a certain leader. As such it should not be entered into lightly (*Agenda for Synod, 2001*, p. 297; *Acts of Synod, 2001*, p. 504).

We do well when we acknowledge both "echoes of Scripture" in the Belgic Confession's references to officebearers:

> they all have the same power and authority, no matter where they may be, since they are all servants of Jesus Christ, the only universal bishop, and the only head of the church.
>
> . . . everyone ought, as much as possible, to hold the ministers of the Word and elders of the church in special esteem, because of the work they do, and be at peace with them, without grumbling, quarreling, or fighting (Article 31).

I. The Offices of the Church

Article 3

a. All adult confessing members of the church who meet the biblical requirements are eligible for the offices of minister, elder, deacon, and ministry associate.

b. Only those who have been officially called and ordained or installed shall hold and exercise office in the church.

The second statement in this article (part b) is the only provision that harks back to the earliest Church Order of the CRCNA. Following the Church Order of Dort, it clearly warned against those who would take upon themselves the office of minister of the Word without having been lawfully called to and ordained in that position. This warning was crafted in the sixteenth century to prevent "roaming priests" who wished to carry on their vocation within the churches of the Reformation from doing so on personal initiative and without thorough examination. But it makes good sense even today.

Internal and External Call

Although Reformed churches have recognized and insisted on the element of "internal calling" felt by those individuals who wished to serve, they have also recognized and insisted on the need for "external calling," the confirming voice of the congregation and, in the case of ministers of the Word and ministry associates, of the entire church. Essentially, Christ calls to office *through* the congregation and confirmation by broader assemblies. Ordination can be defined as that act of the church, liturgically celebrated, whereby, in obedience to the Word, it officially appoints a number of its evidently gifted members to be the organs of Christ's ministry and rule which equips all for service in his kingdom. In this act, it publicly accepts its vocation in the world and acknowledges its complete reliance on the leading of Christ's Word and Spirit.

Requirements for Officebearers

The revised Church Order of 1965 made explicit what had been assumed all along, not only with respect to ministers of the Word but other offices as well: only confessing members of the church who meet the biblical requirements are eligible for office. The reference, clearly, is to passages such as 1 Timothy 3 and Titus 1. The term "confessing members" refers to those who have made a public profession of faith and have affirmed the church's confessions and doctrines. In addition, they are to be adults, and communicant members of the congregation in good standing. God's people have a right to expect that those who will lead and equip them not only have the requisite gifts for service but also subscribe to the church's faith and pledge to uphold it. It is the local council that makes the judgment whether these requirements have been met. With respect to ministers of the Word and ministry associates, however, that judgment must further be confirmed by the broader assemblies as they examine the candidates in light also of additional requirements found in the Church Order (Articles 6-10, 23-24).

Ordination of Women

The only other exception to the freedom of local councils to judge whether requirements have been met has been the injection of the word "male" into this article by Synod 1965. This injection occurred rather naturally, faithfully describing as it did the church's actual practice up to that point. What's more, Synod 1957 had granted women the right to vote at congregational meetings with an explicit assurance that this was "not a matter of assuming leadership over men" and that women "should hold no ruling or teaching office in the church" (*Acts of Synod, 1957*, pp. 313-14). When in later years this latter declaration came to be questioned, however, the prescriptive character of the appearance of the word "male" in Article 3 came to be keenly felt.

Initial studies regarding the issue of permitting women to be ordained and installed to all offices in the church were fairly inconclusive. After a decade of such studies, the CRCNA introduced the possibility of women serving as deacons. Synod 1978 first opened the door and, after a round of serious objections and reversals having to do with the "headship teaching," was followed in this action by Synod 1984. These assemblies thus disentangled the office of deacon from the three others, giving rise to a formulation of Article 3 whereby women could be nominated only as deacons.

Once again, this decision came with an assurance intended especially for those smaller churches that distinguished little, in practice, between elders and deacons. A provisional clause was added as a Supplement to Article 3: "The work of women as deacons is to be distinguished from that of elders." At first glance, this seems utterly obvious. The intent, however, was to assure congregations that a further step toward women in the "leadership offices" of the church was anything but automatic.

Synod 1985 picked up on this and appointed a study committee, in part to "define the work of elders and deacons in such fashion that the local churches will be assisted in carrying out the decision of Synod 1984 that 'the work of women as deacons . . . be distinguished from that of elders.'" The essence of this committee's recommendations was the complete separation of elders' and deacons' functions, in effect even negating an earlier judgment adopted by Synod 1938 that deacons "are warranted in performing presbyterial functions including the right to vote in matters of church government" even though they must then "naturally give due consideration to the judgment of the elders." After Synod 1987 approved the recommendations and adopted significant changes to, among others, Articles 24, 25, 35, and 36, it also saw its way clear to delete the "provisional clause" earlier added as a Supplement to Article 3. The practical implications of that clause, after all, were now firmly anchored in the Church Order, irrespective of whether deacons were male or female.

Synod 1989 adopted a significant statement in the process of not sustaining an appeal. It said: "Decisions made by synod at least since 1978 indicate that the 'women in office' issue has not been regarded as a creedal matter, but as a church order matter" (*Acts of Synod, 1989*, p. 433). This statement was later cited by Synod 1990 in defense of permitting churches to ordain women elders and ministers.

By calling this a "church order matter," synod does not mean that the Scriptures and the confessions are completely silent about the issue, nor does it mean that church order questions can or even must be resolved without guidance from the Bible and/or our creeds. No responsible Reformed church could hold such a position. What it does mean is that although the creeds reflect a time in the life of the church when a woman's eligibility for office was unthinkable, they do not deliberately decide that issue one way or the other. In other words, there is no clear intent to bind the churches on an issue not then even contemplated. Thus, when the English translation of the Belgic Confession says: "when faithful men are chosen, according to the rule prescribed by St. Paul in his Epistle to Timothy," it speaks in a *descriptive* manner (when it says "men") while its intent, *prescriptively*, is to bind the churches to the election of faithful leaders who will serve according to the "spiritual order that our Lord has taught us in his Word." When in the late twentieth century the question of women's eligibility for office was raised, as with any "new" question, the church had to search the Scriptures so as to make a biblically informed decision. But, so Synod 1989 judged, the creeds had no intent to bind us (and therefore do not bind us) to a particular interpretation of the Pauline or any other biblical texts as they may relate to the "new" question we ask. It should be added here that the original French of the Belgic Confession was not gender specific even in its description, using the word *personnages* rather than *hommes*.

In any case, proposals to once again merge Articles 3a and 3b and eliminate the word *male* with respect to all offices were approved by Synods 1990 and 1993 but not adopted by Synods 1992 and 1994. These were turbulent years in a painful and lingering controversy.

Synod 1995 decided to "recognize that there are two different perspectives and convictions, both of which honor the Scriptures as the infallible Word of God, on the issue of whether women are allowed to serve in the offices of elder, minister, and evangelist." Accordingly, it decided to give classes the right, at least until a review in the year 2000, to "declare that the word *male* in Article 3a of the Church Order is inoperative" and to "authorize the churches . . . to ordain and install women in the offices of elder, minister, and evangelist." It did not, however, adopt a change in Article 3. Instead, the decisions to extend this right to classes and to adopt certain regulations associated with it were now placed in the Church

Order as a Supplement to Article 3. A further review in 2005 had a similar result.

The merger of Articles 3a and 3b and elimination of the word *male* from the Church Order was finalized at Synods 2006 and 2007, some forty years after it was first inserted. The denomination ended all restrictions at that time, and Synod 2008 became the first to welcome ordained women ministers and elders as official delegates.

In our church anyone nominated for the office of elder or deacon must sign a statement prepared by the council indicating that person's agreement with the council's position on such issues as "creation and evolution" and "women in office." Is the council within its rights?

No. The Church Order, which has been adopted by previous synods, spells out requirements for officebearers in Article 3. It stipulates, in Article 5, that the Form of Subscription is to be signed, which commits a person only to our creeds and not to (further) interpretations of them. The only exception to this is when a synod (not a person or even a minor assembly) adopts a pronouncement and makes it clear that it will function as an interpretation of one or more of our confessions. In addition, the matter of adopting creeds and possible Church Order revisions (in this case to Article 5) is assigned to synod, not to any one council (Article 47). Councils may demand a healthy respect for synodical decisions on matters such as you raise in your question. But no council has the right, in and of itself, to impose other "hurdles."

Councils would do well to question seriously the wisdom of introducing such extra-creedal requirements. Many of us still remember the devastation caused by this kind of thing in one of our Canadian churches in the 1960s. When led by a minister strongly supportive of the Christian Labour Association of Canada (CLAC), the council refused to install anyone who continued to be a member of a "secular" labor union. Shortly thereafter, led by another minister, the same council refused to install anyone who was a member of the CLAC on the grounds that this organization did not propound a genuinely Christian vision of life. Imagine the consternation!

Does a person's rebaptism automatically disqualify that person from holding office in the Christian Reformed Church?

No, not automatically. The Christian Reformed Church has always held that rebaptism constitutes a denial of the doctrine of infant baptism. Thus, on the level of membership status, the denomination regards those who have themselves rebaptized as being "in error"; they violate our confession. The council must ask such a person if he or she still wishes to be a member of our denomination. If so, it must "faithfully and persistently admonish such an erring member" (*Acts of Synod, 1973*, p. 78). If the unity and wellbeing of the congregation requires it, council may even bar such a member from the Lord's table. Indeed, it must exercise further discipline if he or she "actively disturbs the unity and peace of the congregation." But the clear implication is that the person may well "repent of the error" after such admonition. Then, while rebaptism cannot be undone, full-fledged membership must be gladly given.

This is especially important with respect to those who come to the Christian Reformed Church from a church that routinely rebaptizes its members. Their current views, their desires for their own newborn children, and their ability to celebrate infant baptism with the rest of the congregation must all be considered by council in evaluating their membership status.

With respect to holding office, it seems to me that something similar applies. A person who "errs" on this important matter should under no circumstances be allowed to hold office in the church (*Acts of Synod, 1973*, p. 78). But a person who has "repented of the error" and no longer teaches the necessity of rebaptism should be eligible for office, even if he or she has in fact been rebaptized at an earlier stage in life. If elected, such a person must be expected faithfully to uphold, teach, and defend the church's official doctrine.

Fifteen years ago, my wife and I were divorced on grounds of incompatibility. Two years later I remarried. Do my divorce and remarriage in and of themselves make me ineligible for serving as an elder in my church?

The latest guidelines for the church in this matter—adopted in 1980—do not specifically address your question because they are focused on membership in good standing, not bearing office. They do, however, provide some direction. While upholding the general principles that the marriage relationship is one of permanence and that divorce and remarriage constitute adultery, the Christian Reformed Church also recognizes that there can be circumstances "where the judgment of adultery does not fall upon a person who remarries after a divorce." And even if the person has been culpable in some way, consistories are urged to consider "other factors in the biblical teaching . . . such as repentance for personal failure in the breakdown of the previous marriage, forgiveness of others, understanding of the divinely intended permanence of marriage, and a renewed dependence on the grace of God for the success of the remarriage." In the end, the application of biblical principles "rests on the local consistory, for it has the most intimate and accurate knowledge of the situation."

We must recognize, however, that membership in good standing alone does not make one eligible for office. Aside from such "extras" as special gifts for leadership and mature confessional insight, there is also the matter of being "able to serve effectively." These words are used in Article 84, which deals with the possibility of reinstatement to office after suspension or deposition. Older versions of the Church Order reveal what this ability to "serve effectively" means: it must be evident to the council that a person can serve "without being hindered in his work by the handicap of his past sin and that his restoration would be to the glory of God and for the true welfare of the church." That is the pertinent principle.

I know of cases where councils have made the judgment that a prospective officebearer may be "hindered" because of this "handicap." I also know of cases where councils have made the opposite judgment and, indeed, have insisted that the past experiences in fact have served to further qualify the person for the office of elder. Having gone through divorce and remarriage can sometimes make that person more empathetic and better equipped to deal with those who must also go through this valley of misery.

Thus the straightforward answer to your question is: no, your divorce and remarriage do not in and of themselves make you ineligible for office. It all depends on your particular circumstances, and how you and your church handled the situation. In the end, only the council may judge according to these circumstances whether you could serve effectively as an elder in the church of Christ.

I. The Offices of the Church

Article 4

a. In calling and electing to an office, the council shall ordinarily present to the congregation a nomination of at least twice the number to be elected. When the council submits a nomination which totals less than twice the number to be elected, it shall give reasons for doing so.

b. Prior to making nominations the council may give the congregation an opportunity to direct attention to suitable persons.

c. The election by the congregation shall take place under the supervision of the council after prayer and in accordance with the regulations established by the council. Adult confessing members in good standing shall have the right to vote.

d. After having called the elected persons to their respective offices and having announced their names, the council shall proceed to ordain or install them if no valid impediment has arisen. The ordination or installation shall take place in the public worship services with the use of the prescribed ecclesiastical forms.

The selection of officebearers is a Spirit-led process that can best be described as choosing those who are judged to have the gifts required to equip God's people for ministry.

Meaningful Involvement of the Congregation

The right of the congregation to be involved in this process of selecting its officebearers is clearly rooted in Scripture and the practice of the New Testament church. It is a right that was reclaimed by the Reformation and spoken of in very clear terms in Article 31 of the Belgic Confession:

> We believe that ministers of the Word of God, elders, and deacons ought to be chosen to their offices by a legitimate election of the church, with prayer in the name of the Lord, and in good order, as the Word of God teaches.

On the one hand, this counters the practice of hierarchical appointment; on the other, it prevents individuals from imposing themselves on the church:

> So everyone must be careful not to push himself forward improperly, but he must wait for God's call, so that he may be assured of his calling and be certain that he is chosen by the Lord (Belgic Confession, Article 31).

The call comes from God through the congregation.

A significant number of theologians today, even within the Roman Catholic tradition, are insisting that appointment "from the top down" is a later practice that corrupted the earlier apostolic traditions. Though it is Christ who calls people to office, his call comes through the church under the council's leadership; thus our Church Order insists on congregational involvement from beginning to end. Members "direct attention to suitable persons," says this fourth article, then elect such persons to office.

Discernment of Gifts

While it is important to reject "hierarchical designation," it is timely within our democratic culture to caution against notions of "popular sovereignty." The election of officebearers in a christocratic form of government bears little resemblance to that of members of Congress or Parliament. It is not a popularity contest. There are no power brokers, no campaign managers, no representatives of various "minds" in the church. There is only discernment of gifts in faithful believers necessary for the ministry of equipping others.

Use of the Lot

In recent years, churches have begun to make use of the lot in one form or another. One reason, apparently, is that those not chosen in the congregational election may feel rejected, especially when it happens on a number of occasions. Another reason may be that there simply aren't a sufficient number of gifted persons willing to stand for office. More significant, however, is the argument that casting lots provides relief from possible corruptions of the process such as biased nominating that keeps some people out and campaigning to get the "right" people in. Casting the lot may then be seen as the more spiritual way. Although it recognized this argument, Synod 1989 discouraged the use of the lot in the conviction, apparently, that the leading of the Spirit is as strong in the vote of Spirit-led members as it is in the casting of the lot. It also offered a number of suggestions to increase the involvement of the congregation, thereby clinging to the notion that the call of God is through the church (*Acts of Synod, 1989*, pp. 500-02).

At the same time, Synod 1989 did not absolutely forbid the use of the lot. If it replaces election, it undermines the priesthood of all believers; if it accompanies election, it may be helpful in the process of designation. In accordance with that principle, Synod 2003 declared "that the use of the lot in the election of officebearers is permitted when a congregational vote is part of the process" (*Acts of Synod, 2003*, p. 609).

Article 4 of the Church Order clearly prescribes procedure for election of officebearers, and Synod 1989 discouraged the use of the lot in the selection process. But are these the only two models? Aren't there any creative new models that follow, if not the letter, at least the spirit and intent of this article?

Always, by rule, the congregation is asked to suggest names. Beyond that, here's what I've observed in our churches and, in the italicized parts that follow each item, how I view the practice referred to:

1. The council nominates twice the number to be elected; the congregation elects.

Straightforward Article 4 and the traditional model.

2. The council nominates eight candidates for six positions, or three for two, and so on; the congregation elects by plurality—not necessarily majority—of votes.

A traditional variation on Article 4, probably still in keeping with its intent.

3. The council nominates the exact number to be elected; the congregation votes with a simple yes or no.

Exception allowed by Article 4 but only with an "explanation" to the congregation as to why a single nomination was unavoidable this time, presumably with a pledge to "do better the next time around" and provide at least some choice.

4. The council appoints new officebearers without election or lot by the congregation and without "explanation" but routinely, year after year, possibly with a once-in-five-year confirmation vote on the procedure.

A self-perpetuating council scenario that is surely in clear violation of Article 4.

5. The council nominates four times the number to be elected; the congregation narrows it down to twice the number by way of election during or after the morning service or as an early item on the congregational meeting agenda; the lot determines those selected prior to or during the second service or toward the end of the congregational meeting.

This way nobody knows whether they were "eliminated" by election or lot; honors Article 4 and synodical decisions in that the lot is used when election is still part of the process. Obvious disadvantage: can you find enough nominees?

6. The council nominates twice the number to be elected, whereupon the lot determines those who will serve.

This is surely out of step with synodical decisions in that it removes any meaningful involvement (other than suggesting names) on the part of the congregation.

7. All members of the congregation are sent a letter not merely to solicit possible suggestions but with the request and expectation that every adult confessing member will nominate persons for the offices (twice the number of those needed); the council has veto power but by and large follows the "tally" of the nomination process, then approaches people regarding willingness to serve; the council informs the congregation of those selected and perhaps one or two alternates, and calls for a final congregational vote on the entire slate with a simple yes or no.

Probably in keeping with the spirit and intent of Article 4 since the congregation retains a meaningful role in the selection process. Encourages a focus on giftedness.

8. The council nominates more than needed. The congregation votes and the votes are counted. The nominees that receive a majority of the votes cast are elected but not announced until all selections are made. The remaining positions are filled by lot from among those who have received the most votes (though not a majority). The number of those included in the lot procedure equals the number of unfilled openings plus one. The officebearers selected by majority vote and the lot are announced in alphabetical order. The congregation then votes on the entire slate with a simple yes or no.

An interesting combination of majority vote, plurality vote, and lot; probably in keeping with Article 4 and synodical decisions.

9. The council compiles a list of potential candidates consisting of approximately three to four times the number needed. Council then invites these candidates to a weekend workshop led by the pastor. The

workshop focuses on the congregation's vision, mission, and values; on the roles of elder and deacon; and on discovering gifts. Those who do not accept the invitation are not nominated. Those who attend are called back together at a later date for a time of prayer and determination of their inner calling. Anyone who does not feel called is not nominated. Council confirms the nomination of those who do feel called and are willing to let their names stand. The congregation is informed of the list and votes yes or no for each person. Members are also encouraged in advance to approach the council before the congregational meeting and inform it of any serious reservations so that "no" votes have a context known to council.

If the congregation is asked not merely to suggest names but also expected to nominate the candidates, it might be said to have a meaningful role in the selection process. Voting yes or no on an entire slate might be more appropriate than voting on each person separately, but no doubt the compliance with Article 4 is more obvious this way. Again: can they find enough nominees willing to stand? The most positive feature: people have time to discern an internal calling to the work and to understand what the offices of elder and deacon are really all about. They aren't confronted with it on the spot and requested to respond within just a few days.

After nominating two candidates, our congregation recently decided that a two-thirds majority vote would be required to call a new minister. After the vote on Sunday morning, it appeared that one candidate did have the required number of votes. Both candidates were informed of the result and so was the congregation. On Tuesday evening, however, when the council met to confirm the result and issue the call, we were informed that four absentee ballots had been presented to the clerk on Monday. When these were included in the vote count, the two-thirds majority vanished. There were strong feelings, so we adjourned to think it over. What do we do when we meet again?

First, call the two candidates immediately and explain your predicament, telling both that things are on hold for just a bit. Next, calmly review your rules for election procedures—the bylaws and whatever else has been approved by way of previous council action to the best of your knowledge. Such rules are not found in the Church Order. Each local church adopts them for itself. In most cases, I trust, they are shared with the congregation every time an election of officebearers takes place. From what you tell me, it sounds like your rules do not cover the specific matter of the validity of absentee ballots or proxy ballots and the deadline for their receipt. It also looks like your rules were not announced. In any case, review them. Include the recent decision regarding a two-thirds majority and note that it applies to the election of ministers only, not elders or deacons, if that is indeed the case.

In the likely event that your review does not offer a logical solution to the problem, write each professing member of your congregation a letter in which you announce and explain the unforeseen complications. Be sure to repentantly acknowledge that rules were unclear or nonexistent and, as a result, the election could not be confirmed. In the letter, present a clear set of rules and propose them for approval by the entire congregation. Such congregational approval is not required, but under the circumstances it may be wise. Announce a new congregational meeting where this approval as well as a new election will take place.

Anything short of what I am suggesting may leave a cloud of suspicion about the validity of the call. I doubt anyone would want to begin a ministry that way. Indeed, the very idea of a two-thirds majority requirement adopted in advance and then the confusing result may have already guaranteed that neither minister will accept a possible call.

In general, I am opposed to two-thirds majority requirements. It allows slightly more than one-third of the members to decide an issue.

What should one do in the case of a tie vote when electing officebearers?

Elections for officebearers are governed by local articles of incorporation, bylaws, or any other rules adopted by the local council. If they say nothing about tie votes, my advice would be to decide between two options: (1) have the congregation vote a second time to see if that breaks the tie, or (2) have the council exercise its right to have final authority in such matters (Article 37) and, by its vote, break the tie. If the vote by the council is a tie, the chair of council (who should not be voting in the first round) may break the tie and choose.

The only local article governing this that I have seen that does not call for a reelection is one whereby a tie is broken by having the older person serve. That too is the council's prerogative. But it's probably best not to exercise that option in this case. You must never change the rules during the game. Change them after the game.

Does Christian Reformed polity allow the ordination as elder of a person whose brother is already on the current council as an elder?

Our Church Order does not address this issue. If there are rules pertaining to this, they are locally adopted.

Is the laying on of hands ceremony reserved only for the ordination of ministers of the Word?

In practice it seems to have been. The study committee reporting to Synod 1973, for example, indicated that it is "often associated with the ordination of ministers" (*Acts of Synod, 1973*, p. 714). However, that very same synod indicated that there is "no biblical warrant" for limiting it to the ordination of ministers of the Word (p. 64), a thought more positively formulated by Synod 2001: "Since by the laying on of hands the church recognizes pastoral leadership as such and not a specific office or role, this ceremony is appropriate for all church offices" (*Acts of Synod, 2001*, p. 504). In my congregation, the laying on of hands is always a part of the ordination of elders and deacons, and we have found this to be a very meaningful tradition.

May unordained church members participate in the laying on of hands ceremony associated with installation/ordination?

No, I don't think so. A congregation elects but a council ordains to office. This is the clear lesson of Scripture and church history.

We've just had a service in which elders and deacons were installed. We used the liturgical form found in the *Psalter Hymnal*. As a professional counselor, I noticed that nothing was said about officebearers keeping inviolate all that has been entrusted to them in confidence. In our litigious society, I find this very odd. Any thoughts?

Thanks for a great question. I looked in my *Psalter Hymnal* copy (1987 printing) and verified what you're telling me. I checked the index of synodical decisions and discovered that Synod 1989 did, in fact, adopt changes in the forms of ordination of ministers, elders and deacons (*Acts of Synod, 1989*, p. 469). These changes can be found in the *Agenda for Synod, 1989*, p. 62. It is not surprising, therefore, that *Psalter Hymnals* printed in 1987 do not reflect these changes. The liturgical forms for the ordination of elders and deacons and ministers on the CRCNA website have been updated to reflect this decision.

It is very important that we recall the need for confidentiality in the work of officebearers at the moment they are installed. The congregation can be assured and those in office reminded, publicly, at least once a year. This will not only encourage parishioners to feel free in sharing necessary information with their pastoral leaders, but also function as a powerful defense against any possible lawsuits.

I. The Offices of the Church

Article 5

All officebearers, on occasions stipulated by council, classical, and synodical regulations, shall signify their agreement with the doctrine of the church by signing the Form of Subscription.

The Form of Subscription is the instrument whereby officebearers give their assent to the creeds and confessions of the CRCNA and commit themselves to abide by them in their official tasks. A study committee to report to Synod 2011 is considering asking synod to change the title to "A Covenant for Officebearers in the Christian Reformed Church."

Ever since Peter made the good confession that Jesus is the Christ, the Son of the living God, the church has sought to formulate its faith, saying in words what it believes. It has done so largely for three reasons: to bring witness to those around it what it hears God saying, to teach future generations within it what it confesses, and to ward off heresy in its midst.

Creeds and Confessions of the CRCNA

The Apostles' Creed was probably developed from an early baptismal formula and has remained throughout the centuries a crisp restatement of the Christian gospel. Both the Nicene Creed and the Athanasian Creed elaborated on this elemental doctrine because of the rise of early heresies. Together, the three are normally referred to as the "Ecumenical Creeds."

In the sixteenth century, the Reformation spawned numerous statements of faith in reaction to what it considered to be the corruption within Roman Catholic Church of its time. The CRCNA adopted three of these Reformed confessions as its doctrinal standards. The Belgic Confession was a statement to the King of Spain intended to summarize the faith of the Reformers and convince the authorities and society at large that their doctrines were not politically subversive in any way. The Heidelberg Catechism was developed largely as a teaching aid within the churches. And the Canons of Dort were adopted in 1618-1619 at a synod of the same name in order to counter what it considered to be the heresy of Arminianism.

Contemporary Testimonies

In addition to receiving these three official confessions of the Reformed churches, the denomination has also adopted a "Contemporary Testimony" entitled "Our World Belongs to God." When it did this at Synod 1986, however, it insisted explicitly that this latter document would not have the status of a creed but, rather, must be viewed as "subordinate to our creeds and confessions" (*Acts of Synod, 1986*, p. 679). Subsequent assemblies have not changed this stance. The testimony was recently updated (*Agenda for Synod, 2008*, pp. 209-30; *Acts of Synod, 2008*, p. 458).

Synod 2009 decided to "propose to Synod 2012 the adoption of the Belhar Confession as part of the standards of unity of the CRC (as a fourth confession)." This confession was formulated in the context of post-apartheid South Africa in order to express the biblical themes of unity, reconciliation, and justice. Churches are asked to study this document carefully and remain free to express any agreement or disagreement (*Acts of Synod, 2009*, p. 604). An important consideration will be whether the Belhar Confession should indeed be adopted as a "fourth confessional standard" or function as yet another "contemporary testimony" in addition to "Our World Belongs to God."

Meaning of Creedal Subscription

In the last number of years, the denomination has paid closer attention to the issue of what this required subscription entails and how Article 5 actually functions in our congregations. A study committee dealing with this topic is due to report to Synod 2011. In the meantime, I record here a few personal thoughts on the matter, previously published in the *Calvin Theological Seminary Forum* (Spring, 2008, pp. 9-10).

A story in *The Wall Street Journal* of June 14, 1996, featured a longtime charismatic preacher, the Rev. Chuck Bell, pastor of Vineyard Christian Fellowship of San Jose. One Sunday, quite out of the blue, he announced that God was calling him to a "radically different brand of Christianity" (Eastern Orthodoxy) and that God wanted the entire congregation to join it too. Before long, he began calling himself "Father Seraphim Bell" and transformed half his flock into the St. Stephen Orthodox Church. The other half? They "felt betrayed" and left. As the staff reporter astutely observed, "the very quality that makes many Protestant denominations attractive to parishioners—a lack of central authority—can make these churches unstable. The minister can become a papal figure, his whims unchecked by any higher authority and his hold over the congregation more powerful than that of the denomination."

When a congregation calls and installs a new pastor, the people expect some change—perhaps different approaches to liturgy, or leadership, or pastoral care. But they surely have a right to expect that such change does not go to the core of their identity. That would be like an American president who violates the solemn oath of office and seriously undermines the nation's Constitution. Fundamentally change the outlines of a budget? Sure. Make some sweeping changes in the way intelligence is gathered? Certainly. But you can't declare that an election is null and void. You cannot contradict the essence of democracy: government of the people, by the people, and for the people.

The CRCNA's "constitution" consists of the three ecumenical creeds and three Reformed Confessions (Heidelberg Catechism, Belgic Confession, Canons of Dort). The Form of Subscription officebearers sign is the "oath of office." When they sign it, they declare that the six documents are in harmony with the Word of God. They solemnly pledge to teach these doctrines and not to contradict them. They promise to express any difficulties with them and to submit to the judgment of the assemblies (council, classis, and/or synod) before making such difficulties or contradictory doctrines a matter of public teaching. These doctrines go to the core of our identity.

Most officebearers feel honored to sign the Form of Subscription. They do it heartily as far as the ecumenical creeds are concerned. Some do it less heartily when it comes to the confessions of the sixteenth and seventeenth centuries. This is an understandable sentiment. We all wish that the visible church had remained as one. But history has produced denominations that will probably remain until the Lord returns and unity is finally restored. In the meantime, the officially adopted confessions define our "brand," express what our tradition holds inviolable. Is that tradition "everything"? No, but we believe that it is where the Spirit has led us. So we sign a Form of Subscription. We subscribe to what is at the heart of our faith. And in accordance with that we proclaim and witness to the truth of the Word of God in our time.

Are the confessions equal to the Word? Do they have the same authority as the Word? Of course not. They are human documents, responding to the Word of God, and seeking to summarize and articulate some major doctrines taught in the Scriptures. Although they do that in their own historical context, they express timeless biblical doctrines and therefore have authority, even for us. It would be fitting for a church of the Reformation, like ours, to make this very clear in the Form of Subscription. Instead of saying that "all the articles . . . fully agree with the Word of God," we should begin by saying: "We believe the Scriptures are the Word of God and the only infallible rule for our faith and life." Then we can add that the "points of doctrine set forth in the [confessions] fully agree with the Word of God." This is exactly what the *sola scriptura* of our spiritual ancestors in Europe meant: first, that the Word—not tradition—is the final source of truth; then, that our tradition is and must always be shaped by what the Word reveals.

Affirming the Form of Subscription carries two significant exceptions. First, we do not subscribe to all the words contained in the confessions but to the doctrines that they teach. In signing the Form of Subscription, we are not saying that these doctrines are expressed in timeless words and enduring images. As one of our guidelines (Supplement to Article 5) says, we do not say that these confessions express those biblical doctrines in "the best possible manner" for all times and places. Nor do we say that they cover all that the Bible has to say for our time and forevermore. We are bound only "to those doctrines which are confessed, and . . . not . . . to the references, allusions, and remarks that are incidental to the formulation of these doctrines." Times and contexts change. There are new crises in our time and different battles for us to fight. That's why we need new statements of faith in the midst of new challenges: the CRC's contemporary testimony "Our World Belongs to God," the Reformed Church in America's "Our Song of Hope," the German "Barmen Declaration," and the South African "Belhar Confession." While these do not have the same level of authority as our creeds and confessions (at least not yet), they articulate our cherished

45

doctrines for today. Indeed, the church must constantly be confessing if it is truly alive. That's why many of us still preach "catechism sermons." And it's also why every single one of those <u>sermons had better be in words that folks in 2010 can understand</u>.

Second, as another guideline says, we are not bound "to the theological deductions which some may draw from the doctrines set forth in the confessions." When I was fourteen years old, one of my catechism teachers explained to me what the idea of "reprobation" in the Canons of Dort was all about. We believe, he said, that even before we were born God chose some to go to heaven and others to go to hell and that nothing could ever change that. As a careful listener I concluded that human beings were like wind-up dolls or robots and that God pushed buttons (green and red) to determine our ultimate fate. I also drew from my instruction that I didn't have to go to church. If I "lit up green," I'd get to heaven anyway. If "red," I'd never get there no matter what I did. It took a few years before others assured me that the teachings of the Canons are far more complex and nuanced, and, furthermore, that I'd best go to church. We may have difficulty with the way some express our doctrine. Yet, as it turns out, confessional Protestant denominations do have a central authority. It is not a Pope. It is our sincere attachment to the mutually accepted doctrines in our trusted creeds and confessions, and our submission to the judgments of a council, a classis, or a synod when that becomes necessary. That is what keeps us from suddenly forsaking our "constitution"—from turning "Eastern Orthodox" from one day to the next.

Our congregations should be able to expect that their officebearers will lead them in line with our core identity. To this end, it would be very helpful if the guidelines in the Supplement to Article 5 of the Church Order would actually find their way into the Form of Subscription itself. (As of this writing a new covenant for officebearers is being written for possible adoption.) Perhaps we could sign it with greater integrity and less reservation. Along the way we might simplify the language. And then we might read it aloud once every year, in our council rooms, when new elders and deacons are asked to sign, and talk about what it means—and doesn't mean.

When I was a seminary student, I truly believed that our spiritual ancestors were rigid traditionalists who thrived on legalistic rules that kept everyone on the straight and narrow way. They were stodgy, black-robed clerics, devoid of all compassion and empathy for new generations that were truly "with it." (I exaggerate, of course, to make a point.) Then, in graduate school, I began to study how people in the seventeenth century in fact treated the signing of our Form of Subscription. The Dutch theologian Groen van Prinsterer said it best for me: We hold to our confessions *op onbekrompen en ondubbelzinnige wijze.* In translation, that means, first, that we do so not as cramped legalists who insist on every word and phrase, jot, and tittle; and, second, that we do so single-mindedly, without reservation, and with integrity of heart and spirit.

A candidate for the office of elder has informed the council that he cannot in good conscience sign the Form of Subscription. May we leave him on the ballot?

Not under those conditions, unless the problem can be resolved in a satisfactory manner prior to the election. Sometimes people misunderstand what the signing means or what a doctrine actually is. But if they do understand, and still cannot sign, my answer stands.

Our insistence on having officebearers sign the Form of Subscription to the creeds of the church only encourages hypocrisy and no longer serves any useful purpose. Most of them don't believe everything taught in them. Isn't it about time we recognize this and drop the requirement?

Should we drop the requirement that the President of the United States of America take the oath of office, promising to uphold the Constitution, just because he or she no longer ascribes to certain articles or expressions contained in it?

Maybe I'm wrong, but I rather suspect that some of our members are drifting towards a "No creed but Christ" stance. While this may be popular in certain evangelical circles, it is an impossible position. Ask just one question about who Christ really is, and the first response will be a creedal statement—off the cuff and thus, quite often, without any solid historical or theological foundation.

No, I do not place the creeds on the same level as the infallible Scriptures. But these statements of our faith are priceless gems bestowed on us by the early church and the reformers. We neglect them only at our peril. The church has a right to expect its officebearers to live by its "constitution." To drop this requirement of Article 5 of our Church Order is denominational suicide.

On occasion, I hear a term I don't even know how to spell: *grevamin* (?). Do you recognize it, and, if so, what does it mean?

A gravamen (plural: gravamina) is an official document written by an officebearer who, having once signed the Form of Subscription, now has difficulty with or wishes to revise a doctrine or set of doctrines contained in our creeds. The regulations with respect to this matter were adopted by Synod 1976 in the wake of Dr. Harry Boer's challenge of the biblical support for the doctrine of reprobation supplied in the Canons of Dort. They can be found in the Supplement to Article 5 of the Church Order.

In our tradition the submission of formal gravamina is rare. Aside from Boer's challenge, the only other notable statement of difficulty with the creeds was that of Dr. Dietrich H. Kromminga, who had some questions about our doctrines concerning the last things. In this latter case there was never any final arbitration. Synod 1947 excused itself from this task, explaining that Dr. Kromminga's death rendered a resolution of the matter unnecessary.

The infrequent submission of gravamina should give those of us who are officebearers some pause. Are we taking the creeds seriously enough? Have we signed the Form of Subscription with integrity? Are we making individual judgments about important creedal matters without submitting these judgments to the assemblies for communal scrutiny?

Is there a significant difference between subscription to the creeds (Article 5) and abiding by certain decisions of synod as "settled and binding" (Article 29)? If so, what are the practical consequences?

Yes, there is a significant difference and it does have consequences. Synod is itself bound by the creeds of the church but not necessarily so by prior synodical decisions. These are on different levels of authority. As a study committee of synod once put it:

> Full agreement with the confessions is expected from all members of the church and subscription to the confessions is required of all officebearers by signing the Form of Subscription. While synodical

decisions are "settled and binding," subscription to synodical decisions is not required. Registering a negative vote with regard to a synodical decision is permissible, although this is not tolerated with respect to the confessions. In some instances synod has itself designated the degree of latitude which it permits (*Acts of Synod, 1960*, p. 114), but such decisions should not be applied universally. Guidelines for study, pastoral advice and other decisions of this nature allow for varying measures of agreement (*Acts of Synod, 1975*, pp. 601-02).

Based in part on this committee's report, Synod 1975 actually adopted the following:

The confessions and synodical pronouncements have nuances of differences. They differ in the extent of their jurisdiction, in the nature of their authority, in the distinction of purposes, in the measure of agreement expected, and in their use and function.

The use and function of synodical decisions are explicitly or implicitly indicated by the wording of the particular decision itself: (1) When a synodical pronouncement is set forth as an interpretation of the confession, this is its use and function. (2) When a synodical decision involves pronouncements that are related to the confessions or go beyond the confessions, the use and function of such decisions is to further express the faith of the church without such statements thereby becoming additions to the confessions (*Acts of Synod, 1975*, p. 44).

What I gather from this is that we must have a healthy respect for synodical decisions and consider them settled and binding for our practice, but may also disagree with them. Conscientious disagreement may lead a person to record a negative vote (if able to do so), and approach a following synod with an overture asking for change because the prior decision "conflicts with the Word of God or the Church Order" (Article 29). A relevant synodical statement on this is found in the *Acts of Synod, 1996*, page 528, in connection with the views of professor Hessel Bouma III of Calvin College on abortion: "Article 29 does not preclude faculty discussion, debate, or disagreement with the substance of a synodical decision or position taken."

We do not see synodical assemblies as infallible. Creeds aren't infallible either, but amendments to them are much rarer than amendments to previous synodical decisions. As we honor those who have gone before us, we always want our tradition to be governed and constantly shaped anew by our creeds and confessions, and even more importantly, by the authoritative Word of God.

As we go about our work as officebearers, we may not in our official preaching, teaching, and other forms of public ministry contradict the doctrines taught in our creeds and confessions. We may, however, respectfully disagree with a synodical pronouncement unless synod has "explicitly or implicitly indicated" that its pronouncement interprets the confession. And when we disagree, we should have the humility and the integrity to indicate in what we say publicly or privately that the church currently stands on different ground than we do.

I. The Offices of the Church

Article 6

a. The completion of a satisfactory theological training shall be required for admission to the ministry of the Word.

b. Graduates of the theological seminary of the Christian Reformed Church who have been declared candidates for the ministry of the Word by synod shall be eligible for call.

c. Those who have been trained elsewhere shall not be eligible for call unless they have met the requirements stipulated in the synodical regulations and have been declared by synod to be candidates for the ministry of the Word.

The Church Order now zooms in on the first office "acknowledged" in the CRCNA, the minister of the Word, and devotes to it no less than seventeen articles. Those last three words, "of the Word," though oft omitted, are vital to an understanding of what this office is all about. We use the titles "Pastor Bill" or "Rev. Johnson," but "pastor" and "reverend" don't really get at the heart of what this person does. A shepherd of God's flock? Sure. A teacher of God's people? Of course. An evangelist/missionary? Certainly that too.

All these tasks are reflected in Article 12. But in and through all those functions, and most significantly, in and through crafting and delivering the sermon, the minister of the Word is above all a preacher called "to proclaim, explain, and apply Holy Scripture" (Article 11).

Proclamation and High Standards

Who stands in the pulpit from Sunday to Sunday is no trivial matter. It is through the proclamation of the Word that the Holy Spirit produces faith in our hearts (Rom. 10:13-15), reconciles sinners to God (2 Cor. 5:18-21), and renews our lives (Rom. 12:2). More than that: the pulpit shapes our creed, molds the way we confess the Good News and uphold its truth. The "pure preaching of the gospel," says Article 29 of our Belgic Confession, is the first and most crucial mark of the one true church. This is why, even in New Testament days, the matter was never left to "chance" or even to the spontaneous working of spiritual gifts. Instead, we read in Paul's letters about elders appointed to supervise, and of necessary qualifications for those who would labor especially in the ministry of the Word. The main reason for the emergence of a "hierarchy" in the early church was the importance of guarding the pulpits from heresy. And when the hierarchy went sour, it was precisely the pulpit, and a system of guarding the pulpit, that was restored in the Protestant Reformation. The gospel must be faithfully proclaimed, and those who preach it must be qualified.

Biblical and confessional preaching is at the core of the church's being. Calvin called the ministry of the Word the "knot" that binds the church together—the "strongest means of keeping unity" (*Institutes*, 4.3.1). Thus no person may presume to climb a pulpit without the public and authoritative calling of God and of the church. It is also no surprise that Reformed and Presbyterian church polity has set high standards for ministry and proclamation. Early on, the matter was never left to a local council or session alone. In Roman Catholic polity the task of "guaranteeing" the faith of the local church and of "verifying" the giftedness of the preacher had been entrusted to the bishop. In Protestant churches that task was given to the assemblies such the presbytery or the classis: groups of ministers and elders representing the broader community, functioning as a tribunal of peers.

Satisfactory Theological Education

The Christian Reformed Church continues to highly prize and carefully regulate the theological education of its ministers by its Church Order. A "satisfactory" theological education necessarily has at its core appropriate training in the original languages in which the Old and the New Testaments were written. Good preachers have the tools to "live into" the ancient text, discover with joy and amazement what the Spirit revealed to God's people, and only then know how to bring that message, and no other, in their world today. In addition, ministers of the Word must also learn how previous generations of Christians have confessed the faith and lived before the face of God; how we have come to "organize" biblical truths in various doctrines. Finally, aspiring ministers will be trained in the practical skills of equipping, shepherding, and leading God's people today, and in leading the church in its missionary calling. But it all begins and ends with Scripture, the lifeblood of Christian pilgrims of all ages.

With good reason, therefore, the denomination chooses to own and operate its own theological seminary, and its synod closely monitors the training it provides. It is also with good reason that the denomination further insists that graduates of other theological schools meet the same standards, and that no persons are eligible for call as ministers of the Word in the CRCNA unless they have met the pertinent denominational requirements.

Candidacy Committee

Initially it was the synod itself that directly examined those who aspired to be ministers of the Word. In later years, synod entrusted that task to the Board of Trustees of the seminary. Most recently, synod created its own "Candidacy Committee" that is now entrusted with the task of vetting candidates for the ministry, no matter where they were trained. This committee is also mandated to assist and encourage the classes to establish and maintain ministry leadership committees so that these regional assemblies can identify, accompany, guide, and support future leaders from the very beginning. Even so, the synod itself actually declares candidacy for ministry of the Word in the CRCNA.

Does synod's declaration of candidacy make official that these graduates of our seminary are now ministers of the Word?

No, it does not. Synod has seen to the preliminary testing of the internal call and the required gifts and training, and now announces that these persons are eligible for a call to one of our churches. This is referred to as the "external call." If that is forthcoming and the candidate accepts, he or she will first be subjected to yet another examination by the classis in which that calling church finds itself (Article 10). While the candidate's biblical and theological position is still probed, the exam concentrates on service in that particular region within the CRCNA and that particular congregation, paying attention to local issues and concerns. When that exam is sustained, the classis gives permission to the calling church to ordain the individual to the office of ministry in its midst. Only when that ordination occurs, complete with the "laying on of hands," has the person actually become a minister of the Word.

Article 6b says "the theological seminary" of the CRCNA. Has the denomination ever considered establishing a second seminary? Perhaps in Canada? It would be such a wonderful alternative to the rigours of crossing the border and of meeting all the onerous regulations of the United States Department of Homeland Security.

I love the subtlety of spelling *rigours* your way. I'll bet it was intentional, eh? An attempt was made in the 1980s to begin with a first year of seminary training at Redeemer University College in Ancaster, Ontario, under the auspices and with the direct assistance of Calvin Theological Seminary. Some of us hoped that this could be the beginning of a new seminary in Canada. There was an initial enthusiasm and decent enrollment, but it soon became evident that this satellite program was not sustainable and ought to be abandoned. Apparently our resources were and are not sufficient to sustain two schools. The lives and the training of American students are truly enriched when there is a significant representation of Canadian brothers and sisters. And just between you and me, of course, isn't the opposite also true?

I. The Offices of the Church

Article 7

a. Those who have not received the prescribed theological training but who give evidence that they are singularly gifted as to godliness, humility, spiritual discretion, wisdom, and the native ability to preach the Word, may, by way of exception, be admitted to the ministry of the Word.

b. Those preparing for the ordained ministry under the provisions of this article are required to complete the Modified Ecclesiastical Program for Ministerial Candidacy (MEPMC).

Early History: Need, Yet Giftedness

In the 1570s, when followers of the Protestant Reformation in the Netherlands were finally free from fear of persecution and able to organize their churches for regular weekly worship, there was a sudden and drastic need for ministers of the Word to fill the pulpits. Some preparations had been laid in refugee settings, such as London and Emden, but there were no training centers, no seminaries; instead, there was an abundance of former priests who wished to remain in their towns and cities serving as religious professionals, but no longer within the Roman Catholic Church. While their leadership was often suspect, there was a crying need for it. → Historians also speak of "learned individuals" who wanted to try their hands at ministry. Led by Genevan practice, the churches and classes did their best to deal with the problem by permitting only those who were sufficiently qualified and of "Reformed persuasion" to enter upon the ministry. Some of them instituted private instruction, since appropriate training centers could only be found abroad in places like Heidelberg, Basel, and Zurich. A Dutch national theological faculty was not established until 1575 (at the University of Leiden), and the situation could not be regularized until the following decade.

It stands to reason that the Synod of Dordrecht meeting in 1574 felt the need to provide some clear direction. Since so many were admitted into the ministry who had not received a thorough theological training, they would minimally have to give evidence of "singular giftedness": qualities of godliness, humility, spiritual discretion/superior intellect, wisdom, and a greater than average ability as a public speaker. It was a "line in the sand" while more regular avenues of training for ministry were established with synodical blessing and oversight to provide for the future need of the churches.

This history of great need leading to admission to ministry by way of exception repeated itself first in the wake of the Arminian controversies at the turn of the sixteenth century and again on two occasions in the nineteenth century. In the interest of replacing the Remonstrants with those who would follow its doctrinal position, the Synod of Dort (1618-19) revived the regulation of 1574 and strengthened it to include a period of "internship" or "exhorting" under close scrutiny of the classis. In secessions from the national church occurring in 1834 and 1886 and years following, the spiritual ancestors of the CRCNA once again counted faithfulness to the Scriptures and sound theology of greater value than graduation from an academic program. Yet this too was temporary. As early as 1893, a regulation was adopted that almost made the "exceptional entry" inoperative:

> The Reformed churches acknowledge no other avenue to
> the ministry of the Word than that of theological studies,
> except in those very rare cases where, by way of exception
> and according to His sovereign grace, the Lord bestows
> the necessary gifts in some other way (freely translated).

Modern History: Need, Yet Giftedness

The CRCNA began its denominational life with this same sentiment: a rigid prescription for thorough theological training and the "humility" to acknowledge that a sovereign God might occasionally "override" the church's choice by equipping someone in very unusual measure through other means. It should not surprise us, therefore, that the first ordination to regular congregational ministry by way of this article did not occur until 1918, when J. Balt began his ministry at East Palmyra, New York (*Acts of Synod, 1918*, p. 46). At the time, his tutor stated that he had no knowledge as to dire need in the churches at that time. Classis Hudson just recognized this person's "singular gifts." A second occurrence did not come until J. Joosse was ordained within Classis Chatham in 1960. Clearly, these admissions were not driven by a denominational need for ministers but by "exceptional gifts" detected in such measure that the church felt constrained to ordain.

Synod 1947 reinforced this state of affairs by suggesting, for the first time, that "great need" should be mentioned as a criterion for admission. It reminded the churches that "this article should never be used as a means to ordain all layworkers who may desire such, and whose prestige would be increased by such action." In other words, the church is not necessarily bound to ordain those with "exceptional gifts." Instead, thorough academic training as the "regular door to the ministry" must be "maintained in theory and practice," and Article 7 of the Church Order should "function only in case of great need" (*Acts of Synod, 1947*, pp. 93-94). When a newly revised Church Order was adopted in 1965, the element of need for ministers was no longer merely a descriptive historical fact that automatically leads to a greater use of this avenue but became a part of the denomination's prescriptive regulations:

> Those who have not received the prescribed theological training but who give evidence that they are singularly gifted . . . may, by way of exception, be admitted to the ministry of the Word, especially when the need is urgent.

While it was clearly not the intention of these assemblies, the CRCNA increasingly began to focus on this new clause in Article 7. The element of "exceptional gifts" receded into the background while the element of "need" gained prominence. "Urgent need" came to be defined in ways never previously intended: local need after a long vacancy, the need of congregations arising among ethnic minorities, the need of a "shrinking denomination" to plant new churches—all these led classes to become much more liberal in their application of the article in question. The number of "exceptional admissions" increased so rapidly, in fact, that Synod 1996 ordered a comprehensive review of "routes presently being used to ordained ministry." Admissions by way of theological education at seminaries other than the CRCNA's own, admissions of ministers ordained in other denominations, and admissions of the "singularly gifted" were all in view. The review ultimately led to the establishment of a synodical Candidacy Committee that was given authority beyond the classical level to make judgments about such proposed admissions. It also led to the removal of the need clause in 2004 and returned the focus of the article to its historical roots: "singular giftedness" that on rare occasions "overrides" the church's insistence on a thorough theological education.

My council has encouraged me to consider the ministry. After much prayer and wrestling, I have decided to move in that direction, leaving behind a long and relatively successful career in social work. At my age, going to seminary and learning the classical languages is out of the question, and the council thinks that I could easily qualify via Article 7 of our Church Order. Could you give me some guidance?

I'll try. The first thing to do is to contact the denominational Candidacy Committee. You will note in the Supplement to Article 7 that this committee has a "Journey to Ministry" document that will guide you well.

Second, you should probably contact some ministers in the area and your Classical Ministerial Leadership Team (if there is one) to explore your aspirations with more than just your local council. Chat with them especially about not giving up on Article 6 too quickly. These days there are some very good tools available to assist with learning the languages of Scripture—and that's almost indispensable. The fact is that the prescribed theological training is there for good reason: we believe it to be crucial for the building up of the church but also for the person's own welfare, satisfaction, and success in a new career of ministry of the Word. But if you and those who counsel you in the end still believe you should follow the path of Article 7, by all means proceed down that road.

A note of caution, however. For almost all of our denominational life, those who have traveled this road and gone into ministry had, from the start of their journey, a congregation that was committed to be their "destination church." This group would sometimes first have the person apply for classical permission to exhort (Article 43) for a certain period of time or, if not that, then certainly be willing to serve as the place where that person's ministry is first carried out and evaluated (the "internship" step of the Article 7 journey). There have been only three exceptions to this, beginning in 1999, where classes have declared candidacy without a "destination church" in the picture. Synod 2007 closed that loophole in our regulations and put a definitive stop to this practice, believing that it is the prerogative of synod, not a classis, to establish a pool of candidates for the denomination at large. The result is that a person like yourself must pursue this journey "in the context of a particular congregation's desire and commitment to call that person to serve as minister of the Word" (*Acts of Synod, 2007*, p. 652). You can read this too in the Supplement to Article 7. Remember as you do so that this is nothing but a confirmation of almost a century-and-a-half of CRCNA tradition.

A brief follow-up, if I might. If I find a "destination church" in my own classis, why is it necessary that there be synodical deputies present at the first examination and also when the "pre-ordination" exam takes place in the same classis?

No problem. The CRCNA does not practice "limited ordination." Once you are a minister of the Word, ordained in a congregation, you become eligible for call to any church within the denominational fellowship. It is for that reason that all congregations have an interest in the initial admission, and synod therefore requires the concurrence of synodical deputies.

I. The Offices
of the Church

Article 8

a. Ministers of the Christian Reformed Church are eligible for call, with due observance of the relevant rules.

b. Ministers of the Reformed Church in America are eligible for call to serve in the Christian Reformed Church, with due observance of the relevant rules.

c. Ministers of other denominations desiring to become ministers in the Christian Reformed Church shall be required to complete the Modified Ecclesiastical Program for Ministerial Candidacy (MEPMC).

d. Ministers of other denominations who have not been declared eligible for a call shall not be called unless all synodical requirements have been met.

The last of the three articles regulating preparation for ministry of the Word in the CRCNA deals with those previously ordained as ministers within other denominational fellowships. In addition, the Supplement to Article 8 covers some regulations regarding the nature of the calls themselves—to current CRCNA pastors or to others declared eligible for call.

Ministers from Within

It stands to reason that ministers in the CRCNA, once they have been ordained, are from that time forward eligible for call to congregations throughout the denomination—provided, of course, they remain in good standing. This is why synodical deputies are to be present and must concur with a classis' decision to declare a candidate eligible for call to the first congregation to be served (Article 10). Their involvement represents the interest of all the churches in the denomination to maintain appropriate standards. The deputies' concurrence and synod's approval of their work signifies an "automatic" signal to all churches that these persons are eligible for call during their lifetime of service without additional scrutiny other than the regular oversight to be provided by each council.

Making it easier for congregations to call ministers from within the CRCNA as compared to those in other denominations is a matter of good stewardship of the church's resources. Much has been invested in the training of these persons, individually and collectively, and it is not prudent to show no preference. On the other hand, there are those who argue that just as classes have no "self-interest" in investing in these persons, so the various denominations should have no "self-interest" either: let congregations, whatever their denominational bonds may be, have the freedom to call whom they will. Anything short of that, it is argued, unduly restricts the churches and betrays a "denominationalism" that stands in the way of true ecumenicity. Indeed, in an ideal world that ought to be the situation. In the real world, however, we have to recognize the presence of institutionally separate denominations and the confessional and historical reasons behind them. While the Church Order opens the way to ministers from other denominations by its regulations, a certain preference for those within our fellowship in whom we have invested much seems eminently reasonable.

Examples of the "relevant rules" referred to in section a. are the rules requiring permission to call provided by the classical counselor (Article 9) and on the timing of the call (see below).

Ministers from Other Denominations

The "relevant rules" referred to in section b. currently refer only to the "Orderly Exchange" provisions adopted in 2005 and printed in section D of the Supplement.

The matter of "Orderly Exchange" refers to a special arrangement with the Reformed Church in America reflecting the especially close ties between it and the CRCNA. The arrangement pertains to ordained ministers within the RCA and CRCNA, not to candidates for the ministry. Graduates of Western Theological Seminary or New Brunswick Theological Seminary who wish to become candidates in the CRCNA are instead to follow the provisions of Article 6 under the guidance of the Candidacy Committee and follow the required EPMC program. But for those already ordained, this arrangement provides some excellent opportunities to spend part of one's career in the sister denomination.

A congregation desiring to call a minister who is neither in the CRCNA nor in the RCA will run into further "hurdles" designed to uphold the integrity of the denomination: its unique history, polity, and practice in the midst of the worldwide church of Christ. It will have to prove to the synodical Candidacy Committee, the classical counselor, the classis, and the synodical deputies that "it has put forth a sustained and realistic effort to obtain a minister from within the CRCNA." It must also make a case for the specific need involved: extraordinary qualifications of the minister, long vacancy, specific competence as a new church developer, or a need for indigenous leadership in a multicultural or ethnic minority church setting. Once those "hurdles" are overcome, the minister is examined by way of what is commonly known as a classical *colloquium doctum*, an investigation into the person's doctrinal stance and awareness of CRCNA practice and usage. The members of the congregation (and the rest of the denomination) have a right to know that the one to lead them in ministry of the Word will do so from within their confessional tradition and identity.

Joint Ministry within Two Denominations

The Supplement to Article 8 has provisions for "joint ministry of ministers from churches in ecclesiastical fellowship." This pertains to smaller churches of two denominations that share a minister of the Word when each is unable to fund a full-time position. Such smaller churches should also be aware of options provided under Article 38g and its supplemental material with regard to "union churches."

Timing of the Call

The Supplement to Article 8 has two regulations adopted by synods early on in the history of the CRCNA that place restrictions on congregations with respect to the timing involved in the calling of a minister of the Word. Ordinarily, the minister in question shall have served in a congregation for at least two years before there is eligibility and must not be called twice for the same vacancy within one year. The latter simply protects a minister from harassment from calling churches (which is rare today). The former is important if the theological concept underlying an indefinite call is to be respected: if we believe that Christ has called a minister to serve that congregation, we should grant that four years might be a minimal amount of time for that minister to actually have been of service. It takes at least two years to get started. If the current congregation's indefinite call is not respected, its council might decide not to grant that minister permission to leave (Article 14a). Given the consternation that sometimes results from such refusal, churches would be well counseled to keep covenant on this issue in the first place.

Term Calls

Finally, there is the regulation having to do with "term calls." Circumstances can be such that calls "for a specified term of service" are advisable. Examples are a new church plant project, a temporary military or hospital chaplaincy, a congregation preparing to disband in the not too distant future, or a trial period for a new team ministry in an established church. What is important is that the "end game" is clearly spelled out in the original letter of call. A reappointment might be an option, but so might a termination, complete with an agreed-upon severance. Disasters loom if these matters are not agreed on up front. The procedures with respect to the option of termination closely parallel the provisions of Article 17. Synod 2000 also decided that a term call to a candidate—as opposed to one already ordained—should be no less than two years in duration. This seems only fair when a person is just beginning to hone the skills of the ministry of the Word.

I've taken note of the "Orderly Exchange" material in the Supplement to Article 8. What if a minister in the Reformed Church in America wants not just to serve a CRCNA congregation for an extended period of time but actually to transfer the ministerial credentials to the CRCNA on a permanent basis?

Excellent question! Obviously you have noted carefully that ministers of one denomination who serve for a time in a congregation within the other denomination under the "Orderly Exchange" arrangement do not transfer their credentials but remain ministers in their original denomination. If the intent of the minister you have in mind is indeed to transfer the credentials and join the CRCNA, including its pension plan and the like, then it is not the "Orderly Exchange" provisions that should be followed but, rather, the materials pertaining to "other denominations" contained in section E of the Supplement.

Some of us remember a rule having to do with reimbursement of at least some of the moving expenses of the minister by a new church that has not let a previous church keep that minister for at least four years. Where is this rule to be found?

Such a provision was made by Synod 1884, amended in 1954, and clarified in 1966 as follows:

> If a minister leaves a church within a year, the calling church shall refund the church he leaves expenses in full; if he leaves within two years, three-fourths; if within three years, one-half; if within four years, one-fourth of his moving expenses (*Acts of Synod, 1966*, p. 88).

Synod has never placed this rule in the Supplement to Article 8. What we do find there is the judgment of Synod 1916 that councils "should not place in nomination the names of ministers who have served their present churches less than two years, unless there are very special and weighty reasons." I noticed that the 1966 rule is still found in the *Manual of CRC Government* of 2001, but not in the 2008 revision. I have looked long and hard but have not been able to find out whether synod has ever amended or repealed or replaced this rule. If not—and this seems likely—it may still be in force. In practice, however, the trend has been toward longer periods of service, and it may be that instances to which the rule might still apply have significantly lessened or, indeed, disappeared.

At our Classical Interim Committee meetings, we have been musing for some time about two pastors, both of whom have served their respective churches for more than a decade. They just never seem to get calls to move on for a new start. What we were toying with is to have them simply exchange pastorates. One of us thought that synod had approved such an arrangement and we're thinking it might be refreshing for them and their congregations. Is this possible?

First things first: Synod 1934 considered the possibility, but rejected it as "impractical" and not in keeping with Reformed polity. Previous cases in the Reformed tradition, it said, were not good precedent because they were events that occurred under "abnormal conditions" (*Acts of Synod, 1934*, pp. 64-65). In other words, this would be an illegitimate excursion into an episcopal form of church government.

Synod 1976 apparently had no such reservations. A report of the Ministerial Information Service indicated that many had requested the possibility and proposed a procedure that kept any inquiries in confidence. It envisioned two "single nomination calls" to be approved at congregational meetings of two churches held at approximately the same time, and suggested that if one such vote were to fail, the other church's call would be "nullified." The consideration that this might be an "episcopal detour" was pushed aside by the committee's insistence that these were legitimate calls, not "placements" such as those a bishop would make. Synod agreed. So did Synods 1978 and 1980, when called upon to "review the arrangements." Apparently, there had been only one attempt at an exchange that did not materialize and was "canceled by partial resolution of conditions" (*Acts of Synod, 1980*, p. 363).

The Ministerial Information Service reported to Synod 1983 that it had "worked with the concept" on three different occasions since 1976, but had "not been able to complete any of them." The "concept has many built-in problems," it observed, "and does not seem to have much chance of success at the present time." Synod agreed that no further extension was in order (*Acts of Synod, 1983*, pp. 192, 620). The current Pastor-Church Relations Office that later absorbed the Ministerial Information Service into its operations has never requested a formal renewal of the experiment. What's fascinating is that the episode did not end with the 1934 objection on the basis of principle, but with the pragmatic judgment that it simply wasn't workable. So the answer to your question, I suppose, is that there is currently no synodically authorized way to do what you suggest, but also no inherent reason why you couldn't ask the denomination to revisit the matter with yet another experiment. Are you intrigued enough to draft an overture?

I. The Offices
of the Church

Article 9

In nominating and calling a minister, the council shall seek the approval of the counselor who acts on behalf of classis to see that the ecclesiastical regulations have been observed. The council and counselor shall sign the letter of call and the counselor shall render an account of all matters processed to classis.

Calling a minister of the Word is important business with huge implications for the life and future of a congregation. This is recognized at the local level in the appointment of search committees that spend enormous amounts of time and energy on finding "the right fit." But because ministers play a significant role in matters of the classis and the denomination at large, the broader assemblies have been and continue to be meaningfully involved in local calling procedures. In Reformed polity, we leave as much as possible entirely to the freedom of the local church—but calling a pastor has implications for the whole denomination. Just as in the Roman Catholic Church the bishop confirms the appointment of the priest, so in Reformed circles we insist on appropriate accountability to the classis. This is done partly by way of a counselor appointed by the classis who is mandated to monitor local activities and report to the broader assembly.

The primary responsibility of the counselor is to ensure that all Church Order and synodical regulations applicable to calling procedures are followed in the local setting (see Article 42c). Of course such "supervision" is always closely tied to assistance. Councils should have the freedom to consult with the classical counselor and receive whatever advice is needed to proceed. In addition, counselors may be asked to help with ongoing ministry during a period of vacancy. Perhaps councils would like to have the classical counselor chair important council and congregational meetings. Sometimes councils ask the counselor to help with catechetical work—leading a group of baptized members to making a profession of faith, for instance. Councils should feel free to ask for such assistance. At the same time, classical counselors have their own tasks in their own settings and should feel free to help arrange for assistance rather than providing it themselves.

We are beginning a search for a second minister to enter into a team ministry with our current pastor. Considering we already have one, must we still ask classis to appoint a counselor? Some of us believe that this applies only in the case of a "vacancy." There's also some debate as to whether our current pastor could be appointed if a counselor is required. Can you help?

I hope so. My view is that the use of the words "a minister" in the first line of this article truly means any minister or, better, any vacancy. Your recent decision to add a second minister to the mix implies that you have created a vacancy. In the process of filling that vacancy you will need to have a counselor appointed by the classis to monitor your actions and to sign the letter of call.

Previously I advised questioners that there is no reason why classis could not be asked to appoint your current pastor as the counselor and decide to do so. My rationale was that it's not so much about someone from the outside as it is about accountability for actions taken at the local level. The truth is, however, that the current pastor probably does have a vested interest in whom to call and even in the processes relating to that call. Thus, when a study committee

---

recently addressed this issue and favored "an outside person," I showed appropriate remorse and repented of my previous advice. I now think it best that the classical counselor be one who is not a member of nor credentialed by the congregation calling the second minister. Synod 2010 adopted the current reading of Article 42c and settled that matter (*Acts of Synod, 2010*, p. 903).

The article uses the word "council." In our church we have the "consistory" doing the searching and calling of a new pastor. The deacons are not included. Are we in violation?

I'm afraid you are. Synods meeting in the late 1980s and 1990 approved a number of changes designed to ensure that the right terminology is being used deliberately and consistently in our Church Order. Synod 1987 and the study committee that reported to it made the considered judgment that calling a pastor is the work of council, not just consistory, and changed Article 9 accordingly (*Acts of Synod, 1987*, p. 637).

I should add that the custom of having deacons involved goes back far beyond 1987 to the very beginnings of denominational practice. In their commentary of 1965, Van Dellen and Monsma specifically mention the deacons as signatories of the letter of call even though, at the time they commented on it, the article itself read "consistory." In other words, Synod 1987 merely confirmed a long-standing practice (consistory and the deacons) and introduced nothing terribly new with respect to our calling procedures—it just made it absolutely clear.

I. The Offices
of the Church

Article 10

a. The ordination of a candidate for the ministry of the Word requires the approval of the classis of the calling church and of the synodical deputies. The classis, in the presence of the deputies, shall examine the candidate concerning the candidate's doctrine and life in accordance with synodical regulations. The ordination shall be accompanied by the laying on of hands by the officiating minister.

b. The installation of a minister shall require the approval of the classis of the calling church or its interim committee, to which the minister shall have previously presented good ecclesiastical testimonials of doctrine and life which have been provided by the former council and classis.

Classical Examination

The examination referred to in this article is not the pre-candidacy examination referred to earlier in Article 6 leading to synod's declaration of candidacy for ministry of the Word, nor the ones prescribed in connection with Articles 7 and 8, but rather the post-call or pre-ordination exam conducted by the classis in which the calling church is located. In the tradition, it has often been referred to as the *peremptory* (as opposed to *preparatory*) examination. The terminology is revealing in that one of the most common definitions of the word *peremptory* is "final or decisive." The pre-ordination exam provided for in Article 10 is the truly "decisive" one that can open or close the gate to ordination and, most commonly, a lifetime of service as a minister of the Word within the CRCNA. Hence the denominational interest in the event is expressed by way of the presence of synodical deputies, who must concur in the judgment of the classis.

The "synodical regulations" referred to have undergone significant change in recent years. The examination as prescribed by Synod 1961 would typically last somewhere between seven to eight grueling hours. It included an inquiry into each of the six *loci* of Reformed dogmatics, as well as ethics, church history, Reformed polity, knowledge of the Scriptures, exegesis of both Old and New Testaments, familiarity with the "standards" (meaning creeds and confessions of the CRCNA), and what was referred to as *practica* (meaning matters of life rather than doctrine). Much of this template in effect simply repeated that of final examinations at seminary. Synod 1972 adopted new regulations currently found in the Supplement to Article 10 that more clearly focus on personal readiness for ministry in the particular congregation to which the candidate is being called. There is still some attention to "biblical and theological position," but much of the examination probes personal matters of "relationship to God," "commitment to the ministry," "loyalty to the church," and "relevance of the ministry for our times." Mercifully, the candidate now needs only endure about an hour-and-a-half of questioning. The focus is on how the person will function in ministry within this particular classis. Synod 1978 added for good measure that the earlier "declaration of candidacy may be taken to certify that the candidates have met the academic requirements" and that no further inquiry into them is required at the pre-ordination exam.

The history of "lengthy" inquiry does indicate the seriousness with which the CRCNA takes a person's entry into the ministerial career. None of that seriousness is removed by shorter and more efficient exams. Candidates for ministry via Articles 6, 7, and 8 all endure prior background checks and candidacy exams, and are subsequently held to one and the same standard in the pre-ordination exam provided for in Article 10. The successful examination can be regarded as the signal to the denomination that this person is competent and able to serve in the first congregation and any others yet to follow. All that is additionally required for subsequent installation in new fields of service is "good ecclesiastical testimonials of doctrine and life which have been provided by the former council and classis."

Laying on of Hands

The ceremony of the "laying on of hands" has its roots in biblical passages such as Acts 6:1-6, Acts 13:3, 1 Timothy 4:14, and 2 Timothy 1:6. After examining these texts and sorting through a variety of interpretations, a committee reporting to Synod 1973 offered a "guideline" on this issue that in substance was adopted by that synod as follows:

> The ceremony of the laying on of hands is not a sacrament but a symbolic act by which the church may publicly confirm its call and appointment to particular ministries. As such it is useful but not essential (*Acts of Synod, 1973*, p. 64).

We note, of course, that Article 10 does not leave the matter to choice. Ordination "shall be accompanied by the laying on of hands." A useful (though not essential) ceremony is nonetheless insisted upon!

A candidate has just accepted the call to our church, and we are eagerly planning for his ordination service. Some of us on council believe that only other ministers of the Word who may be present should be invited to join the officiating pastor in the laying on of hands; others believe that the council executive or even all the elders and the deacons ought to be involved as well. Who's right?

Synod 1973 provided a clear answer to this when it decided that "to invite only ministers, and not elders also, to participate in the laying on of hands is a departure from biblical example" (*Acts of Synod, 1973*, p. 64). Since a minister receives the call of God through the congregation, and since that minister's work will be supervised by the council, it seems right and fitting to have the local elders and deacons involved. This would also reinforce our belief in the parity of the offices (Article 2) and our determination that "no officebearer shall lord it over another officebearer" (Article 85).

So when this Article 10 uses the words "by the officiating minister," we understand it to be referring to a minimal requirement and not to an absolute rule that forbids the involvement of other officebearers.

May unordained church members participate in the laying on of hands ceremony associated with installation/ordination?

No, I don't think so. A congregation elects but a council ordains to office. This is the clear lesson of Scripture and of church history.

The candidate we recently examined had already moved into the parsonage with his wife and four children. That put a lot of pressure on the classis to decide that he successfully sustained the exam. Is there no rule to prevent this?

There used to be a rule that such an early move is not permitted. It is no longer in place because, for one thing, there are other legitimate considerations. The oldest child of the candidate you examined needed to be in school a month before the exam. The candidate was open about that, the matter was acknowledged publicly, and apparently the majority of delegates found this reasonable.

A rule still on the books is that "the date of ordination shall be officially announced only after the candidate has passed the examination" (Supplement, Article 10, second rule). So the principle you point to is certainly still valid.

I. The Offices of the Church

Article 11

The calling of a minister of the Word is to proclaim, explain, and apply Holy Scripture in order to gather in and build up the members of the church of Jesus Christ.

This article in its current form was proposed by Synod 1977 and formally adopted in 1978. It seeks to define as clearly as possible the core responsibilities of the office of minister of the Word. Article 12 spells out the various specific tasks the minister may be assigned, but this article lays out the minister's calling in all of those tasks. At its most basic level, the office of minister is that of a minister *of the Word*, that is, of the Scriptures, the Old and New Testaments, the gospel of Christ, the only infallible rule for our faith and Christian life.

The Core of Ministry of the Word

Prior versions of the Church Order had only enumerated certain specific tasks for the minister: preaching, administering the sacraments, leading in worship, teaching catechism classes, pastoral care, the ministry of prayer, and, along with the elders, the supervision of the congregation, the exercise of discipline, and mission and evangelism. These were enumerated without assigning any priority. For as long as the "regular pastorate" in a local congregation was in play, that shoe didn't really pinch. It did begin to pinch when increasingly the denomination had to struggle with the question of whether certain positions other than those "regular pastorates" were, in fact, "non-ministerial" or, alternatively, "in keeping with the ministerial calling." Missionaries and chaplains, it was thought, were clearly within the boundaries. Others were not such an easy call: "Collector" (fund-raiser?) for the Theological School, Educational Secretary, Director of Missions, President of Calvin College or other church-related colleges, teachers and professors at all levels of educational institutions (in Bible, theology, or Christian doctrine, as well as so-called "secular" subjects), editors, theological librarians, or pastoral counselors, to name just a few that became more or less controversial. It fell to synodical deputies to decide whether classical actions in this regard could be concurred in (see Article 12c), and it is not surprising that deputies were not in total harmony on this score. Synods 1977 and 1978 sought to alleviate the resulting confusion by saying that whatever a minister may actually be doing, what is essential is, namely, that this person is proclaiming, explaining, and applying Holy Scripture "in order to gather in and build up the members of the church of Jesus Christ." In the exact wording of the 1977 study committee, "The common denominator for all ministers of the Word is their ministering *of the Word*" (*Acts of Synod, 1977*, p. 647).

It is not without reason that in giving Timothy his final "charge," the apostle Paul begins with a reminder of "how from infancy you have known the Holy Scriptures," proceeds to the declaration that "all Scripture is God-breathed and is useful for teaching, rebuking, correcting and training in righteousness," and then homes in on the "charge" itself: "Preach the word" (2 Tim. 3:14-4:2).

This way of defining the office at its core is not only in tune with the Pauline teaching but also with the theology of the sixteenth-century Reformers. It lies at the heart of Protestantism. When Martin Luther set about redefining the office of bishop, he stripped away all of what it had become in the medieval church and insisted that if it is to be there at all, this office must be about proclamation of the Word of grace and little else. In the same way, John Calvin shifted the function of governance from the bishop to the body of the elders, relegated the administration of the sacraments to a secondary ministerial function, and insisted on the proclamation of the Word of God as the primary means of grace. The sacraments too, he taught, are means of grace, but they assure the congregation of its salvation only when they are confirming "signs and seals" of the "promise of the Gospel" first proclaimed on the basis of the "preaching of the holy gospel." It is by that "preaching" that "the Holy Spirit produces faith in our hearts" (Heidelberg Catechism, Lord's Day 25). In this, as Calvin saw it, lies the "dignity" of the office of minister of the Word.

Gathering In and Building Up

The Church Order here uses the words "proclaim, explain, and apply Holy Scripture" rather than "preaching" to indicate that every function of the minister must be infused with this proclamation of the Gospel. The weekly sermon is surely a primary task within that calling, but the words of Scripture must also be proclaimed through teaching, pastoral counseling, providing leadership, evangelistic outreach, and whatever else may be included in the job description specific to the minister's setting. In addition, the purpose of it all is to "gather in" and to "build up" the members of the church. Noting that "gathering in" precedes "building up," I wonder openly whether that is truly evidenced in our pastors. I also note that these two purposes are in no way in conflict or in competition with one another. What use might it be to "gather in" if we do not also then "build up" those who have now tasted the goodness of the gospel of Christ so that in their further pilgrimage they might be brought ever closer to their Savior and Lord?

Why must we endure the torture of learning the Hebrew and the Greek?

For the long answer, please consult with our professors at Calvin Theological Seminary. You might sense first-hand in what they tell you that they would not describe the training our synod insists on in such drastic terms. But I'll give you the short answer.

There is no way to live into the meaning of the ancient text for the first hearers without reading and hearing that text in its original shape and context, and, therefore, no way to apply that Word with its inherent relevance accurately and reliably to our contemporary world. Without this direct access you will forever be dependent on translators and commentators without any assurance that they actually "got it right." That can't provide much in the way of your being utterly comfortable in what you'll be saying from the church's pulpits.

I promised a short answer so, enough said.

I. The Offices
of the Church

Article 12

a. A minister of the Word serving as pastor of a congregation shall preach the Word, administer the sacraments, conduct public worship services, catechize the youth, and train members for Christian service. The minister, with the elders, shall supervise the congregation and fellow officebearers, exercise admonition and discipline, and see to it that everything is done decently and in order. The minister, with the elders, shall exercise pastoral care over the congregation, and engage in and promote the work of evangelism.

b. A minister of the Word who (1) enters into the work of missions or chaplaincy, or (2) is appointed directly by synod, or (3) whose appointment is ratified by synod shall be called in the regular manner by a local church, which acts in cooperation with the appropriate committees of classis or synod.

c. A minister of the Word may also serve the church in other work which relates directly to the calling of a minister, but only after the calling church has demonstrated to the satisfaction of classis, with the concurring advice of the synodical deputies, that said work is consistent with the calling of a minister of the Word.

Having defined the calling of the minister, the Church Order now parcels out the various tasks or functions of the office in accordance with what lies at its core. In doing so, it envisions three basic categories of ministry: first, those who serve in regular pastorates, then missionaries and chaplains, and finally those who serve in any other work that is "consistent with the calling of a minister of the Word."

Missionaries, Chaplains, Synodical Appointees

The actual functions of missionaries and chaplains are not spelled out in any detail. It is assumed and need not be decided in each case that these persons are serving within the boundaries of the ministerial calling. The church that calls them to that service is to act in cooperation with the appropriate committees of classis or synod. Examples are the Boards of World Missions and Home Missions and Chaplaincy Ministries of the denomination, as well as classical Home Missions Committees, Harbor Ministries, and so on. In addition, the reference is to anyone appointed directly by synod (e.g. the executive director of the CRCNA, Director of Denominational Ministries, and faculty members at Calvin Theological Seminary) and those whose appointment is ratified by synod (e.g. ordained faculty at Calvin College, various directors of denominational agencies, and any others who are appointed by the denominational Board of Trustees). Again, their actual functions are not spelled out in the Church Order but in separate job descriptions. The fact that their appointment or the ratification thereof is accomplished by synod is considered to be a sufficient guarantee that their work is truly in keeping with the office of minister of the Word. In each instance, after all, synod decides directly.

Other Ministerial Work

The Church Order deals differently with those whose work is with what might be called non-ecclesiastical agencies or organizations. Here, the work is defined by such "outside bodies," and the classes must decide that what these folks actually do on a daily basis is in keeping with the ministerial calling. This decision also requires the concurrence of the synodical deputies. The concurrence is reported to synod and that assembly has the prerogative of approving or not approving the work that its deputies have done in each instance. Thus, every year, the *Acts of Synod* records fairly numerous references to job descriptions that have been carefully analyzed in terms of whether the ministry of the Word in its most basic sense is taking place. Recent examples include an instructor of Old Testament at a non-denominational seminary, spiritual care provider at a hospice facility, and president and provost of what is known as the Christian Leadership Institute. In the past, synodical deputies and or synods have drawn the line at professors of philosophy teaching at an independent Christian college, administrators of pastoral care centers who didn't actually counsel anyone but simply ran the operation, and principal of a Christian high school, to name just three of these "rejections." A synod cannot interfere with their appointments, of course, but it can certainly decide that persons who serve in these capacities will not be able to keep or establish ministerial credentials and, thus, that local congregations are not to call them as associate ministers.

Ministry in Congregations

The most common category of ministries, of course, is that of regular pastorate in a congregation. With respect to these ministers of the Word, the Church Order does spell out what ought to be their particular functions.

Just as the first item of business under "The Task and Activities of the Church" is the matter of worship services (Articles 51-62), so here the first reference to tasks of the minister of the Word serving in a "regular pastorate" has to do with what happens in worship: the preaching of the Word, the administration of the sacraments, and the "conducting of" or, better and actually intended, presiding in the worship of the congregation. There is no insistence that the minister "do everything." Members of the congregation may lead in various segments of worship, but it is all at the direction of the minister of the Word, who, along with the consistory, retains responsibility for what takes place in the worship of the church. Delivering the sermon is reserved for the one who has been specifically trained for that important task. And because the sacraments in the Protestant tradition are so closely tied to the proclamation of the Word, the administration of baptism and the Lord's Supper is also reserved for the minister, with some exceptions in cases of special need (see Article 55).

Teaching, "catechizing the youth," or what is later described as "faith nurture" of all members of the congregation stands next in line, followed by "training of members for Christian service." It is significant that the Church Order holds these to be necessary functions of the minister of the Word serving in the local congregation. This does not mean that every minister has to be involved in it, let alone be expected to do all of it. Some churches have specialized staffs, each with functions that match their areas of specialization. It does mean, however, that teaching and training are functions of the ministry of the Word, and thus ought to be carried out under the guidance of the minister of the Word, along with the consistory.

The Church Order then lists activities that ministers of the Word share with the elders: the supervision of the congregation and one another, the exercise of admonition and discipline, the provision of good order, pastoral care, and evangelism. These activities are discussed in connection with eldership under Article 25. That said, it is important to note at this point that most often ministers of the Word are the only ones in the council and congregation to have received formal theological training in these areas. For that reason, and not by any prerogative of the office of minister itself, they should provide adequate training for elders and deacons as they go about their work. Regular discussion of matters of church polity, thorough training in how discipline should be carried out, and arrangements for outreach seminars are the kinds of activities by which ministers can assure that all officebearers are equipped for their special service in the church.

A Christian Reformed minister recently decided he would like to devote a few years to another area of interest, work that admittedly cannot be said to be "consistent with the calling of a minister of the Word" (Article 12c). While he does this, he would like to spend his weekends helping out a small and currently vacant church in our vicinity with any ministerial services it might require. Considering the provisions of Article 15 on "tent-making ministry," does this arrangement allow him to keep his ministerial credentials?

I doubt that this is what Synod 1987 had in mind when it amended Article 15 to allow for "tent-making ministry."

You do not say whether the "small and currently vacant church" has the financial base required to call a full-time pastor. If it does, it should proceed in that direction as quickly as possible. In that case, the services of this minister would not be required. If it does not have the financial base, it may wish to extend a call to the minister involved under the "tent-making ministry" arrangement. This would come at a great time, considering the desire of the minister to both retain his credentials and work in another vocation for at least a number of years.

My understanding of the situation you describe, however, is that this minister's choice to work in another vocation did not come about in conjunction with or after a call to serve this church. For that reason, I believe the proposed arrangement would have far greater integrity if the minister were to follow the provisions of Article 14: be released from office with the approval of council and classis and, when the time has arrived, apply to re-enter the ministry and be declared eligible for call. I trust that he could help the church as long as needed in whatever capacity, and, should that involve the conducting of worship services, the classis would be willing to grant him licensure to exhort. I should add that the addition of what is now Article 14e by Synods 1977 and 1978 has made it easier and more acceptable for ministers who have been released from ministry altogether to be declared eligible for call and re-ordained.

I am a pastoral counselor called by a Christian Reformed congregation via Article 12c to serve in a Christian counseling agency. For the last few years my wife and I have enjoyed worship at a congregation in another denomination. This church has recently asked me to serve as an elder, and that can only happen if I formally join as a member. Could I do this and still be in good standing as a Christian Reformed minister?

No, I'm afraid that is not possible. It is certainly true that membership and ministerial credentials are two different things. So you could remain called and supervised by the current congregation and join another Christian Reformed congregation as a member. But if you resign as a member of a Christian Reformed congregation and join a church outside of the denominational fellowship, you are no longer eligible to hold office in the CRCNA, and you would have to be released as a minister of the Word. As Article 3 states, only "confessing members of the church" are eligible for office.

I. The Offices of the Church

Article 13

a. A minister of the Word serving as pastor of a congregation is directly accountable to the calling church, and therefore shall be supervised in doctrine, life, and duties by that church.

b. A minister of the Word whose work is with other than the calling church shall be supervised by the calling church in cooperation with other congregations, institutions, or agencies involved. The council of the calling church shall have primary responsibility for supervision of doctrine and life. The congregations, institutions, or agencies, where applicable, shall have primary responsibility for supervision of duties.

c. A minister of the Word may be loaned temporarily by the calling church to serve as pastor of a congregation outside of the Christian Reformed Church, but only with the approval of classis, the concurring advice of the synodical deputies, and in accordance with the synodical regulations. Although the specific duties may be regulated in cooperation with the other congregation, the supervision of doctrine and life rests with the calling church.

Local Supervision: Regular Pastorates

It is important to take note of the constant refrain in the three sections of this article: "the calling church." CRCNA polity has deliberately chosen to make its ministers accountable to and supervised by a local council instead of a broader assembly. Other Reformed denominations allow for categories of "ministers in general service," an arrangement where ministers appointed by synod to serve, say, as a missionary or a military chaplain are supervised directly by synod or some synodical committee or agency. Not so in the CRCNA. The matter was hotly debated in the early part of the twentieth century, focusing on whether broader assemblies were even authorized to extend calls to ministers of the Word. And if not, how then shall missionaries and others be properly supervised? The consistent answer has been cooperation with committees or agencies of broader assemblies where necessary, but a local church calls and holds the minister's credentials—all ministers' credentials.

With respect to ministers in "regular pastorates" it seems quite normal to have councils carrying out the local supervisory role even if, from time to time, they are obliged to involve the broader assemblies as well. The most common trigger for such involvement is the exercise of what is known as "special discipline," which consists of suspension or deposition. The denomination insists that such action may not be taken apart from the scrutiny of the classis and synodical deputies. Other issues relating to ministerial supervision may also be referred to the classis by way of appeal, in which case the broader assembly does have authority to hold ministers accountable in the local setting. But on the whole, apart from such special cases, supervision remains at the local level.

Shared Supervision

This choice for local supervision has led to some difficulties and confusion with respect to those whose work lies outside the realm of the calling church. Does a seminary professor answer to the seminary's Board of Trustees or to the council of the church that extended the call? If and when the editor of *The Banner* writes something that leans suspiciously towards "heresy" of some kind, heaven forbid, who must resolve the issue? Synod? The synodical board? The local council? Numerous cases have led the CRCNA to understand that these matters are not taken care of with easy "either or" answers. Any cooperative arrangement with agencies or ministries outside the CRCNA will complicate the system for supervision and accountability. Synod 2002 provided the clearest answer by ruling that the "primary responsibility" for *doctrine and life* lies with the calling church and "primary responsibility" for supervision of *duties* lies with the particular institution or agency involved. The Supplement to Article 13b records the expectation of open channels of communication.

Supervision of Ministers on Loan

Even when a minister of the Word is loaned to a church in another denomination, the calling church within the CRCNA retains the exclusive right to final supervision or final discipline. Again, the outside agency—in this case the other church—has primary responsibility for the minister's duties, but not doctrine and life. The Supplement to Article 13c makes it clear that such loaning can only occur under certain conditions: the congregation to be served is considering affiliation with the CRCNA or wishes to be "strengthened in the Reformed faith," and the broader assemblies must guard against "proselytizing." If the loan arrangement under consideration applies to a congregation of the Reformed Church in America, obviously the rules associated with the "Orderly Exchange" noted in connection with Article 8 take precedence over those in the Supplement to Article 13c.

It is clear that the CRCNA is serious about respecting its ecumenical partners. There have been occasions in which schismatic activity has continued even after official secession: attempts to persuade members and congregations to "reject apostasy" and join the newly formed denomination. There have been times when ministers of other denominations have been loaned to a congregation within the CRCNA for the express purpose of leading it to "more orthodox environments." Some churches have even declared the CRCNA to be their "mission field." It is the sign of a healthy church to permit "loan" arrangements without crossing such boundaries of responsible conduct.

Our council holds the ministerial credentials of a fellow serving in a leadership development organization. His salary is completely paid by that agency. If they were to lay him off, fire him, or release him from duty, would we (his calling congregation) be responsible for supporting him financially? The way I read the Church Order, we would (and should) have that responsibility until such time as he receives another call or loses his ministerial status. Am I reading the Church Order correctly?

Normally, for someone working in a position outside of the calling church (Article 12c, 13b), the calling church's council has issued a letter of call that makes it very clear that the person is being called to work for organization x or y and not to any work within the calling church and, further, that the calling church therefore bears no responsibility for salary and benefits. So everything depends on what the letter of call actually said in this case. I hope it was done correctly and with that kind of clarity. If I am fired from the seminary and get no income, my calling church would not be responsible for any salary and benefits beyond that date either. Its only responsibility would be to declare me available for call.

If your letter of call was not clear on this point, and he is laid off, be sure to at least make his availability for call known as soon as possible and explore what severance package the agency may have made available. Hopefully, solutions short of legal action can be found for the interim. In cases where there is clarity in the original letter of call, such solutions are more a matter of benevolence than of polity requirement.

Sadly, our council has recently found it necessary to request the release of a minister of the Word associated with our church who worked for a nondenominational mission agency. Classis agreed that the minister's resignation was submitted "prior to the conclusion of disciplinary actions" and approved the release. It also agreed to declare that this minister is now "in the status of one deposed" (Article 14). Do we have the responsibility to report this matter to the independent mission agency's board?

Yes. According to Article 13b's supplemental material, you should even be keeping this agency's board up to date *prior to* final resolution by way of an official communication, let alone informing it in writing at the end about the completed action of the council and the classis. What your congregation and the classis have decided might well have repercussions with respect to the agency's hiring and firing policies (and thus with the minister's employment status); simply alerting them to a *fait accompli* seems out of keeping with shared supervisory responsibility.

In providing such information, care must be taken not to reveal matters that have been entrusted to you in confidence. It is best that you refer to minutes of official actions taken by the council and by the classis, without further comment. Inappropriate disclosure of information may come back to haunt you in civil litigation or appeal to the broader assemblies of the church. In other words, you may trust that the agency can seek any further information it may require directly from the minister involved.

I. The Offices of the Church

Article 14

a. A minister of the Word shall not leave the congregation with which the minister is connected for another church without the consent of the council.

b. A minister of the Word who resigns from the ministry in the Christian Reformed Church to enter a ministry outside the denomination shall be released from office by the classis with an appropriate declaration reflecting the resigned minister's status and with the concurring advice of the synodical deputies.

c. A minister of the Word, once lawfully called, may not forsake the office. A minister may, however, be released from office to enter upon a non-ministerial vocation for such weighty reasons as shall receive the approval of the classis with the concurring advice of the synodical deputies.

d. A minister of the Word who has entered upon a vocation which classis judges to be non-ministerial shall be released from office within one year of that judgment. The concurring advice of the synodical deputies shall be obtained at the time of the judgment.

e. A former minister of the Word who was released from office may be declared eligible for call upon approval of the classis by which such action was taken, with the concurring advice of the synodical deputies. Upon acceptance of a call, the person shall be re-ordained.

According to the liturgical forms for ordination, it is God himself who calls ministers of the Word to "their sacred office" through the call of the local congregation, and the call must then be taken seriously enough to elevate it beyond the normal "hiring and firing" of employees in society at large. And if both the denomination and the individual have invested a great of time and resources to prepare to serve as minister of the Word for a lifetime, there must be some mechanism in place that generally honors and protects that investment. It is therefore the expectation in the CRCNA that a minister's coming or going, or choosing to leave the office, is not merely an individual concern but rather a communal one that expects accountability on the part of both partners. This becomes clear in Article 14, which recognizes a "resignation" but insists that the appropriate avenue for it is not merely a "resignation accepted" by the local council, but a "release from office" granted by the classis with the concurrence of synodical deputies. A departure must be for reasons that are "weighty" enough in the eyes of the broader assemblies as well as the local church.

Council's Authority in a Minister's Call

The traditional calling process in the CRCNA is that a minister entertains a call from another congregation, spends time in information gathering and in fervent prayer, and then decides at the end of three weeks of deliberation whether to stay or move on. The congregation currently being served shows a measure of empathy without much fervor or, alternatively, showers its pastor with a barrage of pleas to stay, thus warmly confirming its original call. What has often been ignored is that ministers are *not* totally free to decide one way or the other. The council that currently has supervision must be involved in the deliberative process. And the question is not how well the pastor is liked or appreciated, but whether local circumstances are such that the minister is free or not free to move on. Perhaps the pastor's presence continues to be essential to the ministry in which the community is engaged. Even after the pastor has made a decision to leave, the council may withhold its consent, though it must certainly have very weighty reasons for doing so. Pastors are not "free agents" who inform the new calling church of their decision even before the current council has been consulted or informed. If they behave in that fashion, the assemblies may call them to order.

Release to Another Denomination

It was not until the mid-1990s that the current Article 14b was introduced into the Church Order of the CRCNA. Prior to that time the matter of a minister leaving to carry on ministry in another denominational setting would have been "unthinkable" and therefore was "not codified." In cases where this actually happened, the council and the classis would usually apply what is now Article 14c. In fitting modesty, we now regulate such an exit. The only reservation in it at all has to do with whether the minister involved has made the decision based on personal conscience or whether, in addition, the minister has also engaged in conduct designed to take as many parishioners as possible into the newly chosen denomination or independent setting—behavior that could be characterized as "schismatic." The classis is asked to make that judgment and to provide all the churches with the outcome by designating the person as "honorably released" or just "released" (positive), or as "dismissed" or "in the status of one deposed" (negative). These categories were not invented in 1995; they were drawn from decades of use as possible declarations regarding ministers who resigned, either for good and honorable reasons or in the face of threatened disciplinary measures.

Release to a Non-Ministerial Vocation

Ending ministry of the Word by taking on a non-ministerial vocation has sometimes been viewed negatively as a forsaking of the calling and "no longer wishing to serve the Lord." It is now commonly understood that God and his kingdom can be served in a variety of settings, not just in the institutional church. If, for example, after some time spent in ministry, a person finds that some doors seem to be closing while others seem to be opening, it is beneficial to have some appropriate avenue whereby release from the ministry of the Word is possible. It is not done on a whim and without adequate wrestling, but it may be the better part of wisdom. Article

14c regulates the matter when the minister requests the release; Article 14d does so when there is no such request, but a council informs the classis that in its judgment the person no longer functions in ministry of the Word. Classis must then make a decision within a one-year time frame. At the same time, Article 14e has been added to make it easier for the person to return.

Loss of Privileges

Reformed church polity usually differs from Presbyterian or Episcopal polity in that it does not recognize the principle that ordination is for life, regardless of the specific tasks in which a minister is engaged. Lifetime ordination is considered to be a wise move (given the denominational investment in ministerial preparation) but it is not a given that lasts for as long as no special discipline is applied. Thus release is possible. And when, therefore, ministers are released from the ministerial calling, they no longer have the authority to conduct worship services or perform any other official act of the ministry. A classis would have to grant such authority in a separate action regulated by Article 43.

I recently accepted a call to serve another congregation. When I notified the council of my decision, they voted unanimously not to let me go. I know I've only been here three years, but can they do that? And what will our relationship be now if I stay?

Article 14a leaves no doubt that they can do that. The last time this rarity occurred, the minister confided in me that he had apologized for not consulting the elders sufficiently and that relationships were actually much improved after the run-in. He served with great effect for another three years before moving on, this time with the council's blessing.

A minister who was released from office under Article 14b and served for about a year as pastor of an independent congregation has had second thoughts and now wishes to return to the CRC ministry. He is asking our classis to declare him eligible for call. The classical interim committee feels uncertain about how to proceed. Does Article 14e apply in this case?

If this person was ordained in a congregation not affiliated with the CRCNA, then this article does not apply. Article 14e applies only to those who once left the ministerial office altogether, that is, entered upon a non-ministerial vocation, and who now wish to return to the ministry. When it adopted Article 14b, Synod 1994 reminded "councils and classes that Article 8—not Article 14—is to be followed" in cases such as these: entry into the CRCNA ministry from another denomination.

I have only encountered one situation where the minister was released under Article 14b but then, as it turned out, was never ordained elsewhere even though that was the intent. In that case, I suppose, a classis could (retroactively) change its previous action to one under Article 14c and then proceed to declare eligibility for call under Article 14e.

In the Supplement to Article 14b, synod calls for "a proper resolution of dismissal" when a minister resigns and asks classis to "make a declaration reflecting the resigned minister's status that is appropriate to the way and spirit in which the minister acted during the time leading up to and including the minister's resignation from office." From what I have seen in practice, this seems to give classes every opportunity to be vindictive and "fire a parting shot." What are we to make of these four options: "honorably released," "released," "dismissed," and "in the status of one deposed"?

First, you should take careful note that these four possible declarations were not invented by Synod 1998. This assembly was the first to apply them to ministers resigning in order to serve in another denominational context or in an independent congregation. But the declarations actually functioned in practice much before that year. All along, there have been those, for example, who resigned by reason of a growing conviction that they could no longer assent to the church's confessions ("honorably released") or those who resigned under the pressure of special discipline instead of following the process through and looking toward repentance and restoration. In the case of the latter, it is better to declare such persons to be "in the status of one deposed" than to depose them after a resignation has been submitted (something the courts would not judge to be appropriate).

Next, as you suggest, we need to acknowledge that vindictiveness has no place in making these declarations. In fact, it is not so much a declaration to and about the person involved as it is a signal to the church at large. Congregations need to know whether they should ever invite such a person to mount a Christian Reformed pulpit again. If the assemblies have said that a person is "dismissed" or "in the status of one deposed," congregations would normally not extend such an invitation. If it was an "honorable release" or just a "release," the broader assemblies might allow for a preaching visit or even a possible reentry into the denomination.

We should also observe that it is primarily the classis that makes the determination with respect to the kind of declaration that is appropriate. The reason for this is that the classis is in a far better position to make these judgments than the synod would be. Even if, for example, a resigning minister has made some problematic statements in the news media that perturbs synodical delegates, the classis would still have a much clearer and more balanced view of that minister's past service. Synod 1998 acknowledged that fact in an action with respect to one such resigning minister by attaching the following note: "In the broader context of denominational life a declaration of 'released' might have been more appropriate than that of 'honorably released'" (*Acts of Synod, 1998*, p. 431). Still, it approved the work of synodical deputies who concurred in the judgment of the classis that, on balance, the person should be given an "honorable release."

I. The Offices of the Church

Article 15

Each church through its council shall provide for the proper support of its minister(s). By way of exception and with the approval of classis, a church and minister may agree that a minister obtain primary or supplemental income by means of other employment. Ordinarily the foregoing exception shall be limited to churches that cannot obtain assistance adequate to support their minister.

In the midst of articles that govern a minister's exit from the ministry, the appearance of this provision for "proper support" may seem at first glance to be totally out of place. It makes sense, however, when we consider that the original Reformed church orders saw the ministerial calling as a true covenant: if the person was to commit to a lifetime of ministry, the church should also commit to a lifetime of support. This is why councils may not dismiss the minister without the approval of broader assemblies. It is also why the denomination provides for a pension and insists on adequate material provisions, including appropriate salary and benefits.

The Church Order also makes provision for "tent-making ministry" with an explicit regulation for the protection of both parties involved in such an arrangement.

It is assumed that churches have "local autonomy" in these matters. The denomination does publish information regarding the average salary and benefits provided in various regions of the two countries and other such advice, but this has no binding force among us. At the local level it is a budgetary matter that by reason of the articles of incorporation and Article 37 of the Church Order must be proposed by the council and adopted by the congregation.

For the last three years, the council has proposed that my salary be decreased. I have now lost about 10 percent of my income ($2,000 per year). The congregation has adopted these budgets, and I am told by friends that it has been adequately informed of the reasons for this. It is always "the current economic climate" or "the financial tightrope." I'm beginning to think that they just want me to leave. What do you think? Is this fair?

It's not for me to judge your council's motives, so I'll not go there. What I do hear in your description of the situation is the need for honest communication. In most churches that I'm familiar with, the council has a "pastoral relations committee" that seeks to effect better communication between the minister and the council—in both directions. If there is no such committee, then surely you and your council can sit down together and thoroughly discuss the matter. I've learned in my ministry that the couple fighting over the color of the refrigerator probably needs some help discovering what's really going on in their marriage. It's high time to be more open with one another. Classical church visitors might be an instrument to help you and your council work through the situation.

We have been forced to suspend our pastor. We have the consent of the neighboring church and we will, of course, consider lifting the suspension or recommending to the classis that he be deposed, depending on how he responds. But that may be months off, and some of us are concerned about ongoing payments with no service

in return. Now that he is under discipline and therefore inactive, must we continue to support him financially?

Yes, you continue to have an obligation until the matter is resolved. Every suspension must be temporary in nature, even without the financial considerations. If a deposition occurs, should that be the outcome here, you may still have to provide a reasonable severance package, and, after that, at a minimum, provide diaconal assistance for him and his family for as long as that is needed and they remain members of your church. Request help from the classis if this is absolutely not feasible in your local setting.

I should add that this continued responsibility for financial support dictated by Article 15 has led some churches to lift the suspension and invoke Article 17 separation instead. If and when there is no good reason for lifting a suspension, such churches are not keeping covenant with others in the denomination when they choose this route.

I. The Offices of the Church

Article 16

A minister who for valid reasons desires a temporary leave of absence from service to the congregation must have the approval of the council, which shall continue to have supervision over the minister. In all cases of a temporary leave of absence the minister shall return to service in that congregation.

It was not that long ago that Article 16 appeared without that last sentence. In some instances, the matter of return to service was not obvious, or it was obvious only to one of the two parties involved. Article 16 came to be used as an "intermediate step" leading to situations intended to be regulated in Article 17 instead: a total severance from a congregation. The procedure was much simpler. After all, Article 17 requires the involvement of the classis and the synodical deputies, while Article 16 has no such provision—it is simply an arrangement between pastor and council at the local level. But the instances of resulting confusion and pain and the lack of honesty in the church-classis relationship led Synod 1998 to adopt the stipulation that after any temporary leave the minister "shall return" (*Acts of Synod, 1998*, pp. 399-400). That clarity has been a blessing.

This article provides for approved sabbaticals, time granted for healing after a breakdown, continuing education activities, and the like. The broader assemblies have not been involved other than in the form of general encouragement to see to the professional enrichment of the denomination's ministers of the Word.

Our minister is seriously considering spending a few years working for a Christian organization that is not church related, then returning to ministry in the CRC. At our last council meeting he applied for a "temporary leave of absence." We feel uncertain about how to proceed. Can you help?

With the term "temporary leave of absence," Article 16 envisions such things as a leave for further study, a temporary time of healing, or an extended vacation of some sort. The clear intent of the article is that the minister will return to serve the same congregation. If the understanding is that you will call another minister to replace him, this article does not apply.

My advice to your minister is to follow the provisions of Article 14c and 14e, release to enter upon and return from a nonministerial vocation. If he believes strongly that the work he will be doing "is consistent with the calling of a minister of the Word," he must demonstrate this to your council—and your council must demonstrate this to the classis and the synodical deputies—and you or another church may thereupon call him to that work under the provisions of Article 12c. If the work is truly nonministerial, then Article 14c is the honorable way to do this.

About a half a year ago, we granted our minister a leave of absence for further study. The agreement was that he would return after a year. For that year, the council arranged for "stated supply," a seminary intern whose work has been greatly appreciated. In fact, a majority of the council and congregation has now become convinced that our minister should not return. One elder has proposed that we ask him to apply for "termination from service" and, if he refuses, that we release him under Article 17a. Is this legitimate?

Technically speaking, yes, I suppose it is. Article 17 was written precisely because it sometimes occurs that ministers can no longer serve their congregations with blessing. This used to be referred to as an "intolerable situation." And I do believe that the edification of the congregation is a greater value than the well-being of one minister. But if your minister hasn't served for half a year, how could an "intolerable situation" have arisen during that time? Are people just comparing the work of the intern to what your minister used to do? Is that entirely fair?

I raise these questions because your council does have a moral obligation to stand by its covenant with your minister. You invoked Article 16 and the agreement was that he will return. So this will probably come to him as devastating news. Given some intensive and, above all, loving conversation with him, he may become convinced that the council's newly laid plans are best for all involved, including himself. As a bare minimum, you must certainly provide for his support until, also with your active help, he has found another place to serve. Note that Article 17 requires that the "financial arrangements" must receive the approval of the classis and that there is a minimum severance package that kicks in only after that approval is given. Note also that it might be wise to give your pastor some time to "seek another call" before (or while) Article 17's procedures are invoked. But before we worry about all of that, is it still within the realm of possibility that you take him back as agreed in the first place? You might be surprised!

I. The Offices of the Church

Article 17

a. Ministers who are neither eligible for retirement nor worthy of discipline may for weighty reasons be released from active ministerial service in a congregation through action initiated by themselves, by a council, or jointly. Such release shall be given only with the approval of classis, with the concurring advice of the synodical deputies, and in accordance with synodical regulations.

b. The council shall provide for the support of a released minister in such a way and for such a time as shall receive the approval of classis.

c. A minister of the Word who has been released from active ministerial service in a congregation shall be eligible for call for a period of two years, after which time the classis, with the concurring advice of the synodical deputies, shall declare the minister to be released from the ministerial office. For weighty reasons the classis, with the concurring advice of the synodical deputies, may extend the eligibility for call on a yearly basis.

d. In some situations, the classis may decide that it cannot declare the released minister eligible for call after the minister has completed the process of evaluation and assistance. The classis, with the concurring advice of the synodical deputies, shall then declare the minister to be released from ministerial office.

In the vast majority of cases, a person's ministry in a particular setting comes to an end by way of the acceptance of a call to another place of service (Articles 8, 14b), a release (Article 14c, d), or a retirement (Article 18). It does happen, however, and increasingly so, that the council or the minister or both request a separation or release from the particular call. Retirement is not indicated, discipline is not warranted, and no call to another place is forthcoming. Article 17 regulates such a release.

Removing the Stigma

This avenue of ending service in a particular place used to be referred to among us as the "intolerable situation" clause, carrying with it the negative stigma that in every case a particular minister was in whole or in part to blame for the difficult circumstances that led to a forced separation. In recent years, attempts have been made to remove that stigma. Invoking this article need not in every case reflect negatively on the minister or the congregation at all, nor does it necessarily imply that an "intolerable situation" even exists. Ministers may simply want to further their education, for example, and not insist that the congregations they are serving grant them a long sabbatical and then take them back (as Article 16 provides). There may be times when other personal or family circumstances trigger the need for a solution that requires a move elsewhere. An example that comes to mind is where a pastor's daughter suffered a rare illness that had to be addressed initially by way of the family's move to a more suitable climate. In such cases the council and classis should make it abundantly clear in their minutes that the release is granted by reason of further study or personal or family circumstances.

Denominational Interest in Release

The reason for the involvement of the classis and synodical deputies in cases of release is to hold councils accountable in "ousting" their ministers. There must be reasonable and adequate cause, not a wanton exercise of an "employer's power." The denominational investment in the person's ministerial career is still at stake and requires protection. More importantly, the theology of a divine call to ministry suggests that the withdrawal of external calling is a serious matter that implies more than just the simple issuance of a pink slip to an "at-will employee." Of course, congregations need protection as well. While the exercise of special discipline is sometimes the natural instrument for ending a ministry, serious issues that do not warrant such disciplinary measures may also need to be addressed. And such serious issues may have a bearing on future as well as present ministry. A classis may find it necessary to agree to a separation for the benefit of its member church and may even have to insist that corrective measures be taken before the person can be declared eligible for call to another congregation. That too is an expression of legitimate denominational interest and concern in the matter.

An Active Role of Classis

The request for a particular release from ministry to be presented to the classis must clearly indicate whether separation comes about through one party's insistence or through a joint or mutually acceptable arrangement. It must indicate whether there is agreement on a severance package and, if not, a clear presentation of the options preferred by either party so that the classis has an opportunity to come to reasonable conclusions in the matter. Congregational and classical minutes must indicate whether this is a positive circumstance that in no way reflects on the minister's performance, or whether it is indeed a case of dysfunction. If the latter, it must additionally be clear whether some form of evaluation or follow-up is requested. This might involve addressing the minister's conduct and suggested steps for professional growth, or, for that matter, the congregation's past conduct and steps to see to it that the next minister to be called does not suffer a similar fate. The dysfunction may exist on either side or both, and the classis is free to decide to implement certain corrective measures it judges to be necessary, usually by way of appointment of a special ad hoc committee as stipulated in the Church Order Supplement. In CRC polity, the classis has the authority to force a delay in the congregation's announcement that its minister is eligible for call, and it also has the authority to force a delay in the congregation's calling of its next minister of the Word (see Supplement, Article 17a).

Our church is feeling a financial pinch and the council is proposing to downsize from three pastors to two. It plans to rewrite the job descriptions for the pastors and then, based on the result, decide which two of the pastors to retain, or to which two of the three to extend a new call. Can this be done like they are proposing? Is not a call to a pastor indefinite, unless otherwise specified? Under which article of the Church Order would the third pastor in this scenario be released from his call?

You are correct that a call to an ordained minister of the Word is considered to be indefinite unless at the time of the call it was said to be a term call under the provisions of the Supplement to Article 8.

If all three pastors received an indefinite call, in this case one would have to be released and declared eligible for call under Article 17, unless one of them received and accepted a call to another position in some other place prior to classis dealing with the request. Barring that, Article 17 would be invoked by the council (by reason of downsizing), either with one of the pastors' consent or without it. A severance package would need to be in place with the approval of the classis. The declaration of eligibility from your council should clearly state the reason, financial difficulties, in order to make it clear to all the churches why this had to occur and that it had nothing to do with performance issues.

We are taking joint action to request the release of our pastor. Both parties are agreed, in principle, but now want to come with a reasonable proposal for the severance package. Is there a guideline for what is appropriate?

The regulations adopted by Synod 1998, noted at the end of the Supplement to Article 17, have a "minimum requirement." Beyond that, I know of no regulation that is binding beyond the more general concern expressed in Article 15. This is more a matter of "common law" in that certain precedents are set in specific situations and subsequently followed in further cases. The rule of thumb I've seen employed the most has been the formula that a minister is entitled to continued salary and benefits at the rate of one month of such severance pay for every year served. You would need to explore whether this is reasonable and acceptable in your setting.

Why is there this regulation of a two-year period of eligibility for call? And what would qualify as a "weighty reason" to extend that period of time?

The two-year period is considered to be adequate time to determine whether there is still an external call to ministry within the denominational context to accompany the person's insistence that he or she continues to feel the internal call. It is crucial, of course, that the announcement of eligibility is made early and as often as necessary to make this a true test. Every avenue should be employed, not the least of which is the denomination's own ministerial information services housed within the Pastor-Church Relations Office.

If the two-year period is indeed considered to be adequate time for this determination, it seems that the only weighty reason for an extension is a demonstrable "call in the making." There is a congregation about to vote on a nomination for call, for example, or an agency that has expressed interest in hiring the pastor for duties consistent with the ministerial calling, but not the person's explanation alone. In all of this, the ruling principle is that Reformed polity requires an external call for a person to remain in office. It should also be remembered that once the release is final, it is not final in an ultimate sense. The person released from ministry altogether may apply at a later time to be declared eligible for call and, having received and accepted one, be reordained to the ministry of the Word. This matter is regulated in Article 14e.

Is a pastor released by way of Article 17 still authorized to preach and administer the sacraments?

Absolutely, for as long as the pastor continues to be eligible for call. While the new "external call" is sought, the pastor has authority to perform official acts of ministry (preaching and administering the sacraments included) in all Christian Reformed congregations. This denomination-wide authority to do so is withdrawn only if and when a final release from office is implemented by the classis.

I. The Offices of the Church

Article 18

a. A minister who has reached retirement age, or who because of physical or mental disability is incapable of performing the duties of the office, is eligible for retirement. Retirement shall take place with the approval of the council and classis and in accordance with synodical regulations.

b. A retired minister shall retain the title of minister of the Word and the authority, conferred by the church, to perform official acts of ministry. Supervision shall remain with the church last served unless transferred to another congregation. The supervising church shall be responsible for providing honorably for the minister's support and that of qualifying dependents according to synodical regulations.

c. Should the reasons for retirement no longer exist, the minister emeritus shall request the council and classis which recommended the retirement to declare the minister eligible for call.

With these provisions, the church regulates retirement from ministry of the Word by reason of age or disability. Synod 1956 declared that ministers may request retirement at age fifty-five and Synod 1993 regulated the "reduced pension scale" involved in early retirement. Most do not request it before the age our governments designate as normal retirement age.

Retention of Title and Authority

A minister of the Word retains the "title" of the office and also the "authority . . . to perform official acts of ministry." This recently amended description clarifies what the traditional language of "honor and title of minister of the Word" actually meant: ongoing authority for the ministerial duties voluntarily engaged in anywhere within the denomination. Supervision with respect to those duties naturally falls to the council of the congregation last served. It may be shifted elsewhere, according to the Supplement, and this often happens when the retired minister transfers membership to another congregation. It should be said that this is not a necessity. Ministerial credentials and church membership are two separate matters.

Removal of Title and Authority

The "title" accorded a retired minister and the authority to perform official acts of ministry can be removed for good reason as a parallel to the "special discipline" of deposition from office. Retirement does not confer lifetime status. To insure fairness and objectivity, it is recommended that the procedures relating to "special discipline" (Articles 82-84) be followed even if technically it is the removal of title and authority rather than deposition from active ministry.

Disability Retirements

Finally, with respect to medical disability retirements, there is the possibility for a council and classis to recommend that the minister be declared eligible for call and thus return to active ministry. Needless to say, classis should have sufficient objective evidence to approve such return.

If I'm not mistaken, our denomination's Ministers' Pension Fund used to be organized on a "pay as you go and according to need" basis. We just estimated the cost for the next year and set the ministry share at the appropriate level. The system was easy to understand, there were no questions about the propriety of our investments, and we were never subject to sudden huge losses in the stock markets. Why did we ever change things?

I'm no expert in financial matters, but I've been informed that such "pay as you go" pension arrangements are now illegal. Even nonprofit organizations like churches must run their operations in conformity with the law that requires "setting aside up front" what is needed to "guarantee" an annuitized income down the road. There are times when governments may have to be disobeyed; when, for example, it might in some misguided way restrict our ministers in what they proclaim from the pulpit on Sunday morning or engage in even more blatant persecution. But an insistence on responsible financing for retiring personnel that simply reflects good stewardship is definitely not one of those times—in my humble opinion, of course.

May a minister of the Word insist on postponing retirement until he is, say, seventy or seventy-five?
That happens, yes, but ministers who desire to remain in active service beyond the "usual" retirement age would be wise to enter honest conversations with the supervising council to determine whether this decision fits the congregation's needs as well.

I. The Offices
of the Church

Article 19

> The churches shall maintain a theological seminary at which persons are trained for the ministry of the Word. The seminary shall be governed by synod through a board of trustees appointed by synod and responsible to it.

Part of our denominational covenant is to "maintain a theological seminary" whose primary mission is to train ministers of the Word and other specialized congregational leaders. To state the obvious, seminary professors are to do that training. But they must do more. They must also give theological leadership to the church at large. As Article 20 states, they must "expound the Word of God and vindicate sound doctrine against heresies and errors." The language goes back to the time of the Reformation. It may strike us as a bit quaint and archaic, yet this second role is also crucial in the life of the church, especially so in a day of growing biblical and theological illiteracy.

The Seminary: Training People for Ministry

A colleague of mine once remarked that he could only vote yes for a ministerial candidate if he could also answer yes to this question: would

I want this person to be my daughter's pastor? That brings the seminary's task close to home. Seminary professors' sacred obligation is to do all they can to model, encourage, teach, disciple, and train so that we need not be anxious about that part of our sons' and daughters' spiritual journeys.

Training people for ministry is a broader task than it may seem. A seminary education must open up new worlds of thought, new horizons of ideas, and new expressions of faith—expressions that restate in relevant ways the truth once revealed and long confessed. It must hone the skills required to preach, lead, teach, and counsel with wisdom, effectiveness, and integrity. It must model genuine spirituality that is infectious in others.

To do that well, the seminary must listen to the church, be attuned to its experience, understand its current needs, and bring what it learns to the task of training new leaders. At the same time, it must itself be leading. It must keep the church's focus on what is most important: the truth of Scripture, the mission of God, the gospel of grace, the time-honored witness of the universal church, and the cherished creed of that part of it known as the Christian Reformed community. That is an awesome task.

Yet we who do the training of pastors are struck by how the seminary is only a small part of the training process. There's a sense in which all professors can do is chip away a little, sculpt a little, inject some new notes into an already well-known melody. The bulk of preparation for meaningful professional ministry happens in the formative years from the days of childhood to the day of college graduation and beyond. It is done in the home, in the school, and in the parenting congregations. As such, it is the task of the church as a whole. Indeed, the seminary and the church have a strategic partnership in this training venture.

The Seminary: Theological Leadership for the Church

The seminary not only trains pastors for ministry, it teaches and gives theological leadership to the church as a whole. In a fascinating article entitled "Teachers and the Teaching Authority" (*The Ecumenical Review*, April 1986, pp. 152-202), Willem Visser 't Hooft, former General Secretary of the World Council of Churches, looks in broad strokes at the entire history of the Christian church and traces within it the relationship between the *magistri*, the theological teachers, and the *magisterium*, the authority responsible for the true teaching of the church, in our case, the synod. Having recounted a "somewhat tumultuous history of the relations between" these two, Visser 't Hooft concludes that "they need one another" because "both are in danger of forgetting the limits of their task" and "both need a constructively critical partner." "Great moments in the history of the church," he continues, "have been those when the *magisterium* [the synod or bishop or church] called upon theologians to make their contribution, or when they [theologians] came spontaneously to the rescue of the church."

So, for example, as the Third Reich developed in 1934, Karl Barth and others rescued a Protestant church "overwhelmed by a wave of syncretism" by publishing the Barmen Declaration of Faith. Today we might add the more recent example of South African theologians drafting the Belhar Confession, urging synods of Reformed churches to back away from defending apartheid policies on so-called biblical grounds. *Magistri* (theological teachers) keep the *magisterium* (synod, church) honest. They point it, when they must, to the heart of its historic faith.

One should not make grandiose claims about the contributions of our seminary professors in the history of the CRCNA. But who can deny the influence of a David Holwerda putting his hand to a report on "Neo-Pentecostalism" (1973) or an Andrew Bandstra to a hermeneutical report (1978) and a summary of the exegetical debate (2000) on women's ordination? Examples like this abound. Peter De Klerk's *Bibliography of the Writings of the Professors of Calvin Theological Seminary* happens to be a two-inch-thick volume with nothing but a listing of books and articles, often written for the church. It is no exaggeration to say that many have significantly sacrificed their academic careers to be of service to the denomination. And although they are less outspoken today than in the past, faculty advisers continue to contribute to synod's deliberations in June and serve on many of its study committees on an ongoing basis.

Here too the relationship between the seminary and the church is a two-way street. The church must also keep professors honest. It appoints them, reappoints them, and occasionally fires them. As congregations play out their witness in a constantly changing world, they often tug at the professors in two directions, both vital: first, challenging them to stay within confessional boundaries, and, second, reminding them that the practice of faith has outraced their cherished formulations of doctrine and theology. Here too the seminary must listen to and learn from the church in order to provide theological leadership. In a very real sense, experienced pastors become their seminary teachers' teachers on matters of church and ministry. Ideally, the seminary and church live in such a mutually serving and teaching relationship with one another so that we all attain "to the whole measure of the fullness of Christ" (Eph. 4:13).

Does the denomination have some principle in mind for having a separate seminary where theology is pursued apart from the other academic disciplines? Why not incorporate it into a university setting? I recently heard a sermon on Genesis 1 and 2, be it an enthusiastic one with some valid points, but one that displayed a definite ignorance about obvious scientific facts. . . .

There have been some serious debates or controversies about this matter in the early stages of our denomination's life. Followers of Abraham Kuyper argued that his approach of teaching theology as one discipline among many at a Christian university should be our guiding principle. But those who traced their heritage to the earlier Secession of 1834 in the Netherlands, Professor Foppe ten Hoor, for example, argued that the church must itself train its future ministers and that professors of theology are nothing other than ministers of the Word with a special task. Proponents of this position even sought to base their arguments on biblical texts such as 2 Timothy 2:1-2, where Paul was said to be giving that charge to his "son" in the faith. I must say I have considerable difficulty interpreting the text that way.

Personally, I believe that even if it were preferable, the American environment makes the realization of Kuyper's vision a terribly difficult one to implement. I also believe that the CRCNA is committed to both "principles" or concerns: a seminary that is under no other control than that of its own synod and, at the same time, a seminary that does not teach theology in seclusion from what its students have already absorbed in other subjects such as the natural sciences and psychology.

I. The Offices of the Church

Article 20

The task of the ministers of the Word who are appointed as professors of theology is to train the seminary students for the ministry of the Word, expound the Word of God, and vindicate sound doctrine against heresies and errors.

Professors at the denominational seminary are here said to be "ministers of the Word" with a special task to train students and guide the confessional orientation of the CRCNA. It is true that some professors were not ordained as ministers (the late Dr. Marion Snapper is a good example), but in those cases the church has also insisted on additional training to add certain competencies considered necessary in the absence of any formal theological preparation or prior ecclesiastical service. Early Church Orders carried with them a fourth office of "doctor," but provision for this was never implemented and all reference to it was dropped in 1965. There is no question, however, that many of the functions envisioned for that fourth office are carried out by seminary professors.

"Expounding the Word of God" refers to teaching based on a thorough knowledge of biblical languages, of doctrine, of systematic theology as it organizes the truths of Scriptural revelation, and of "practical theology" as it trains persons in the competencies required for successful ministry in the midst of our congregations.

The church has a right to expect that its seminary professors will provide leadership in evaluating the "confessional currents" of our time. They often serve on standing committees like the Candidacy Committee or the Ecumenical and Interfaith Relations Committee, as well as ad hoc study committees. A timely reminder of the tenets of certain cults, a helpful article on what predestination actually means, an "awakening of concern" on developments in our culture that threaten our heritage—these and others like it are much-needed contributions to the life and ministry of our congregations. The seminary currently produces a Theological Journal as well as a more popularly written publication known as the Calvin Theological Seminary *Forum* in which faculty seeks to stimulate and lead the church at large.

It has also been a matter of synodical procedure that some seminary professors serve as advisers to the denomination's annual assembly. The current rule calls for "selected members of the seminary faculty," in recent years interpreted to be seven in number, as well as the president of the seminary, "who shall be present at every synod."

Is it true that a seminary professor was once fired for attending a movie at a local theater?

Indeed it is. Synod 1928 referred to such activity as involvement in a "worldly amusement" and declined to reappoint B.K. Kuiper as professor of historical theology after determining that he was guilty of the offense (*Acts of Synod, 1928*, pp. 84ff.).

You should not, of course, rest in your merriment about this fact of history, but update yourself on where the CRCNA currently stands on "worldly amusements." A good place to begin would be to read a study committee's report on "Church and the Film Arts" prepared for Synod 1966 (*Acts of Synod, 1966*, pp. 316-61). If you don't happen to have that handy, I'd be happy to send you this report in .pdf format. Contrary to a rumor going around, I have it on the good authority of the current editor of *The Banner* that Adobe Acrobat is not a worldly amusement.

I. The Offices of the Church

Article 21

The churches shall encourage individuals to seek to become ministers of the Word and, in coordination with classis, shall grant financial aid to those who are in need of it.

The article begins with "encouragement" of "individuals" to choose the ministry of the Word as their career, their life's work. "Encouragement" means many things. It means the occasional prodding to consider ministry because the gifts for it are recognized by a pastor, a teacher, a parent, a friend. It means helping people find the most appropriate ways to prepare for it, then accompanying them in their journey with prayer, interest, and support. Accordingly, the recent appointment of a standing committee at the denominational level known as the Candidacy Committee included a mandate to work with classes in such a way that the rather limited "Student Fund Committees" be upgraded to become "Classical Ministerial Candidacy Committees" whose task fully reflects the intent of this article.

This encouragement should also take the form of financial support. The requirement that seminary students receive financial support is as old as the first synodical assemblies of the Netherlands in the latter part of the sixteenth century. The Church Order adopted in Middelburgh in 1581, for example, spoke of the need to provide for them *ex bonis publicis*, referring specifically to a governmental fund amassed from what had been Roman Catholic property. That language remained in use in the CRCNA until 1914, even when in the context of the separation of church and state in North America the state was definitely not involved. Synod of that year rephrased the article to fit the new realities. To this day the classes of the CRCNA are required to set aside funds that it obtains by way of ministry shares for this important cause.

In practice, the level of encouragement and support varies widely from one classis to the next. That a number of them do so little in this regard is unfortunate in a day and age when other careers that are far more lucrative or "professionally promising" are claiming more and more of our brightest and best. Perhaps the time has come for some standardization adopted by synod. The church will continue to be in great need of those who will excel as ministers of the Word.

As a seminary student, I find it very difficult to make a go of it when my classis supports me with what amounts to little more than the cost of my books. I worry about the totals of my student loan accounts to be repaid with a somewhat meager minister's salary. Are there no denominationally determined "minimum levels" of support for us?

Indeed there are not. We have generally allowed classes the freedom to proceed as they saw fit. I assure you that there are a number of classes that are far more generous than what you tell me about yours. One that I'm aware of actually has a written rule that the support must cover all tuition and related educational expenses. I should also mention that some classes with no or few students to support have come to the aid of other classes that work with far more students from their areas. This generosity has led some of us to dream about a denominational student fund that could standardize things so that there is no injustice of any kind.

As a member of our classical student fund committee, I'd appreciate your opinion on whether we should support those who are being trained for some form of unordained ministry in the CRC. Doesn't our Church Order limit support to the area of ordained ministry?

It is true that this article limits classical financial aid to future "ministers of the Word," a specific term referring to *ordained* ministers. We do not yet have a parallel article providing for aid to future *ordained* ministry associates. Classes may well consider that possibility and synod may well approve a parallel article in due time. Since *unordained* ministry (e.g. youth pastors with an M.A. degree in educational ministry or ministers of evangelism with an M.A. degree in missions and church growth officially employed in a local church and not ordained as ministry associates) is a relatively new phenomenon, however, one cannot reasonably argue that the Church Order *intentionally* excludes the unordained professional. That each classis must now review its policy in the light of the new reality is unavoidable. In doing so it must search for the *principle* underlying this article and seek to apply this to the current situation. Since classes are coming to totally different conclusions on the matter, it would be beneficial if we could review it soon at the synodical level. A measure of uniformity will help prevent injustice, often a subject of debate among ministry associates and seminarians as well as unordained workers.

I. The Offices of the Church

Article 22

Students who have received licensure according to synodical regulations shall be permitted to exhort in the public worship services.

Like declaration of candidacy, licensure to exhort in the churches was originally given to students by synod directly, then by the Board of Trustees of the seminary, and, most recently, by the denominational Candidacy Committee. After academic requirements are met and the appropriate recommendations are received, students are interviewed for this purpose by panels made up of committee members and enlisted pastors. We note that this licensure of persons preparing for ministry of the Word—in distinction from that referred to in Article 43—is denomination-wide, not restricted to a particular church or region. It permits students to practice preaching and worship leadership during their time of preparation. Such permission is temporary and is typically replaced at the conclusion of the study programs by the declaration of candidacy and then by ordination as minister of the Word, both of which carry within them their own authority to perform some or all of the "official acts of the ministry" (Article 53).

We note that this article does not say "permitted to lead in worship and preach the Word." Instead, it uses the word "exhort." The nuanced difference between "exhort" and "preach" is lost on many people, if only because the function looks exactly the same. The person mounts the pulpit, announces the text, proclaims God's Word, and applies it to people's lives. On the other hand, the person has not (yet) received an external call, is not (yet) ordained, and has not (yet) been authorized to administer the sacraments nor to engage in official acts of ministry beyond what "exhorting" involves. There are in fact differences in functions but, more significantly, differences in authority received from the church that amounts to a "lesser permission" than that granted upon ordination. This is not just a quibbling over words. It is appropriate recognition of the meaning of being ordained to ministry of the Word, what Synod 2001 called an "enactment of a pastoral relationship between Christ and the church, mediated in a certain leader" (*Acts of Synod, 2001*, p. 504). Personally I found that there was indeed a great deal of difference between exhorting in various churches "on the run" as a student and in serving "steadily" as an ordained minister in one congregational setting. Nonetheless, these "on the run" experiences were invaluable as preparation for a ministerial career.

Licensure to exhort is granted to students at Calvin Theological Seminary but also, in the context of the Ecclesiastical Program for Ministerial Candidacy, to students studying at other seminaries. Students at other schools should not seek licensure to exhort from the classis in which they find themselves. Aside from the fact that the student would be limited to exhorting within the bounds of that classis, such licensure regulated in Article 43 is meant for those who do *not* aspire to ministry of the Word, and classes will likely respect that provision and deny the request.

In addition, licensure is also granted to international students as provided for in regulations adopted by Synod 1961.

As an EPMC student at [a seminary in Canada] now licensed to exhort, I find it very difficult to know where the boundaries are in terms of what I am permitted to do and what I am not permitted to do. I would like to do only that which is appropriate and to be humble enough in my conduct so as not to give offense. Please provide some guidance in this area.

I am happy to do so. In a document we prepare for students at Calvin Theological Seminary, we enumerate seven items from tradition and Church Order that we deem to be "official acts of the ministry" (Article 53): the greeting or salutation, the blessing or benediction, the assurance of pardon, the reception or dismissal of members, the ordination of officebearers, the preaching of the Word, and the administration of the sacraments. The preaching of the Word is a recent addition by Synod 2001, and students, of course, are licensed to proclaim it, to "exhort." The other six items do not all carry the same weight. Our advice about them follows.

Do not raise your arms and pronounce the salutation and the benediction. You will undoubtedly upset someone if you do. Instead, change these pronouncements into prayers: "The Lord bless us and keep us . . ."

The assurance of pardon is undoubtedly a word of Scripture, and the student pastor is perfectly free to read it. Say, "The Lord says in Isaiah 1: 'Though your sins are like scarlet, they shall be as white as snow.'"

Reception or dismissal of members is really the act of the consistory as a whole. I see no reason why you couldn't welcome people into adult confessing membership on behalf of the elders who have met with them. This makes good sense, especially if you were the one who, as an intern, led a number of young people to make public profession of their faith. It makes less sense for you to announce dismissal if you have not been involved in discipling the person(s) involved.

Ordaining elders and deacons is also the act of the local council. If you are involved in that, the council must give its permission, and it must be clear to the congregation that it's really the council doing the installing. Involve the chair of the elders and the chair of the deacons to make the point visibly. Have them—not you—do the laying on of hands, for example, since they are ordained and you are not.

The sacraments, given our theology, are clearly to be administered by ordained persons, either a minister of the Word, a ministry associate, or—as a legitimate exception—an elder identified by the classis as having the authority to do so if no minister or ministry associate is available. We advise you as a student not to administer baptism or the Lord's Supper.

Finally, remember that you are not licensed to solemnize a marriage. Conducting funerals is another matter and, if it makes good sense, feel free to do so if requested by the family.

Does the church provide any supervision of student exhorters? I noticed that the Church Order doesn't say anything about this, and I'd sure like to report on something a student said in his sermon last Sunday.

I hope it wasn't anything too disastrous. Yes, the church definitely provides such supervision. Not to do so would be as irresponsible as sending medical students to perform surgeries at local hospitals without a professional mentor to guide them before, during, and after.

First, your consistory is in charge of worship services at your congregation (Article 52). You should bring your concern to an elder. Second, students usually bring evaluation forms provided by the seminary and distributed to members of the church. Perhaps you could have one of those given to you by the elder and fill it out so that the seminary is alerted to your observations. The seminary's Mentored Ministries Office monitors all field education and receives the formal as well as informal evaluations. Third, at Calvin Theological Seminary, each student is in a "Mentoring Group" where mutual accountability is built into the fabric of training for ministry; its leader would likely be happy to receive your concern. Finally, and most important, address the student directly, yourself, with just the right sense of timing (not right after the service, please) and an appropriate measure of sensitivity. Most budding preachers I know are happy to receive such comments. And besides, I believe there's something in Matthew 18 about first communicating with them directly.

I. The Offices
of the Church

Article 23

a. Ministry associates shall be acknowledged as elders of their call-
    ing churches with corresponding privileges and responsibilities.
    Normally, their work as elders shall be limited to the ministries
    in which they serve as ministry associates.

b. Ordinarily, the office of ministry associates who serve in emerging
    congregations will terminate when a group of believers becomes
    an organized church. However, upon organization and with the
    approval of the newly formed council and the classis, ministry
    associates may continue to serve the newly organized church
    until an ordained minister of the Word is installed or until
    they have served the newly organized church for a reasonable
    period of transition. Ministry associates who continue to
    serve a newly organized congregation beyond this reasonable
    period of transition must seek the permission of classis with the
    concurrence of the synodical deputies.

c. Ministry associates may also serve in organized congregations
    along with a minister of the Word and may serve as chaplains in

institutional settings in the community. Ministry associates who have served an organized congregation along with a minister of the Word may, in exceptional circumstances, with the approval of classis and the concurrence of synodical deputies, continue serving that congregation as a solo pastor after the minister of the Word has left.

d. Ministry associates may be called to serve as solo pastors in organized congregations if the classis, with the concurring advice of synodical deputies, ascertains that such congregations are from a ministry context where the standards for pastoral preparation required by Articles 6, 7, or 8 are not presently practical.

e. Ministry associates who desire to serve beyond their specific field of labor must secure the approval of their consistories and classes.

The Church Order now focuses on a second office "acknowledged" in the CRCNA, namely, the ministry associate, and devotes two articles to it.

Article 23 circumscribes the office by indicating its status or place within our structures as well as the particular fields of service that are envisioned for it. Ministry associates are "acknowledged as"—deemed to be—elders with a particular calling to serve either within or outside of the organized church that ordains them. Within that church they might serve as a director of church education, a minister of congregational life, or a worship coordinator, though not as a "regular elder" (as defined in Article 25). Sent by that church, they might serve elsewhere as an evangelist, a church planter, or a chaplain. They are "associates in ministry" specialized in these or other particular functions of the ministry of the Word.

Article 24 focuses more clearly on the exact calling or task of the ministry associate and spells out the necessary channel of accountability.

Lay Workers in Evangelism

The historical roots of this office of ministry associate in the CRCNA lie in what used to be called "lay workers in evangelism." In the early part of the twentieth century, these folks were given assignments to work in inner city centers, town or country chapels, and mission posts in faraway places proclaiming the glad tidings of the gospel. They functioned very much like ministers of the Word but were not similarly trained and thus typically referred to as "evangelists." They were said to hold an "extraordinary office," as John Calvin had described the evangelists of the apostolic era long ago, meant only to reach "unbelievers" in "special times," and never to be confused with the "ordinary offices" designed to equip the organized church for ministry. They were believers sent on a mission, not ordained officebearers. It is telling that Synod 1920 provisionally adopted a pension plan for these unordained workers (*Acts of Synod, 1920*, pp. 22-23). And when some twenty-five years later it was suggested once again that these people be ordained, the church was quick to point out that the "prestige" of ministers of the Word would be significantly compromised. Ordaining these lay workers, said the Board of Missions at one point, would encourage the "fallacy" that "men of lower standards of preparation" can do what ministers do and do it just as well. Synod 1946 agreed and insisted that no "proof of the validity and necessity" of an office of evangelist had been presented (*Acts of Synod, 1946*, pp. 74-75, 296-98).

In the meantime, of course, more and more lay workers played an increasingly visible role in the denomination's missionary endeavors. There were even some calls for an "official examination" to set some minimum standards—an ironic development with respect to those for whom no office could be found in the structures of the church. The primary argument against ordination was that the Scriptures permit three and only three offices. In keeping with Christ as prophet, king, and priest, the New Testament church has the minister, the elder, and the deacon, period. Evangelists were to be none of the above—they functioned in the "office of all believers," it was said, and no special office was available to them. But then by what authority were they proclaiming the Word of God?

It became evident that the only way out of the predicament might have to involve a thorough study of the meaning of office and ordination. Such a study was commissioned in 1969 and presented to synod in final form in 1973. This assembly considered some "guidelines" on ordination that suggested, among other things, that "the Scriptures do not present a definitive, exhaustive description of the particular ministries of the church" and that, therefore, "the Bible leaves room for the church to adapt or modify" its office structures. Synod itself, however, was more cautious in its decisions on the matter. It insisted that the "guidelines" do not "re-define the basic types of service currently assigned to deacons, elders and ministers" and do not now "authorize anyone other than ministers to administer the sacraments along with the preaching of the Word." Instead, any changes in the polity of the church on these matters can only be introduced by formal revision of the Church Order. Sensing, apparently, that after all this lengthy and thorough study it had done nothing to settle the question of possibly ordaining the evangelists, the same synod appointed yet another committee to study the implications of the guidelines, "especially as they relate to 'lay workers in evangelism'" (*Acts of Synod, 1973*, pp. 62-64).

A Fourth Office: The Evangelist

It took the denomination another five years before the matter was settled. All the options for ordaining lay workers were revisited: an elder with an extraordinary task of evangelism, a licensed evangelist, a minister of the Word with limited ordination, a minister of the Word via Article 7, a minister of the Word-evangelist, and a classically licensed exhorter who is also an elected elder of the calling church. In the end, the rigid threefold office concept was abandoned and the CRCNA settled on a fourth office of "evangelist" acknowledged as an "elder" of the calling church, but set aside for a ministerial function in an "emerging congregation" (*Acts of Synod, 1978*, pp. 74-78). Arrangements were made for the evangelist to be examined by a classis and officially ordained in the midst of a local congregation.

As it turned out, this introduction of a fourth office did not settle the matter but only invited a process of evolution of it that continues to the present day. Synod 1978, after all, only provided for the function of church planting. It said nothing about what would happen to the evangelist after the organization of the group; nothing about mission work that is not primarily concerned with the establishment of a congregation; nothing about chaplaincy; and nothing about possible responsibilities within the home church itself. So it was that Synod 1987 regulated the church planter's service to a newly organized church for a "reasonable period of transition" (*Acts of Synod, 1987*, p. 582). Synod 1994 expanded the functions within the office to include possible service in "an organized congregation along with a minister of the Word" consisting of equipping "fellow believers to participate in the work of evangelism" (*Acts of Synod, 1994*, pp. 488-89).

Ministry Associates: An "Umbrella" Office

Next, Synod 2001 expanded functions even further by asserting that the office "may be understood to have the character of pastoral extension." It is an "umbrella office," in other words, that covers a variety of specialized ministry positions: "chaplain, pastor of education, pastor of youth, minister of congregational life, and so forth." The same synod was also the first to propose permitting evangelists to administer the sacraments (*Acts of Synod, 2001*, pp. 506, 508), a privilege given final approval the following year (*Acts of Synod, 2002*, p. 537). At the request of CRCNA Chaplaincy Ministries, Synod 2003 approved a change in title from "evangelist" to "ministry associate" to avoid the impression of proselytism (*Acts of Synod, 2003*, p. 611). Finally, Synods 2007 and 2008 decided on when and under what circumstances a ministry associate might be permitted to serve as a "solo pastor" in an organized congregation (*Acts of Synod, 2008*, pp. 519-20). It is widely recognized that many more changes may be in the offing as the "fourth office" continues to evolve.

Ministry Associates: Qualifications, Standards, Limitations

Standards of "character, knowledge, and skill" for ministry associates were approved in 2004 (*Acts of Synod, 2004*, p. 619). They reflect the full range of functions envisioned for the office. So does the provision for examination by the classis—an examination that has some uniform components but is also flexible enough to fit a variety of tasks in different positions. A coordinator of worship, for example, need not present a sermon for classical scrutiny if the job description does not call for preaching. Precise regulations for formal training have not been developed.

Ministry associates serving in emerging congregations may remain when such congregations become organized (Article 38) for a "reasonable period of transition." Going beyond that "reasonable" period is possible only with permission of the classis and the concurrence of synodical deputies. Similarly, a ministry associate serving in organized congregations may "continue serving that congregation as a solo pastor after the minister of the Word has left," but only in exceptional circumstances and, again, with the approval of classis and the concurrence of synodical deputies. The reason for these provisions is the concern that established congregations have the Scriptures "proclaimed, explained, and applied" (Article 11) by those who have received more extensive formal training than a ministry associate, namely, the ministers of the Word. The denominational Candidacy Committee spells out certain differences in standards between these two offices that reflect the extent of formal training and reviews those standards periodically. This reflects diversity in the office structures of the denomination and is not intended to negate the parity of office acknowledged in Articles 2 and 85.

It is possible, of course, that the higher standards for ministers of the Word expected in the "dominant culture of the denomination" prevent "raising up indigenous leadership" in congregations with significant differences in ethnicity, language, or economic circumstances from that "dominant culture." Article 23d and its Supplement now provide for the possibility that a ministry associate may serve as a "solo pastor" in an organized congregation for a significant period of time.

Ministry associates may also serve as "chaplains in institutional settings in the community." The reference is to chaplains in hospitals, industry, the military, and the like, and it was determined by Synod 2003 that "the mandate, characteristics, and guiding principles that define chaplains ordained as ministers of the Word are applicable to chaplains ordained under Article 23." Among other things, this means that ministry associates can now receive denominational certification just as ministers of the Word receive it. Such certification is generally a professional requirement in any field of chaplaincy service.

Finally, we note that ministry associates are not "automatically licensed" to preach or to administer the sacraments in settings other than their own fields of service. There is no parallel to ministers of the Word who, by virtue of their ordination in one congregation, are eligible to preach and administer the sacraments in any congregation within the CRCNA. Thus, ministry associates must "secure the approval of their consistories and classes" if they "desire to serve beyond their specific field of labor."

I notice in the Supplement to Article 23a that "the concurrence of synodical deputies is not required for the examination of a candidate for the office of ministry associate." Why not?

As it is now, at least, the office of ministry associate is inherently "local" and temporal, not denominational and for life, like that of minister of the Word. The fact that this person is "acknowledged as an elder" means, among other things, that when a time of service is concluded in, say, a church plant that has now become an organized church, the ministry associate is no longer in office, in exactly the same way that elders and deacons are no longer in office when their terms have come to an end. If this person is now to serve elsewhere, a new calling church will request its classis to examine the candidate for the new position. The classis may "waive" that examination and accept its own or another classis' previous action in this regard, but it may also decide not to do that. One good reason for the latter would be a significant change in function that requires different competencies. Since there is no "automatic" credentialing for a lifetime of ministry such as we find in the examination for ordination of ministers (Article 10), the concurrence of the deputies reflecting the interest of the entire denomination is not required.

I remind you, however, that the synodical deputies do have a mandate to examine the job description for a proposed ministry associate position. They must concur in the judgment of the classis made prior to the examination that this job description is in keeping with the guidelines adopted for the office of ministry associate in 2001. The concurrence of the deputies is also required to decide on the length of a "reasonable transition" after a church has been formally organized. But as you can see, synod's intent here is to protect the "boundaries" of the office, not the credentialing of the person for a lifetime.

My friend served as a ministry associate for six years and was then promptly "fired" for no apparent reason. I truly believe that the council's action was wanton and arbitrary. How is it that the Church Order protects ministers in this regard, but has no such regulation for ministry associates?

I'm glad you asked. Synod now requires classes to "ensure" that ministry associates receive sufficient support for their ministry and just recently decided that "a calling church that terminates the service of a person in an approved ministry associate position must seek the concurrence of the classis in which approval was given." You can find these regulations in the Supplement to Article 23a. My guess is that even more will be adopted in the future to ensure greater parity among ministers and ministry associates.

I. The Offices of the Church

Article 24

a. The task of the ministry associate is to bear witness to Christ through the preaching of the Word, the administration of the sacraments, church education, pastoral care, evangelism, and other ministries in order that believers may be called to comprehensive discipleship and unbelievers may be called to faith.

b. Ministry associates shall function under the direct supervision of the council, giving regular reports to it and being present at its meetings, particularly when their work is under consideration.

Specializations in Ministerial Tasks

Article 24's listing of the tasks of ministry associates looks a great deal like the listing of tasks applicable to ministers of the Word in Article 12. The ministry associate is called to preach, to administer the sacraments, to teach, and to engage in pastoral care and evangelism. That is so because this wording was initially adopted for the fourth office of "evangelist." It has never been updated in any substantial way as the office has evolved and even been given a new name. The understanding, however, is that not every ministry associate will accomplish all these tasks, but that most will specialize in some or even just one. A chaplain, for example, will probably only preach, administer sacraments, and engage in pastoral care. It is often not appropriate for the chaplain to engage in overt evangelism. Similarly, Directors of Church Education might be limited to a teaching role and perhaps a bit of leadership and administration. "Ministry associate" is an umbrella term used in the Church Order but not necessarily in practice. The chaplain's office door will not say "John Doe, Ministry Associate" but "John Doe, Chaplain" and the Director of Church Education will have that title on the door, not the umbrella term. In this way the CRCNA is able to maintain just four offices and avoid a confusing multiplication of offices beyond those four.

Distinguishing the offices of minister of the Word and ministry associate in this way is in line with two principles adopted by Synod 2000 (*Acts of Synod, 2000*, p. 702). The first is the principle of proportionality: the greater the level of responsibility assigned, the greater should be the level of understanding, skills, and training. The second principle is the CRCNA's commitment to a theologically well-trained ministry of the Word. As Synod 2001 put it, the office of ministry associate "may be understood to have the character of pastoral extension" (*Acts of Synod, 2001*, p. 506).

Whatever the tasks a particular ministry associate is given in a particular setting, the heart of the office is "to bear witness to Christ," to call believers to "comprehensive discipleship," and to call "unbelievers to faith." This more clearly differs with Article 11's designation of the heart of ministry of the Word—not in the parts about discipleship and evangelism, but in the "bearing witness to Christ" as opposed to "proclaiming, explaining, and applying Holy Scripture."

Article 24 does not here repeat the requirement in the Supplement to Article 23 that the particular job description requires the approval of classis and the concurrence of the synodical deputies. But that requirement is in place. Focus of this scrutiny is whether the package of tasks fits the guidelines for the office adopted by Synod 2001. The substance of these "guidelines" is found in the current Supplement to Article 23a.

Ministry Associates as "Elders"

Finally, according to the earlier article, ministry associates are "acknowledged as elders of their calling churches," no matter what specifically they do. The intent of this provision of the Church Order is to place the office within the official structures of the local council, later defined in Article 35 as the assembly of ministers, elders, and deacons. As Article 24 now adds, "acknowledgment as elders" is meant to provide the channel of accountability. The work of the ministry associate is "under the direct supervision of the council" that expects "regular reports." The intent is not to suggest that as elders they are responsible for the things the other elders are called to do in their home congregation. Ministry associates are typically present at consistory or council meetings only when their work is on the agenda of those assemblies.

Is a ministry associate of a neighboring CRC congregation permitted to administer the sacraments in our church?

No, that is not permitted, unless the consistory and the classis have given special permission for the ministry associate to serve beyond the "specific field of labor" (Article 23e).

Our worship coordinator, who was recently ordained as a ministry associate, comes to every council meeting and enthusiastically participates in deliberations on every issue that is placed on the table. Is this appropriate?

I understand your concern and usually prefer to answer it by saying that such involvement in every issue on the table is legal but not always wise.

Note that ministry associates are expected to be present at council meetings "particularly when their work is under consideration." It does not say "only when their work is under consideration." Most ministry associates I know do not in practice come to every meeting of the consistory and/or the council. They are present at certain times when they are expected to report. If the consistory is engaged in a complete overhaul of worship, perhaps the worship coordinator should be invited to that as well, over and above the routine reporting. If ministry associates take it to be important to their work to be present at every consistory and/or council meeting, there is no law against it. But it may not be wise to be heard often on matters outside of their particular calling.

Consistent with our principle of parity of office (Articles 2, 85), ordination to an office—any office—guarantees membership in council and in consistory or diaconate. It even qualifies for receiving the privilege of the floor at classis meetings (Article 40). This right may not be infringed upon. Without going that far, a chair of council might nonetheless have a brief discussion with your worship coordinator to indicate that just as elders often defer to deacons' judgments about issues of benevolence and stewardship, and deacons often defer to elders' judgments about issues of liturgy and pastoral care, so too ministry associates might just defer to other officebearers on issues not directly related to their area of expertise and functioning. Enthusiasm, of course, remains appropriate, and I trust the brief discussion I recommend doesn't dampen it.

I. The Offices
of the Church

Article 25

a. The elders and deacons shall serve for a limited time as designated by the council. As a rule a specified number of them shall retire from office each year. The retiring officebearers shall be succeeded by others unless the circumstances and the profit of the church make immediate eligibility for reelection advisable. Elders and deacons who are thus reelected shall be reinstalled.

b. The elders, with the minister(s), shall oversee the doctrine and life of the members of the congregation and fellow officebearers, shall exercise admonition and discipline along with pastoral care in the congregation, shall participate in and promote evangelism, and shall defend the faith.

c. The deacons shall represent and administer the mercy of Christ to all people, especially to those who belong to the community of believers, and shall stimulate the members of Christ's church to faithful, obedient stewardship of their resources on behalf of the needy—all with words of biblical encouragement and testimony which assure the unity of word and deed.

The Church Order now takes up the third and fourth offices "acknowledged" in the CRCNA, namely, the elder and the deacon. It treats them in this one single article that concludes the first section on The Offices of the Church.

Limited Tenure

It may surprise us initially that the very first part of this article deals with the issue of limited tenure and not, as we might be forgiven for expecting, a positive listing of the calling and tasks of elders and deacons found in the two parts that follow. The explanation is to be found in history—in the history of the Protestant Reformation generally as well as that of the CRCNA specifically.

The Reformers in the sixteenth century focused enormous attention on the elimination of a hierarchy gone sour. The "aristocracy" of popes, cardinals, and bishops had become a barrier between believers and their Lord instead of a channel of ministry bringing them closer together. Its self-perpetuating character trampled on the rights accorded Christian believers in New Testament times, especially the right of church members to play a meaningful role in selecting their leaders in ministry. John Calvin believed that lay elders and deacons with a specified term of office would be the pawns with which to checkmate the pope (an image I encountered in the writings of Dutch theologian O. Noordmans). What future theologians might characterize as "overkill" or "overly reactionary," namely, to severely limit the tenure of officebearers, was perhaps quite appropriately high on the "to-do list" of the Protestant Reformation. Today it remains a "prominent feature" of many denominations who carry the Reformation banner. One must not only eliminate a hierarchy gone sour but also eliminate the possibility that it will ever happen again.

But what was keenly felt as a need in Geneva was not experienced with the same intensity elsewhere. The Church of England, for example, had its influence on the development of Presbyterianism in the British Isles and in North America: a tradition of lifetime ordination. The Reformed Church in America featured permanent tenure from the very beginnings of its existence and to this day speaks of elders for life, active or inactive. According to minutes of Classis Holland covering the period 1848-1858, "the calling and election of God are without repentance" and these gifts to the church must never be "set aside merely on the basis of practical concerns." In other words, even among the continental Reformed in

Europe and their spiritual descendants in North America, the motto "once an elder, always an elder" was never totally absent from the scene.

When certain congregations left Classis Holland and thus also the Reformed Church in America to form the CRCNA in 1857 and years following, a choice for limited tenure was considered to be one good justification for leaving. Serious controversy in the Grand Rapids congregation involving elder Gysbert Haan strengthened the new denomination's resolve in this matter. At one point, Classis Michigan declared a person ineligible for the office of elder because he favored permanent tenure. The minutes that record the incident indicate that it was even considered to be a confessional issue: the elder holding such a view—we now read with puzzlement—would not be able to sign the Form of Subscription. There were notes of caution on this issue in years that followed, but the Church Order of 1914 left no room for misunderstanding:

> The elders and deacons shall serve two or more years according to local regulation, and an equal number shall retire each year. The retiring officers shall be succeeded by others, unless the circumstances and the profit of some church render a reelection advisable . . . (Article 27).

Note that the only exception beginning with the word "unless" is not whether they shall retire after a number of years but whether they might be eligible for reelection.

The Depression era seems to have ushered in a time when the disadvantages of a rotary system could not be ignored. In 1935, the editor of *The Banner*, H.J. Kuiper, called attention to the inefficiency of mandatory retirement, pointing especially to the often painful lack of experience in consistory rooms and the decline in quality among the elders. He favored a more Presbyterian system and wondered out loud if one could prove from Scripture "that there was anything in the early Church resembling the constant shifting and changing in the consistory which we have today" (*The Banner*, October 25, 1935). His public call for change on this issue was not the only one. Some twenty years later the same sound was heard from Canadian churches, newly organized among Dutch immigrants, probably for lack of those who might provide the necessary leadership in reasonably fluent English. When, therefore, the Church Order was revised in 1965, the tone was slightly less insistent:

> The elders and deacons shall serve for a limited time as designated by the consistory. As a rule a specified number of them shall retire from office each year.

Note that the exception now pertains to the retiring as such, not just the eligibility for reelection. On the other hand, the words "as a rule" leave little to the imagination and indicate a clear choice for limited tenure as fitting for a church that tends to follow the practice of Geneva.

The Scriptures, of course, do not speak to the issue of permanent or limited tenure of elders and deacons with any great clarity. In fact, honest students of the Word will admit that, if anything, the apostolic witness in the book of Acts and in the pastoral epistles probably leans toward permanent tenure instead. On the other hand, not all elders and deacons are able to serve well permanently, if only because for most of them it is an avocation, a part-time function voluntarily exercised. Having a "natural" end to a term is a powerful practical reason for limited tenure. So are other practical matters: the full use of all members gifted to serve in a leadership role, avoiding new hierarchies among us by allowing fresh insights within the walls of the council room, and so on. It remains an interesting fact that Synod 1978 allowed an exception for the First Korean Presbyterian congregation of Toronto, Ontario, upon its entry into the CRCNA (*Acts of Synod, 1978*, pp. 34-35) and permitted it to maintain a strong cultural tradition of permanent tenure. But just as interesting that only a few years later this same congregation, having "tasted the Reformed tradition" in denominational fellowship, decided that limited tenure is not as objectionable as it first appeared to them and thus changed course.

The Elder's Calling

At the heart of the office of elder is that they are to be the "overseers" or "shepherds of the church of God" (Acts 20:28). As our liturgical form for ordination states, they are "responsible for the spiritual well-being of God's people." They are to see to it that Christ's ministry in and through the congregation remains vibrant and alive, that the Word is faithfully proclaimed, the sacraments are rightly administered, and the church's nurture of its members truly equips them for service in the kingdom of God. Together with the minister(s) and the deacons, they are to govern the church as responsible leaders who know what it means to provide good order and direction and be of service at the very same time. They are to guard the church's confession and see to it that this faith professed is lived

135

by the members and also awakened in the lives of unbelievers through vital outreach programs. They are to provide faithful counseling and, if necessary, solid discipline so that they truly "bear up God's people in their pain and weakness, and celebrate their joys with them" (Form for Ordination).

The Deacon's Calling

At the heart of the office of deacon is that they are to "inspire faithful stewardship" in the congregation (Form for Ordination). They are to lead in the exercise of showing mercy by having those who have "plenty" supply others with what they need (2 Cor. 8:14). They are to be prophetic critics of injustice in society at large, courageously addressing its most vital needs and boldly encouraging appropriate service of God's people to the community and to the wider world. They are to be good stewards of the church's resources as these are received and distributed with discernment and a generous spirit. They also are to see to it that Christ's ministry in and through the congregation remains vibrant and alive. Together with the elders and the minister(s), they are to govern the church as responsible leaders who know what it means to provide good order and direction and be of service at the very same time. Deacons especially are to set the tone of servanthood in the church, the church that belongs to the one who washed his disciples' feet and told them to do as he did (John 13:12-17).

We will deal with the issue of the deacon's delegation to higher assemblies in Article 40 (p. 235).

We're becoming increasingly disillusioned about Reformed polity dictating a high turnover rate in the offices of elder and deacon. It seems like people are just "warming up" to the job when they must leave in favor of others. In the case of one of our deacons, frankly, we were glad to see him go. But most of the time we seem to be trading in our "gifted performers" for "bungling novices." What's to be done?

My sense is that you are not the only one yearning for greater continuity. There's a great deal to be said for longevity in office when gifted people are making ministry happen. The chairperson of a nearby diaconate complained to me recently that her deacons never seem to grow out of apprenticeship status. No business corporation, she said, would ever tolerate such inefficiency. What's the use of casting visions for true diaconal outreach in the community only to have your hopes for it dashed in the Christian Reformed council room version of musical chairs? Elders tell me discipline just doesn't work when there's always a "stranger" attempting the outreach.

As I pondered your question for a while, I began to appreciate your honesty about the one whose exit gave you joy. At the very least it is a glimmer of appreciation for limited tenure. A slated retirement is certainly less traumatic than a resignation or dismissal for lack of performance.

The truth is that the practice of limited tenure has certain advantages. The more frequent the rotation, the more people we can use to serve in office. The gifted should have that opportunity. And if terms are reasonably short, more will be willing. Fresh insights and approaches sometimes enliven the council room as well as our congregational life. We avoid all semblance of hierarchy or domination by a particular group and lay no particularly heavy burdens on relatively few.

You will counter immediately, of course, with the disadvantages you point to. Practice makes perfect, and the earlier we release from office, the less perfection we attain. Pastoral bonds are important and take time to be developed. Gaining a vision for particular ministries doesn't happen overnight. Growing in confidence doesn't either. This phenomenon is especially noticeable at our broader assemblies where ministers generally rule the roost simply because they have the experience.

Practical considerations alone cannot settle this issue among us. But the fact that Scriptures do not address the issue directly and that fear of hierarchy is at the root of our choice has made us somewhat cautious about binding the church's practice in the extreme, about becoming "ultra-Reformed" in the matter. This caution, I suppose, is what I would like especially to bring to your attention as you ponder what's to be done in your congregation. The fact is that Article 25a does not bind us half as much as our established customs do. And we must never equate those two.

Please note carefully that Article 25a does not spell out exactly how long the "limited time" must be. Such a time must be "designated by the council." It could be two years, three years, four years, or even five years. It could be half of council, a quarter of council, or even an eighth. Thus, in a twenty-member council, you could have two elders and two deacons retiring every year, while the other sixteen members continue on their five-year terms. The article indicates that "the retiring officebearers shall be succeeded by others," but goes on to say that exceptions are possible if "the circumstances and the profit of the church make immediate eligibility for reelection advisable." Those reelected must then "be reinstalled." But as you can see, one person could serve for ten years straight.

At the heart of our limited tenure provision is not the detail but the principle that the congregation must remain meaningfully empowered to choose its officebearers. This, it seems to me, is what we must hang on to at all cost because it appears to be the lesson of Scripture, Reformed history, and Reformed polity. At the same time, the Church Order provides far more room in these matters than the local rules most of us have adopted as our own. What's to be done? We should review them.

In our church, deacons are very little more than "elders in waiting." They learn the ropes of church government a little, but busy themselves more with "material" than with "spiritual" things. Every time a big decision about the church's ministry is to be made, they are told they must "defer to the elders." Is this true elsewhere in our denomination?

Your church is certainly not alone in such a disposition toward the deacons. It is also true that many other churches have redefined what ordination and leadership are really all about and militate against what you're experiencing. It's been that way for as long as the CRCNA has existed. The tensions have never been totally resolved.

Just for the fun of it, I'll give you a taste of both sides in our historical narrative.

The minutes of Classis Holland, meeting on April 30, 1851, tell of a certain Mr. Paul Van Vulpen of Grand Haven who "declined the election to the office of deacon, being angry that the office of elder had not been entrusted to him." Four years after the CRCNA came into existence, Classis Michigan ruled that a deacon presently serving a term could be placed on nomination for the office of elder;

if elected, nominations for a new deacon would follow; if not, he would simply serve out his term (February 6, 1861, p. 15). You hear nothing, of course, about an elder being nominated to the office of deacon. It sounds a whole lot like what you call "elders in waiting." H. Beuker, seminary professor, taught that elders may do the work of a deacon, but not vice versa, based on the theory that the diaconate finds its roots in the "seven" of Acts 6. And the spin on that text was that the ruling offices (apostles) are focused on the "spiritual," the serving offices (deacons) on the "material" (*Wenken over Kerkrecht en Kerkregeering*, p. 25).

On the other hand, William Heyns, also a seminary professor, once applauded the formation of diaconal conferences, but insisted that these were "insufficient solutions" because they had no authority to act on behalf of the churches. The ideal solution, he said, would be to delegate deacons to major assemblies with the power to deal with all matters brought before them that concern the ministry of mercy (*Gereformeerde Amerikaan*, January, 1909, pp. 54-57; September, 1909, pp. 484-88; October, 1909, pp. 497-502; December, 1913, pp. 542-58). More recently, Trinity CRC of Iowa City admitted to a "long-standing practice" of having "the elders conduct annual home visitation accompanied by deacons." The consistory flatly denied that in this way the deacons were doing the work of the elders. On the contrary, "in a congregation with a large number of students in which there is rapid turnover and [there are] cases of acute, short-term financial need," such an arrangement actually helped the deacons "in fulfilling *their* office." Upon hearing of it, Classis Pella declared that this practice was "in violation of the Church Order" since Church Order Article 65 "assigns the task only to ministers and elders" and the council promptly appealed. Synod 1981 was perplexed enough to "withhold action on the appeal" even though it hinted that, technically speaking, deacons on home visitation might well constitute a "deviation" (*Acts of Synod, 1981*, pp. 101-02).

There are many more such stories recorded in the annals of our denomination, some of them quite delightful. Very notable is the unauthorized "experiment" on the part of Classis Muskegon in the 1970s to have its churches delegate deacons to a governing assembly, and the subsequent recommendation of a minority report to the

Synod of 1980 to carry that experimentation into the rest of the denomination. That recommendation was ruled out of order (*Acts of Synod, 1980*, pp. 105-06) and twenty-two delegates had their negative votes recorded. Just seventeen years later, synod changed course and permitted the delegation of deacons to classis (*Acts of Synod, 1997*, p. 621). I could go on and on.

Instead, I'll just remind you that the offices do not differ in "dignity and honor" (Article 2) and that by our common consent, "no officebearer shall lord it over another officebearer" (Article 85). I would hope that a greater sense of that parity might penetrate the walls of your church.

II. The Assemblies of the Church

The first section of the Church Order dealt with the *who* of the institutional church: they are its leaders, given by Christ "to equip his people for works of service, so that the body of Christ may be built up until we all reach unity in the faith and in the knowledge of the Son of God and become mature, attaining to the whole measure of the fullness of Christ" (Eph. 4:12-13).

This second section deals with the *how* of the institutional church: officebearers do their work in mutual accountability and in recognition and pursuit of the unity of the body by way of its assemblies.

II. The Assemblies of the Church

Article 26

> The assemblies of the church are the council, the classis, and the synod.

Assemblies Defined

The assemblies are church governmental structures that are deliberative in nature. The adjective is not in common use. It is derived, of course, from the verb *deliberate*, which my dictionary defines, in part, as "to think carefully or attentively." In the history of Reformed churches, however, it has come to mean much more than that. It is not simply a matter of thoughtful reflection, or even of wise judgment, but of discerning the will of the Lord. It is prayerful decision-making in the conviction that God will rule and lead his church by his Spirit.

Officebearers rule and lead in concert, never as autonomous individuals. They assemble or gather to deliberate in the same way that the leaders described in Acts 15 gathered at Jerusalem. They do not lord it over each other (Article 85). They come to listen carefully to one another and to discern what the will of God might be, how the Spirit is leading them. That is the reality of Christ's presence in the midst of the church's affairs just as he promised it: "surely I am with you always, to the very end of the age" (Matt. 28:20). In the humility of bearing office, in communal discernment of God's will, church leaders see to it that Christ remains "the only universal bishop and the only head of the church" (Belgic Confession, Article 31).

The list of assemblies (council, classis, and synod) recognizes the organic wholeness of the church. The Scriptures present the church as both local and universal, not one or the other. It is the body of Christ, the people of God, gathered in many different places but bound together as a spiritual organism, a new creation in him. This is certainly how the apostle Paul describes the church in the first chapters of Ephesians and Colossians. For Paul, this idea was more than a moot point of doctrine. He insisted, for example, that churches throughout Asia Minor demonstrate their oneness with the "mother church" in Jerusalem by way of offerings (1 Cor. 16:1-3).

The Protestant Reformation remained faithful to this biblical notion of catholicity even while it rejected a hierarchy gone astray. In its objections to papal authority, it did not resort to the obvious weapon of a supposed "autonomy of the local church." Instead it fought for a universal church renewed, restored, and purged of evils. Luther and Calvin did not wake up one day and decide then and there to leave the Roman Catholic Church and "establish" new denominations. They sought to renew the church that was. Thus the Belgic Confession too speaks of "one single catholic or universal church" that "is not confined, bound, or limited to a certain place or certain persons" but "is spread and dispersed throughout the entire world" (Article 27).

Today it is tempting to view the local congregation as an independent entity free of outside control. Denominations were designed to express the organic wholeness of the church as broadly as possible, but contemporary thinking increasingly views them as an "outside interference." It can be dangerous for the local church to lack accountability to the larger church. It is not surprising, then, that those who have studied the phenomenon of pastoral abuse testify to the fact that most churches within which abuse occurs tend to be independent, autonomous groups not subject to a system of checks and balances. The transition from independent church to dangerous sect is not as giant a leap as we would like to believe. Our own tradition teaches us not to be naïve on this score.

The Functions of Assemblies

The assemblies are governmental bodies designed to express the rule of Christ through officebearers. These bodies do not constitute the church, but only the governmental structures that provide leadership within the church. They do not themselves, for example, worship or administer the sacraments or engage in faith nurture or pastoral care. They do ministry only when such ministry "is beyond the scope and resources of the local churches" (see, for example, Article 75). While assemblies in other Reformed denominations (e.g. presbyteries in the PCUSA or classes in the RCA) sometimes celebrate communion of their own accord, the assemblies of the Christian Reformed Church only celebrate communion when a local congregation sponsors the worship and its members are also invited to attend.

Though limited in this way, assemblies still govern on behalf of the Lord of the church. They are gatherings of officebearers. When a local council approves a new ministry program, adjudicates a dispute, or moves to excommunicate an unrepentant member who refuses to heed its admonitions, that council acts with the authority of Christ himself. Similarly, when a classis permits that same council to proceed with the excommunication of that member (a requirement of Supplement, Articles 78-81) or when a synod takes a stand on a major doctrinal or church political issue and expects all churches to accept that position (a requirement of Articles 29, 47, and 86), these assemblies act with the authority of Christ himself.

The roles of the various assemblies and their relationship to one another are fleshed out in the articles that follow. At this point it is important to observe that we tend to follow what some have called the principle of subsidiarity. Briefly stated, this principle holds that we allow the local congregation to do all that it is able to do by itself, reserving for broader assemblies and the larger church that which the local congregation cannot do all by itself, or that which requires broader adjudication, or that which lies within the common interest of all the churches. This does not mean, however, that the local congregation (and its council) is completely autonomous. The genius of assemblies in the Reformed system is that they bring us a structure of accountability to the broader church and, through that broader church, to Christ.

Do all churches of Reformed persuasion use the terminology of council, classis, and synod?

No. Presbyterian denominations, for example, usually feature the local "session," regional "presbytery," and the "synod," with a "general assembly" to boot. These are also "geographical" designations respecting the catholicity of the church. It should be clear, however, that they are not exactly the same in constitution and in mutual relationship. The Presbyterian minister, for example, is ordained by a presbytery, not a local church. The minister is a continuing member of a presbytery as well as a member of a session of the local congregation. The session does not include deacons, just the minister(s) and the elders. The "synod" (we would say *particular* or *regional* synod) is made up of "commissioners" (we would say *delegates*) from presbyteries. So is the general assembly (we would say *synod*), but it is a much larger body, in most Presbyterian denominations made up of more than one synod.

There are many other variants. Sometimes Reformed denominations use the same terminology but incorporate different features in the governmental structures referred to. So, for example, the Reformed Church in America's classis sometimes resembles a presbytery in more ways than ours does.

I am surprised to find that only three assemblies are listed. Aren't there at least three more, namely, the consistory, the diaconate, and the congregational meeting?

You raise a very good question. Article 35 does indeed introduce the "consistory" (minister and elders) and the "diaconate" (deacons only), but these are considered subsets of the "council" and not separate local assemblies. That is not just my opinion. Two synods deliberately addressed this precise issue. Synod 1988 actually proposed a revision to Article 26 that listed five assemblies, including the consistory and the diaconate (*Acts of Synod, 1988*, p. 609). The following synod, however, did not adopt this change based on these revealing grounds:

> The church in Belgic Confession Article 30 confesses
> that the council (comprised of ministers, elders, and
> deacons) governs the church.

Historically the Church Order has recognized the council (formerly the general consistory) as the only local assembly.

To adopt the proposed change in Church Order Article 26 and 27 would confuse the appeal and overture procedure.

Of the three local bodies listed in Church Order Article 35 it is the council which is assigned the "common administration of the church." Hence, in enumerating the assemblies of the church at large, it is necessary to refer only to the council as the assembly of the local church (*Acts of Synod, 1989*, p. 523).

As for the congregational meeting, it is actually considered to be a meeting of the council to which all confessing members are invited in order to express their judgment on items presented to them by that council. The council retains the final authority in "making and carrying out final decisions," with some exceptions (Article 37). Minutes are typically approved at the next council meeting, not the next congregational meeting. In Reformed church polity, church government is not in the hands of all members but only of those who have been elected and ordained to office. On this issue it is perfectly analogous to what we find in civil government: senators, representatives, members of parliament, premiers, and state governors are in charge, not all citizens.

Has the CRCNA ever considered establishing regional synods?

Yes, regional or "particular" synods are part of the CRCNA's roots in the churches of the Netherlands. The Church Order referred to them in this article until 1965, although the words "the particular synod" were placed in parentheses from 1914 until 1965. The parentheses indicated that they just hadn't been implemented by reason of the size of the denomination rather than any confessional or theological reason.

This issue might qualify as a promising nominee for the most recurring debate within the denomination. I don't want to bore you with a listing of all the synodical assemblies that dealt with it for an entire century, from 1894 to 1995. The reason why relatively few feathers have been ruffled over it is that argumentation on both sides is more pragmatic than principial. I should add, however, that it did take on a tinge of nationalism when it became enveloped in discussions on the distinctiveness of the Canadian and American segments of the CRCNA.

The denomination first sought to resolve the tensions surrounding this matter of national distinctiveness by establishing the Council of Christian Reformed Churches in Canada (CCRCC). This assembly, made up of delegates from the Canadian classes, was in place from 1967 until 1998 and was even given a church orderly foundation in 1993—not as a regional synod but as a "council" formed by cooperation of certain classes (see Church Order, Article 44b and *Acts of Synod, 1993*, p. 574). Frustration with the limitations of this body's authority was without any doubt the driving force behind synod's latest address to the issue of regional synods because that address occurred in that same year: 1993. After considering an extensive study committee report, synod declared that "the introduction of regional synods is not advisable at the present time." Grounds for that declaration were as follows:

> There is little indication that the present ministries of the church would be made more effective by the introduction of regional synods.
>
> The implementation of regional synods would be disruptive and costly and would necessitate duplication of office and staff in each of the regions.
>
> Adding another ecclesiastical level in addition to councils, classes, and synod will place unnecessary burdens on a relatively small denomination like the Christian Reformed Church (*Acts of Synod, 1993*, p. 573).

II. The Assemblies of the Church

Article 27

> a. Each assembly exercises, in keeping with its own character and domain, the ecclesiastical authority entrusted to the church by Christ; the authority of councils being original, that of major assemblies being delegated.
>
> b. The classis has the same authority over the council as the synod has over the classis.

Part b of the article is the "classic formulation" of the relationships involved, adopted in 1581 by the Synod of Middelburg in the Netherlands. It is important to note that it does not spell out just what this "authority" involves and where it comes from. The silence on this matter may well be deliberate, presupposing that all authority in the church is of Christ, sole bishop of the church, and that no person may rule in his stead. It is also explicitly acknowledged that the broader the representation, the greater the authority. This is to honor the principle of the catholicity of the church.

In 1857, the CRCNA received this provision from its traditional sources without any fanfare and formally held to it until the Church Order was revised in 1965. The accent on synod's authority over that of the minor assemblies, however, soon led to major struggles focusing on the question whether broader assemblies may depose a council.

Authority of Broader Assemblies

On three separate occasions, in 1861, 1864 and 1870, Classis Michigan of the CRCNA sought to end local controversy by simply "dissolving" the councils of Grand Rapids, Zeeland, and Noordeloos, respectively, and calling for the election of new ones. Even more brazenly, Classis Hackensack avoided the euphemism and decided in 1899 to depose the entire council of the Ramsay, New Jersey, church, an action which it was later forced to recall by Synod 1900. The more intensive struggles, however, had to do with three major controversies in a decade of turmoil from 1918 to 1926. Classis Muskegon deposed the council of First CRC in Muskegon in a doctrinal dispute known as the "Maranatha Case." Next, Classis Sioux Center deposed a seven-member majority of the council of Sioux Center in a dispute involving the church education program. The seven were later restored to office by Synod 1922. Finally, there was the secession in the Grand Rapids and Kalamazoo, Michigan, areas involving the doctrine of common grace, the resolution of which led to the beginnings of what came to be known as the Protestant Reformed Churches. The different viewpoints on the church political question involved in this latter case were expressed quite clearly in two vastly different judgments. Classis Grand Rapids East "declared that the consistory of the Eastern Ave. CRC had left the fellowship of the denomination," while Classis Grand Rapids West deposed the consistories of the First CRC in Kalamazoo and the Hope CRC of Grandville.

In the debates surrounding these struggles, one could detect two different models. The "congregational model," espoused by A. Kuyper, J. Robbert, I. Van Dellen, J. Van Lonkhuyzen, and others, held to

- church government from the bottom up;
- authority of broader assemblies derived from councils;
- suspension and deposition the prerogative of the local church alone; and
- assemblies limited to a "declaration" that a local church has withdrawn from denominational fellowship.

The "denominational model," espoused by H. Bavinck, F.M. Ten Hoor, W. Heyns, G.D. De Jong, and others, held to

- church government from the top down (though not hierarchical in the Roman Catholic sense);

- authority of broader assemblies original (Christ-given), not merely derived;

- suspension and deposition the right and even the duty of a broader assembly; and

- assemblies with a "sacred calling" to discipline when the welfare of the local church is at stake.

It should be noted carefully that Synod 1926, while it did not condemn the action of Classis Grand Rapids East, deliberately chose for the latter model when it upheld the right of Classis Grand Rapids West to depose the two councils mentioned above (*Acts of Synod, 1926*, pp. 141-43).

With these major struggles within the denomination in mind, and cognizant also of similar struggles within denominations in ecclesiastical fellowship with the CRCNA, the Church Order Revision Committee felt the need to amplify on the existing provision. In 1957, it presented the following draft reading:

> Minor assemblies delegate to major assemblies the authority to deal with matters of common concern. The classis has the same measure of authority over the consistory as the regional synod has over the classis, and the general synod over the regional synod.

Four years later, it came up with yet another draft:

> a. Each assembly exercises, in keeping with its own character and domain, the ecclesiastical authority entrusted to it by Christ.
>
> b. The classis has the same authority over the consistory as the synod has over the classis.

The subtle shift away from "derived" or "delegated" authority evoked overtures like the one from First CRC of Kalamazoo, which argued that "there are no grounds to assume that any authority was entrusted directly by Christ to any major assemblies" and that the "autonomy of the churches is a matter that we feel we must safeguard at all cost." Ecumenical discussions with the Orthodox Presbyterian Church, among others, led to a similar request: "that Synod re-study and reconsider the authority which is now ascribed to our major assemblies." An advisory committee of Synod 1963 became the first to suggest what the Church Order Revision Committee presented as its "final draft":

> Each assembly exercises, in keeping with its own character and domain, the ecclesiastical authority entrusted to *it* by Christ, the authority of consistories being original, that of major assemblies being delegated (italics mine).

The final round of the revision process centered on the word *it*. Classis Hackensack, for example, perceptively spoke of a "manifest contradiction." In its words: "If Christ entrusted to each assembly an ecclesiastical authority that is in keeping with each assembly's own character and domain, then such authority cannot be spoken of as delegated, but must in each instance be original." At its bidding, Synod 1965 substituted the words "the church" for "it" and adopted the article as it currently stands.

But in this way the CRCNA chose the road of compromise. It sought to alleviate the fears of those who demanded deliverance from "synodocracy" or "collegialism," top-down hierarchical rule, by speaking of "original" and "delegated" authority. At the same time, it sought to avoid the extremes of congregationalism by retaining the current Article 27b. The result is not without some inconsistency, especially so if the word "delegated" comes to mean "derived."

As for the right of broader assemblies to depose local councils, the controversy reappeared briefly in the early 1980s. In a dispute at Goderich CRC involving its elders and its minister over against two deacons, Classis Huron suspended the majority of the council of this congregation. Upon appeal, Synod 1980 ruled that the classis had acted hastily and without adequate investigation and asserted that it should lift the suspension. However, it also ruled that Classis Huron

> did not exceed its authority when it engaged itself with the situation at Goderich CRC. Christ gave authority to the church as a whole and thereby entrusted authority to the occasions of its exercise in classis and synod as gatherings of the churches to maintain the unity of the congregations in both doctrine and discipline (*Acts of Synod, 1980*, p. 28).

151

When Classis Sioux Center subsequently appealed from this ruling, Synod 1982 simply noted:

> The Synod of 1980 declared that it is indeed proper according to Reformed Church polity for either classis or synod to intervene in the affairs of a local congregation, if the welfare of that congregation is at stake (*Acts of Synod, 1982*, p. 55).

In other words, Synod 1982 reaffirmed the legacy of Synod 1926.

Relative Autonomy of the Local Church

In view of this history, not only, but also of more contemporary controversies surrounding the church's hymnody, the installation of women elders at a time when such was not permitted, and the selective withholding of denominational ministry shares, to name just three, the considerations that follow should be kept in mind.

Reformed church government does recognize a measure of "autonomy" of the local church. L. Berkhof, for one, argues in his *Systematic Theology* that this means, first, "that every local church is a complete church of Christ, fully equipped with everything that is required for its government" and, second, "that, though there can be a proper affiliation or consolidation of contiguous churches, there may be no union which destroys the autonomy of the local church," so that "it is better not to speak of classes and synods as higher, but to describe them as major or more general assemblies." But such "autonomy" of the local church, says Berkhof, is clearly a relative autonomy. As he goes on to explain:

> the autonomy of the local church has its limitations in the relation in which it stands to the churches with which it is affiliated, and in the general interests of the affiliated churches. The Church Order is a sort of Constitution, solemnly subscribed to by every local church, as represented by its consistory. This on the one hand guards the rights and interests of the local church, but on the other hand also, the collective rights and interests of the affiliated churches. And no single church has the right to disregard matters of mutual agreement and of common interest. The local group may be even called upon occasionally to deny itself for the far greater good of the Church in general (pp. 589-90).

While we may disagree, as I do, with the statement that every local church is *"fully* equipped with everything that is required for its government" (emphasis mine), Berkhof's insistence on a "relative autonomy" within the broader denomination is to be applauded. In my personal view, the local church is *fully* equipped for its government only after it is blessed with channels of accountability to the broader church. But this much is clear: Reformed church government does not recognize an absolute "autonomy" of the local church, a word, we should remember, that literally means "a law unto itself." No congregation is an island.

Denominational ties are not created merely by the good will of local councils voluntarily uniting while retaining the right to withdraw whenever that seems indicated. Just as believers are "obliged to join and unite" themselves with the "holy congregation . . . of those who are saved" (Belgic Confession, Article 28), so local churches are *obliged* to concretize what Christ not only willed for his people but also gave to his people: "that they may be one" (John 17:11).

Ecclesiastical office is not local *or* denominational. It is both. The elders' responsibility, for example, extends beyond the local church when they are called upon also to oversee the affairs of their denomination. The reason why no local church shall lord it over another (Church Order, Article 85) is not that it and all others have an "original authority" within themselves but rather that Christ is Lord of all and "the only universal bishop" and "head" of the church (Belgic Confession, Article 31).

In their Revised Church Order Commentary of 1965, Van Dellen and Monsma indicate that only "councils" are "essential to the church's being" and "permanent" in character, while classes and synods are "temporary in character" and "essential not to the being, but to the well-being or welfare of the churches" (p. 114). Do you agree with them?

With all due respect, I don't agree. These trusted experts in church polity themselves say on the very same page that although in principle "churches can exist without holding major assemblies," "this would be abnormal and far from ideal." The claim that assemblies are "temporary in character" is true enough if you look only at the issue of the gathering of the delegates. Assemblies begin with prayer and roll call, and they end with more prayer and with the closing gavel.

153

But synod and classes carry on ongoing ministries that lie beyond the resources of local congregations; they have "interim committees" that function on a permanent basis (see Article 33), and they most certainly represent the constant interests of the entire denomination by way of classical church visitors or synodical deputies assigned, say, to attend examinations for the ordination of ministers. Indeed, the claim that assemblies are "temporary" applies equally to the local council. While pastors, elders, and deacons are constantly ministering in the midst of the local congregation, that assembly meets only once a month, if that.

In my view, the local church has the council as its governing assembly; the regional church has the classis as its governing assembly; and the (bi)national church has the synod as its governing assembly. The denomination as a whole, in unity and harmony, settles in its Church Order what belongs to the authority of each of these. But "the classis has the same authority over the council as the synod has over the classis" (Article 27b). That's the only thing that goes back to the Synod of Dort of 1618-19. Broader assemblies have an "accumulated authority," a ministering authority of all the ordained leaders in the CRCNA that is extended to them by Christ who, when he distributes it, remains the only universal bishop of the church.

This view of Reformed church polity has been held by many esteemed theologians in our tradition. It approaches the church from the point of view of its organic unity that is given by Christ rather than its many local manifestations. As seminary professor D.H. Kromminga once put it: to claim "that the consistory is the supreme authority in the church is to set our church government on its head instead of on its feet" (*The Banner*, Feb. 27, 1942, p. 197).

The reason why we have these two models of church government that seem rather contradictory is that they are both drawn from one of the earliest of church polity experts in the Reformed tradition, seventeenth century Dutch theologian G. Voetius. In his thought and works (*Politica Ecclesiastica*) both of these "truths" existed side by side and in perfect harmony. Office is not either local or universal. It is both. People began scooping from the vast well of his thought only that which was helpful to them in their polarized settings and thus sought to "slay" their worthy opponents. Come to think of it, that's happened on so many fronts in so much of the history of the Christian church!

If it is synod's task, among other things, to adopt and revise the Church Order, how is it that in 1995 synod allowed the classes to decide whether or not the word "male" in Article 3 shall be "operative" within its bounds? Isn't Article 27 quite clear on synod having authority over the classes and classes over the councils?

A very perceptive question. In normal circumstances, given our system of Reformed church government, synod would have decided the issue as to whether or not the word "male" should continue to appear in Article 3. Article 47 gives synod that prerogative with respect to the entire Church Order. But Synod 1995 did not make its decision in the context of normal circumstances. Synodical assemblies from 1990 to 1994 had made very contradictory rulings on the matter. This resulted in frustration, anger, confusion and, perhaps more importantly, a lack of synodical credibility—one that had the potential of going far beyond the issue of the ordination of women alone and tearing apart our denominational fellowship in the process.

In a very real sense, Synod 1995 surrendered its legitimate final authority on an interim basis when it allowed classes to decide on women's ordination. It was felt that a classis was closer to what was happening in each local church and could make more pastorally informed judgments. It was also felt that this "temporary surrender" was necessary until synod could regain its credibility and greater denominational unity could be found.

The decisions of Synods 2006 and 2007 to delete the word "male" essentially constituted the end of the "surrender." At the same time, synod was careful to build in the appropriate cautions, just as it did in 1957 when women were given the right to vote. According to the Supplement to Article 3, no local council is forced to ordain women against its will, no classis is forced to accept women delegates, and no person is forced to participate in actions that would contradict that person's convictions, and so on.

II. The Assemblies of the Church

Article 28

a. These assemblies shall transact ecclesiastical matters only, and shall deal with them in an ecclesiastical manner.

b. A major assembly shall deal only with those matters which concern its churches in common or which could not be finished in the minor assemblies.

c. Matters referred by minor assemblies to major assemblies shall be presented in harmony with the rules for classical and synodical procedure.

Having named the assemblies of the church and stipulated their relationship, the Church Order now indicates what is legitimately on their agenda. When officebearers deliberate and make decisions, it asks, what are the sorts of issues that are appropriate or inappropriate to the nature and purpose of these assemblies? The answer is that they shall transact "ecclesiastical matters only."

Ecclesiastical Matters Only

The limitation that the council, classis, and synod are to deal with "ecclesiastical matters only" is not intended to mean that the assemblies may deal only with "spiritual" matters as opposed to "temporal" or "material" matters. Councils, after all, decide on the annual budget and then present it to the congregation for approval (Supplement, Article 35a). When a council and congregation decide to disband, one of the issues appropriately on the table is what to do with the assets—how to distribute them. The council must even consult with classis before any final decisions on this "material matter" are made (Article 38d). The same requirement holds with respect to a congregation's disaffiliation from the denomination (Article 38f). On appeal, even synods have made decisions on disposition of property. Classes have decided that the level of severance support proposed by the council for a minister to be released by way of Article 17 is insufficient. The fact is that the organized church is a human institution even if, theologically, we refer to it as the "mystical" body of Christ. The separation of "spiritual" and "material" or the distinction of the "secular" from the "sacred" does not help us catch what this article means.

What the Church Order does intend here is to distinguish the church from other human institutions such as the state, a business enterprise, a family, or a school. Each of these societal spheres has its own unique competence. The church is concerned with such things as Christian worship, the proclamation of the Word, the administration of the sacraments, the nurture of the faith of God's people, pastoral care, and mission efforts. These matters are within the assemblies' competence. The state has no competence in these matters and, rightly ordered, will not interfere in them. The state's appropriate concern, on the other hand, is with enacting the laws that govern a pluralistic society, protecting the rights of the individual and the community, providing for the security and safety of its citizenry, and ensuring justice and equity for all. In principle, the church and its assemblies have no competence in these areas. Or take the matter of church and school. Our Church Order no longer insists, as it once did, that local councils directly supervise the Christian day school's curriculum to ensure that "the biblical, Reformed vision of Christ's lordship over all creation is clearly taught" (Article 71). Instead, the councils "encourage the members of the congregation to establish and maintain good Christian schools." They concede that they are not competent in that area. Mature Christians look after these matters outside of the confines of the organized church. School boards, in consultation with parents, address the educational enterprise.

It is not enough, however, merely to distinguish between these different societal spheres or areas of competence. Life is too complex for that. Public schools might make curricular decisions that constitute a denial of the rights of Christian believers in sufficient measure for the church to take a stand. Similarly, the state may, at times, enact certain laws that clearly touch on doctrinal or ethical issues. It is conceivable that such laws directly contradict or, when further developed, come to contradict what the church proclaims from the Scriptures, what it publicly confesses in its creed and advances in its ministries.

Take, for example, the laws that for a long time regulated apartheid in South Africa: a social policy that saw to the deliberate separation of the races in every respect. The Reformed church there could legitimately be said to have been a "coconspirator" in tolerating this political situation. It was silent for the longest time. Some even justified that eloquent silence by hiding behind the traditional church political insistence that the assemblies may deal only with "ecclesiastical matters." Encouraged by the worldwide communion of Christian believers, however, it eventually felt constrained to publicly uphold the dignity of every human being—each one created in the image of God. The matter had now reached *status confessionis*, the church judged, meaning that this stance was not in tune with God's will for humanity as expressed in the confessions, and therefore falsified the proclamation of the gospel. The church's assemblies decided that any theological justification of an "apartheid system" is heresy. Note that they did not decide that all members of the church ought to take up arms and rise up against the existing government and its laws. That would be disobedient to Scripture (Rom. 13) and creed (Heidelberg Catechism, Lord's Day 39). But they did decide within their area of competence to no longer provide support to that particular social arrangement based on a so-called "biblical" witness that they now branded as heresy. In this way they contributed to the healing of society.

Or take two more examples. The state regulates whether or not it will administer capital punishment and when that is appropriate. That lies within its competence. But the question of whether the state has the right to take the life of a convicted criminal given a system of justice that is often flawed clearly has an ethical dimension. Sometimes the church has no alternative but to address it, and its assemblies have done so. A number of synods addressed the matter. The CRCNA ultimately wound up taking the position that modern states, though not obliged to do so, may institute and practice capital punishment if it is exercised with utmost restraint: it is to be employed only under exceptional circumstances and not routinely (e.g. *Acts of Synod, 1981*, pp. 72-73, 490-91). The same course of action was followed with respect to issues regarding war. Just prior to the Second World War, for example, the synod of the CRCNA discussed "Our Attitude to War" and justified the legitimacy of that agenda item when it declared that

> political, social, and economical questions are ecclesiastical matters only when doctrinal and ethical issues of sufficient moment and magnitude are involved according to the Word of God and our standards (*Acts of Synod, 1937*, p. 11).

Here we note the limitation of competence that is acknowledged as well as the unique circumstances that make the church's involvement appropriate. Subsequent discussions on selective conscientious objection and on pacifism have also been addressed in a similar manner.

In fulfilling the church's task, the CRCNA may occasionally address the governments of Canada and the United States of America and, indeed, has done so through its assemblies. When it has done so, it has typically sought to limit itself to matters within its own competence. When it was believed that these appropriate limits are not observed, members and minor assemblies have often sent protests to the broader assemblies. The reason for that is obvious: going beyond demonstrably biblical proclamation to embrace a particular political philosophy or strategy runs the risk of equating that point of view with the gospel of Christ. When the church becomes too closely identified with a particular political point of view it compromises its foundation in the prophetic and liberating Word of God.

Similarly, local church councils have traditionally seen to it that those who preach do not proclaim a preference for certain nominees for political office, whatever their politics or party. They often refuse to permit the signing of certain petitions within the church's precincts, especially when such petitions have nothing whatsoever to do with any significant ethical issues. While at times sponsoring congregational discussions on issues in political campaigns, or particular "propositions" that appear on the ballot, they do so only to equip the church's members to take seriously their Christian faith and their responsibilities as Christian citizens of their country without forming them into a particular political mold.

Assemblies do well to ensure that members of the CRCNA can readily find themselves in the church's statements on ethical matters within the body politic, seeing to it that such statements are clearly rooted in the truth of Scriptures.

In instances where the church's assemblies move beyond these boundaries of their competence, members of the denomination do well to call them back to the restriction that they ought to "transact ecclesiastical matters only."

Ecclesiastical Manner

Article 28 also insists that the assemblies of the church shall deal with such matters "in an ecclesiastical manner." Once again the purpose is to distinguish the church from other institutions. Assemblies must not run their meetings in the way that corporate boards do their business. They must not use Roberts' Rules of Order or any other set of regulations and procedures that were designed for the United States Senate or the Canadian Parliament or the local school board. The church has its own rules of procedure. It has its own *modus operandi* more appropriate to its sphere. Indeed, this goes far beyond just what rules we follow. This has to do with cultures of governing.

Cultures of governing are modes of operation that have developed in a particular society consistent with that society's purposes. If government in democracies is rule "of the people, by the people, and for the people," it is clear that representatives must follow the will of the people back home, and that the people have their ways to influence or "lobby" their representatives. It is not just special interests that have lobbies to try and steer political leaders in certain directions. Natural constituencies do the same thing—be it at town hall meetings or in telephone calls. Polls are conducted, and it is taken for granted that the majority's position prevails. Popular sovereignty is the name of the game.

The culture of governing in the church is different. It is not democratic but christocratic. Leaders humbly seek to discern the will of the Lord of the church in particular settings. Their primary allegiance is to Christ, to the Scriptures, to the good confession of God's people. Only secondarily do they "listen to" and represent their "constituency." An elder might explain how most people in her district believe the church should approach this particular issue. The council listens and pays heed, but then steers its deliberation in the direction of what the Lord might be insisting upon. Accountability in its decision-making is to God first and to the congregation second. This means, in distinction from more democratic cultures, that the council might well decide in favor of a small minority just because it's the right thing to do. Sometimes minorities point the church in the right direction. The elder may have voted against what her own district expected of her because she too finally agreed it was the right thing to do. Come to think of it, we may even find ourselves wishing from time to time that our Parliament or Congress would do things that way too. The same scenario can be played out for classis and for synod. Delegates to these assemblies may not be bound by the home constituency. If that were true there would be no purpose for any deliberation. They could all stay home and take the vote by fax. Delegates meet in assemblies to discern God's will together.

In the CRCNA, synod has its own rules of procedure, routinely printed in the back of the Church Order booklet. Every classis has the right to adopt its own set of rules and many have done so. They may look much like the synod's version, and almost always have their own unique features with respect, say, to deadlines for appeals, manner of committee reporting, ways of managing specific ministries, and the like. Local councils tend to do things in less formal ways. Instead of officially adopting specific rules, they almost always have traditional ways of doing things that most ministers and elders "remember." That makes it easier to work towards unanimity, which is the goal all assemblies strive for. Indeed, it is not unheard of, when a motion on a significant issue barely passes, that the chair of council says, "We're not going to live with it this way—let's continue our deliberations and see if we can get a clearer majority." In the end, of course, 50 percent plus one might carry the day. But at least the attempt at unanimity is made. You can't run a major corporation that way, as many astute business leaders keep reminding us. But, as we may and ought to respond to them, the church is different territory. That's what Article 28 intends to say.

Matters of Churches in Common

The Church Order further stipulates that a classis or a synod "shall deal only with those matters which concern its churches in common." Obvious examples are the maintenance of a seminary, declaring candidates for ministry of the Word, adopting official liturgical forms, regulating hymnody, deciding on what the church takes to be its official creeds and confessions, and the like. Other examples are a classis discussing "at least one ministry issue" that it "considers to be especially important in the life and ministry of member congregations," as Article 41 maintains, or a synod deciding "which denominations are to be received into ecclesiastical fellowship" (Article 49). In almost all cases, the Church Order spells out what fits within this category, but assemblies are free to count as legitimately on the table whatever they believe to be in the common interest of the churches.

Subsidiarity

Article 28 then says that a "major assembly shall deal only with those matters . . . which could not be finished in the minor assemblies." As much as possible, local councils and regional classes should "finish" issues without always feeling the need to pass them on for broader consideration. Classes and synods are thus given the option of refusing to deal with a particular matter on the grounds that they could have and should have been "finished" in the minor assemblies. Conversely, classes and synods are free to decide that certain matters are legitimately before them because they are in the "common interest."

What may not be declined by major assemblies are matters of appeal. It is always possible for a member to ask a council to reconsider a particular decision. But if councils refuse, appeal to classis is reasonable. Similarly, a council may appeal from a decision of classis to the following synod. Obviously the lines of accountability are at stake, and major assemblies must accept their judicial role. They must deal with and decide on such appeals—sustain them or not sustain them—because by their very nature they "could not be finished in minor assemblies."

Orderly Procedures

When, finally, the article speaks of matters having to be presented to major assemblies "in harmony with the rules for classical and synodical procedure," several issues are targeted. One is that appropriate deadlines are observed. An appeal must usually be filed within a certain period of time; the length of these periods of time may well differ from classis to classis. By their nature, synodical rules on deadlines for appeals are decidedly different. Anyone venturing into these areas should consult with the Stated Clerk of a classis for relevant rules and, when synod is involved, take careful note of Article 30 and its Supplement.

Another consideration here is for rules of synodical procedure pertaining to the acceptability of overtures and communications. A synod will typically declare an overture to be out of order when it has not first been considered at the classical level. Not so if the classis agreed. And if a classis has decided not to adopt the overture as its own, the council submitting it may then expect that synod will consider the overture legally before synod. If communications are repetitive and appear to come from one and the same source through multiple channels, the executive director of the CRCNA is free "to omit such items from the printed *Agenda*" (Rules for Synodical Procedure, V.B.3.c).

Article 28 speaks of "minor" and "major" assemblies. What is actually meant by these adjectives, and is this the best way to refer to the council, the classis, and the synod?

Indeed, in Reformed polity the classis and the synod are referred to as "major assemblies," and the council and classes are referred to as "minor assemblies," even in the Church Order itself. The intent is not so much that classis and synod have a higher authority than that of the council of the local church, although that is secondarily and derivatively true. It is higher only because it is cumulative. The primary intent is to honor the principle of catholicity: the greater the geographical spread of churches represented, the more significance we attach to the decisions made.

In the classis and in the synod we are dealing with the phenomenon of accumulated authority. For the local council, there is accountability to the broader church. It is for this reason that you will often hear the expression "broader assemblies" in our circles. I admit that we don't often hear the term "narrower assembly." But the adjective "broader" does say more precisely what "major" refers to.

I am tired of church agencies "lecturing" my government on issues of national and world poverty. Why don't we just stick to the business of proclaiming Christ and the salvation he brings?

I hear you loud and clear. I have sometimes wondered if all the detail that comes with these "lectures" doesn't go beyond what the church is competent to express. I remember when controversies over what the Council of Christian Reformed Churches in Canada's Committee on Contact with the Government testified at a parliamentary gathering in Ottawa were splattered all over the *Christian Courier*. It also sparked some hefty debate at the meetings of classis. People often said, "Let's stick to 'ecclesiastical matters,'" while others would say it's not that simple.

For example, the topic of "faith-based initiatives" is very much alive in the White House and Christian political think tanks in the United States. The church is called to a diaconal ministry and must show in its benevolent outreach that Christ has compassion for the poor. The state is called to address the same issues of poverty within its particular focus. The debate concerns how these two structures in society—church and state—might meaningfully relate and cooperate when addressing similar problems. It is very legitimate for local deacons to take up contact with a government's social work agency. They must become aware of needs that the church's programs might meaningfully address. I could ask you to reflect in the same way about issues like war and peace, nuclear disarmament, and the like. While our tradition honors "sphere sovereignty" among various institutions, the boundaries are not always clearly drawn.

Is it at all legitimate for our council to have a conversation with representatives of the local Christian school board to talk about how we might coordinate our separate educational programs?

In my view such coordination is not only legitimate but absolutely necessary. I understand that there are specific purposes for church and school, but it is crucial that one institution does not duplicate the other. I learned that the hard way. Young people have attended catechism classes of mine and indicated on more than one occasion that they'd "already learned this in school" and were "bored to tears."

It is also obvious to me, by the way, that a church that finds itself in a community where the emergence of a Christian school is out of the question should focus its mission in such a way as to absorb as much as possible what a Christian school would contribute if that were possible. In the same way one would expect parents (the family) to do the same. In other words, the distinctions between church and school and school and family may have to be drawn less clearly in that setting.

II. The Assemblies of the Church

Article 29

> Decisions of ecclesiastical assemblies shall be reached only upon due consideration. The decisions of the assemblies shall be considered settled and binding, unless it is proved that they conflict with the Word of God or the Church Order.

As indicated in the earlier commentary on Article 26, assemblies are church governmental structures that are deliberative in nature. They are to be engaged in thoughtful reflection and wise judgment, but, most importantly, in discerning the will of the Lord.

Due Consideration

Officebearers rule and lead in concert, never as autonomous individuals or representatives of pockets of opinion within the church. They assemble or gather prayerfully to deliberate in the same way that the leaders of Acts 15 gathered at Jerusalem. In the humility of bearing office, in communal discernment of God's will, church leaders see to it that Christ remains "the only universal bishop and the only head of the Church" (Belgic Confession,

Article 31). This is at the heart of what Article 29 means when it says that decisions "shall be reached upon due consideration."

For the last two decades we have witnessed a regrettable development towards the kind of "lobbying" that many of us tend to deplore even on Parliament or Capitol Hill. Conservatives and progressives compete for the honor of representing all members that are "the constituency" and then, as a sort of "natural" expectation, proceed to vote as these folk in majority would demand of them. Not that long ago, in fact, a classis adopted a resolution expressing dismay that its elder delegates to a synod had voted contrary to a classically agreed upon stand on a thorny issue. To avoid such "disasters" in the future, the classis decided that henceforth the election of delegates must be preceded by a time for "declaration of views on issues judged to be important by classis" and, in the case of nominees not present, the assembly must have a "prepared statement" prior to the voting. But where then is the prayerful eye and ear raised to heaven in the company of officebearers representing many other constituencies, where the willingness to bow to others in our denomination, where the challenge to work toward the unity that is Christ's gift? It makes no difference whether the issue is controversial or moot, obviously at the heart of our confession or more routine. It is Christ's rule and the "broadness" of his church that should be honored. To the extent that our assemblies are characterized by a spirit of humble deliberation, to that extent our Savior will be allowed to rule among his people.

Try to imagine how the rest of the narrative in the Book of Acts might have read if the Gentiles had been forbidden entry into the covenant. How disastrous if the representatives of the Jerusalem church had followed and absolutely insisted upon the will of the people back home. The explosive conflict would have torn into the delicate fiber being woven into the temple of God's Spirit. Instead, Peter refused to follow his natural inclinations; James put aside vested interests of the Jewish-Christian congregation; and "the apostles and the elders, with the whole church," tasted something of the grandiose plans the Savior had in order to bless *all* the true descendants of Abraham. Thus, as Acts 15 reports, when people in Antioch read the decision, they were "glad for its encouraging message" (v. 31). A major decision reached after "due consideration" has that potential.

Similarly, for the last number of years we have seen classical and synodical delegates rushing to complete their responsibilities, airline tickets burning in their pockets, car engines running, looking for efficiency at the expense of thorough and wise decision-making. Agreed—only too often we become entirely inefficient, and that makes for equally impoverished results. But in the end, the church will suffer. We have no right to demand that decisions of assemblies are "settled and binding" if they are not made with "due consideration." This is the careful balance that avoids hierarchical rule from above as well as anarchy from below.

Settled and Binding

"Settled and binding" means that local councils have agreed to be in denominational fellowship and will respect the decisions of the broader assemblies when they are made with "due consideration" and in tune with the accepted confessional standards and Church Order. The officebearers of all congregations belonging to that classis or the denomination as a whole will respect these decisions publicly and privately—in their mutual conversations, yes, but more especially in their official duties of preaching, teaching, and providing leadership. But again, the "balance" of Reformed church government comes to the fore. It is foreseen that some may not be able, in good conscience, to respect these decisions because they are deemed to be "in conflict with the Word of God or the Church Order." In other words, there is always the right of appeal, of proving the assembly wrong (see also Article 30), and of requesting "revision of a decision" previously made (see Article 31). Once that is understood, the provision that decisions must be "settled and binding" seems eminently reasonable. Without it, there is no denominational bond.

At the same time, we must recognize that settled and binding decisions of our assemblies are not on the same level of authority as our creeds and confessions. A delegate appearing at a classis or synod who wants openly to differ with or record a negative vote on, say, the Heidelberg Catechism's approach to the sacraments, will clearly be ruled out of order. Article 5 spells out the "given" that all officebearers have signed the Form of Subscription and agreed to operate within creedal constraints. On the other hand, a delegate to an assembly, be it the council, the classis, or the synod, has the freedom to record a negative vote on any issue that is decided. The *Acts of Synod* are filled with such recorded negative votes. So are the minutes of councils and classes. We permit that. This guarantees the right of that delegate to "respectfully disagree" and seek, perhaps, to request a revision of the decision at a later time. In the meantime, the delegate must still respect the decision made by the majority and thus the assembly as a whole. But there is a greater measure of latitude, because these decisions do not carry the same freight as creeds and confessions do. Of course, delegates do not have the freedom to "respectfully disagree" if they do not record their negative votes. The rule remains that the minority always bows to the majority.

This recognition of different levels of authority is something synod itself has pointed to. When Synod 1996 wrestled once again with the excruciatingly difficult issue of abortion, this time in the context of challenges to the public views of Professor Hessel Bouma III of Calvin College, it adopted the following interpretation of the Church Order's provision:

> Article 29 does not preclude faculty discussion, debate, or disagreement with the substance of a synodical decision or position taken (*Acts of Synod, 1996*, p. 528).

There must be a healthy respect for what previous assemblies decided with respect to such a vexing issue by officebearers and members alike. But even a "settled and binding" decision does not rule out academic freedom. Synods themselves recognize that they are not infallible. They do not take a stand and muzzle all opposition. They provide responsible leadership based on Scripture and creed and are open to correction.

Furthermore, not all synodical decisions are of equal weight. Synod 1975 made this very clear when it spoke of synodical pronouncements as having "nuances of differences," differing "in the extent of their jurisdiction, in the nature of their authority, in the distinction of purposes, in the measure of agreement expected, and in their use and function." If the decision itself claims to be interpreting the confession, it has the same level of authority as the creed and no officebearer may differ with it. But if it involves "extra-creedal" positions or "guidelines" or "pastoral advice," it is in the category of "settled and binding" (*Acts of Synod, 1975*, p. 44).

It is significant, for example, that Synod 1973 twice framed all of its "statements" on homosexuality, including its "ethical stance," as "pastoral advice" (*Acts of Synod, 1973*, p. 51). It intentionally avoided referring to them as an "interpretation" of the Heidelberg Catechism's use of the term "unchastity" in Lord's Day 41. The possibility that this creed meant to include what the synod referred to as "homosexualism" is not denied. It is not being claimed that the Bible permits homosexualist behavior. It is just that the assembly chose not to be that resolute. It merely wanted to establish the "ground rules" for how all officebearers within the CRCNA ought to approach their pastoral responsibilities to those struggling with same-sex orientation. It expected a "healthy respect" for its decisions, not creedal attachment. Officebearers would not be subject to dismissal from office based on unorthodox views, but only on disrespect for what the synod decided.

Avenues of Appeal

Assemblies are not infallible. In the Reformed tradition they have never wanted their decisions to be a foreign yoke imposed upon believers' necks. This awareness of their own fallibility has prompted the rule that individual believers and/or the minor assemblies may seek to "prove" that a certain decision of synod "conflict[s] with the Word of God or the Church Order." Obviously, the proving must not be done to oneself, or to one's council, or to one's classis, but to synod. If it were otherwise, we would once again be left with "autonomous individuals" or "autonomous local churches." Within a denomination, however, such matters must be proven to a subsequent synodical assembly. If that assembly deems the matter to be proven, it may take a "new" decision on the matter or arrange for a further "revisiting" of the issue involved. If not, the previous decision stands. Then, if the individual or the assembly still can't live with it, that individual or assembly must nonetheless not militate against the decisions but rather be respectful of them.

A recent overture to our classis wanted the assembly to "declare that participating churches of classis are under the power and authority of their local churches" and "that decisions of classis are binding only insofar as they are accepted and approved by the local church." Is that in line with our polity?

No, it is not. This is seriously out of touch with our belief in the unity and catholicity of the church. Individual congregations have the right to appeal from a decision of a classis or a synod if they believe that such a decision is in conflict with the Word of God or the Church Order. But assemblies have the right to decide on such an appeal and thus also on whether such a conflict in fact exists. The decision on the appeal is then binding on all of their member congregations.

You wrote in *The Banner* that if individuals or councils object to a synodical decision, they must "prove there is a conflict" with the

Word of God or the Church Order and that they must "demonstrate it to the satisfaction of the broader assemblies." I don't necessarily disagree, but I am struck by the fact that Van Dellen and Monsma seem to be saying the opposite in their *Revised Church Order Commentary* (p. 125): a church or an individual may "withhold submission when that church or individual is fully convinced that the conclusion reached is unbiblical, even before the assembly concerned has reversed its conclusion." Let me guess: you're right and they're wrong?

Frankly, yes. I don't mean to be arrogant or show any disrespect. It's just that if this were all they had written on this issue, they would essentially be claiming that the CRCNA's synod is like a Baptist convention: advice, but no binding force for local congregations. Clearly that is not their view. We must read them in context.

Further down on that same page, they indicate that

> those who disagree with a decision reached by any assembly should submit themselves to the decision involved while they petition the assembly to alter its decision. Such submission and conformation is altogether reasonable. Only in those rare instances in which the party or parties involved would feel themselves to be sinning against God could they be expected to be excused from rendering such temporary submission.

They then go on to say that if the assembly is not persuaded, if it does not recognize the conflict between its decision and the Word of God, if that has not been proven to its satisfaction,

> then the churches must bear with the aggrieved brother, if at all possible. If, however, the matter be of far-reaching import, then the aggrieved brother should be asked to conform and submit as long as he remains to be a member of the church concerned. If his conscience will not at all permit this, he should

ultimately affiliate with a church not so binding his conscience.

What Van Dellen and Monsma claim, therefore, is that if push comes to shove, an individual believer, or perhaps even a local council, must obey God rather than a synod. True enough. But assemblies have the right to say, "No, this decision we have made does not conflict with the Word of God, you haven't proven it to our satisfaction and, furthermore, sadly, we cannot bear with your disagreement—it is too important a matter, and we will have to part ways." That person or that council then essentially steps out of the denominational fellowship. This is the clear import of what has been a foundational element of Reformed church government since the sixteenth century: "the classis has the same authority over the council as the synod has over the classis" (Article 27b).

I have observed that a number of denominations work with a system of "ratification" whereby a significant decision of the synod or general assembly must first be approved by the classes or regional assemblies before it is deemed to be in effect. Does the CRCNA have similar procedures?

No, it does not. Our rules seek to ensure that minor assemblies have sufficient time to consider important matters before synod meets and to present any viewpoints they may have by way of overture or communication. Any item in the printed *Agenda for Synod* is "fair game" in this respect. Once synod is constituted, of course, the minor assemblies are all present by way of delegation to make a final decision.

II. The Assemblies of the Church

Article 30

a. Assemblies and church members may appeal to the assembly next in order if they believe that injustice has been done or that a decision conflicts with the Word of God or the Church Order. Appellants shall observe all ecclesiastical regulations regarding the manner and time of appeal.

b. Synod may establish rights for other appeals and adopt rules for processing them.

c. If invoked, the Judicial Code shall apply to the processing of appeals and written charges.

If broader assemblies are not infallible, and if—as Article 29 indicates—they must be open to the challenge that their decisions are "in conflict with the Word of God or Church Order," it follows that there ought to be established avenues for members and minor assemblies to take if and when the need arises. This is why Articles 30 and 31 now regulate appeals as well as requests for the revision of a decision.

Appeals

Article 30's treatment of appeals actually broadens the playing field significantly. It is not just a matter of reacting to prior decisions of the assemblies. It is also possible that in the ongoing ministry of the church an injustice is done to a person or to a minor assembly. Church polity must provide the framework within which any such injustice may be challenged.

The Rules for Synodical Procedure define an appeal as "a procedure by which a decision or action of an assembly, board, agency, or committee is brought to the appropriate assembly for review in the light of existing policies and standards of the church" (V.A.1). The executive director of the CRCNA typically designates appeals received as "regular" or "personal"; the former are usually printed in full in the *Agenda for Synod*, while the latter are only listed. The difference between these two categories obviously has to do with confidentiality, the protection of individuals involved in an alleged injustice. Beyond that, the issue is whether the appeal clearly has significant implications for the rest of the church and its polity. Classes and councils typically have similar rules in this regard.

It is important to note that a "protest" lodged against a decision of an assembly is actually defined by synodical procedures as a "communication" rather than an "appeal." This means that the assembly that receives such a protest "is not required to take any action with respect to a communication" (V.A.2). If an assembly decides not just to receive it as information but to deal with it in some way for the benefit of the church, often a wise move, the procedures with respect to the handling of appeals are usually followed. This means among other things that a responding assembly must have time to prepare its case, that both parties in the dispute have a right to be represented, and that they must both be granted access to the classis or synod dealing with the protest.

Rules dealing with the format of an appeal, the deadlines for an appeal, the submission of the respondent's materials, and the assembly's handling of an appeal are found in the Supplement to Article 30a. In this case, rules do not just pertain to synod but also to procedures at the classical level. Classes are free, of course, to add desired provisions as long as these do not contradict the synodical directives.

Article 30b governs regulations that apply to two specific types of appeals:

- appeals of those who are not being recommended as candidates for the ministry of the Word; and

- appeals challenging the course of conduct of agencies, boards, or committees of the CRCNA by employees of same, or by individual members who are "substantially affected" by such conduct, or by the assemblies.

With respect to the second, it is noted in the Supplement to Article 30b that the "Judicial Code may be invoked," in which case the rules and procedures of that code found in the Supplement to Article 30c must be followed instead.

Judicial Code

People sometimes find that rules pertaining to appeals get very confusing at this point. The Judicial Code takes up some eleven pages in the Supplement to Article 30c and, what's more, the specifics found in that code are not always the same as those recorded in the much simpler rules for "regular appeals" found in Articles 30a and 30b. It may be helpful to clarify this situation as much as possible.

The code was adopted in 1977 to "encourage greater uniformity of procedure throughout our denomination when charges must be adjudicated" and "to insure just treatment of those who are involved in the judgments and decisions of the church" (*Acts of Synod, 1977*, p. 53). A careful study of the history of the CRCNA reveals some serious incidents where "just treatment" was definitely lacking. Even when that is allowed to happen for some supposed "greater good," the protection of true Reformed doctrine from heresy, for instance, the Scriptures are clear that we are not to show partiality or favoritism under any circumstances (1 Tim. 5:21; James 2:1, 8-9).

The Judicial Code says about itself that it is "intended to be a dispute-resolution mechanism of last resort." Its use must never displace prior attempts to resolve issues amicably nor eliminate the use of trained facilitators or mediators to reach agreement before the "last resort" kicks in. When it is finally resorted to, the Judicial Code functions as a rule book to ensure that the rights of both complainants and respondents are scrupulously observed. You could say that the code launches the assembly concerned into the appropriate mode that ensures it will be just, fair, and resolute. Sometimes, even in the church, that is exactly what is needed before things fester too long.

The code applies only when "written charges are filed" and "when either party to the dispute requests a judicial hearing or when the assembly first hearing the charges determines to constitute a formal hearing." Charges must be specific and clearly indicate with sufficient detail exactly how an injustice has been done. Further, the Judicial Code must be invoked by either the complainant or the respondent. When that occurs, the use of the code is not automatic "just by reason of the invoking." It is left to the judgment of the assembly whether "sufficient informal means have been exhausted," or, to put it differently, whether the invoking of the code by one or both of the parties in the dispute is reasonable. It is also within the prerogative of the assembly to decide to hold a formal hearing without either party necessarily requesting it. Presumably the assembly would do that in order to put a quick and merciful end to the conflict while also leaving the legacy of a formal resolution achieved with justice and fairness.

Article 10 of the Judicial Code articulates the additional requirement that the assembly must first decide whether the written charges "are substantial enough to warrant a [formal] hearing." The complainant must demonstrate to the council, classis, or synod that a person or an assembly has committed an offense against God's Word, the creeds, or the Church Order—the "existing standards" functioning within the CRCNA. Or, as a second possibility, the complainant must demonstrate that something an agency, board, or committee of the denomination has done constitutes an injustice. In the case of an employee there must be proof that what has occurred "substantially affects him or her directly, either materially or personally." There is room for assemblies to make the judgment that a formal hearing is not (or not yet) warranted.

To put it as simply and briefly as possible, the assemblies of the church are here given a tool that they may use at their discretion. They may use it fairly quickly, sensing that informal means will not resolve the issue. Sometimes that is actually more healing to the parties involved. Or they may use it as a last resort when all else has failed and resolution must come by way of a formal hearing that settles the matter once and for all, whatever the impact. But assemblies are never forced to use this tool; it's purely a matter of wise and discerning judgment.

Since local councils meet frequently, they usually conduct the formal hearings directly with all officebearers present and gathered in full session. Their findings may be appealed to classis. Similarly, classes typically conduct these formal hearings in full session and their findings may be appealed to synod. Since synod meets only once a year, this assembly has a standing committee known as the Judicial Code Committee, whose task it is, when so requested by the executive director of the CRCNA, to determine whether a formal hearing should be held, and, if so, to hold it in advance of the following synod. The committee's recommendations in the matter are then dealt with at the broadest assembly. Synod retains the right to hold its own hearing. This seldom occurs. It happened in 1991 because that year's synod judged that the matter was too urgent to postpone or delegate to its own Judicial Code Committee or any other standing committee. An advisory committee of synod actually conducted the hearing at a grueling (Sunday!) session and then brought its recommendations to the floor the following day. If anything, this demonstrated that working through the Judicial Code Committee is prudent whenever it is possible and ensures even more that every attempt is made to come to fair and just resolution.

Appeal to Assemblies Next in Order

Article 30 indicates that "assemblies and church members" have the right of appeal to "the assembly next in order." With respect to decisions of council, this is the classis. With respect to decisions of classis, this is the synod. And with respect to decisions of synod, this is a following synod, a year later or even beyond. Once an appeal has been dealt with at a following synod, there is, humanly speaking, no "higher court." There is then only the provision of Article 31 that provides for requesting a revision of the decision taken. But, as we shall see, the bar within that provision is higher.

If a council makes a decision and I wish to appeal it, must I first appeal to the council or may I appeal directly to the classis?

In their *Revised Church Order Commentary*, Van Dellen and Monsma indicate that "it is often advisable that an appeal is first made to the next session of the assembly against which an appeal is being made" (1965 edition, p. 127). On the other hand, they also indicate that the appellant is "at full liberty" to go directly to the classis. I agree entirely. Whether or not to present your appeal to the next meeting of the council is a question of wisdom. You have the right not to do that. If you do present your appeal directly to the classis, however, you must ensure that your council receives a copy in sufficient time for it to formulate a response. If you don't, you run the risk of the classis postponing its decision.

I have often heard of other denominations settling things in their "judicatories" or "judicatory bodies." Do we have similar organizations in the CRCNA?

Actually these terms almost always refer to assemblies themselves (like our council, classis, and synod), but then acting in their capacity to hear and to rule on certain charges or appeals. We seldom use this language, but there's nothing to stop us. When synods hear a case, they function at that moment in their role as adjudicators of disputes rather than, say, their role as legislative bodies enacting church law. Our synod does have a standing Judicial Code Committee, but since this body doesn't make the decisions for synod, it is not itself a "judicatory body."

Does the assembly's ruling on a specific appeal constitute a new law for all to follow? In other words, is there the equivalent of what is known in the Anglo-Saxon legal tradition as "common law"?

Not in the CRCNA. Let me give you an example.

I have heard it said that persons who agree with all that we stand for except our doctrine and practice of infant baptism are nonetheless eligible for confessing membership in our churches. People who say this most often base this opinion on a decision of Synod 1964.

The 1964 case involved a protest treated as an appeal. Classis Muskegon advised Bethany CRC of Muskegon that a "middle-aged couple of Baptist background" could be admitted as confessing members because "they do not share the Arminian, Dispensational viewpoint." They had some difficulty "accepting our proof for infant baptism" but did "affirm that they find the only true communion for their souls in our church." The matter came before synod because the Rev. C. Holtrop submitted a protest against Classis Muskegon's "favorable advice." He argued that the denomination's subscription to Article 34 of the Belgic Confession and Lord's Day 27 of the Heidelberg Catechism ruled out the couple's admission. Synod disagreed. It

177

acknowledged "the right and duty of a consistory to evaluate each case of admittance according to the special circumstances of the persons requesting such admittance." It observed that the couple was "willing to be further instructed in the Reformed doctrine of baptism" and that they had "promised not to propagate any views conflicting with the doctrinal position of the church" (*Acts of Synod, 1964,* p. 63).

Does this now set a precedent? No, especially since this assembly referred to "special circumstances" in this case. Presumably, the issue of whether or not to present an infant child for baptism would not arise in the case of a middle-aged couple. Also, the couple was apparently able happily to celebrate the sacrament with the rest of the congregation whenever a new child was presented. The only point of disagreement, said the synod, had to do with something very specific: "the point of direct biblical evidence for the doctrine of infant baptism."

We need to remember that other persons applying for confessing membership may be in a similar situation and have similar reservations. But it is highly unlikely that these cases are exactly like the one in 1964. This synod's ruling applied only to one particular protest, one particular judgment, and one particular couple's request. It may not be broadened into existing law when that law would almost certainly contravene the creeds and Article 56 of the Church Order.

I am writing you anonymously for good reason. Please call me "Karen" and use the P.O. Box I have supplied. I have been sexually abused by a pastor. I don't want to get into the details of him doing this to me right now. I'm probably to blame too. But I feel so cheap, so used, and so depressed. I don't think I can keep living with this without doing something about it. I don't know where to turn—if and when I do get up the courage. Can you help? If so, please share with me all the ins and outs of what I should do. I want to know what I might be getting into.

Dear "Karen":

I'm so sorry to hear this story from you. You are not alone. Unfortunately, there are many others with a similar story. Like you, those people do not know what to do either or where to turn. I'll do my best to describe the "ins and outs" as you requested.

First of all, my response depends on your age. I cannot tell from your letter whether you are an adult, so I am going to describe a response to a minor and then a response to an adult.

If you are a minor (under age eighteen in most states and provinces), you should know that sexual abuse of a minor by an adult is a crime whether or not the abuser is a pastor. If the abuser is a pastor, the abuse is also a serious form of church leader misconduct, a violation of professional ethics, a betrayal of your trust, and a sin. Although it might be very difficult for you, you should tell a parent or a stepparent what has happened. If you cannot tell your parent or stepparent or if they do not believe you, then tell your story to an adult—perhaps an elder of your church, a youth leader, or a school teacher—it doesn't really matter who, as long as it is an adult that you trust. If you live in Canada, all adults are legally responsible to report the allegation. If you live in the United States, some adults must report an allegation of abuse because of their professional responsibilities while other adults do not have to report.

Then two things should happen to prevent the sexual abuse from happening again. First, the adult you confide in should report your allegation to the local police. By law, the adult should report the allegation within twenty-four hours of hearing about it. Second, that same adult or the police should inform the church's executive or leadership group of your allegation. You didn't say whether he's your pastor or the pastor of another church. But that doesn't matter. The church needs to be told.

The police will interview you and the pastor separately, and they will interview others as well. It takes some time to conduct a thorough investigation. After all the interviews are done, it is possible that criminal charges will be filed. There could be a trial, especially if the pastor claims he is innocent. If he is found guilty of abusing you or if he pleads guilty to abusing you, he will likely be punished. I can't say what the punishment might be, but you should understand that any punishment is the result of *his* abuse and not because you reported the abuse.

The church's leaders should take action too. The church should at least suspend him for a period of time, or they should remove him from the pulpit and prevent him from being a minister again in that church or another church.

Throughout this experience, you will find it helpful to have a counselor to talk to. Your friends will be very supportive to you, but you may not want to share all the details with them. Besides being a good listener, a counselor can also help sort through all the feelings you'll have through the investigation and trial.

All this may sound scary and overwhelming to you. I am not trying to frighten you. There really isn't another way to prevent you from being hurt again by the pastor, or to prevent him from hurting someone else. I hope you find the courage to tell someone, and that the abuse stops. This is my advice if you are a minor.

If you are an adult, I am just as saddened and disturbed by your story as if you were a child. My advice, however, is a bit different.

First of all, I hope you'll make an appointment with a counselor or therapist as soon as possible. Please don't delay. Depression is a very natural reaction to the sexual violation and the betrayal you have experienced. But depression, anger, and sadness can also be overwhelming at times, so you should not face these emotions alone.

As an adult, you have different choices than does a child. One of your choices is to go to the police with your story. If the events took place a long time ago, the police may or may not be able to investigate your story. The laws in your community may also affect whether or not charges can be filed.

Another choice is to approach the Christian Reformed Church. The churches in the denomination have been challenged to understand the gravity of your situation, and the classes in the denomination are providing Safe Church Teams so that you have a safe place to go with your story.

The conduct you describe might be sexual misconduct. Sexual misconduct occurs when a minister does not observe appropriate relationship or physical boundaries. Sexual misconduct usually includes exploiting a person for the power and control that it gives the other person. While it may look as if the relationship between the two people is "consensual," in fact it is not because the minister is in a position of power and authority over a parishioner and has violated the sacred trust of his office by his conduct. The minister is always responsible to safeguard the relationship with the parishioner. When boundary violations occur, the minister should be held accountable.

This is a very serious matter. And I hope my indication of the road to take now, even if it is a difficult one for you, is the right one for you and for the church.

If this person is guilty of sexual misconduct, he must not be allowed to continue in office. Despite your own pain, we hope you will help us prevent further hurt and humiliation to even one more person. Unfortunately, once ministers cross these boundaries, more incidents usually follow.

The Christian Reformed Church has a network of Safe Church Teams that are convened to hear stories like yours. If a team is not located near you, your expenses to travel to that team's location will be provided for you. In addition, Safe Church Teams offer claimant advocates to assist those who have allegations of sexual misconduct committed by a minister. To get started and bring your story forward, you may contact a claimant advocate, a Safe Church Team chairperson, or the chairman of the church council to whom this pastor is accountable. If the offender is your minister, you may feel more comfortable calling a claimant advocate or team chairperson, but you certainly may approach someone on your council that you can trust. If the offender is a minister of another congregation, you can call either the claimant advocate, team chairperson, or a person on that church's council. Usually the claimant advocate makes the call, but you could choose to make the call.

If all of this begins to sound too difficult or impossible in some way, please know that the claimant advocates and Safe Church Teams are made up of professionals who are knowledgeable in sexual misconduct dynamics. You do not have to worry about confronting the minister alone or at all.

The Safe Church Team will form a panel that will meet with you, accompanied by the claimant advocate, and then they will meet separately with the accused minister.

When both parties have been fully heard, the panel will consider whether your allegations are more probable than not. You and the minister will be notified of the panel's findings; the panel also notifies the executive committee of council. The council will then meet to decide on what should be done. Once again, the claimant and the minister do not meet face to face, but they will both be notified of the council's decision.

If the council judges that the allegations are more likely than not to have occurred, the council should initiate steps of discipline. It is likely that the minister will then first be suspended. If he claims to be innocent, a formal hearing will be held. If he pleads guilty or it is determined that he is, in fact, guilty of an offense, it is likely that he will then be deposed. If, on the other hand, the council judges that the charges you have brought are not likely to have occurred, then the matter could end. However, the chairperson of the advisory panel and the claimant advocate might challenge the decision of council. They could submit a copy of the panel's report and of the council's action to the Interim Committee of the classis. This committee presents a report to the next meeting of that classis. This is done to make sure that there is no partiality in the way that your allegations have been responded to in a "more local" setting.

When this difficult road of appeal has been followed, and still no action is being taken against the minister for whatever reason, you and your claimant advocate still have the right of appeal from what the classis has decided in the matter. That appeal may be addressed to the synod of the Christian Reformed Church. It meets once a year and has a special committee that can hear the case in confidence. It will then provide the following synod with well-formulated recommendations. So you have representatives from the entire denomination at your disposal to address this serious matter.

"Karen," I've just given you a lot of stuff to digest. If you have any further questions, please know that you may contact me at the telephone number listed below my signature. I will keep our conversations confidential and not reveal them to anyone. Or you may write back. Either way is fine.

I also encourage you to contact the denominational Safe Church Ministry at 616-224-0735. The ministry has a website with information on how to contact a claimant advocate or a Safe Church Team chairperson. I wish you much strength in all of this. I understand that this minister has hurt you. I hope you will experience a church that wants to end that hurt. The church does not want to bury its head in the sand. It wants and needs the opportunity to help you now. Just getting the word out to others will be difficult but, in the end, I am confident it will lighten your load and lead you on new roads to joy.

Grace and peace to you.

II. The Assemblies of the Church

Article 31

A request for revision of a decision shall be submitted to the assembly which made the decision. Such a request shall be honored only if sufficient and new grounds for reconsideration are presented.

Request for Revision of a Previous Decision

Article 31 permits confessing members or the minor assemblies to file a request for revision of a decision previously made. Any past decision of a local council is eligible, provided, of course, that it is the member's own council. So is any decision of a classis (the member's own, the council's own) or any decision of a prior synod. Members of minor assemblies may present the request directly to the assembly that made the decision. This permission to bypass the assemblies in between is somewhat unusual and applies only to revision requests.

Synodical rules do not allow members to bypass the assembly next in order if a "new decision" is called for by way of an overture. In that case, members must necessarily first submit such an overture to their council. The council may then pass it on to classis or the member may present it to the classis if the council has not consented to it. Similarly, the classis may pass it on to synod or, alternatively, the member's or the council's overture may be presented to synod if the classis has not consented to it. If members or councils bypass the assembly next in order, the result is almost always that the overture is declared out of order. I say "almost" because it remains true that "all other matters may be considered which synod by a majority vote declares acceptable" (Rules for Synodical Procedure, V. B.11).

The request for revision of a decision, however, is not an overture or a new matter. It is by definition a "conscientious objection" to a prior decision and a heartfelt plea for change. Hence, these petitioners do not need to follow the steps involved in presenting an overture. They are certainly permitted to do so, presumably to gain some support and add some weight to the request, but this is not required. Broader assemblies are obliged to receive any and all requests for revision legally on their agenda and must deal with them. They can only consider their decisions "settled and binding" because they provide an opportunity for conscientious objection to them.

The request for revision of a decision is also the last avenue for one who has pursued the way of appeals (Article 30) and has now come to the very end of that road. Recall that members and assemblies may appeal to the assembly next in order. If one synod has decided not to sustain the appeal and a following synod (the assembly next in order) confirms that judgment, the only thing left to an appellant beyond this is to request a revision of that last decision of synod. In fact, some commentators believe that the first appeal to the next synod is itself already a request for revision, not an appeal. I differ with them. What's quite clear, however, is that whether it is then considered an appeal or a request for a revision, the bar becomes very high.

Sufficient and New Grounds for Reconsideration

If decisions of broader assemblies are taken "only upon due consideration" (Article 29), after careful and prayerful deliberation, it stands to reason that requests to revise them must meet a fairly high standard. The petitioner, says this article, must present "sufficient and new grounds for reconsideration." The requirement for "new grounds" means that the burden of proof is on the petitioner to show that certain valid and pertinent arguments or insights, such as biblical directives or ecclesiastical regulations, were neglected by the prior assembly. These grounds must also be "sufficient," that is, weighty enough to demonstrate that the petitioner's conscience is inappropriately infringed upon by the assembly.

The assemblies respond to these requests in two stages. These stages clarify the differences between "reconsideration" and "revision." It must first be decided whether there are "sufficient and new grounds for reconsideration." If, after appropriate discussion, the assembly is not persuaded of that and so indicates by vote, the matter ends. If it is persuaded and so indicates by vote, the request for reconsideration is honored and the assembly then proceeds to revisit the issue. A new and more comprehensive discussion is held, this time about the substance of the issue now "under review": whether to revise the previous decision or not. The assembly may then uphold the previous decision by denying the request for revision or it may overrule the previous decision by negating it or revising it in some way. The Rules for Synodical Procedure indicate that the most recent decision on a matter stands:

> A succeeding synod may alter the stand of a previous synod; it may reach a conclusion which is at variance with a conclusion reached by an earlier synod. In such cases the most recent decision invalidates all previous decisions in conflict with it (VIII.I.2).

There is no rule in the polity of the CRCNA that limits the number of times a request for revision of a decision may be submitted. Article 31 says nothing about it. Neither do the Rules for Synodical Procedure. Technically, therefore, the synod has no Church Order ground to rule a repeat request out of order. On the other hand, the higher bar of "sufficient and new grounds for reconsideration" protects our synods from exhausting their resources on a single member or assembly over and over again. An advisory committee need only recommend to the full session that the matter not be reconsidered because the petitioner has not advanced sufficient and new grounds. On the other hand—and this remains at the heart of Article 31—synods must never dispense with a request so precipitously if it is not a "repeat" but a genuinely new and significant conscientious objection.

In a church that professes to be Reformed, it is the assemblies' sacred obligation to maintain openness to new understandings of the confessions and the Scriptures.

Aha, we finally caught you red-handed! What you've been teaching us in class about permission to bypass minor assemblies with these requests directly contradicts a decision of Synod 1983. That decision is right there in the Church Order booklet itself, in the Supplement to Article 31. How could you miss it?

Well done, observant ones! I didn't miss it. I respectfully disagree with it.

Synod 1983 indeed decided to "advise the churches that a request for revision of a decision of a major assembly must be processed as far as possible in the minor assemblies before coming to the major assembly." In providing its grounds, the synod asserted that such a request falls within the category of "overtures." Hence, it too must proceed step by step. It further asserted that this will enable minor assemblies to refine the request, clarify it, and remove any possible "errors or misconceptions" (*Acts of Synod, 1983*, pp. 653-54). I respectfully disagree with these assertions.

To be honest, I find this restriction puzzling in view of the principle of conscientious objection. I am not aware of any other commentators on our church polity who agree with this synod's decision. If it had advised that a request *may* be processed as far as possible in the minor assemblies, I would have no problem with the advice. It is the word *must* that I object to. As Van Dellen and Monsma correctly observe (1965 edition, p. 130), CRCNA polity has never required this precisely because an "overture" is deemed to be "a new matter," whereas a request for revision is an expression of a member or assembly's objection and "inability" to treat a prior assembly's decision as "binding" upon the churches. A member or council would be wise to gain some support on the way "up the ladder." A member or council might also find it wise not to try that route, presumably because a negative judgment along the way would also speak volumes to the broader assembly. This ought to be left to the member's or council's discretion.

Had I been a delegate to Synod 1983 I would definitely have registered my negative vote. Even now I am not persuaded by its grounds. I respect its decision, of course, because no decision negating it or revising it has been made since. It is in force and, therefore, rightly brought to the continuing attention of the churches in the Supplement to the Church Order. Members and assemblies should pay attention to it in making requests for revision and not follow my lead unless and until it is negated or revised. You would run the risk of having it summarily ruled out of order. On the other hand, and purely as a commentator, I here retain the right of disagreement and truly believe I am in good company.

Come to think of it, perhaps I should be the one to request a revision of the 1983 decision. . . . Of course, I'd first have to persuade my council, and then . . . well, you get the idea.

The Canadian Reformed Churches are sometimes referred to as "Article 31 churches." Is this a reference to the article on requests for revision of previous decisions? That doesn't make much sense to me.

You're right. That wouldn't make much sense to me either. Actually, the reference is to a prior version of what we currently have in Article 29: "The decisions of the assemblies shall be considered settled and binding, unless it is proved that they conflict with the Word of God or the Church Order." In the Church Order of the applicable Reformed churches of the Netherlands (GKN), this prior version in force in 1944 was numbered Article 31 and, in our English translation of it that we adopted in 1914 on this side of the ocean, this article then read as follows:

> If anyone complain that he has been wronged by the decision of a lesser assembly, he shall have the right to appeal to a greater assembly, and whatever may be decided by a majority vote shall be considered binding unless it be proved to conflict with the Word of God or with articles of this Church Order, as long as they are not changed by the General Synod.

The "polity side" of the conflict that came to a head in 1944 had to do with the question of whether synod has the right to bind officebearers to its decisions, even when these officebearers individually or collectively at the local level deem such decisions to be in conflict with the Word of God. For synods of the CRCNA these days, that remains a clear word of caution from our past.

How does anyone know whether an assembly did or did not consider certain things in coming to its decision? The minutes of classis or the *Acts of Synod* are often so cryptic and do not record all the thought and debate that has gone into it.

You're right, of course, although assemblies are well advised to offer grounds that do in fact indicate or cover the entire territory of debate in some way. Since 1979 all of synod's general sessions (omitting executive sessions) are recorded, and an official audio recording is maintained in the office of the executive director. *Acts of Synod* since that time indicate that the recording is for the purpose of verifying the written record of synodical proceedings. Upon request, the executive director may grant the right to anyone wishing to determine whether proposed grounds are "new and sufficient" to listen to the official audio recording.

II. The Assemblies of the Church

Article 32

a. The sessions of all assemblies shall begin and end with prayer.

b. In every assembly there shall be a president whose duty it shall be to state and explain the business to be transacted, and to see to it that the stipulations of the Church Order are followed and that everyone observes due order and decorum in speaking. There shall also be a clerk whose task it shall be to keep an accurate record of the proceedings. In major assemblies the above named offices shall cease when the assembly adjourns.

c. Each assembly shall make proper provision for receiving communications, preparing agenda and acts, keeping files and archives, and conducting the financial transactions of the assembly.

d. Each assembly shall provide for the safeguarding of its property through proper incorporation.

One might well ask why the first regulation on prayer is even necessary. It seems so utterly obvious. Perhaps so, but that's not a good argument against it. If nothing else, it is a reminder and further insistence on the theme of Articles 28 and 29, namely, that assemblies are for "deliberation," a thoughtful discerning of the will of the Lord for his church that is appropriately to be bathed in prayer.

Officers of Assemblies

Our Church Order speaks of only two assembly officers: the president and the clerk. This is not a "limiting" requirement but a "minimal" one. There is no intent to forbid an assembly from electing a vice-president, a second clerk, a treasurer, or any other functionary. It is just that minimally there must be someone to lead the proceedings and there must be one who accurately records them.

Along these lines, three subsequent articles in the Church Order also refer to assembly leaders. Article 36 says about the local council, consistory, and diaconate that "each body shall select its own president and other officers." Typically, these others are the vice-president and the clerk; in the case of the diaconate, often the secretary and the vice-all. Article 40 says regarding the classis that "ministers shall preside in rotation, or a president may be elected from among the delegates." Classical rules of order differ somewhat, but a classis typically has a president, vice-president, and a clerk (often in addition to the Stated Clerk who handles all communications and permanent record-keeping). Article 46 says that "officers of synod shall be elected." Synodical rules currently call for the election of a president, vice president, first clerk, and second clerk (I.C.3).

Temporary Leadership

Article 32 now insists that these "offices shall cease when the [major] assembly adjourns." A similar claim is made in subsequent articles only with respect to the classis, namely, that "the same person shall not preside twice in succession" (Article 40c).

Officers of assemblies in the CRCNA have a temporary leadership responsibility. They preside only for as long as the classis or the synod is in session. The executive director of the CRCNA is deliberately listed as a "nondelegated synodical functionary." The person holding this office is a servant of synod, never a delegate, and, accordingly, never its president (Rules for Synodical Procedure, III.A). Instead, a president of synod is elected from among the delegates (see commentary on Article 46). The responsibilities of that office cease when the closing gavel sounds with only one exception: the past president serves on a Program Committee that meets the next spring to make plans for the following summer's annual synod.

In this matter, the CRCNA differs not only from the hierarchical traditions within the Christian church generally, but also from the polity of other Reformed denominations. Many Presbyterian churches (including the PCA, PCUSA, EPC), the Reformed Church in America (RCA), and Protestant churches in other countries tend to have a "moderator" or "president" who functions on a permanent basis (even if only for a designated term)—not just during but also before and after the assembly's annual sessions. In the RCA, for instance, "the immediate past president of the General Synod shall be the moderator" and, in that capacity, an "officer of the General Synod Executive Committee" for a maximum of six years (Bylaws of the General Synod, Sections 1 and 3). Responsibilities go far beyond one synod's closing gavel.

An increasing number of people have called us to focus a bit more on the benefits of continuity in gifted leadership. The Church Order says nothing regarding a minister, elder, or deacon as permanent chair of local assembly sessions, month after month, often for much longer than just one year. It limits its insistence on temporary office to leaders of "major assemblies." So why, the claim goes on, should there be such concerns with respect to these broader assemblies?

As a matter of fact, many classes have begun choosing presidents for one-year terms (either two or three sessions), despite the fact that such a practice is in direct violation of Article 40. As far as I know, none has yet been challenged on the issue. This may be because the terms remain limited (usually to a year), just as they do in the RCA, and there is little activity outside of the actual sessions themselves. As one person recently told me, "It's not like we're returning to lifetime bishops and cardinals."

Indeed, all this seems perfectly analogous to developments with respect to limited tenure of elders and deacons (see Article 25). One imagines that reflection on these matters will continue down the road. For the sake of good order, however, current rules should not be violated. If it's worth doing in the eyes of one classis, why not share the newly discovered riches with the rest of the denomination, acknowledge where the shoe pinches, and, by way of overture, request a synod to adjust our rules?

Rules of Order

The matter of "due order and decorum in speaking" is clearly laid out in Section VIII of the Rules for Synodical Procedure. By design, there are "a few general rules of order" that fit well within the bounds of dealing with issues only "in an ecclesiastical manner" (Article 28). They are not detailed parliamentary rules, like Roberts' Rules, or any other such instrument, but rules that serve us well in the setting of a deliberative assembly. Classes follow the same synodical rules of order, or slight variants thereof that they have adopted for their own use. Councils do the same, in theory, but those who preside in local assemblies tend to be less formal in leading the discussions and bringing matters to a vote.

Local Articles of Incorporation

Finally, the Church Order raises the issue of "safeguarding . . . property through proper incorporation." This issue is actually much more significant for the life of our churches than its brevity and its placement would indicate. People overlook it until their congregation is suddenly confronted with the phenomenon of schism or disaffiliation. Emotions run high when members who have worshiped together for years can suddenly no longer engage in a civil conversation and face off against each other, sometimes in civil court, in order to claim the property and the assets in part or in whole. This may be unthinkable to some, but it has been a bitter reality for others. Broader assemblies increasingly understand the need to help their constituent congregations with "proper incorporation."

The most critical is the need to "safeguard" property at the local level. A bit of history in this regard might be helpful.

For the first seven decades of its existence the CRCNA frowned on legal incorporation for fear that the state would infringe upon the affairs of its congregations. Put differently, the denomination refused to acknowledge the "positive role" of the state and was therefore utterly unprepared for the legal consequences of possible schism. Synod provided no help. But two cases of schism or irreconcilable division changed all that.

The "Maranatha" case involved First CRC of Muskegon. Minister, elders, and deacons were all deposed when they refused to follow the classis in condemning the "premillennial" views of that minister, the Rev. Harry Bultema. The few members who sided with the classis and wished to remain within the denominational fellowship were subsequently awarded all property and assets in civil court. Without synod's guidance, and ironically so, the congregation had actually incorporated itself in 1902 with the following provision:

We irrevocably appropriate to the maintenance of our confession and government forever, such real and personal estate as this church now has or may hereafter acquire, and that to these objects alone it shall be applied. And that in case of any departure from the above established standards of doctrine and government by any portion of this church or congregation, such estate shall be held and enjoyed exclusively by those who adhere to said standards hereby declared and established as the basis of our church and congregation.

This provision became the basis for the court's decision. The court also voided the earlier attempt on the part of the officebearers to amend the articles of incorporation in favor of the majority of members. In its words, this is nothing but "an effort to set up in this church of presbyterial form of government a congregational form of government" (Borgman *v.* Bultema 213 *Michigan Reports*, March 1921, pp. 690-91, 700).

The "Common Grace" case involved the council of Eastern Avenue CRC of Grand Rapids. After Synod 1924 judged that the Rev. Herman Hoeksema's views on common grace were "out of harmony" with the confessions of the denomination, this minister was suspended, then deposed. When the consistory declared its refusal to abide by synod's decision, the classis declared it guilty of "insubordination" and insisted that by its action the consistory and all members sympathetic to this refusal had "broken ecclesiastical relationship with the Christian Reformed Church." As in the "Maranatha" case, the minority of members that sided with the classis was eventually granted control of church property and assets (Holwerda *v.* Hoeksema, [1925] 232 *Mich.* 648, 206 N.W. 546-565).

In view of these sad developments, Synod 1926 finally adopted a model for congregational articles of incorporation (*Acts of Synod, 1926*, pp. 59, 310-14). There was no requirement placed upon the churches to use it; synod just provided some guidance. The model's section on schism read much like that of First CRC of Muskegon and was thus based on the theory of "implied trust": when members contribute to the budget, they are deemed to be giving such funds for the purpose of maintaining a CRC congregation, one that holds to the creeds and form of church government adopted by that denomination. In the event that the council and broader assemblies collide, those members who take their lead from the classis and/or synod, no matter their number, are the "lawful congregation."

Synod 1963 took it one step further. It adopted a very similar model and asked classical church visitors to "review the matter of proper incorporation with each church." The intent, clearly, was that regardless of local variations required by differing laws in states and provinces, basic articles such as the one on schism should be included in the articles of every congregation. It would now be a requirement. The church visitors were to ensure compliance with this denominational covenant (*Acts of Synod, 1963*, pp. 50-52, 343-44).

From 1970 until 1997, the denomination tried a different model. It envisioned the *pro rata* distribution of property among the parties involved, regardless of decisions of broader assemblies with respect to faithfulness to creeds and church government. Broader assemblies must pronounce that a schism has occurred and must help "to achieve a just and fair division of property" in order that settlement might be made "according to the scriptural injunction of 1 Corinthians 6," but the ownership of property is solely in the hands of the "autonomous" congregation, and both parties have legitimate claim on some of it (*Acts of Synod, 1970*, pp. 104-06, 468-83). The belief was that in this way an already heated controversy would not be heated even more by matters of property and assets. The hope was that parties would never need to go to civil court to settle the matter. Division, after all, is purely a matter of arithmetic that follows the number of members in each group.

This hope proved to be overly optimistic. In further cases of schism, most notably the one occurring in Mount Hamilton CRC in Ontario (1992-1993), it became obvious that the "pro rata distribution" arrangement in fact does not prevent the parties from looking to the civil court for arbitration. Prompted by new occurrences of this, Synod 1997 returned to the pre-1970 state of affairs. It adopted a model that once again provided that classis (or synod on appeal) has the exclusive determination regarding which group of members "shall be the lawful congregation" and shall thus have exclusive rights to property and assets. It added, however, that there is nothing to prevent the classis from determining that "more than one group of confessing members . . . are each a lawful congregation" and dividing property and assets between such groups. In addition, Synod 1997 also adopted a clear procedure for disaffiliation from the CRC to be followed by a local congregation. It is now a Supplement to Article 38f of the Church Order (*Acts of Synod, 1997*, pp. 612-20).

By decision of Synod 1997, the executive director (then general secretary) of the CRCNA is to "send a biennial inquiry regarding the congregations' current articles of incorporation and to recommend that the churches adopt articles that faithfully reflect the model contained in the Church Order Supplement to Article 32d." Note that the word "recommend" is a bit softer than the "compliance" expected by Synod 1963. On the other hand, any congregation receiving financial assistance from synodical agencies or newly affiliating with the CRC is *required* to faithfully "reflect the model adopted by synod" (*Acts of Synod, 1997*, p. 619).

Considering that the model articles and the new procedure for disaffiliation have served the denomination well in subsequent cases of schism and resultant court cases, most notably the sad divisions occurring in Lamont, Michigan (1998-2007), churches are well advised to keep their articles and bylaws updated and in tune with synodical direction, even if, by God's grace, no schism ever occurs within their congregations. The CRCNA now fully understands that civil government has a legitimate role to play in some regulation of the church's affairs and that the denomination's broader assemblies provide helpful guidance with models and expectations. Councils should understand, on the other hand, that in any court case everything will depend on what particular congregations have in fact adopted and filed as their own articles of incorporation.

Incorporation of Broader Assemblies

We have seen that issues of incorporation at the local level are significant. There remain the affairs of the regional and (bi)national church.

The CRCNA as a denomination was incorporated in the mid-1970s as a Michigan and a Canada corporation. The pertinent articles and bylaws protect property and assets consisting of the denominational buildings in Grand Rapids, Michigan, and Burlington, Ontario, as well as property and investments owned worldwide by synodical agencies.

Classes within the CRCNA typically own no property but may do so occasionally on a temporary basis. A good example would be the purchase of a piece of land destined to become a home for a new church plant in its midst. In more recent years, classes have nonetheless also incorporated themselves in order, for instance, to make it possible to insure against any liability that may arise out of lawsuits directed at Safe Church Panels or any other classical agency.

We have discovered the hard way that elders don't always make good clerks. Could a deacon be clerk of council? Do you have other suggestions?

The Church Order specifically gives you the right, at the local level, to select whomever you wish as officers of the council, the consistory, and the diaconate (Article 36). Typically, these are officebearers. Selecting a deacon to be clerk of council is certainly possible. Most councils prefer to have the clerk serve for both council and consistory. That would make the selection of a deacon a bit more problematic since deacons don't serve on the consistory. But it is entirely your prerogative.

My other suggestion would be to indicate that it is also possible to appoint a capable person not serving in office to do the actual work of recording and correspondence under the guidance of the selected elder clerk. For example, I have seen retired persons who once served as elders now serve in this capacity with great joy and enthusiasm. You could ask such a person to make a "vow of confidentiality," and use their time and energy to everyone's benefit.

When family visits are reported I am very loathe to write in the minute book, for example, that X's marriage is falling apart or that Y is "consumed by hatred." We have resorted to a "destructible 'scandal'/progress sheet" to remind us of action to be taken, etc. In your opinion, what should and should not be recorded in the minute book?

My personal inclination is to advise councils, consistories, and diaconates of the local church, as well as broader assemblies, to maintain two sets of minutes. The first is general in nature, communicated freely, open to all, and contains all actions taken in "open session." A second set records deliberations and decisions which were held during "executive session." For the local consistory, this would include the kinds of confidential matters you refer to. This second set of minutes is then kept in a secure place (church safe or safety deposit box) and is accessible only to officebearers who have publicly pledged a vow of confidentiality and require the information to do their pastoral work.

The general minutes record, for example, that the elders discussed family visits made to X and Y and that details of these visits are found in File #9035 of the minutes of executive sessions. Since the second set is not generally accessible, clerks are free to record matters in as much detail as they believe would be required by members of the consistory to prepare adequately for future contacts.

Has any council ever successfully taken a congregation out of the fellowship of the CRCNA with a majority of the members and all of the properties and assets?

I know of at least one such council. As they say in the news business, I have not independently verified all the details. What I know of them comes from ex-parishioners who shared their story with me. I believe they are trustworthy witnesses. At a congregational meeting, the council in question received the majority's assent to set up a new corporation and abandon the old. Apparently this occurred before people clearly understood what was about to happen. Sometime later, the council openly decided that the denomination was "apostate" and declared the congregation to be "independent." In the one overlapping month, the old corporation (CRC) sold the property to the new one (independent) for a dollar. It appears that even here the articles of incorporation in force at the time may have been violated, but this matter was never brought to a civil court and therefore never determined.

I still recall the many tearful conversations with members of the minority. Many were retired folk who had contributed to the church's budget their entire life, only to have everything taken away from them in one fell swoop. They were told to join the exodus or else go worship in some other church. I noted that it was precisely these longstanding members who took seriously the admonition of the apostle Paul to the Corinthians that we should settle these matters "among us." Perhaps that's why it never went to court. Yet there was no ecclesiastical way for these people to challenge the council. It was now independent and simply would not answer to a Christian Reformed classis, even if an appeal were to be sustained. I still wonder if this is what the apostle had in mind.

II. The Assemblies of the Church

Article 33

a. The assemblies may delegate to committees the execution of their decisions or the preparation of reports for future consideration. They shall give every committee a well-defined mandate, and shall require of them regular and complete reports of their work.

b. Each classis shall appoint a classical interim committee, and synod shall appoint the Board of Trustees, to act for them in matters which cannot await action by the assemblies themselves. Such committees shall be given well-defined mandates and shall submit all their actions to the next meeting of the assembly for approval.

"Execution" of the assemblies' decisions means implementing their specific decisions as well as carrying out the applicable ongoing ministries for them on a more permanent basis. "Reports" to be prepared for "future consideration" can be on those activities or, alternatively, on issues that are too vexing to solve at any particular session of classis or synod. Our broader assemblies have distinguished between standing committees, advisory committees, and study committees.

Denominational Committees

Standing committees of synod include all the so-called boards: Boards of Trustees of Calvin College and of Calvin Theological Seminary, Boards of World Missions, Home Missions, World Relief, and so on. These boards routinely govern the particular ministries assigned to them on a continuing basis and bring annual reports and recommendations to the synod via the denominational Board of Trustees. The standing committees also include what are collectively called "Service Committees," such as the Ecumenical and Interfaith Relations Committee, the Historical Committee, and the Candidacy Committee. A complete listing is published in the annual *Yearbook* of the CRCNA together with all the appropriate contact information.

Study committees of synod are appointed on an ad hoc basis, usually for a three-year term. Because of synodical rules for timely submission of agenda items, these committees typically only have two of those three years to do the bulk of their work. Study committees with work in progress, as well as any that are newly formed, are listed in the concluding articles of the annual *Acts of Synod*. Regulations pertaining to all the committees of synod are found in Section VI of the Rules for Synodical Procedure.

Advisory committees function only during the meetings of the broader assemblies, not before or after them. Their role is defined in the Rules for Synodical Procedure. Classes also make use of committees for pre-advice; their role is often defined in these classes' own rules of procedure.

Regional and Local Committees

The same situation pertains to every classis and council. There are classical Home Missions Committees, for example, and the classis is free to appoint any other standing committee or study committee of its choosing. At the local level, councils typically have Evangelism Committees, Fellowship Committees, Administrative Committees, and the like. Members of such committees need not be officebearers, though ordinarily they must be confessing members of that congregation. The only thing the Church Order requires of all three assemblies is that any and all committees they appoint must submit "regular and complete reports of their work." The assemblies, in other words, made up solely of ordained officebearers (Article 34), must remain in charge as the governing bodies of the ministries and activities of the church. That is the principle on which Article 33 is based.

Interim Committees

Interim committees are necessitated by a church governmental structure that deliberately limits assemblies to the times of their meeting. Christian Reformed polity does not feature a "permanent" assembly of any kind. The local council often meets an evening a month; classis three times or two times a year for an evening, a day, or two days; synod once a year for a week. Interim committees are authorized to act on behalf of the assemblies that appointed them in matters that "cannot await actions by the assemblies themselves."

The classical interim committee typically prepares agendas for classis meetings, endorses ministers of the Word who have accepted a call to another church, holds preliminary interviews with those who request licensure to exhort, and the like. It almost always limits its activities to "routine matters," avoiding whenever possible any decisions or actions that are likely to be controversial. This is what the regulation means when it refers to submission of all actions to the next meeting and to "well-defined mandates."

What used to be known as the synodical interim committee is now called the denominational Board of Trustees. This board typically prepares the agenda for the following synod, endorses interim appointments to membership in synodical boards and committees, regulates and carries out denominational ministries in line with prior synodical decisions, appoints and supervises employees and personnel, and the like. Over the years, agenda items for this board have increased significantly. Its actions are sometimes viewed with suspicion and it is often accused of taking too much authority upon itself. The fact is that it ordinarily functions within the well-defined mandate adopted and amended by synod, and it remains accountable to the assembly in all of its activities. As "synodical interim committee," the board should exercise the same kind of caution that the classes demand of their interim committees: submitting all truly important matters to the following synod for its decision.

Do local councils have "interim committees"?

Yes, they do. They have what often goes by the titles Executive Committees or Administrative Boards. Typically, these groups implement councils' decisions between meetings and prepare agenda for the following meetings. The Church Order nowhere offers an "ideal" or "required" committee structure at the congregational level. Unregulated as it may be, there is no question that good committees with clear mandates at the local level are beneficial in the life of the local church and that Article 33 provides the juridical basis for them.

My favourite sport is hockey, the way we play it north of the border, of course. Is it true that the favourite sport of the Christian Reformed Church is shoving all important issues into study committees?

Yea, verily, it is played frequently and with much gusto. For what I take to be mysterious, yet, upon reflection, excellent or even ingenious reasons, the emotional level of CRCNA members that attends the issues involved tends to wane as the study takes its time and toll. This in direct contrast to the way you raucous Maple Leaf fans increasingly explode as the season on ice progresses. Why do you approach it so fanatically anyhow? Here in the U.S. we just have hockey teams for commercial reasons. Fodder for a new study committee? Wait, no, Article 28, "ecclesiastical matters only"!

II. The Assemblies
of the Church

Article 34

The major assemblies are composed of officebearers who are delegated by their constituent minor assemblies. The minor assemblies shall provide their delegates with proper credentials which authorize them to deliberate and vote on matters brought before the major assemblies. A delegate shall not vote on any matter in which the delegate or the church of which the delegate is a member is particularly involved.

In our consideration of Article 26, we noted that assemblies are church governmental structures that are deliberative in nature and are designed to express the rule of Christ through officebearers. Ordained members provide Spirit-led leadership to the church, strive for its unity, and do that together in mutual accountability. This applies to all levels of church government: local, regional, and (bi)national. Before focusing in on the local council, the Church Order concludes a section on the assemblies in general by carefully distinguishing the major assemblies from that local body—focusing on what makes the classis and the synod unique. Whereas every officebearer functioning within a particular congregation is by reason of ordination alone a member of the local council, the classis and the synod are gatherings of those who have been "delegated by their constituent minor assemblies." In other words, Reformed church polity insists that major assemblies are constituted by way of representation.

Government by Representation

It was not always that way in the history of the CRCNA. Both in the "forerunner" of the denomination, namely, Classis Holland of the RCA, as well as in the earliest broader assemblies of the CRCNA itself, there is evidence that all officebearers gathered to do the work. There simply weren't enough congregations and classes to warrant a representational system. Even the deacons were included. The rationale was that in small churches they performed "presbyterial functions" along with elders by way of exception, and this exception was then to be extended to the broader assembly level as well. Sufficient numbers for good accountability was considered an overriding value. Minutes of the classis covering more than a decade indicate that "Rev. X and Consistory" (today we would say council) were present. But these early assemblies recognized that this practice would soon become unwieldy. More important, they interpreted Reformed church polity in principle to hold that voting rights at classis and synod should be limited to a certain number of ministers and elders (not deacons) delegated by constituent councils and classes:

> In order more closely to observe the church order, it is resolved that henceforth, from each consistory, in addition to the minister, two elders shall be sent to the Classis with credentials, and that voting shall be confined to them. Nevertheless, it is considered very desirable and commendable that all brethren not delegated shall take part in the meeting (*Classis Holland, Minutes 1848-1858*, April 29, 1852, p. 90).

By the end of the nineteenth century, councils routinely sent a minister and one elder (or, in the absence of a minister, two elders) as delegates to the classis. Deacons were received as voting members only by way of exception, most commonly when no elder was available. Synod was made up of exactly the same representation from councils until a system of delegation by classes was ordered in 1882 and finally implemented in 1894. Delegation of deacons as a regular (non-exceptional) feature of classis meetings was not permitted until more than a century later (*Acts of Synod, 1997*, p. 621; see discussion of Article 40). Their delegation to synod is quite another matter: it is still nonexistent (see Article 45).

In the polity of the CRCNA, therefore, two things make persons eligible to be voting members of the major assemblies, and both are necessary: ordination and delegation.

Ordination Required

There have been and are those who assert that ordination is not absolutely necessary. Major assemblies, they say, are gatherings of churches, not individuals, and this is important because the authority of the council is original, while that of the broader assemblies is delegated. The offices belong to the church's being (*esse*), while the broader assemblies are there only for the well-being (*bene esse*) of the church (see discussion of Article 27).

Advocates of this view are fond of citing the example of two men who were not ordained but nonetheless delegated to attend the famous Synod of Dort (1618-19). It is an early indication, they say, that the right to be seated at synod is intrinsic in the delegation alone (see, for example, *Agenda for Synod, 1987*, pp. 413-15). The truth is, of course, that Willem van Brouckhuysen and Jan van der Lauwic were sent to the Synod of Dort by the provincial synod of Overijsel along with four ministers because it could not find a full complement of six ordained officebearers able to follow the official proceedings: they were to be held in Latin. It is an obvious exception. The Church Order approved at that same Synod of Dort itself insists that ministers and elders are sent to classis and synod (Articles 41, 47, 50). The Church Order of the CRCNA rightly summarizes all of this in its revised version of 1965 by stating in this article that "major assemblies are composed of officebearers. . . ."

Delegation Required

Broader assemblies are made up only of those officebearers who are properly delegated by their local council or classis. This requirement arose out of the historical necessity of warding off possible intruders to the earliest official synods of the Reformed church in the Netherlands. But even with that unlikely event out of the picture, it is simply a matter of good order for delegates to classis to carry with them the "proper credentials" that list them as official representatives of their council. The same holds for delegates to synod. The credentials authorize them to deliberate and vote on all matters "brought before the major assemblies."

Conflict of Interest

The article ends by stating that "a delegate shall not vote on any matter in which the delegate or the church of which the delegate is a member is particularly involved." Van Dellen and Monsma call this "a matter of common sense and fairness." And so it is. We must avoid all conflict of interest. If the assembly is deliberating and voting on an appeal alleging wrongdoing of the delegates' council or classis, obviously there is no objectivity and they ought then to abstain when the vote is taken. They may represent that council or classis, of course, usually before a committee of the assembly, but in full session they ought to withdraw voluntarily from the discussion and vote. The clerk should see to it that the abstention is duly recorded in the minutes.

Do all ministers within the boundaries of a major assembly have the right to participate in its deliberations and vote on all matters before it?

With respect to the voting, no, they don't. Christian Reformed polity operates with a system of representation at this level of church government. Only those officially delegated by constituent assemblies have the right to vote.

On the matter of participating in the deliberations apart from the right to vote, the matter is a bit more nuanced. Article 40a does provide for the possibility of granting other officebearers (elders and deacons as well as ministers) an "advisory voice" (privilege of the floor), but that applies only to the classis. There is no analogous provision in connection with the synod. At classis, furthermore, the matter is not "automatic." It happens only when a classis deliberately decides to grant certain non-delegated officebearers the privilege of the floor. That is done by vote of the body or by a ruling of the chair.

None of this, of course, prevents a major assembly from granting the privilege of the floor to anyone of its choosing for good and necessary reasons. Such privilege is then typically limited to a specific item on the agenda.

Is it appropriate for a council or classis to instruct its delegates to broader assemblies to vote on a given issue in a particular way?

Older versions of the Church Order spoke of credentials *and instructions* (e.g., pre-1965, Article 33), and some people have indeed chosen to interpret those last two words to mean that such "binding" of votes is therefore appropriate. I emphatically disagree.

These "instructions" (*litterae mandati*, i.e. letters of mandate) referred to the specific matters on the agenda of the broader assembly that the delegates were being authorized to deliberate and vote upon. Often they indicated a matter or two that were to be added to the assembly's already established agenda: last-minute overtures, communications, or requests. Reformed churches have always made a sharp distinction between these *litterae mandati* and the so-called *mandat imperatif* to clarify that this has nothing to do with the latter: binding delegates to a particular vote. The "instructions" involved what they were to do, not how they were to do it. Even Van Dellen and Monsma, known for their insistence on the priority of local congregations, make it quite clear that such binding would disallow true deliberation and ultimately reduce the role of delegates to that of "voting machines" (*Revised Church Order Commentary*, 1965 ed., p. 146).

Even in our democratic forms of government, members of congress or parliament are not deemed in principle to be bound on any given issue. They are sometimes forced to vote a certain way by their party, but that never seems to happen on issues that involve a moral position. In such sensitive matters, they are allowed to vote as their conscience dictates, even if a majority within their home constituency thinks differently on the matter.

It is understood, however, and probably worth repeating, that delegates to broader assemblies of the CRCNA *are* bound to transact all business within the framework of their obedience to the Scriptures, subscription to the creeds and confessions, and attachment to the Church Order (see Article 5).

II. The Assemblies of the Church

Article 35

a. In every church there shall be a council composed of the minister(s), the elders, and the deacons. Those tasks which belong to the common administration of the church, such as the calling of a pastor, the approval of nominations for church office, mutual censure, meeting with church visitors, and other matters of common concern, are the responsibility of the council.

b. In every church there shall be a consistory composed of the elders and the minister(s) of the Word. Those tasks which belong distinctively to the office of elder are the responsibility of the consistory.

c. In every church there shall be a diaconate composed of the deacons of the church. Those tasks which belong distinctively to the office of deacon are the responsibility of the diaconate. The diaconate shall give an account of its work to the council.

Previously we defined the assemblies as church governmental bodies designed to express the rule of Christ through officebearers. The body that provides this leadership at the local level is known as the council.

Composition of Council

The council consists of all those who are ordained as officebearers to minister within their local congregation. Those who are ordained by a council but called to minister outside the boundaries of the local congregation are not deemed to be members of the council. Examples are professors of theology, chaplains, or ministry associates involved in church planting. These become members of council only when in addition to their main calling they are also ordained as elders or deacons set aside to serve in that capacity within their local congregation. All who are ordained to serve within the local congregation are *ipso facto* members of the council: the minister(s), elders, and deacons. In this, the Church Order faithfully reflects a requirement within one of the CRCNA's Reformed confessions:

> We believe that this true church ought to be governed according to the spiritual order that our Lord has taught us in his Word. There should be ministers or pastors to preach the Word of God and administer the sacraments. There should also be elders and deacons, along with the pastors, to make up the council of the church (Belgic Confession, Article 30).

Council, Consistory, and Diaconate

For much of its history, the denomination referred to the "council" as the "consistory" in order to be absolutely clear that the reference was to ecclesiastical as opposed to civil government; in other words, to have people understand that this assembly is nothing like the "city council." It made a distinction between the "general consistory" (now "council") and the "restricted consistory" (now just "consistory") or, at other times, spoke of "the consistory" and of the "consistory and the deacons." The current reading of Article 35 was proposed in 1987 and adopted the following year (*Acts of Synod, 1988*, p. 552). This was done in the context of sharply distinguishing between the tasks of elders and deacons, but it had the broader effect of clarifying and standardizing the terminology used for the local assembly: it is known as the council. The consistory and diaconate are the council's subsets.

As previously discussed under Article 26, we do not have three assemblies at the local level but just one, as the word "subsets" indicates. The key words in Article 35 are "common administration" and "tasks which belong distinctively" to the offices of elder and deacon. These latter tasks form the context for consistory and diaconate meetings. Ministry associates serving within the organized congregation along with the minister of the Word are "acknowledged as elders" and belong to the consistory as well as the council. In most circumstances, they are present only when their work is on the agenda (the limitation in Article 23a), but everything depends on their specific mandate. Ministers of the Word have their own unique or distinctive functions, but also have others they share in common with the elders. For both of these reasons, they belong to the consistory as well as the council. Obviously, some functions of the ministers of the Word are also shared with the diaconate, and there is nothing to prevent them from attending diaconate meetings when that is called for. Such cooperation is often appreciated by ministers and deacons alike.

Division of Responsibilities

All officebearers share in matters of "common administration." The Church Order here gives us some examples: nominations for officebearers, mutual censure, accountability to classis in the form of meeting with church visitors. But there are many others. Often the Church Order itself indicates when it is a matter for council rather than one of its subsets. Admonition and discipline of members ("general discipline") is in the hands of the consistory (see Article 80), while discipline of officebearers ("special discipline") is in the hands of the council (see Supplement, Articles 82-84). The consistory regulates worship (see Articles 52, 60) but the council regulates mission and evangelism (see Articles 73, 74). Sometimes the boundaries aren't quite so clear. Budgets for worship (stipends for choir director and organist, purchasing wine and grape juice for communion) fall within the area of "common administration," while specific liturgical issues like the order of worship should probably be a matter for the consistory alone. A good rule of thumb in cases of doubt is simply to have the council rule on division of responsibilities.

The Place of the Deacons

It may be helpful at this point to present a brief overview of the place of the deacons in the CRCNA's local assembly structures. The same will occur in articles on classis and synod, focusing then on delegation to broader assemblies.

At the very beginning of CRCNA history, deacons were full-fledged members of the "consistories." Their office, it is true, was seen as one of lesser importance than that of the minister of the Word and the elders. Thus, the accepted Church Order provided that a consistory is composed of the minister(s) and the elders, and that deacons meet separately to transact their business. To prevent oligarchy in smaller churches, however, a further stipulation was made that there the deacons might be "added to the consistory." Since all churches were small, that option was exercised universally. Oligarchy was deemed to be a greater "evil" than having deacons serve as assistant elders.

For the first three decades of the twentieth century, there was much debate as to whether deacons, when added to the consistory in this way, should have the right to vote on matters pertaining to their office only or should have the right to vote on all matters on the agenda. In the end, Synod 1938 ruled that "the phrase, 'added to the consistory,' can mean only that the deacons become members of the Consistory, and as such they are warranted in performing presbyterial functions." This assembly also ruled that when this occurs, "deacons, in matters of church government, should naturally give due consideration to the judgment of the elders" (*Acts of Synod, 1938*, p. 81). The assumption of that decision is that "governance" belongs to the office of elder, not the office of deacon.

Wherever this assumption holds sway in the CRCNA, any move toward granting deacons greater influence in leadership is viewed as an "incursion" on the authority of the minister(s) and the elders. Of course, another assumption can also hold sway, namely, that all officebearers are called to provide leadership by reason of their ordination, and that in this respect the deacons are at full parity with the minister(s) and elders. All have distinctive tasks, but all are involved in "common administration." Elders nurture, equip, and disciple, while deacons show mercy and lead members in the ways of exercising stewardship and striving for justice. Both provide leadership in ministry shared by all, and there is no unauthorized "incursion" one way or the other. The current reading of Article 35, adopted in 1988 but in principle already back in 1965, definitely leans toward this latter assumption (*Acts of Synod, 1965*, p. 67). As Richard De Ridder put it, "what was previously regarded as the exception now became a general rule." In his mind, it further "blurred the traditional distinctions" and "gave the deacons a much larger role in the general government of the congregation" (*Delegation of Deacons to Classis and Synod*, 1982, p. ii).

Attempts have been made at several significant junctures in the history of the CRCNA to settle this debate once and for all by way of arguments from Scripture. In 1970, for example, H.G. Arnold wrote that

> the pattern of the New Testament shows it to be a fact that the elders governed the church. On the other hand, the very origin of the deacon's office indicates that it was to "serve tables." . . . In the record of the New Testament no instance is given of the deacons' ruling. . . . all application of biblical and theological truth must always be limited by explicit directives of Scripture (*The Threefold Office of Christ in Its Bearing on the Office of Elder*, 1970, pp. 97, 108).

The *Agenda for Synod, 1987* also dwells on the biblical "origin of the deacon's office." A majority report noted that the office's origin has almost always been located in the words of Acts 6. "The responsibility assigned the Seven by the apostles for meeting peoples' physical or material needs later came to be institutionalized in the office we now know as 'deacon.'" Thus, "as representatives of the church, deacons have throughout history been entrusted with tasks focusing on works of mercy, justice, etc." On the other hand, a minority report countered with the observation that in listing required qualifications for the "seven," Acts 6 fails to even allude to care for the poor but rather calls for deacons to be "full of the Spirit and wisdom." Thus, "the apostles continued to devote themselves to preaching and prayer, but the managerial coordination of the communion of the saints in the homes was now turned over to others." In view also of 1 Timothy 3:8-13, one must conclude that "the elder is responsible for supervisory leadership, while the deacon is responsible for coordinative service" (*Agenda for Synod, 1987*, pp. 390-91, 408-09). Similar battles have been fought over the proper interpretation of 1 Timothy 5:17 ("no mention is made of deacons in the presbytery") and of Acts 15 ("only apostles and elders gave leadership"). The common mistake in all these attempts is to assume that the Scriptures provide a ready-made "church order," a clear mandate for ministers, elders, and deacons for all time.

Arguments of this kind are not helpful. We must do much more than simply consulting all biblical references to "elders" and "deacons." In biblical times, as in ours, officebearers have a distinctive function but they also share a unity of function, a common goal: nourishing and equipping the church of Christ for ministry in the world. Within that "general calling" are dimensions of proclamation, of pastoral care, and of leadership in acts of mercy and stewardship. That is at the heart of Article 35: a council for "common administration" and a consistory and diaconate for the unique dimensions of bearing office.

Should ministers (who are essentially "paid employees" of the church) chair council meetings or even be members of the council?

A minister is an elected officebearer, set aside by the congregation as Christ's representative to exercise spiritual oversight and to equip members of the congregation to fulfill their calling in the church and in the world. As our Belgic Confession makes clear in Article 30, ministers of the Word together with the elders and deacons "make up the council of the Church." This confessional basis must translate into organizational/administrative reality. I am not fussy about ministers having to *chair* council meetings. That requirement is more common in Presbyterian polity and in the RCA. For the CRCNA, there is a selection process in Article 36, recognizing that certain elders or deacons may be more gifted for that position. Broadly speaking, churches may never exclude ministers from membership in the council.

I fully understand that certain tax regulations or other government regulations applying to nonprofit corporations or charitable institutions may suggest or state outright that this amounts to a clear instance of conflict of interest: a "paid employee" on the board. This, however, should not lead us to the extreme of forbidding ministers from being seated on the council in clear violation of the confessional basis and the text of our Church Order. In most cases, it is possible to exclude the minister from all decision-making that involves ministerial salary and benefits and other agenda items that such government regulations clearly envision. In fact, this has been our traditional practice at both council and congregational meetings.

Local articles of incorporation could even spell out that the church has a council (all officebearers) and also a board (all officebearers minus employees, including ministers). The latter would be responsible for all matters relating to the remuneration or employment of staff, if not the entire budget.

May an unordained youth worker attend and/or participate in council/consistory meetings?

In principle, assemblies are open for anyone to attend. The officebearers may declare executive session, of course, and ask the visitors to leave, especially when persons are discussed or dealt with. However, such declarations should be used as little as possible. It is important for members to be involved and for officebearers to realize that they must wrestle with issues and make decisions "in the open."

This matter gets a little "stickier," however, with the elders and consistory. These meetings so often feature discussions of persons that we assume (be it informally) they are always in "executive session." It is the same with meetings of the diaconate. In small congregations, council meetings and consistory meetings sometimes "fuse into one," and there too the members may have such assumptions. In that case, by the way, I would strongly advise separating them clearly, even if only by way of separate times on the same evening, just to give members as much opportunity as possible to attend and become more interested in the government of their church. Attendance is one thing, participation another. Observers must not speak unless they have been extended the privilege of the floor. Nonmembers do not have the right to vote at our assemblies.

But now more directly to your question. To answer it, we can learn from Article 23a of the Church Order when it states that the ministry associates' work as elders is normally "limited to the ministries in which they serve as ministry associates." Along these same lines I think it would be entirely appropriate and even necessary for the council to allow an unordained youth worker (who is not a member of council per se) to participate in deliberation on matters relating to his or her function, short, of course, of a right to vote.

With respect to voting rights, my judgment is that these are granted only to ordained members of council. Our Belgic Confession says clearly that it is pastors, elders, and deacons who form the council of the church, not whomever else the council might wish to invite as members.

Article 35 calls on the diaconate to "give an account of its work to the council," but no such demand is made of the consistory. Are the deacons on a lower level of authority?

Frankly, yes. Part of our tradition seems to categorize elders as those who "rule" and deacons as those who "serve." I'm not sure how universal it was and is, but it's there. Perhaps, as our Church Order evolved, that part of our tradition had the upper hand in shaping it. In any case, there is also another part of our tradition that fights for the recognition of the diaconal office as a full-fledged ministry of Christ among us.

The imbalance you observe in this article can easily be resolved by adding to section b: "The consistory shall give an account of its work to the council." Why not test the mind of the denomination and see which part of our tradition currently has the upper hand by sending an overture through the assemblies? In the meantime, I would strongly advise you to adopt the practice in your own congregation without delay. There's nothing here that forbids it. Now that I think of it, this was the actual practice in all the congregations I've served as pastor. We just assumed that it was important for the deacons to know what the elders were up to. One note of caution: here too the matter of confidentiality and "executive session" should be respected. Elders should not reveal personal matters unless, in their judgment, deacons must know about them in order appropriately to fulfill their calling.

II. The Assemblies of the Church

Article 36

a. The council, consistory, and diaconate shall ordinarily meet at least once a month, at a time and place announced to the congregation. Each body shall select its own president and other officers.

b. The council, at least four times per year, shall exercise mutual censure, in which officebearers assess and encourage each other in the performance of their official duties.

Frequency of Meetings

In 1581, it was once a week; in 1914, it was once a week "as a rule, at least in larger congregations"; in 1965, it was once a month; and in 2004-5 it became "ordinarily" at least once a month. Synod 2004 explained that the provision on frequency of meeting should "reflect current practice" and offer "greater flexibility." It also adopted the following ground:

> Church visitors can ensure that the number of meetings held are sufficient for the ministry needs of the congregation (*Acts of Synod, 2004*, p. 542).

This is an obvious reference to what Synod 1942 added to Article 41 (in its pre-2006 reading) on accountability to classis, namely, whether the council meetings are "held regularly according to the needs of the congregation" (*Acts of Synod, 1942*, p. 111). That significant phrase probably best reflects the original and lasting intent of this regulation on frequency. For the sake of accountability it also remains wise to add some specificity. Councils, consistories, and diaconates should "ordinarily meet at least once a month."

Openness of Meetings

The article next speaks of the need to announce "time and place" to the congregation. This may seem odd, at first glance, since members of the congregation do not typically meet with the officebearers unless asked to do so for the annual congregational meeting (Article 37). Upon further reflection, one might conclude that there is a measure of accountability to the congregation as well as the classis. More specifically, it is important for members to take note of the council's leadership, its specific decisions, and guidance for ongoing ministries. Without question, it also provides the necessary information for purposes of possible members' appeals and communications. In addition, these meetings of officebearers are in principle open to the membership unless they are declared to be in executive session. The latter happens routinely at meetings of the consistory and the diaconate (when particular members and their circumstances are discussed each time) and it happens occasionally when a council feels the need. A good example of that would be a discussion on nominations for elders and deacons. Nonetheless, meetings of council, certainly, are typically open, and it is good when members of the congregation take an interest and attend as visitors.

Officers of Local Assemblies

Article 36 goes on to provide that each body (council, consistory, diaconate) "shall select its own president and other officers." This is a relatively new reading. The earliest of sixteenth century Church Orders of the Reformed Church in the Netherlands already held that the minister of the Word or, if more than one, the ministers in turn should preside (e.g. *Synod of Dordrecht, 1574*, Article VIII). The CRCNA inherited this provision, changing it in 1965 only to the effect that an elder might preside in the absence of a minister of the Word. Synod 1973 introduced more drastic change. Acting on an overture from Classis Eastern Canada, the assembly inserted the word "ordinarily" on the grounds that "there are experienced elders who are quite capable of chairing" and that "the offices of minister and elders as rulers are equal" (*Acts of Synod, 1973*, p. 82). Synod 1996 took it one step further with its proposal to eliminate the preference for ministers presiding altogether and to add the reference to "other officers," this time at the urging of Classis Chatham. The ground offered for that action asserted that "officers of council should be chosen on the basis of gifts, talents, and abilities" (*Acts of Synod, 1996*, p. 580). The proposed and now current reading was officially adopted the following year (*Acts of Synod, 1997*, p. 612).

Mutual Censure

In Reformed circles the practice of mutual censure was introduced to provide a means of adjudicating complaints about the doctrine and life of the officebearers, especially ministers. Any such complaints would be dealt with in the (temporary) absence of the accused and, if necessary, he would be admonished upon his return to the meeting. It was one way of coping with lack of training as well as loose morals on the part of the clergy. The custom, in other words, was immediately endowed with a negative tone. As early as 1586, however, the Dutch Reformed Church sought to change that tone by providing in its Church Order that the discharge of office, not doctrine and life, was to be the focus of such mutual censure. This more positive formulation has remained with us ever since. Mutual censure is concerned with assessment of and encouragement in "the performance of . . . official duties."

There has always been an insistence that mutual censure take place on a regular basis. The Dutch Synod of Dordrecht (1578) first implemented this principle by way of a specific reference to the celebration of the Lord's Supper. In 1586 reference to the sacrament was dropped from this provision of the official Church Order. It seems obvious that, once again, consistories were given the room to decide for themselves exactly when the matter would appear on the agenda.

Christian Reformed synods extended the courtesy until 1914, when the first English version of the Church Order was adopted. In that year, it was decided to include the phrase "before partaking of the Lord's table." Perhaps the church was only making explicit what had become a well-established custom. In any case, they reached back to a span of only eight years of linkage in Dutch tradition to do it. A study committee reporting to Synod 1947 suggested that "there is no connection between *censura morum* and the Lord's Supper." The assembly agreed, but argued that official "disassociation . . . is apt to cause neglect." The newly revised Church Order, in force since 1965, still specifies the need to exercise mutual censure "at least four times per year" but no longer mentions the celebration of the sacrament in this connection.

The only advantage of a link with the sacrament is that it ensures regularity. A serious disadvantage is that it confuses "general" and "special" discipline. The former applies to all members of the congregation, the latter only to officebearers. If an elder is at odds with a deacon to the point where celebrating communion together is unthinkable, the matter ought to be attended to immediately on the level of "general" discipline. They shouldn't sit through even one regular worship service under those conditions. If, on the other hand, that elder can accept the deacon as a brother or sister in Christ, yet have some reservations about the way in which that deacon is performing the official duties of ministry, the elder might well wait until the council agenda calls for mutual censure.

There are ways in which councils could make mutual censure a more edifying experience. Councils could change the emphasis from scrutiny of the individual to communal self-examination. Doctrine and life still have a bearing, but the focus is on the performance of official duties. Councils could arrange for regularity of discussion but do away with the link to the Lord's Supper. Mutual censure is more appropriate, say, after the reading of elders' and deacons' minutes and the pastor's report. Councils could ask in what ways their fellow officebearers are meeting or not meeting the needs of the congregation. They could use the time to adjust present goals and objectives if necessary. Councils could structure each occasion thematically. They could focus on, say, evangelism, pastoral care, proclamation, benevolence, political awareness, church education, stewardship, or discipline, and discuss these matters in depth. In preparing for a classis meeting or for the arrival of church visitors, councils could use the appropriate guides for these events to launch the discussion. Councils could use this slot on the agenda to discuss needs of the congregation when a pastor leaves and a mandate for the search committee is to be drafted. In any case, councils should never place the matter toward the end of a meeting. They should take sufficient time for meaningful dialogue and focus on the positive as well as the negative.

Article 36 says that "the council, consistory, and diaconate shall ordinarily meet at least once a month." Would it be in violation of the Church Order if council meets one month and consistory meets the next? Is that in keeping with the once-a-month practice? We are thinking of meeting as council one month and consistory and diaconate the next month. If there are any pressing council matters on the months when consistory meets, we would have a brief council (elders and deacons) meeting prior to consistory and, similarly, with consistory matters on a month when council meets.

Technically, that surely is a violation, especially if it is done on a permanent basis. Our Church Order speaks to this issue with obvious specificity and then adds the flexibility of the word "ordinarily." This is understandably puzzling to some people. But when you study the history of the provision, it becomes clear what the Church Order basically intends to say: the frequency must be sufficient to meet the needs of the congregation. In fact, that is the language used in early versions of Article 41. Delegates were to be asked at classis meetings whether council meetings were held "regularly" and "according to the needs of the congregation."

Prior to 1965, the provision called for *weekly* meetings as a rule, especially so in larger congregations. Now that it's once a month, I've never heard of a church being admonished for skipping a July meeting. On the other hand, some of the arrangements made these days go too far in the other direction. We find that some churches have council meetings only twice a year for "visioning," leaving the rest to executive councils and the like. You have to wonder whether officebearers can exercise sound leadership that way. The "exception" you have in mind—six times a year with a brief council meeting possible when consistory and diaconate are to meet and vice versa—sounds eminently reasonable because, in my judgment at least, you can be fairly certain that the needs of the church are being met. In other words, my view would be that you're not unduly stretching the flexibility of the word "ordinarily." That's key here, not the mere technicality involved.

II. The Assemblies of the Church

Article 37

The council, besides seeking the cooperation of the congregation in the election of officebearers, shall also invite its judgment about other major matters, except those which pertain to the supervision and discipline of the congregation. For this purpose the council shall call a meeting at least annually of all members entitled to vote. Such a meeting shall be conducted by the council, and only those matters which it presents shall be considered. Although full consideration shall be given to the judgment expressed by the congregation, the authority for making and carrying out final decisions remains with the council as the governing body of the church, except in those matters stipulated otherwise in the articles of incorporation or by law.

The congregational meeting is a council meeting to which the congregation is invited. This must be done at least annually, with sufficient notice, and usually centers around two main items: election of officebearers and adoption of the church's budget. The former is specifically mentioned here as a reminder of the requirement contained in Article 4; the latter is the most common "other major matter" presented by the council for congregational consideration. Both of these, furthermore, require congregational voting. In other matters, councils are not bound to call for a vote. The congregation's "judgment" can be ascertained without it: a thorough discussion, for example, before the council makes a "final decision" as "the governing body of the church."

Councils are well advised to choose carefully which matters it presents, how it presents them, and when to call for a vote. It is usually unwise to put other matters, besides elections and budget, to a congregational vote when a council meeting to follow could very well decide the matter differently. In that case, the council should stick to a "listening mode" in order to keep faith with the congregation. If matters are put to a vote, reasonable amendments from the floor are acceptable. Such amendments must be precisely that: minor change within a major matter. Proposals for major change at the meeting itself should be ruled out of order. They may then become a reason for voting for or against the main motion on the floor, or the council may choose to take back the entire issue for re-presentation at a future meeting.

It stands to reason, of course, that elections for officebearers are not open for discussion prior to the vote. Procedures for such elections might be discussed, but not the giftedness of nominees or perceived lack thereof. Councils should ensure that members have sufficient information on nominees. This typically means that those being considered for call as minister(s) have been introduced and have led at least one worship service. At a minimum, a search committee's summary, with only the needed and most useful information approved by council, should be passed along to the membership. It should also never be assumed that nominees for elder and deacon are well-known. If only as a matter of courtesy to those who have most recently joined the congregation as new members, the council might well do something similar in their case.

The Church Order insists that matters of "supervision and discipline" are not to be placed on the agenda for congregational meetings. The reference is to matters that fall within the unique functions of the elders and probably gets at the very same distinction made in Article 35 between such functions and the "common administration of the church."

For much of denominational history, the obvious tension between this article of the Church Order and the articles of incorporation in matters of property and assets, as well as the annual budget, remained unresolved. In other words, the final clause that specifically refers to these articles of incorporation was not there. This way, the council retained its "final authority" even in decisions on budgetary matters taken after the congregational vote. There are numerous stories of some very unpleasant events that took place when councils actually chose to depart from the decision of the members. Synod 2010 decided to resolve the tension and eliminate that possibility (*Acts of Synod, 2010*, p. 901).

Are there some rules about a quorum for congregational meetings?

Certainly not in the Church Order nor in its Supplements. However, synod approves a Model for Articles of Incorporation, which includes language like this: "a meeting of such members of this church or congregation present and entitled to vote, duly and specially called for that purpose by notice given for two successive Sundays at the usual place of meeting." In other words, it is envisioned in this model that decisions are made by a majority of those present. One can reasonably assume that if only 20 percent of the adult confessing members happen to be present, 10 percent plus one would carry the day. One would hope for a better turnout. But this is merely a model. The real answer to your question can only be found in the actual articles of incorporation and bylaws of your own local church, duly and legally approved.

Councils are also well-advised to have in place and constantly hold before the congregation the rules on voting with respect to proxy voting and absentee balloting. They should be printed in every meeting's agenda. Generally, we assume that with respect to any matter to be deliberated at the meeting, absentee balloting and voting by proxy is not permitted. If no discussion is called for, say, in electing officebearers, these might be permitted.

The minutes of our council meeting have this notation regarding council's budget recommendation to the congregation: "Elders *A*, *B*, and *C* wish their negative votes to be recorded so that they can speak and vote against the motion at the congregational meeting." Does the act of recording their negative votes in council's minutes give these officebearers the right or opportunity to speak and/

or vote against council's recommendation at the congregational meeting?

Yes, it does. That is precisely what they need to do to retain that right. The chair may wish to explain at the congregational meeting that this has occurred, that normally the minority bows to the will of the majority and no negative votes are recorded, that those who now did are focusing on just a part or some parts of the budget, and that they have promised the chair that as demurring council members they will state their objections with utmost respect and civility (which hopefully will be the case). As chairperson, I would then also make sure that the thinking of the majority of council members is clearly conveyed before any motions are voted upon. It is important, however, that those who have recorded their negative votes should not discuss the matter with members outside of, before, or after the scheduled congregational meeting.

Not a big issue, but we had quite a discussion last night at council meeting about whether it was appropriate for council to approve the minutes of a congregational meeting. Shouldn't that be done by the congregation whose meeting it was? Is it right for one body to approve the minutes of another body?

The congregational meeting in our system of church government is actually a council meeting to which the congregation is invited. In our churches the council approves the minutes and they are sometimes distributed, sometimes just summarized and distributed in point form, sometimes read in their entirety at the next congregational meeting. So yes, it is appropriate for the council to approve these minutes.

II. The Assemblies of the Church

ARTICLE 38

a. Groups of believers among whom no council can as yet be constituted shall be under the care of a neighboring council, designated by classis.

b. When a council is being constituted for the first time, the approval of classis is required.

c. When a non-Christian Reformed congregation wishes to affiliate with the Christian Reformed Church, including the transfer of its pastor and other ministry staff, the procedure and regulations established by synod shall be followed.

d. When a council and congregation decide to disband or revert to unorganized status, the approval of classis is required. If any distribution of assets is required, the congregation and council shall consult with classis.

e. When two or more councils and congregations decide to merge, the approval of classis is required.

f. When a council decides to disaffiliate from the denomination, the set process for disaffiliation adopted by synod shall be followed.

g. Particular churches of the Christian Reformed Church in North America may unite to form union congregations with one or more particular congregations of churches in ecclesiastical fellowship, with the approval of classis.

Constituting a New Council

The first two sections of this article have been in place since the sixteenth century. At the time, the context was that of a classis supporting Reformed believers in areas where persecution by a prevailing Roman Catholic culture was still rampant. Whenever such persecution began to subside and sufficient numbers could gather for worship, the classis would formalize that support by approving organization, seeing to the election of officebearers, and thus constituting a council. The CRCNA inherited these same procedures. The only real change was introduced in 1914, when the synod of that year decided to have a classically designated "neighboring congregation" provide the support instead of the classis itself.

Today, the context is almost always that of a church plant that has flourished sufficiently to become an organized congregation. In most situations, a supervising council is in place when classis agrees to take on the mission effort and, from the very beginning, that council does for the new group what it does for its own members: provide support for the discipling process, call a church planter for the work of gathering, hold memberships of those who join, and so on. In some cases it has not been a supervising council but a home missionary who has done these things. Synod has allowed for that possibility since the adoption of a Home Mission Order in 1959 (*Acts of Synod, 1959*, pp. 77, 206). In any case, classis must approve organization and permit the election and installation of officebearers when the group is of a self-sustaining size. Definitions of that self-sustaining size are not precise, but the factors that play a role have to do with self-sufficiency in leadership gifts, full-fledged ministry, and good prospects for continued growth (see Supplement, Article 38b).

Affiliating, Disaffiliating, Disbanding, Merging

The last five of seven sections of this article were introduced in the past two decades by synods recognizing new realities. They were facing the following facts:

- some congregations left the denomination in the midst of disputes over contentious issues and became independent and/or joined other fellowships;

- others joined the CRCNA after disaffiliating from their own denomination;

- still others disbanded, reverted to unorganized status, merged, or formed union churches by reason of decline in membership in situations where hoped-for growth did not materialize.

These things happened in sufficient numbers so as to warrant some regulation.

As of 1997, councils that decide to lead their congregations out of the denominational fellowship are required to follow the procedure contained in the Supplement to Article 38f. The main burden of that procedure is that classis will be given the opportunity to have representatives meet with the council and congregation before final decisions are made. In the end, classis is free to "acquiesce" if the congregation persists in withdrawal, but then not until "disputes between differing factions" within that congregation, if any, are settled. As we noted in the treatment of Article 32d, it is expected that churches within the fellowship of the CRCNA have made this possible by way of appropriate language to that effect in the articles of incorporation. The hope is that rightful ownership of property and assets can be determined without resorting to a civil court.

The regulation of an entire congregation joining the CRCNA began at a classical level and has only recently been adopted by synod (*Acts of Synod, 2006*, p. 680). The most common context is that of first-generation immigrant congregations looking to find a denominational home. But it could also involve a congregation forced to leave its prior fellowship by reason of conscience. Traditionally the CRCNA deliberately avoids proselytizing at all cost. This is its ecumenical responsibility. But it is also hospitable to those who have taken the initiative of looking for a new denominational home.

In an increasingly mobile society and a culture that values the institutional church less and less, it is not surprising to see a significant number of congregations struggling to survive. Articles 38d, 38e, and 38g, along with their supplemental materials, provide the regulated options available to them. The common denominator is approval by the classis.

> **A new Christian Reformed church plant in our area is attracting a number of our members who seem excited about its potential and want to help. We regret their desire to leave us, of course, but also have no objections to their transferring their membership. But is that proper procedure?**
>
> In some cases, home missionaries have held membership until the church plant has become an organized congregation by an action of the classis. More common, however, is that the classis has appointed a supervising or sponsoring congregation and that the council of that church holds membership until that organization occurs. In any case, a "steering committee" cannot receive attestations or transfers of membership, and the formal organization of the emerging church is required before there is a council in place that has the authority to receive these.
>
> **A small church in our classis has decided to disband. Its council is now asking the classis to be the trustees of its assets until all is resolved. How should the classis respond?**
>
> Assuming that the option of becoming an unorganized church under the care of a neighboring council has been explored and rejected, the classis takes note of the church's decision, sees to it that all memberships are appropriately transferred to other congregations, and, when asked, gives advice about financial matters. It should be carefully noted, however, that the local articles of incorporation and bylaws may already provide for the possibility of dissolution and the disbursement of all assets. If so, these provisions must be carefully followed—by the church itself and also by the classis. If not, and those who remain confessing members are so inclined, classis may gain the right of trusteeship only upon a clear vote to that effect at a congregational meeting prior to the disbanding. Such trusteeship must be temporary. As a rule, classis does not own property.

When a church disbands, what is the status of the ministers involved? Do we need to follow Article 17 and involve the deputies, or are they simply declared eligible for a call, or . . . ?

The 2001 edition of the *Manual of CRC Government* prepared by David Engelhard and Leonard Hofman, page 242, features the following statements by the authors (presumably in the absence of specific regulations):

> If the congregation has a pastor at the time of dissolution, provision should be made from the remaining assets of the church for the support of the pastor, his residence, pension, insurance, as well as the length of time and amount of support. This should be done in accordance with the provisions of Church Order Article 17.
>
> Announcements should be made at appropriate intervals of the pastor's availability to receive a call to another church.
>
> The pastor's ecclesiastical credentials should be transferred to the care of another council in consultation with the pastor, the advice of classis, and the assent of that council. The extent and nature of the receiving council's responsibility to the minister whose credentials it will hold should be clearly understood by all parties.

The more recent *Manual* (2008) has omitted this material. I tend to agree that this is formally an Article 17 matter. If it is at all possible to anticipate the event, it would be preferable for everyone involved if the minister would receive a call and accept it prior to the disbanding, rendering moot the provisions of Article 17.

One of the options our small and dwindling congregation is considering is whether or not the church should become unorganized. Would this step require the approval of classis? Under whose supervision would the congregation be should this step be

taken? What are the advantages and the disadvantages of taking this step? What responsibility would we have to the denomination? At what point might it be wise for such a decision to be made?

Article 38d itself insists that "when a council and congregation decide to . . . revert to unorganized status, the approval of classis is required." The unorganized church then comes under the supervision of a nearby congregation designated by the classis. The group may provide classis with a preference, but classis decides. The members then technically become members of the neighboring church and the council then becomes a "steering committee" under the authority of the council of the neighboring church.

The advantages of taking this step are that the group need not look for new officebearers all the time because the Church Order's insistence on limited tenure no longer applies. There are no expectations for meeting denominational obligations such as ministry shares. Truthfully, none of the Church Order's rules apply, except of course that one would hope for new growth, restoration to organized status, and then one would want the "emerging group" to look like a CRC congregation following its polity. In short, reverting to unorganized status removes obligations and opens some doors for renewal. The disadvantages are that the neighboring council must now do all the "official" things. For example, its elders (who have never served within the group) must carry out any needed disciplinary actions. The unorganized congregation now sends delegates to classis only if a member of the steering committee happens to be ordained as an elder by the supervising church or a ministry associate remains in place, both of which are unlikely. In addition, a request of classis to permit extending a call to a new minister will not usually be granted until all conditions are ripe for return to "organized" status. In short, it tends to isolate the group, and only a classical Home Missions Committee can counter that with constant attention.

The unorganized church continues within the "fold" of the CRCNA, and the new group would still have some obligations to the denomination. But various options can be considered, including merger with another church (CRCNA or RCA), sharing a minister with another church, closing the church altogether ("disbanding" of 38d), or working with CRCNA Home Missions to find creative ways for growth and opportunities.

Wisdom on this? For me the real wisdom has to do with a congregation being so small that it really has no potential for good leadership any more, i.e. it has an insufficient number of people who could serve on council with others and truly provide what it takes for the group to flourish. In the end, the wisdom of Supplement to Article 38d is a matter of facing reality: a church with fewer than forty-five active confessing members probably is no longer viable, and new options need to be entertained. I share that view. But, of course, I'm just a faraway bystander. . . .

II. The Assemblies of the Church

Article 39

A classis shall consist of a group of neighboring churches. The organizing of a new classis and the redistricting of classes require the approval of synod.

Previously, we defined the assemblies as church governmental bodies designed to express the rule of Christ through officebearers. The body that provides this leadership at the regional level is known as the classis.

Alignment of Classes

The classis (plural: classes) consists of officebearers who have been delegated by the constituent church councils to represent them in the deliberations and decisions. Those who are ordained by a council but called and set aside to minister outside the boundaries of the local congregation are typically not deemed to be eligible for such delegation. The only exception is that officebearers serving in the setting of an emerging church may be delegated to classis as representatives of the emerging church if the classis has decided to permit the practice and the supervising congregation that has ordained them so decides (see commentary under Article 34). Any other officebearers ordained by the constituent church councils "may also attend classis and may be given an advisory voice" (Article 40a), but they are not official delegates and therefore do not have the right to vote.

Realignment of Classes

The classis itself typically approves the formation of a council in an emerging congregation that is ready for organized status and welcomes its delegates to its meetings (Article 38b). On the other hand, Article 39 holds that only the synod may approve the formation of a new classis or the redistricting of classes. This usually occurs by way of overture(s) to synod. Proximity is the main factor. Some classes simply become too large and a reasonable split is desirable. But as the Supplement to this article indicates, Synod 1996 ruled that a council's request for transfer to another classis "may include grounds that go beyond the sole matter of geographic proximity" and that "synod is at liberty to consider such grounds in its disposition of the request." The obvious context is the issue of the ordination of women and their delegation to the assembly. The same synod, however, also decided against formation of a classis "based on theological affinity" (*Acts of Synod, 1996*, p. 561). Proximity remains the main criterion.

Could you help me understand what a "classis contracta" is? I ran across that term in an article on the ordination of women as ministers but I can't find it anywhere in our Church Order.

When a classis gathers for a regular meeting, all of the constituent churches are expected to send delegates. If a church fails to do so, it is automatically approached for the reasons why, just to ensure that the congregation is not withdrawing from denominational fellowship and going independent. We need one another.

Sometimes a classis holds special meetings that are unavoidable. A good example is when one of the churches has just called a candidate for ministry to be its pastor, and now that candidate needs to be examined for ordination. The congregation shouldn't have to wait until the next regular classis meeting takes place, and the matter is too important to simply deal with at a classical interim committee meeting. So a special meeting is held. When the constituent churches of a classis are within easy reach of each other, as for example in

---

Grand Rapids East or Toronto, all churches tend to appoint delegates who attend. When, on the other hand, the constituent churches of a classis are widely dispersed, as for example in Classis Rocky Mountain or British Columbia North-West, the classis sometimes insists on delegation from a certain grouping of churches in close proximity to each other but "excuses" congregations at great distance from the place of meeting. These may send delegates, but do not have to do so. Needless to say, there should be a quorum: at least 50 percent plus one of the churches must have delegates present. Typically the agenda for the special meeting consists of only the one item that occasioned its need.

Geography, however, is not the only factor at stake. There is one additional trigger having to do with an ordination exam for a woman candidate or the transferring of credentials of a woman minister. This exception actually uses the words "classis contracta"—not, as you say, in the Church Order itself—but rather in the Supplement to Article 3. Synod 2007 recognized the need for all classes to "respect the prerogative of its constituent churches to call and ordain officebearers according to their own biblical convictions." If a council only has officebearers who feel that they cannot in good conscience participate in the examination of a woman candidate, that council is excused from sending delegates, and the examination will thus take place in a "classis contracta." There is the further stipulation that the classis may even invite representatives from churches outside its boundaries in order to "achieve the equivalent of a quorum."

II. The Assemblies of the Church

Article 40

a. The council of each church shall delegate a minister and an elder to the classis. If a church is without a minister, or the minister is prevented from attending, two elders shall be delegated. Officebearers who are not delegated may also attend classis and may be given an advisory voice.

b. The classis shall meet at least every four months, unless great distances render this impractical, at such time and place as was determined by the previous classical meeting.

c. The ministers shall preside in rotation, or a president may be elected from among the delegates; however, the same person shall not preside twice in succession.

Constitution of the Classis

As we noted with respect to Articles 25 and 34, the CRCNA has insisted from the end of the nineteenth century that ministers and elders qualify for delegation to the classis by reason of their mandate to "govern" and that the delegation of deacons who "serve" should occur only by way of exception.

In keeping with this insistence, deacons have been delegated to classis only when elders were not available. This practice of seating the deacons "by way of exception" is still often recorded in classical minutes as a separate decision taken at the time of the constitution of the assembly.

Delegation of Deacons

As the Supplement to Article 40a indicates, however, Synod 1997 has approved the delegation of deacons to the classis, provided that the classis so decides. If so, the classis will receive a minister, an elder, and a deacon at all meetings, and the deacon will receive "identical credentials." It can be argued, therefore, that the CRCNA is gradually moving toward the view that it is a person's ordination as such and not his or her specific office or mandate that qualifies that person for delegation to the classis. Or, to put it another way, the CRCNA may finally be drawing the logical conclusions regarding the parity of the offices (Articles 2, 85). The only thing that gives one pause in coming to this conclusion is that Article 45 still does not permit the delegation of deacons to synod, not even by way of exception.

It is important to note that this decision of 1997 was no sudden novelty. A study committee reporting to Synod 1966, for instance, judged that in light of the biblical givens and Reformed church polity "there are no lawful objections to the delegation of deacons" and proposed that this become the practice of the synod as well as the classis. "Any half-way house," the committee said, "will only prolong the process" (*Acts of Synod, 1966*, pp. 22-23). The proposal was not adopted at the time but it placed on the table what a significant minority had been arguing throughout the denomination's history. Indeed, as we have previously noted under Article 25, Classis Muskegon even conducted an open but unauthorized "experiment" with diaconal delegation in the 1970s. When asked to regularize the practice, Synod 1980 did not oblige. It would take an additional seventeen years for a synod to begin to move in that direction.

It is true that ministers, ministry associates, elders, and deacons have different functions to perform. But they share the calling that together they are to "equip [Christ's] people for works of service" (see Eph. 4:11-13). Church government is all about mutual accountability and encouragement in this equipping work. Many issues dealt with at meetings of the classis tend to have a diaconal dimension and it is fitting that deacons are present to help deliberate on them. For that reason, synod might well consider revising Article 34 to read as follows:

The major assemblies are composed of officebearers who are delegated by their constituent minor assemblies. The minor assemblies shall provide their delegates with proper credentials which authorize them, *in a manner consistent with the uniqueness of their particular office,* to deliberate and vote on *all* matters brought before the major assemblies. A delegate shall not vote on any matter in which the delegate or the church of which the delegate is a member is particularly involved.

This would lay the appropriate foundation for the further revision of Articles 40 and 45 to include the delegation of deacons as a regular feature of church government in the CRCNA.

Privilege of the Floor

Article 40 proceeds to indicate that all non-delegated officebearers may attend classis and may be given an "advisory voice." This is more popularly known as the "privilege of the floor." Note that it says "officebearers" and that, therefore, deacons are included. This wording was adopted in 1965 and quite consciously broadened the provision beyond what had been the case in Reformed polity since 1618-19, namely, that only ministers could be given such an advisory voice.

Frequency of Classical Meetings

As a general rule, classis meetings must be held three times a year. This has been the ideal throughout the history of the CRCNA in order to provide sufficient exercise of mutual accountability and leadership among the congregations. Synod 1914 was the first to provide for an exception pertaining to "great distances." A recent task force appointed by the Board of Trustees indicates that "over 50 percent of churches belong to classes that meet only two times per year." It is an interesting case of obvious noncompliance with what the Church Order so clearly prescribes. When asked, a relatively recent synodical assembly steadfastly refused to revise this article so that classes might decide the issue of frequency of meeting for themselves (*Acts of Synod, 1993,* p. 506). Presumably the assembly relied on grounds that were recorded in defeating an earlier attempt at revision:

The advantages to three meetings a year that should not be given up except for good cause are: the opportunity to respond to the agenda of synod, more frequent contact among the churches, closer supervision of the work of classis, and the distribution of the burden of the work over three meetings instead of two (*Acts of Synod, 1985*, p. 725).

Officers of Classis

As for the provision on those presiding at meetings of the classis, it begins with the option of "ministers presiding in rotation." Limiting the pool of eligible persons to ministers was the practice of the CRCNA from 1857 until 1984, at which time it was broadened to "officebearers" (*Acts of Synod, 1984*, pp. 231, 573). The consensus was that there were "gifted elders" who could well serve in that capacity. Nonetheless, the option of "ministers presiding in rotation" remains in place. It appears to be a fairly common practice to allow ministers to withdraw from such rotation if they feel less than qualified to preside. In other areas, the rotation method has been abandoned completely. For the further limitation that no person shall serve as president twice in succession, the reader is referred to comments on that issue pertaining to Article 32.

Do all ministers within the boundaries of a major assembly have the right to participate in its deliberations and vote on all matters before it?

With respect to the latter, the right to vote, no, they don't. Christian Reformed polity operates with a system of representation at this level of church government. Only those officially delegated by constituent assemblies have the right to vote. Article 40a does provide for the possibility of granting other officebearers (elders, ministry associates, and deacons, as well as ministers) an "advisory voice," but does so only with respect to the classis. There is no analogous provision with respect to the synod. With regard to participation in the deliberations of a *classis*, the answer is that this happens only when that classis so decides, most commonly by a ruling of the chair.

Now that Synod 2007 approved the delegation of leaders from emerging churches to the classis, are those churches free to send representatives of their choosing?

No, this permission came with two often-missed restrictions. The first is that a classis must agree in principle to allow this. Thus, the Supplement to Article 40a says, "if a classis so desires, it may . . ." The second restriction—less conspicuous in that Supplement but nonetheless there—is that the representatives, two maximum, must be ordained officebearers in keeping with Article 34 of the Church Order.

Assemblies are by definition made up of those who are ordained. This previously applied only to those who have been ordained to serve in an "organized congregation," one that has been accorded that status by a classis (see Article 38a and 38b) and now regularly sends delegates to broader assemblies. But Synod 2007 has expanded that now to include those who have been ordained to serve in an "emerging church," defined in Article 38a as a "group of believers among whom no council can as yet be constituted." It did so to "create a greater sense of community and ownership" and to "enrich the ministries and meetings of classis" (*Acts of Synod, 2007*, p. 595). They have typically been ordained by the council of the supervising organized congregation that has set aside an elder or called a ministry associate to serve within that emerging church setting.

Members of emerging churches that do not have any ordained elders or ministry associates among their leaders may attend the meeting of classis and may even be given the privilege of the floor, but they do not have the right to vote. Do remember, on the other hand, that in broader assemblies that strive for unanimity, the privilege of the floor is probably more significant than the vote itself.

II. The Assemblies of the Church

Article 41

In order to assist the churches, the classis shall allocate sufficient time at its meetings to respond to requests for advice or help from the churches and, at a minimum of one of its meetings annually, shall allocate sufficient time to discuss at least one ministry issue that the classis considers to be especially important in the life and ministry of member congregations in the denomination.

When followers of the Protestant Reformation emerged from the structures of the sixteenth-century Roman Catholic Church to organize a new church life, the primary means of supervision of the local parish was suddenly gone: there was no bishop. The chosen solution for that dilemma was mutual supervision of local congregations within the classis. This mutual supervision was exercised at the regular meetings of the classis by the chair and, secondly, by way of appointed church visitors. These two instruments of supervision are the subject matter of Articles 41 and 42.

Mutual Accountability

Since bishops were the "guarantors" of orthodoxy and order, classes had to determine whether local officebearers represented by their delegates were indeed committed to the Reformed faith and willing to abide by the polity and rules of order gradually being developed among them. We can imagine that the one presiding at a meeting of the classis would take the time, right up front, to "ensure" such faithfulness and commitment with utter seriousness. We can also imagine that over time, when issues of doctrine and order were becoming well established, the urgency of the public inquiry would slowly disappear. That is the refrain of our denominational narrative as well.

Traditional Inquiry

Within the CRCNA, for almost all of its history, the following questions were prescribed in the Church Order, here in their most recently altered version (Article 41, Church Order of 2005):

- Are the council, consistory, and diaconate meetings regularly held according to the needs of the congregation?

- Is church discipline faithfully exercised?

- Does the diaconate faithfully lead and stimulate the congregation in obedient stewardship of its resources on behalf of the needy?

- Does the council diligently promote the cause of Christian education from elementary school through institutions of higher learning?

- Have you submitted to the secretary of our Home Missions Board the names and addresses of all baptized and communicant members who have, since the last meeting of classis, moved to a place where no Christian Reformed churches are found?

- Have you informed other councils or pastors about members who reside, even temporarily, in the vicinity of their church?

- Have you, having been informed yourself of such members in your own area, done all in your power to serve them with the ministry of your church?

- Does the council diligently engage in and promote the work of evangelism in its community?

These questions actually appeared on the credentials the delegates carried to the meeting of classis. An advisory committee would peruse the material written at council meetings in days prior and report to the general session that "all is well" or, alternatively, note any unusual or unacceptable responses. The method often took on a legalistic tone and failed to implement the principal purpose of mutual supervision envisioned in the sixteenth century in any meaningful way.

Current Form of Supervision

After numerous attempts to alter these questions, change the methods of inquiry, or make the practice more meaningful, Synod 2006 finally took the bold action of prescribing a totally new instrument of supervision for the classes. Adequate opportunity to seek advice is to be given at every meeting, and classis must take time, at least once a year, to wrestle with one important ministry issue that then becomes the focus of mutual supervision and encouragement (*Acts of Synod, 2006*, pp. 725-26). In addition, the credentials now feature the written testimony that the council "faithfully adheres to the doctrinal standards of the Christian Reformed Church and diligently and effectively attends to ministry within our congregation, community, classis, denomination, and the broader kingdom of God" (Supplement, Article 41).

II. The Assemblies of the Church

Article 42

a. The classis shall be responsible for appointing persons to provide counsel and advice to churches. The classis shall appoint church visitors to visit each church in classis on a yearly basis. The classis shall appoint classical counselors to provide advice to any church in the process of calling a minister of the Word.

b. The church visitors shall consist of one or more teams of officebearers chosen for their experience and counsel, with teams composed of two ministers or one minister and one elder. Their task shall be to ascertain whether the officebearers of the church faithfully perform their duties, adhere to sound doctrine, observe the provisions of the Church Order, and promote the building up of the body of Christ and the extension of God's kingdom. Churches are free to call on the church visitors whenever serious challenges arise that would benefit from their advice. The church visitors shall provide classis a written report of their work.

c. The classical counselor's task is to ensure that a church in the process of calling a minister of the Word observes ecclesiastical regulations and sound process. The counselor shall be an officebearer, normally a minister of the Word, whose ministerial credentials or membership resides in a congregation other than the church in the process of calling a minister. The classical counselor shall provide classis a written report during and after the calling process.

History of Church Visiting

[This material by the author also appeared in the *Manual of Christian Reformed Church Government* (2008 Revision) as an introduction to its Appendix D containing the Guide for Conducting Church Visiting adopted by Synod 2000.]

Church visiting has its roots in apostolic tradition. Peter "traveled about the country" and, among others, visited the "saints in Lydda" (Acts 9:32). Paul "went through Syria and Cilicia, strengthening the churches" (Acts 15:41), ascertaining how they were doing (Acts 15:36), and delivering "the decisions reached by the apostles and elders in Jerusalem for the people to obey" (Acts 16:4). His epistles are filled with references to previous or future visits (e.g. 1 Cor. 16:5-9; 1 Thess. 2:1; 2:17-3:10) designed to build up the saints of God.

There are very few references to the practice in descriptions of life in the early Christian church. It is clear, however, that by the fourth century there was a regular pattern of diocesan visits made by bishops or their representatives in the Eastern Orthodox tradition. In the centuries that followed, especially in the Western church, these visits increasingly assumed the character of hierarchical supervision. Indeed, by the beginning of the sixteenth century, if done at all, they had degenerated into judicial inquiries or occasions for the clergy to heap abuse on the local parish. It is no surprise, therefore, that the Reformers initially saw them as part of a corrupt system desperately in need of renewal.

Despite early hesitations, Martin Luther eventually urged the Elector of Saxony to require church and school visits in every place. As Williston Walker observes in *A History of the Christian Church*, "'visitors' were appointed by the elector to inquire into clerical doctrine and conduct on the basis of articles drawn up by Melanchthon in 1527, and enlarged the following year" (p. 440). The focus in these articles was indeed on "clerical doctrine and conduct," but the document included areas such as confession, discipline, and liturgy. Indeed, this "constitution" also provided for the appointment of "superintendents" who visited churches on an annual basis, not only in Germany but throughout the Lutheran world. An element of hierarchy remained, but the practice was largely restored to its original purpose of strengthening the congregations.

Similar developments took place in other areas where the Reformation flourished. John Calvin introduced annual church visits in Geneva and surrounding areas in 1546. They were done by two city council members and two elected ministers of the Word. Eventually the practice found an enduring place in the Genevan Church Order (the *Ordonnances ecclesiastiques*) adopted in 1561. In Scotland, John Knox instituted a temporary office of "superintendents" who were to visit all the congregations to ensure a healthy development of church life. His idea was that the office should cease as soon as there were a sufficient number of preachers. Due largely to Episcopal influences, the practice took on a more permanent character and, once again, there were traces of illegitimate hierarchical intrusion into affairs of the local parish.

The attempt to avoid all hierarchy in such a practice was most successful in the Reformed churches of France and the lowlands. The Synod of Emden (1571) adopted the principle still found in Article 85 of our current Church Order: "No church shall in any way lord it over another church, and no officebearer shall lord it over another officebearer." When the Synod of Middelburg was asked a decade later whether it wouldn't be beneficial to appoint superintendents to conduct annual church visits, the assembly expressed its fears about such arrangements and decided that they were unnecessary. But the need remained, apparently, and just five years later the Synod of the Hague (1586) eventually permitted *visitatores* appointed by regional bodies (classes) while at the same time the institution of "superintendents" was forbidden. This decision became the model for the practice of church visiting in the Netherlands and, ultimately, what is now Article 42 of the Church Order. It also provided the basic structure for what we know as the "Guide for Church Visiting" that has been developed throughout the history of the Christian Reformed Church in North America.

In this way, the churches of the Reformation sought to return to apostolic example by arranging for annual visits of congregations designed to strengthen the local church and its officebearers. The practice acknowledges that the local church is not an island unto itself. It provides an avenue of accountability—not as if the officebearers must answer to superiors, but by acknowledging the accumulated authority of the broader assembly called the classis, which designates those who conduct church visiting and counsel congregations in the process of calling a new minister. In addition, those who visit provide a reasonably objective "ear" for members who have grown disillusioned with their leadership and need the assistance and advice of others. In this way, congregations have a constructive way to deal with tensions that may arise.

Annual Church Visits

As we saw in the previous article, mutual supervision and encouragement is exercised at meetings of the classis. But it is here extended beyond those occasions to annual church visits. Two (or teams of two) experienced and competent officebearers are appointed by classis for that purpose. The genius of this arrangement is that it is not merely the two or three classical delegates who experience the regional collegiality but all members of the local council who do so in their home setting. This is why we should be cautious about experiments that have been conducted by some classes in the CRCNA in which this form of church visiting was abandoned in favor of what is now the practice prescribed in Article 41 or, alternatively, regular discussions at classis with the focus on one or more particular congregation's ministries, in turn. The problem is the absence of all non-delegates at meetings of the classis. At a time when it is difficult enough to avoid an isolationism or independentism on the part of our congregations, such experiments are inadvisable. Every officebearer should have an annual "taste" of mutual supervision in action. Synods 1975 and 1990 were both asked to prescribe these visits "once every other year" instead of annually, but refused to oblige on the following still pertinent grounds:

> It is readily acknowledged that the practice of church visitation has not always been as effective or as meaningful as it might have been. In many instances church visitation has been conducted mechanically, hastily, and with relatively little profit. On the other hand, many have found church visitation to provide a meaningful setting for receiving genuinely helpful counsel and needed fraternal advice, as well as an opportunity for pastoral and consistorial growth.

Since church visitation has the potential for providing significant benefits for every [council], it is important that the practice of regular visitation be strengthened rather than weakened. Those churches which are at some distance from others within classis surely need the stimulation and fellowship provided by church visitation as much as, or even more than, others. The expenditure of time and money which may be involved is surely justified by the potential results of a well-executed program of visiting. Consequently, rather than diminishing the number of visits which are to be made, the classis should diligently continue the practice of yearly visitation while seeking to make each visit a meaningful and spiritually enriching experience for all those involved (*Acts of Synod, 1990*, pp. 591-92).

Councils are free to call upon the church visitors for advice even apart from the annual visit. This is especially helpful at times of intense struggle—within the council, or between council and congregation in whole or in part. At the same time, classes are free to make use of church visitors on what these assemblies may consider to be necessary special visits. Pleading with a church to bring itself in conformity with a classical or synodical decision or at least give it more respect is one good example of such a visit.

It is important that the church visitors present classis with a written report that may or may not be confidential. The council should be provided with a copy in advance of the meeting to which it is submitted. In this way the full circle of accountability is completed.

Classical Counselors

Finally, this article governs the appointment of classical counselors who oversee the process of calling a minister of the Word to congregations in its midst. Their duties have already been discussed in our treatment of Article 9.

Do classical church visitors have the freedom to meet with members of our congregation without the presence of at least a delegation of our council?

Not until the council has given its blessing to that arrangement in the interest of resolving difficulties in a pastoral manner, and certainly not without a report to the council as well as the classis of what transpired.

The current provision gives *churches* the freedom to call on church visitors, not members in general. If members wish to speak with them, they must receive the council's permission and abide by the arrangements the council makes.

In my experience, there is much wisdom in a council allowing such meetings to take place when members request it. Difficult situations have been defused before they might have exploded. In our system, you might say, leaders who "must give an account" (Heb. 13:17) do so by way of the classis, and it never hurts to show the congregation in concrete ways that they are willing to be accountable for how they lead.

Classical church visitors recently took sides in a local dispute within our congregation by laying blame on the pastor and advising the council to begin Article 17 release procedures. In my judgment, this only served to increase the tensions. Do classical church visitors have the right to adjudicate a dispute in this way?

No, they don't. Article 42 deliberately uses the word *advice*. Only the classis (and/or synod) has the right adjudicate if and when that becomes necessary.

At our last church visit, the visiting minister announced that he would chair the meeting and that his elder colleague would be drawing up the minutes for presentation to classis. Our own minister seemed surprised but chose not to object. Is this synodically prescribed?

It was, once, back in 1922. That year synod adopted "Rules for Church Visitation," one of which read as follows: "At the meeting one of the visitors functions as president, and the other as clerk" (*Acts of Synod, 1922*, pp. 79, 250). More recent guides do not include this provision. In my experience, the chair of council always presided while giving

247

church visitors every opportunity to do their work, to guide the discussion in the way that they choose, and to lead in closing prayer. This places a nice accent on the fact that we are involved in mutual supervision, not a checkup from higher authorities.

II. The Assemblies of the Church

Article 43

a. Every classis shall maintain a student fund and a Classical Ministerial Leadership Team (CMLT) to provide support and encouragement for individuals preparing for ministry in the Christian Reformed Church.

b. The classis may grant the right to exhort within its bounds to persons who are gifted, well-informed, consecrated, and able to edify the churches. When the need for their services has been established, the classis shall examine such persons and license them as exhorters for a limited period of time.

The first section of this article was adopted by Synod 2010 (*Acts of Synod, 2010*, p. 903). It reflects the reality of new structures in place at the classical level for those wishing to become ministers of the Word, namely, the Classical Ministerial Leadership Teams. These teams were already envisioned when Synod 2004 adopted an entirely new process whereby the synodical ministerial Candidacy Committee (not the seminary's Board of Trustees) licenses students and proposes to synod the declaration of their candidacy for ministry of the Word. The idea is to have all classes make the transition from having (mere) classical student fund committees to having a Classical Ministerial Leadership Team appointed to identify potential leaders and journey with them. That journey begins with wrestling through the training options available to a particular individual and continues with ongoing counsel and encouragement and the preparation of appropriate recommendations to the classis. The understanding is that these teams will be in place as soon as possible.

In our treatment of Article 6, we noted that who is on the pulpit from Sunday to Sunday is no trivial matter. Biblical and confessional preaching is at the core of the church's being. The CRCNA has chosen to "guard the pulpit" carefully. It does not approve of "lay preaching" as one might find, say, in the Mennonite tradition. More precisely, it recognizes that while there may be "need" for the unordained to lead in worship and proclaim the gospel, it insists that these persons first be examined and licensed by the classis and then continue to be monitored by way of licensure renewal. "Need" refers to the absence of a minister of the Word (vacancy or temporary absence) and the lack of availability of any other minister or ministerial candidate in the area. We note that classes commonly assign the ministers of their constituent churches to preach in churches with vacant pulpits until such vacancies are filled, but even then such classical assignments typically do not cover every worship service.

There are regions within the CRCNA where this need is fairly common on a regular basis and where "gifted persons" are readily available to "edify the churches." These might be professors, experienced retired elders, recognized community leaders, or any other members who are not ordained. They must be persons who have no intention of entering into the ministry of the Word. That is how this classical licensure to exhort differs from that described in Article 22. Upon recommendation by a council, these persons are then examined for giftedness and faithfulness to the creeds of the church. Approval is always for a limited period of time so that ongoing supervision is in place. We note also that this is not the only way to fill the need. Article 53 has regulations for those not ordained nor licensed to lead in worship and, in doing so, to "read" a sermon prepared by a minister and previously approved by the consistory. But even that article speaks of "persons licensed to exhort" and thus recognizes that the use of gifted individuals in these circumstances might be more edifying than having someone read a sermon.

There is no prescribed method for the examination of these individuals. Each classis operates within the framework of its own accepted procedures.

The presumption is that applicants are tested on their knowledge of Scripture, confessional fidelity, Reformed exegesis, and ability to communicate well in public address.

We recently hired an unordained youth director. He has offered to preach whenever I am not available. The elders believe he needs to go before classis to be examined for licensure if that is to take place. I thought that if council approves he is free to preach but then only in our church, not in other churches within the classis. Who's right?

I need to side with the elders. This person must be licensed by the classis to exhort in any of the churches within its bounds, and that includes your congregation.

The Stated Clerk of our classis has been approached by a person studying at a nearby Reformed seminary (not Calvin) who is requesting a classical licensure to exhort. Since the student intends to enter into ministry in the CRCNA, this seemed to our classical interim committee like a reasonable request, and they are scheduling an interview for our May meeting. Is this appropriate?

No, it is not. Any person wishing to enter into ministry in the CRCNA currently studying at an "alternate seminary" must be pre-enrolled in the denomination's Ecclesiastical Program for Ministerial Candidacy administered by Calvin Theological Seminary. It is through that program that such persons receive licensure to exhort as provided for in Article 22 of the Church Order. This licensure is for all congregations in the CRCNA.

Article 43 of the Church Order also provides for licensure to exhort, but it does so only for congregations within a particular classis (not other classes) and, more important, only to those who have no intention of entering upon ministry in the CRCNA or any other denomination. This regulation provides "quality control" over the individual who mounts the pulpits within the regional boundaries of the classis on the basis of need, namely, on those occasions when an ordained minister or other denominationally licensed person is not available to lead in worship.

II. The Assemblies of the Church

Article 44

a. A classis may take counsel or joint action with its neighboring classis or classes in matters of mutual concern.

b. Classes engaging in matters of mutual concern may organize themselves into an ecclesiastical assembly that will function on the level of classis, with freedom to determine the delegation from the constituent classes and the frequency of meetings. Such an assembly's authority, jurisdiction, and mandate shall be approved by synod. It shall have direct access to synod in all matters pertaining to its mandate.

Historical precedent for inter-assembly cooperation or joint action was focused on regional or particular synods. When all reference to "particular synods" was removed from the listing of broader assemblies in 1965, synod adopted Article 44a to make room for cooperation among the various classes instead.

As we shall see in articles that follow, the normal way for classes to be engaged in matters of "mutual concern" is through the annual synod of the denomination. That is because most such matters are of concern to all classes, not just a few. The shaping of the church's confession and liturgy, decisions on the polity of the church, and the handling of appeals or administration of church discipline are all matters that should not be treated in an assembly any narrower than the full synod. On the other hand, the Church Order makes room for certain ministries to be carried out by two or three classes. Classis Eastern Canada and Classis Quinte have shared responsibility for the Harbor Chaplaincy in Montreal, a project that could be taken up by agencies of the general synod but thrives on its own because of intense regional interest. The same could be said of Harbor Chaplaincy in Vancouver or San Francisco. Cooperation also need not be limited to ministries. For example, it could consist of the churches' shared response to moral dimensions of social or political issues raging only within a certain state or province.

Issues such as these gave rise to the establishing of the Council of Christian Reformed Churches in Canada (CCRCC) in 1967. This was a gathering of delegates from all Canadian classes called together to deal with ecclesiastical, social, and political issues particular to Canadian churches. When requests to form regional synods did not find favor at the general synod, the CCRCC became the vehicle of choice for cooperation and combined action. The council met for three decades and produced its own "Agenda" and "Acts." A keenly felt lack of authority eventually led, in 1993, to synod's adoption of Article 44b as a constitutional basis for the CCRCC. Note that direct access to synod is guaranteed but also that any such council or gathering must have its "authority, jurisdiction, and mandate" approved by synod. Also note that no such council or gathering currently exists since the CCRCC was disbanded in 1998. All the same, the foundation for cooperation among classes in a particular region of the denomination remains.

A classis recently called on other classes to help form a "conference of the concerned." The matters to be addressed include the denomination's position on women in ecclesiastical office and its relationships with churches in the Netherlands. The proposal appealed to Article 44b as the "legal basis" for this gathering. Does this article actually offer such?

No, it does not. The two issues mentioned are of equal concern to all classes. "Women in ecclesiastical office" is an issue of Church Order and dealing with it at any assembly other than synod violates the requirement of Article 47 that it be dealt with in the broadest assembly of the denomination. The matter of ecumenical relations is under the jurisdiction of the Ecumenical and Interfaith Relations Committee and, thus, also of synod, to which it reports.

I fully understand that people striving for a particular cause want to broaden their circles in order to have more influence on the rest of the denomination, but there is no Church Order basis for such a gathering. It would be based on theological affinity instead of geographical and cultural bonds. Calling for it also comes perilously close to planting seeds of schism.

II. The Assemblies of the Church

Article 45

> The synod is the assembly representing the churches of all the classes. Each classis shall delegate two ministers and two elders to the synod.

Previously, we defined the assemblies as church governmental bodies designed to express the rule of Christ through officebearers. The body that provides this leadership at the (bi)national level is known as the synod.

Constitution of Synod

The synod consists of officebearers who have been delegated by the constituent classes to represent them in the deliberations and decisions. The classes are at liberty to delegate anyone ordained as an officebearer by their constituent church councils, regardless of whether they serve within or outside of their particular congregations, with the deacons being the only notable exception: the article speaks only of ministers and elders. Ministry associates are "acknowledged as elders" (Article 23a) and hence also eligible to serve as elder delegates to synod. Further, if a ministry associate is serving as a solo pastor of an organized congregation, that person may be sent as a ministerial delegate (*Acts of Synod, 2007*, p. 665) if the classis so chooses.

(On the delegation of deacons to synod, see p. 235 under Article 40)

Issues of Size, Fairness in Representation, and Women Delegates

Two other issues regarding the constitution of synod have been raised in the past and probably linger as concerns. The first is the sheer size of the assembly: currently 188 delegates from 47 classes. The question there is whether this is conducive to a truly deliberative process (see, for example, *Acts of Synod, 1987*, p. 624). The second is whether delegating an equal number of ministers and elders is fair, given the fact that local assemblies have far more elders than ministers. The concern is that the "clergy" dominates the "laity." To this, Synod 1993 replied that "the denomination has never based representation on a formula related to size." Indeed, a "smaller classis has the same representation at synod as a larger classis" (*Acts of Synod, 1993*, pp. 506-07).

Synod 2008 was the first to receive women delegates. Those who oppose this practice have the right to have their protests recorded on the credentials from their classis and in the minutes of synod (Supplement, Article 45).

Is a minister whose work lies outside of a local congregation, our university chaplain for example, eligible for delegation to synod?

In principle, yes. Some classes, however, have rules which prevent it. There, only ministers serving within a local church setting are eligible. The classis is free to adopt such rules. But I suspect that for most classes, these ministers of the Word in "extraordinary positions" are indeed eligible for delegation to synod.

May a minister be sent to a synod as an elder delegate?

In principle, no. That would destroy the intended balance of clergy and lay members, a precious good of the Reformation. If, however, a minister whose ministerial work lies outside of a local congregation, a professor of theology, for example, is in fact also currently serving as an elder in a local church, that minister could be sent as an elder

---

delegate, provided that this is not forbidden by rules a classis may have adopted on its own. There are some strong feelings on this issue.

If deacons should really be delegated to synod and, at the same time, we need to reduce the assembly's size, why don't we just have each classis send a minister, an elder, and a deacon? Behold, the number is down from 188 to 141.

Great question. Very creative. The thought has occurred to synodical delegates over the years. I've noticed that the suggestion doesn't find much favor among ministers of the Word. It doesn't take long for them to figure out that this would destroy the present balance of clergy and lay members, putting them very much in the minority. Is it naughty of me to assume that this will therefore never happen?

Our classis has introduced a new "rotary" method of choosing delegates to synod. One minister delegate is still chosen from all who are eligible, but the other is picked "automatically" according to a schedule of rotation by alphabetical order of the churches' names. Is this permitted?

Yes, it clearly is, but the question is whether it is advisable. Many commentators in the Reformed tradition believe that they should be chosen by free election (Bouwman, Jansen, Monsma, VanDellen); they reject the rotary method accordingly. I agree. As I look at the specific rules you sent to me, it appears that ministers not serving in the churches themselves but, rather, as a university chaplain, are eliminated from consideration for that second slot. In addition, the classis is not bringing to bear on its choice of delegates the issue of who is most competent to serve. It is a mistake to think that all ministers will make an equally valuable contribution to a deliberative assembly.

II. The Assemblies of the Church

Article 46

a. Synod shall meet annually, at a time and place determined by the previous synod. Each synod shall designate a church to convene the following synod.

b. The convening church, with the approval of the Board of Trustees of the CRCNA, may call a special session of synod, but only in very extraordinary circumstances and with the observance of synodical regulations.

c. The officers of synod shall be elected and shall function in accordance with the Rules for Synodical Procedure.

Synod met once a year for the first three decades of the denomination's existence; from 1890 until 1936 once every other year; and since 1936 back to an annual gathering. The frequency of meeting has been debated by the Board of Trustees just recently in the midst of financial pressures, but no recommendations for change have been submitted. In an age where denominational ties seem to be loosening more and more, keeping it an annual event seems wise.

Synod typically meets on the campus of Calvin College and Calvin Theological Seminary in Grand Rapids, Michigan. The main reason for that choice is that the denominational building is located there as well, eliminating the need for consultants and advisers who work and live in Grand Rapids to travel elsewhere. On the other hand, synods have also been held from time to time on the campuses of Dordt College (Sioux Center, Iowa), Trinity Christian College (Palos Heights, Illinois) and Redeemer University College (Ancaster, Ontario). A decision to meet on the campus of The King's University College (Edmonton, Alberta) for Synod 2010 was reluctantly reversed at Synod 2009 for financial reasons. Having synod meet in different sectors of the denomination from time to time expresses its desire to show that it truly represents all the member churches of the CRCNA. Of course, new technology allows any member who is interested to follow the deliberations of the plenary sessions by way of streaming audio and video. A convening church appointed by the previous synod arranges for the next one in cooperation with the office of the executive director.

Special sessions are rare in the Reformed tradition. In 1967, synod was "reconvened" for two days at the end of August in order to complete its deliberations on the "love of God" controversy involving Professor Harold Dekker. But even that was not technically a "special session" because synod itself decided to return and finish the work. A special session would be one where a convening church, with the approval of the Board of Trustees, would call the churches' delegates together "in very extraordinary circumstances." This has never happened in the CRCNA and probably won't if the practice of annual synods continues.

Officers of synod are, for the convening, a President Pro Tem (usually the minister of the convening church) and, thereafter, the President, the Vice-President, the First Clerk, and the Second Clerk. Their mandates are recorded in the Rules for Synodical Procedure. Under the guidance of the President Pro Tem, these officers are elected by synodical delegates from a list of nominations received from the delegates and prepared in advance by the office of the executive director. All delegates are eligible, but receiving nominations from the delegates in advance of the meeting allows for a more thoughtful and effective process.

Where does one find the Rules for Synodical Procedure?

These rules are found in the back of the annually printed *Church Order and Rules for Synodical Procedure* and, online, under "synodical resources" at www.crcna.org. Beginning in 2010, they appear online separately from the Church Order. The rules cover functionaries, agenda items legally before synod, and parliamentary procedures.

II. The Assemblies of the Church

Article 47

The task of synod includes the adoption of the creeds, of the Church Order, and of the principles and elements of worship. Synod shall approve the liturgical forms, the *Psalter Hymnal*, and the Bible versions suitable for use in worship. No substantial alterations shall be effected by synod in these matters unless the churches have had prior opportunity to consider the advisability of the proposed changes.

Adoption of Creeds

As noted with respect to Article 5, the creeds of the church are the "constitution" of the CRCNA, at the core of all that it does—in its worship, its faith nurture, its pastoral care, its outreach, and its discipline. From its beginnings in 1857, the denomination deliberately chose the Confession of Faith (or Belgic Confession), the Heidelberg Catechism, and the Canons of Dort as its confessions, along with the early Christian creeds: the Apostles', Nicene, and Athanasian. It is currently considering whether to adopt the Belhar Confession as well (*Acts of Synod, 2009*, pp. 606-07). All churches are involved in the consideration, but synod alone—the broadest assembly of the church—has the authority to adopt or amend this creedal "constitution." In distinction from other traditions, the CRCNA does not have "ratification" procedures where classes (presbyteries) or even local churches must agree before synodically approved changes are in effect.

Adoption of Church Order, Liturgical Materials

In similar fashion, synod alone has the authority to adopt or amend the Church Order. Article 86 makes explicit that "any revision thereof shall be made only by synod." In addition, the churches agree that synod may also insist on certain "principles and elements of worship." Practically speaking, that means that synod approves "liturgical forms, the *Psalter Hymnal*, and the Bible versions suitable for use in worship" (see Article 52). The provision is one that recognizes the power of liturgy. Our Christian reflection and walk of life is profoundly affected by our weekly worship. Music and songs "invade" our minds and hearts and cling to them throughout our lives, even more so than the spoken word. Synod has the solemn responsibility of ensuring that the liturgy of the congregations can be truly Christian and truly Reformed. In doing so, it need not place local consistories and its committees in a straitjacket with regard to every detail. But it must "serve" the churches with responsible approval of what turns out to be much-needed "confessional direction" in regulating the worship of God's people.

Prior Opportunity

The last sentence of this article is extremely important. The Church Order here insists that all churches must have "prior opportunity" to deliberate on proposed changes and to express their points of view to the synod. For that reason, every standing committee, study committee, or advisory committee of synod must indicate whether what it is proposing to change in these matters is to be considered a "substantial alteration." If synod agrees that it is or decides that it is in spite of what is being recommended, it must guarantee that congregations have had this "prior opportunity." As the Supplement to this article indicates, the deadline for getting any proposals of this kind to the churches is November 1 of the year before synod meets. If this deadline cannot be met, the action of two synodical assemblies will be required.

Prior to the mid-nineties, the language used for enacting changes in these matters defined the action of the first of two synods as "adoption" of a change, the action of the second as "ratification." For the sake of clarity we

262

now speak of the first synod "proposing" and the second synod "adopting" the change involved. For as long as the change is not yet finally adopted, it may not be implemented. This is the covenant we have together for the sake of the unity of the church (Eph. 4:3).

Status of Material in the Church Order Supplements

It should also be carefully noted that changes in the Supplements to articles of the Church Order are not included in these procedures. Supplements are nothing more than synodical decisions that the assembly has decided to keep before the continuing attention of the churches. These decisions are also "settled and binding" (Article 29), but as the Rules for Synodical Procedure make clear:

> a succeeding synod may alter the stand of a previous synod; it may reach a conclusion which is at variance with a conclusion reached by an earlier synod. In such cases the most recent decision invalidates all previous decisions in conflict with it (VIII.I.2).

What congregations must know, therefore, is that their comment on any proposals made for such changes in the Supplement appearing in the *Agenda for Synod* (typically available in April) must be sent immediately through as many appropriate channels as possible. It is precisely for this reason that synod permits "late overtures" and considers them legally before it when such overtures "deal with matters relevant to reports found in the printed *Agenda*" (V.B.8).

Other Tasks of Synod

Article 47 has never purported to be a complete statement of what synods are called upon to do. It touches only on some of the broadest assembly's core responsibilities. It does not, for instance, say anything about its judicial role in dealing with appeals and protests. In this case as well as others, the role of synod is found in other articles.

If changes to the Supplement require only one synod and changes to the Church Order itself often require two, couldn't you then have a situation where supplemental material doesn't even have a basic article or provision to which it can be attached?

Brilliant question. You should probably be in law school but, now that you're here in a seminary, we're grateful you'll be in a position to bless many others with your insight. The church needs that in you and others. I'll answer your question with a case in point. Synod 1997 adopted a process to be followed by a council desiring to disaffiliate from the denomination. It was a synodical decision, supplemental material, but for one year it did not have its "basis" in the Church Order itself. Article 38f was proposed in the same year but not adopted until Synod 1998. Nonetheless, churches were obliged to follow the process in the interim because the decision of 1997 was binding on them pursuant to Article 29. A court in West Michigan recently agreed with that interpretation of our rules. And that judge did go to law school.

Note: The following question and answer, received and answered in December 2005, aptly illustrates how this legislation in Article 47 actually works.

An RCA minister has accepted a call to a church in our classis. He has already been working there for a couple of months. Prior to Synod 2005, he had decided to ask that an exam be set up for him so that he can become a CRC minister. But now we have that new arrangement for RCA pastors. I know it was only proposed and must be adopted at our next synod, but how critical is it for us and for him to schedule this exam now? If he decides to remain RCA, he could hold off a year, just be on loan to this church for a few months, and then continue that service with synodical blessing after it next meets. If he does want to switch to the CRC, would a *colloquium doctum* still be required?

Section d in the Supplement to Article 47 is utterly clear on this point: "A proposed change may not be implemented until it is adopted by a following synod. It has no effect on any other synodical decisions until it is adopted." Synod 2005 proposed this revision to the following year's synod in that awareness, arguing that it is a substantial change.

If and when Synod 2006 adopts this change in the Church Order, a *colloquium doctum* procedure (Article 8) will no longer be necessary for RCA ministers who wish to serve in a Christian Reformed congregation and remain credentialed in the RCA. There will be an "orderly exchange" between the CRC and the RCA. The exam will still be required for those who wish to transfer their ministerial credentials to the CRC, but not for those who wish to serve in the CRC only for a time. The point to be noted: prior to the actual adoption of this "orderly exchange," the requirement of a *colloquium doctum* remains in place.

It is within the realm of possibility that Synod 2006 will reject this proposed change in the Church Order. We need to respect the process.

In my opinion, classis would err if it permitted his installation (or even his "on loan status") and, if appealed by someone, that error would have to be acknowledged and that would be highly embarrassing to both minister and congregation. I do recognize, of course, that he currently does not have the choice of serving this Christian Reformed congregation and remaining credentialed in the RCA. And you will undoubtedly accuse me of legalism. But if you were one of those who did not favor the proposed revision, how would you feel if others within our denominational covenant were already implementing it? I hasten to add that this same question of procedure comes up almost every year, in one form or another, on widely divergent issues, and that might include one that you have very strong feelings about. In that case, my "legalism" might be perfectly acceptable to you.

II. The Assemblies of the Church

Article 48

a. Upon the nomination of the classes, synod shall appoint ministers, one from each classis, to serve as synodical deputies for a term designated by synod.

b. When the cooperation of the synodical deputies is required as stipulated in the Church Order, the presence of at least three deputies from the nearest classes shall be prescribed.

c. Besides the duties elsewhere stipulated, the deputies shall, upon request, extend help to the classes in the event of difficulties in order that proper unity, order, and sound doctrine may be maintained.

d. The synodical deputies shall submit a complete report of their actions to the next synod.

The Church Order insists that certain matters pertaining to ministers of the Word are not merely for classes to decide but require synodical approval as well. These include all admissions to ministry—of those with or without the prescribed theological training (Articles 7, 10), those who come from other denominations (Article 8), and those who were previously released, deposed, or had earlier resigned (Articles 14, 17; Supplement, Articles 82-84). They also include deciding that proposed work outside of a local church is "consistent with the calling of a minister" (Article 12), acquiescing in all resignations from ministry (Article 14), releasing from ministry to a particular congregation (Article 17), and deposing from the ministerial office (Supplement, Articles 82-84). The Church Order insists on this because all churches have a stake in such decisions. Ministers, after all, are in principle eligible for call throughout the denomination for as long as their service lasts. Synodical deputies must also concur in certain decisions of classes relating to the mandate of ministry associates (Article 23 and its Supplement). In this way, synod assures compliance with its regulations for that office.

Requiring approval from synod itself in each classical action of this nature is unreasonable. Classes meet three times a year, sometimes twice; synod only once. It cannot act in a timely manner and cannot itself be "on the scene." For that reason, classes nominate and synod appoints ministers, one from each classis, to serve as synodical deputies. Three of these synodical deputies from neighboring classes must be present for each occasion where such matters are dealt with. The deputies observe the deliberative process involved, sometimes seek information they might require, and then withdraw to formulate their opinion. If, upon return to the classis meeting, it appears that the classis has acted in line with their opinion, their concurrence in the action of classis is noted in the minutes and reported to synod by way of the executive director. If, on the other hand, it appears that the classis has come to an opposite conclusion, the deputies' non-concurrence is duly noted. Classis or the deputies are thereupon free to continue deliberation and alter these decisions. If agreement is not forthcoming, the action of the classis is thereby invalidated and deputies report their lack of concurrence to synod. When it next meets, synod then decides the matter by approving or not approving of the deputies' work.

Synodical deputies are sometimes also invited to attend a classis meeting for their advice on very thorny issues. In that case, classis is free to make decisions on its own and no formal concurrence is sought. The purpose of such incidental attendance is the same as with required attendance: it is always to maintain "proper unity, order, and sound doctrine" within the denomination. These deputies, therefore, do what archbishops or cardinals do within the diocesan structures of the Roman Catholic Church, guaranteeing the orthodoxy of those who are to be ordained and making judgments about their doctrinal stance. In the Reformed tradition, however, we acknowledge this need for a measure of "superintendence" with due caution: "No officebearer shall lord it over another officebearer" (Article 85). Deputies need to be mindful of that.

A classis may nominate—and synod may appoint—a female minister to serve as synodical deputy. In that case, there must also be a male alternate to accommodate a neighboring classis that may have decided not to permit women officebearers to function as delegates. This is how we have covenanted to live together with differing understandings of the biblical position on women's roles.

Do synodical deputies concur *in* a decision or *with* a decision of a classis?

As far as I can tell, the Church Order conveniently sails around this linguistic problem. If pressed, however, I vote for *in*. My dictionary defines concurrence as "accordance *in* opinion." Etymologically, the *con-* in the word *concur* is a variation of *com-* when it appears before all consonants except *b, h, l, p, r,* or *w* and thus means *with*. You might say that a subsequent use of the preposition *with* is then repetitive or clumsy. See, I *was* awake in English 101.

Since we are in the "hinterlands" of the denomination, we often run into situations where synodical deputies must come a long way and at great expense to approve our actions. This seems right when important issues need resolution. But some of the issues seem like no-brainers. Could we just do this by conference call?

I agree with you that when important issues are on the table, especially those that involve persons (release of a minister, discipline of an officebearer), synodical deputies should be present for the deliberative process of the classis and have the opportunity also to ask questions they will need answered in order to formulate their concurrence or non-concurrence.

I also agree with you that some issues are so little in need of such intense deliberation that leaving the deputies at home and doing things by phone might seem the better part of wisdom. An example might be a request to declare that a certain hospital chaplain's position is consistent with the calling of a minister of the Word (Article 12c).

But we do need to be careful here. Suppose the request to make such a declaration is not with reference to a hospital chaplain but to an administrative position of some kind in a counseling agency. And suppose further that the job description doesn't really have a whole lot in it that resembles ministry of the Word. Members of the classical interim committee and synodical deputies might even agree that on paper this really doesn't fly and that the request should be denied. It's open and shut, so why invest the time and resources to have the deputies present for the occasion? The trouble is that the local church requesting the declaration and perhaps the person involved may well come with vehement argumentation that it is in fact work that is consistent with the ministerial calling. The synodical deputies, it seems to me, should be involved in that deliberative process.

Perhaps the Stated Clerk of your classis might be given some authority to consult with the deputies and have the four of them decide in each instance with some of these principles in mind. In any case, I have no objection to some kind of videoconference or teleconference in cases where distance and relative ease of the decision allows.

What happens if the synodical deputies cannot agree?

The opinion of two out of three is the official result. The third may file a separate minority opinion or append an appropriate note to the official report of the others. This is precisely why the rules require the presence of three.

What happens when synod does not approve of the work of the synodical deputies?

We hope this doesn't have to happen too often. But sometimes it does, and it certainly has in the past.

If synodical deputies concurred in an action of classis and the synod then decides not to approve their concurrence in it, the matter classis decided upon is "overturned." So, for instance, if classis approved of the deposition of a minister and the deputies concurred, synod not approving the work of the deputies means that the deposition is not effective (even if the local council had already taken that action).

Alternatively, if synodical deputies decided not to concur in an action of classis and synod then decides not to approve their non-concurrence, the matter classis wanted to have approved is, in fact, approved. So, for instance, if classis approved the deposition of a minister and the deputies did not concur, synod not approving the deputies' work means that the local council is now permitted to depose the minister.

II. The Assemblies of the Church

Article 49

a. Synod shall appoint a committee to encourage ecumenical relationships with other Christian churches, especially those that are part of the Reformed family, as articulated in the synodically approved Ecumenical Charter of the Christian Reformed Church so that the Christian Reformed Church may exercise Christian fellowship with other denominations and may promote the unity of the church of Jesus Christ.

b. Synod shall designate the churches with whom the Christian Reformed Church is in ecclesiastical fellowship, the churches with whom the Christian Reformed Church is in dialogue, and the ecumenical organizations in which the Christian Reformed Church holds membership or significantly participates.

Truth Trumping Catholicity

Articles 49 and 50 make provision for the exercise of ecumenical relations. The fact that such regulations first appeared in the Church Order in 1965, more than a full century after the denomination's beginnings, is our first clue to how the CRCNA has fared in seeking unity with other Christian churches. In his book *Catholicity and Secession*, published in 1991, Henry Zwaanstra eloquently summarizes his answer to this question:

> During the twentieth-century ecumenical age, the CRC has remained faithful to the truth as it perceives it. The authority of God's Word has been respected and esteemed at a time when in many churches the Bible's authority has been undermined. Ironically, the clear testimony of Scripture and the creeds to the catholicity of the church has made little impact on the CRC, and the church for the most part remains unaware of the fact that loyalty to the truth includes commitment to the ecumenical dimensions of the Christian faith (pp. 123-24).

Hopeful Signs

It is not as if the CRCNA has not been able to articulate a biblical vision of catholicity and point the way to its implementation. A remarkable report to Synod 1944 and the adoption of an Ecumenical Charter at Synod 1987 are abundant evidence of that (*Acts of Synod, 1944*, pp. 330-67; *Agenda for Synod, 1987*, pp. 170-75; *Acts of Synod, 1987*, pp. 588-90). Both documents even draw the concentric circles of fellowship beyond just the nearest Reformed kin to all Christian churches. Nor is it that none of this has been put in practice. There is now an agreement, for example, between the CRCNA and the Reformed Church in America known as the "Orderly Exchange of Ordained Ministers" (see material on Article 8); the CRCNA publishing agency (Faith Alive Christian Resources) is now the "official resource provider" for the RCA; and there is provision for union churches (see Supplement, Article 38). These efforts are also not confined to Reformed circles. The CRCNA no longer binds its officebearers to the polemic section of Q&A 80 of the Heidelberg Catechism dealing with the Roman Catholic Mass, the result of months of intense discussion between Roman Catholic Bishops in both Washington, D.C., and Ottawa, Ontario, and a study group appointed by the Interchurch Relations Committee (now Ecumenical and Interfaith Relations Committee). That episode in its history has also landed CRCNA representatives a seat in the United States Roman Catholic-Reformed Dialogue currently discussing the sacraments. These are hopeful signs. On balance, however, Zwaanstra's conclusion may still be fairly accurate at the end of the first decade of the twenty-first century. No denomination has a corner on truth, and walking together with others as we strive for greater unity can bring us closer to it. The CRCNA will hopefully find new ways to accomplish this. We confess one holy catholic church.

Bilateral Relationships

Article 49—for the most part—governs bilateral ecumenical relations. Article 50 then focuses on participation in ecumenical organizations. Currently the CRCNA maintains ecclesiastical fellowship with only three groups in North America: the RCA, the Associate Reformed Presbyterian Church, and the Evangelical Presbyterian Church. It also maintains ecclesiastical fellowship with ten churches in Africa, five churches in Asia, Australia, and Indonesia, one in Europe, one in Latin America, and two in South America. In addition, there are eight additional denominations with which the CRCNA maintains what is known as "formal dialogue." These are the "official" bonds of fellowship. It must be remembered that there are literally hundreds of a more local and regional nature: ongoing ecumenical relationships that do not involve a committee of synod but are simply played out in the midst of church life. On the other hand, the "official" bonds do determine different ways in which members are received into the fellowship of the CRCNA (see Article 59d).

Other Ecumenical Features

There are other ecumenical touches in the Church Order beyond just these two articles, such as the Supplement to Article 8. But it is very significant, for example, that the CRCNA holds valid the baptism of "one who comes from another Christian denomination" as long as it was administered "in the name of the triune God" and "by someone authorized by that denomination" (Article 58). There are no further requirements for this. It also bears mentioning that Article 74 on outreach ministries specifically mentions "cooperation with one or more neighboring churches" in the enterprise of evangelism and the ministry of mercy.

All officebearers should be familiar with the Ecumenical Charter first adopted in 1987 and subsequently revised. It matters in the way they minister at home. It also matters as they care about and become involved in the affairs of the classis and the denomination. In this charter one finds the rules governing ecclesiastical fellowship currently in force. A thorough reading of the annual report of what is now the Ecumenical and Interfaith Relations Committee in the *Agenda to Synod* will also be helpful. But it is especially synod itself that has the task of providing leadership in "exercising Christian fellowship with other denominations" and "promoting the unity of the church of Jesus Christ."

How do we know at any given time exactly which churches are in ecclesiastical fellowship with the CRC?

The synod of the CRCNA decides on these relationships upon the recommendation of its Ecumenical and Interfaith Relations Committee (previously known as the Interchurch Relations Committee). In recent years, this committee has reported annually to synod exactly which churches are in ecclesiastical fellowship with us by reason of prior synodical decisions. You can find that information in the *Agenda for Synod* of each year. It is also available on the denomination's website (www.crcna.org) under "Ecumenical Relations."

I know that being in ecclesiastical fellowship with other churches makes a difference at the broader assembly level. Synods, for example, receive fraternal delegates and they address us there. But does it really make any difference at the local level, in my congregation, for example?

Yes it does. When you invite a minister of another denomination into your pulpit, the consistory is obliged to "examine" the person to ensure that Reformed doctrine and ways of understanding the Scriptures are not publicly contravened or ridiculed. A Baptist minister, for example, should take pains not to militate against infant baptism or the interpretations of the Bible and theological doctrines on which that practice is founded. If the minister is from a church in ecclesiastical fellowship with us, the consistory's examination is not required.

Another example: when members of churches in ecclesiastical fellowship with us appear on our doorstep with an "attestation" or "statement" of membership, the consistory can feel confident about the option listed in Article 59, namely, admitting them directly rather than by way of public reaffirmation or profession of faith.

The Greek Orthodox priest in our monthly ministerial get-together insists that Reformed people at the mall on Sundays are forbidden to use the escalator. Is that true of the CRCNA? (The question is only half in jest, of course.)

Why no, how ill-informed he is. A tragic misunderstanding. The truth is that CRCNA people may use the mall's escalator but only downward. To go upward is to require the efforts of another on the day of rest. (The answer is half in jest, of course. Like you, I do hope we represent each other's views with honesty and integrity.)

II. The Assemblies of the Church

Article 50

a. Synod shall send delegates to ecumenical bodies in which the Christian Reformed Church cooperates with other Christian denominations, particularly those sharing the Reformed perspective.

b. Synod may present to such gatherings matters on which it seeks judgment of churches throughout the world.

c. Decisions of ecumenical bodies shall be binding upon the Christian Reformed Church only when they have been ratified by its synod.

Ecumenical Organizations

As we have seen, Article 49 deals with bilateral relationships between the CRCNA and other denominations. Article 50 deals with ecumenical "bodies," organizations, networks. The distinction is very significant. The CRCNA's participation in, say, the National Association of Evangelicals does not imply that it is in a relationship of ecclesiastical fellowship (as defined in Article 49) with all other member churches of that organization.

What it does imply is that the CRCNA is seated at the table, a member on the same podium, a participant in discussion of important issues, a colleague in Christian witness to the outside world that will, at the same time, increase mutual understanding and hopefully lead toward greater unity among the people of God.

If this distinction is duly noted, officebearers in the CRCNA need not be so anxious about losing our Reformed distinctiveness in the interaction with other Christian churches. We should insist on the rock bottom basis of our faith: that all participants truly affirm the Apostles', Nicene, and Athanasian creeds. Beyond that, we can confidently address the issues of the day, standing with both feet on the further foundation of the Reformed confessions that we need not deny as we commune with Christians of other persuasion. Indeed, we can even stand with both feet on the ecumenical creeds and the Reformed confessions when we testify of our faith to and dialogue with groups representing non-Christian religions. This in part explains why the denomination's Interchurch Relations Committee is now known as its Ecumenical and Interfaith Relations Committee.

Early Limitations in the Provision

It is telling that for far too long the Church Order has limited our participation to "Reformed ecumenical bodies," "Reformed churches," and denominations that "confess and maintain the Reformed faith." By 1944 the CRCNA had already acknowledged that our vision should be extended beyond those boundaries to all churches that confess Christ as Lord. It is to be expected, of course, that our fellowship with churches of Reformed persuasion will be fuller and more intimate. But that should not keep us from our obligation to be a witness to and with all others where God has led us in our journey of faith. We can be grateful for the action of Synod 2010 to adopt new versions of Articles 49 and 50 that significantly broaden our perspective to all Christian denominations and ecumenical organizations (*Acts of Synod, 2010*, pp. 826-27).

The CRCNA has learned over the years that true ecclesiastical fellowship is discovered not so much in debates on significant issues, be that an important endeavor, but in the day-to-day ministry of members of two denominations sharing in a common mandate to be a witness to the world. It is in the running of a food bank, say, sponsored and operated by a CRCNA and an RCA congregation together, that we begin to understand how little our differences are when compared to the greater commonalities

found in shared discipleship. The CRCNA has also learned that it has
nothing to fear in joining, say, the Canadian Council of Churches or the
Evangelical Fellowship in Canada. We can stand firm in our traditions even
as we engage with those of others.

Federal Council of Christian Churches and National Association of Evangelicals

The CRCNA was a member of the Federal Council of Christian Churches
(FCCC) from 1918 until 1924. As Henry Zwaanstra observes in
Catholicity and Secession, this "did not arise out of a deepening ecumenical
consciousness" but to be better positioned, at the end of the First World
War, to place military chaplains in the armed forces (pp. 21-22). Fears
of "liberalism" within that council became "the overriding concern and
reason" (p. 24) for the withdrawal decided on by Synod 1924 (*Acts of Synod*,
1924, p. 112). In 1943, the denomination joined the National Association
of Evangelicals (NAE), developed at that time as a "more orthodox"
alternative to the FCCC. Fears of "Arminianism" and "fundamentalism"
within the association led Synod 1951 to terminate that affiliation as
well (*Acts of Synod, 1951*, p. 79). At the time, the denomination became
more interested in developing international contacts with churches of
similar Reformed persuasion. Synod 1988, having been convinced by the
Interchurch Relations Committee that nothing in the NAE's Statement
of Faith contradicted the Reformed character of the CRCNA, decided
to rejoin this organization (*Acts of Synod, 1988*, pp. 516-17). According
to Henry Zwaanstra, this was the first time in almost forty years that the
denomination "stepped out of its isolationist tradition" (*Catholicity and
Secession*, p. 105).

Reformed Ecumenical Synod (Council), World Alliance of Reformed Churches, World Communion of Reformed Churches

Along with the Dutch Reformed Church in South Africa (RCSA) and
the Reformed Churches in the Netherlands (GKN), the CRCNA was
instrumental in the formation of the Reformed Ecumenical Synod. This
international assembly gathered for the first time just after the Second
World War, in August 1946, in Grand Rapids, Michigan. Over the years,
this organization grew significantly, mostly by admitting to membership
Reformed churches in Africa, Asia, Europe, and South America. At a

certain point, the body felt it necessary to change its name to "Reformed Ecumenical Council" in order to make it clear that its decisions were "advisory" and not necessarily binding on member churches (see Article 50c above). In June 2010 the REC merged with the World Alliance of Reformed Churches (WARC) into an ecumenical body known as the World Communion of Reformed Churches.

North American Presbyterian and Reformed Council

Early in 1974, the newly formed Presbyterian Church in America (PCA), after seceding from the Southern Presbyterians (PCUSA), initiated a discussion with the CRCNA as well as the Orthodox Presbyterian Church, the Reformed Presbyterian Church (Evangelical Synod), and the Reformed Presbyterian Church in North America (sometimes referred to as the Covenanters) to explore the possibility of an "organic union." When delegates of these denominations gathered in Pittsburgh in October of that year, the result was less than what the loftier goal envisioned, yet nonetheless a hopeful development: the North American Presbyterian and Reformed Council (NAPARC) was formed. In practice, however, that hope weakened in subsequent years. The organization spent more time on examining its member churches for a strict adherence to the teachings set forth in Reformed confessional standards than on exploring ways toward greater organic unity and common ecumenical outreach. Eventually, the CRCNA was thus examined and found wanting, largely because of its position on women in ecclesiastical office. Its membership was suspended in November of 1998 (*Agenda for Synod, 1999*, pp. 188-90).

World Council of Churches

Although Synod 1967 gave very serious consideration to joining it, the CRCNA has never become a member of the World Council of Churches (WCC).

If our synod is the governing body of the church as a whole (meaning the CRCNA), why don't we just go all the way, as it were, and have our synod be accountable to a "super-synod" representing all denominations? Why insist on ratification of our own synod for decisions to be binding?

Great question. I wish we could go all the way. I wish we could have a Reformed or Protestant "Vatican," or, to go even further, an international synod whose decisions would be settled and binding for all of the Protestant, Orthodox and Roman Catholic churches. What better way to demonstrate the unity of the catholic and apostolic church of Christ worldwide and respond to Jesus' prayer that his church may be one (John 17:21)? It is significant that in their beginnings our sixteenth-century Reformed ancestors in the Netherlands were not isolationists. They very much valued cooperation with Lutheran and Calvinist Protestants in Germany, Switzerland, France, and the British Isles. Indeed, delegates to Reformed synods in the Netherlands were asked to affirm the "Confession de foy" of the French churches as well as the Belgic Confession. The great Synod of Dort (1618-19) included delegates from these other lands to help the Dutch decide on the pressing doctrinal issues of the day.

In short, it is my firm belief that the Reformers were out to reform the one, holy, catholic church, not to start hundreds of additional denominations. They would probably have rebelled against calling them "Lutheran" or "Calvinist" and having them divide and splinter in future centuries. Currently, realistic or not, we should have no lesser vision than that of a universal church. That's why I feel strongly about retaining a binational CRCNA and firmly hope for huge strides in visible church unity.

III. The Task and Activities of the Church

The first section of the Church Order dealt with the *who* of the institutional church: they are its leaders, given by Christ "to equip his people for works of service, so that the body of Christ may be built up until we all reach unity in the faith and in the knowledge of the Son of God and become mature, attaining to the whole measure of the fullness of Christ" (Eph. 4:11-13). The second section dealt with the *how* of the institutional church: officebearers do their work in mutual accountability and in recognition and pursuit of the unity of the body by way of the assemblies.

This third section deals with the *what* of the institutional church: its worship services, faith nurture, pastoral care, and missions.

III. The Task and Activities of the Church

Article 51

a. The congregation shall assemble for worship, ordinarily twice on the Lord's Day, to hear God's Word, to receive the sacraments, to engage in praise and prayer, and to present gifts of gratitude.

b. Worship services shall be held in observance of Christmas, Good Friday, Easter, Ascension Day, and Pentecost, and ordinarily on Old and New Year's Day, and annual days of prayer and thanksgiving.

c. Special worship services may be proclaimed in times of great stress or blessing for church, nation, or world.

Mission Statement

The content and order of the four activities of the church (worship, faith nurture, pastoral care, and missions) is significant. One might say that the mission statement of a CRCNA congregation is contained in them. We are to bring our praises, prayers, and offerings and hear the Word of God proclaimed from week to week so that our lives between these days of rest are blessed with the presence of Christ and spent in his service.

Next, we are to share our commitment with future generations and all who enter the community. The Spirit alone gives faith but, as with any healthy plant, the church must nurture it. Then, we are to shepherd all of God's people in their joys and sorrows so that they are truly prepared for healthy discipleship. Finally, thus equipped, we must gather the lost, reach the poor and destitute, and draw them into the community of faith. All this happens simultaneously—with one no more important than another.

Worship: Frequency and Core

The task or activity mentioned first is that of worship. Worship is the lifeblood of the church of Christ. As the Westminster Shorter Catechism puts it, "the chief end of man is to glorify God and to enjoy Him forever." This applies to all of human life, but the glorification and enjoyment flow from the wellspring of weekly worship. Thus, the congregations "shall assemble for worship, ordinarily twice on the Lord's Day." Since the days of the apostles, the New Testament church has done this primarily on Sunday, fittingly referred to as the "Lord's Day," the day Christ arose, the day of our "new birth into a living hope" (1 Pet. 1:3).

In the mid-1990s, when the word *ordinarily* was inserted here, synod affirmed "the rich tradition of assembling for worship twice on the Lord's Day" and encouraged the continued "embrace [of] this tradition." It also insisted that any "alternatives to the second service" must be "part of a strategic ministry plan with full accountability to [the] classis" (Supplement, Article 51a; *Acts of Synod, 1995*, pp. 766-67; *Acts of Synod, 1996*, p. 455).

Our annual worship pattern is to be organized around the central events of our salvation: Christ's birth, ministry, death, resurrection, and ascension as well as the Spirit's coming. In other words, we are bound to the liturgical seasons of Advent, Christmas, Epiphany, Lent, Easter, and Pentecost. In addition, members will ordinarily gather to observe the passing of another calendar year, celebrate "annual days of prayer and thanksgiving," and attend any "special worship services" that may be "proclaimed in times of great stress or blessing for church, nation, or world."

Do you have any good ideas for a meaningful and better-attended second service?

I don't know how good they'll be, but this is what I've heard and seen. What I do not recommend is that the second service be almost exactly like the morning service. In some cases, the difference has involved no more than substituting the call to confession and assurance of pardon with a recitation of the Apostles' or Nicene Creeds. Our increasingly diverse denomination needs to consider variety.

Consider the teaching service. Early Reformed "second services" were educationally focused. That's one reason why our Catechism is divided into 52 Lord's Days and why ministers are asked "each Lord's Day . . . ordinarily [to] preach the Word as summarized in the creeds and confessions of the church, especially the Heidelberg Catechism" (Article 54b). In the past, synod has even encouraged the use of the contemporary testimony ("Our World Belongs to God") for this purpose. I sometimes think that members in our churches are confessionally illiterate. Teaching services, creatively planned and well executed, might be just the ticket.

Consider other possibilities as well. A contemporary music service once a month that truly appeals to the young and the young-minded. Perhaps a service in the style of Taizé with its contemplative stillness. A service focused on healing. An "end of the year" service on the Sunday evening before the 31st to remember those who passed on, those who were born or adopted or brought into the church membership, and/or the cardinal moments in nation and world. An intergenerational worship service of one kind or another. For great ideas check with the Calvin Institute of Christian Worship or consult back issues of *Reformed Worship* magazine (both with a rich online presence). Or arrange for smaller gatherings in homes where people either form a community and tackle each other's challenges with biblical insights and shared prayer or deliberately disciple new members into our fellowship—or both of these together. In that case, be sure that "such alternatives are part of a strategic ministry plan with full accountability to [your] classis" (Supplement, Article 51a).

All this is not radically new territory. Synod 2005, for example, decided to "remind the churches that the second worship service may be a teaching service, employing models such as small groups, house churches, and various congregational gatherings characterized by learning together, dialogue, and interaction" (*Acts of Synod, 2005,* p. 720).

Christmas 1995 fell on a Monday. Our council decided that we would have our regular two services on Sunday, December 24, and none on Monday, December 25. This, quite frankly, ruined my Christmas Day celebration and suggests to me that giving thanks to God for his great gift to us in Christ is no longer of much importance to my congregation. Isn't there a church law that requires a Christmas Day service?

Article 51 of the Church Order says that "worship services shall be held in observance of Christmas." Note that it does not say that they shall be held on Christmas Day but "in observance of Christmas." I take that to mean in observance of Christ's birth. There is definitely some room here for what your council has done. Did they consider one service on the 24th, and one on the 25th? You would probably have been just fine with that.

By the way, some sixteenth century Reformed congregations held services only on Sundays, and councils refused to call their members to assemble on what they called festival days, including Christmas, when they fell on a weekday. A century later, they held services not only on the first Christmas Day but also on the second Christmas Day in order to prevent "reveling" on public holidays. Surely that illustrates how the context dictated this more than some principle of Scripture or tradition. That's why our law is written the way it is.

One question that remains is why our Church Order departs from this pattern and insists that worship services shall ordinarily be held on New Year's Eve and New Year's Day (not "in observance of" those days). For fifteen years of my ministerial career, that meant I had to preach on my birthday! When I tried to invoke the "ordinarily" part on that basis, the elders didn't deem that sufficient cause. They did, however, permit the appearance of a birthday cake after the morning service. OK, yes, it's New Year's Day, but the hour of my birth was 6 p.m. Thus, as far as I know, my mother made no headlines in our postwar city near Rotterdam, the Netherlands.

Do you approve of synod's designating certain Sunday services for "special causes" like All Nations Heritage Day and the like?

Yes, I do, provided that these designations are kept to a minimum and the events of Christ's redeeming work remain dominant in our yearly worship.

III. The Task and Activities of the Church

Article 52

a. The consistory shall regulate the worship services.

b. The consistory shall see to it that the principles and elements of worship approved by synod are observed, including the use of liturgical forms, songs, and synodically approved Bible versions. If liturgical forms are adapted or additional psalms, hymns, and spiritual songs are used in worship, these elements should conform to synodical guidelines.

It may be useful to refresh our memory on the use of the terms "council," "consistory," and "diaconate" as commented on under Article 35. It is the local assembly of minister(s) and elders that is given the authority to arrange for and supervise the congregation's worship. Obviously, its primary concern will be the guarding of the pulpit and the proper administration of the sacraments. But the consistory holds final responsibility for everything involved in worship. Most often it will exercise this authority with the help of a hands-on worship committee.

At the same time, the Church Order acknowledges an appropriate role for the synod. The order of worship, "the principles and elements of worship," liturgical forms, hymns, Bible translations—these are significant components of congregational worship, powerful in how they shape our life of faith from week to week, year to year. For that reason, we leave it to the broadest assembly to guide our local churches in these things.

Since it provides the way to find all the material specifically mentioned in Article 52b, we insert below the actual wording of Supplement, Article 52b adopted by Synod 2010:

Bible versions recommended by synod for use in worship services are listed online at www.crcna.org and include the King James Version (KJV), the American Standard Version (ASV), the Revised Standard Version (RSV), the New International Version (NIV), the New Revised Standard Version (NRSV), Today's New International Version (TNIV), the English Standard Version (ESV), and the New Living Translation (NLT).

Liturgical forms, songs and elements of worship approved by synod are contained in the latest edition (currently 1987) of the denomination's *Psalter Hymnal*. Forms, subsequent revisions of forms that are synodically approved, and other such resources are made available on the denomination's website (www.crcna.org) under "Synodical Resources."

Synodical guidelines pertaining to the *adaptation of liturgical forms* are found in the *Acts of Synod, 1994*, pages 493-94 and in the *Manual of Christian Reformed Church Government* (2008 Revision), pages 224-25.

Materials on the *principles of, elements of, and guidelines for worship and music* are found in the "Introduction to the Psalms, Bible Songs, and Hymns" contained in the latest edition (currently 1987) of the denomination's *Psalter Hymnal*, pages 11-13, in the *Acts of Synod, 1997*, pages 664-68, and in the 1997 Committee to Study Worship Report available on the denomination's website (www.crcna.org) under "Synodical Resources."

Synodical approval of Bible versions specifically refers to the Bibles obtained for and placed *in the pew* (or chairs, as the case may be). There is no law against the minister using another, perhaps more "popular" version, for the call to confession or the assurance of pardon. There is no law against citing another translation as more faithful to the original text, either when reading the text for the sermon or while preaching the sermon itself.

In order to avoid possible confusion, we note that Synod 1982 approved the New American Standard Bible (NASB) not as a version for official use in worship but "for Bible study only" (*Acts of Synod, 1982*, pp. 69-70).

You said in class the other day that doctrinal error can "creep in stealthily," often without intent, especially when it comes to our liturgy. I know that's true of hymns having to be scrutinized for Reformed content. But you were even more specific: you said you heard bad theology with your own ears in a "prayer of consecration" when you last celebrated the Lord's Supper. Can you tell me exactly what you heard and why it was a departure from sound doctrine?

I'd be happy to. I even alerted our pastors to it. The written liturgy identified as the "Prayer of Consecration" had the congregation saying: ". . . so that we may be joined to Christ the Lord, receive new life. . . ." But the congregation is not "joined to Christ the Lord" by the Holy Spirit through the breaking of the bread. It does not receive new life through the drinking of the wine. It is joined to Christ and receives new life even apart from sacramental celebration. As the Belgic Confession states, Jesus instituted the Supper in order "to nourish and sustain those who are already born again and ingrafted into his family: his church" (Article 35). If one insists on carrying the thought into sacramental liturgy, it would be more acceptable to say that the congregation is joined to Christ the Lord by the Holy Spirit through the administration of baptism, not the Lord's Supper. According to Heidelberg Catechism Lord's Day 29, we are *nourished* by his crucified body and poured-out blood, we are *assured* by a visible sign that we share in his true body and blood. This sacrament is about nourishment of and assurance for those who are already joined to Christ.

In my humble opinion, this is not nitpicking. Perhaps my pastors thought so. But sometimes these things can be significant in faith formation without anyone really noticing. Notice that it is easier to say what I quoted earlier than to say it correctly: ". . . so that, joined to Christ the Lord, we may receive assurance of new life. . . ." Perhaps somebody just intended for the congregation to have to recite the prayer less clumsily—who knows? Liturgy, especially repeated liturgy, has a way of being an effective teacher and I honestly believe, in this case, a teacher of bad sacramental theology.

In our church, an elder shakes the hand of the minister at the beginning of the worship service and again at the end. One Sunday morning the elder on duty refused to shake the hand of the minister after the benediction because he did not agree with the sermon. Is this standard procedure?

What this particular elder did is neither standard nor correct procedure. The practice itself is still found in a number of our churches and is clearly rooted in our tradition. It symbolizes that the consistory bears responsibility for the preaching of the Word of God, that the minister is given authority to proclaim it, and that the consistory takes back that authority when the minister is done with the proclamation. This means that the consistory (the minister and the elders too) will deal with any and all criticism should that come from any quarter. It also means that no individual elders can take it upon themselves to make that decision on the spot. The handshake is not intended to indicate approval but just the consistory's taking back the authority. I wonder if incidents like this caused most of our churches to abandon this traditional practice.

Your question reminds me of the time when I, as a fairly young minister, was assigned to preach at a church some 150 km (95 miles) away. Much to my chagrin, I was advised that I was not free to go home right after the service, but that I would first have to meet once more with the consistory. It turned out that the elders took their responsibility seriously and reviewed the sermon right there and then when it was still fresh on everyone's mind. The result of the review was by no means devastating, nor was it totally confirming. For a while, on the way home, I resented the fact that these elders pounced on a young visiting minister without any regard for the heightened vulnerability that would have ebbed away by Tuesday or Wednesday. It didn't take long for me to change my mind. This "quaint custom," one I had not previously experienced, was just their way of exercising their God-ordained duty to guard the pulpit. I don't necessarily advocate the exact same practice, but at least they were doing it. In other churches I served or observed, no such custom existed at all. There, I actually had to take initiative and solicit review of my preaching by asking for—at the very least—a consistory-appointed committee. I also insisted that at least one of the four-per-year occasions of "mutual censure" (Article 36b) focus on the minister's responsibility of writing and delivering the sermons. That helped to alleviate my loneliness in proclamation.

Is it proper to have the American flag and the church flag in the sanctuary during the worship service on Sunday?

By "church flag," I assume you mean the flag of the CRC, the "cross on the triangle" symbol. I believe it might be considered appropriate for a congregation of members who have all made a profession of faith and indicated their consent to hold to the creeds and confessions of the CRC denomination and who have all submitted to the discipline of that church to symbolize the community in which they stand to worship by having the symbol/flag appear in church during worship. There is certainly no law or rule that I know of that forbids it. The symbols, after all, refer to the object of our worship: the crucified Lord and the holy Trinity.

The presence of the national flag is a matter of a totally different nature. It has been hotly debated in a number of congregations that I know of. It involves, of course, the need to distinguish church and state in our thinking, and a discussion of Article 36 of the Belgic Confession might be helpful in such debates. Like displaying the church flag, this is a matter of wisdom and discretion. There is no rule or law or synodical pronouncement on this issue that I know of, nor am I aware of any denominational study or synodical decision that would give guidance to our congregations. I'll just observe here that the presence of the flag may relativize our unique allegiance to the Lord and further confuse the already confusing issue of church/state relationships. I do hope this issue is not terribly divisive in your setting.

If it is indeed the local consistory that must regulate the worship services, how is it that the classis, the synod, and the Church Order impose their will on what we do on Sundays?

Your point of view on this has deep roots in our tradition. Indeed, the very first assembly of the newly Reformed churches in the Netherlands (an unofficial synod held in 1568 at Wesel, Germany, while leaders were still in exile) insisted that

> insofar as possible in all circumstances things which by their nature are indifferent and which have no firm foundation in the doctrine and example of the apostles and which also have no necessary and unavoidable reasons may not tie the freedom of the churches down by any prescribed form (Convent of Wesel, I.9).

One example of such indifferent matters given by this assembly itself is whether, during the administration of the Lord's Supper, believers shall receive the elements while reclining at a table, standing, or walking.

Of course, the point of view that assemblies may "impose their will," as you call it, also has history on its side. The very same Convent of Wesel goes on to mention

> things which are of a completely different character because they are grounded either in God's Word or in the usage and example of the apostles or for continuing and very important and necessary reasons undergird the practice of the church. [In these things,] one shall not deviate lightly from the general consensus of the churches and their deep-rooted customs (Convent of Wesel, I.11).

The Church Order and synod rightly insist on obedience to Scripture, on following the ways of the New Testament church, and on upholding customs that have been adopted for "very important and unavoidable reasons." An example of such a custom is that we worship weekly. We must "spur one another on toward love and good deeds, not giving up meeting together . . ." (Heb. 10:24-25). Assemblies may hold us to that. That's why we have them.

This tension of the denomination insisting on principles when it must and permitting freedom in local practice whenever possible is one that persists throughout all the regulations on the tasks and activities of the church. The church is both local and universal.

III. The Task and Activities of the Church

Article 53

a. The worship services shall be led by the ministers of the Word and others appointed by the consistory.

*" giving +
taking away
of authority"*

b. Worship services may be led by persons <u>licensed to exhort</u> or by those appointed by the consistory to <u>read a sermon</u>. Such persons, however, shall refrain from all official acts of ministry, and only sermons approved by the consistory shall be read in a worship service.

The claim is often made that Reformed churches have never been completely purged of the evils of sacramentalism. It is argued that the clergy-laity distinction is maintained illegitimately and that we have <u>not fully</u> honored the <u>priesthood of all believers</u>. Those who make this claim often argue in favor of the practice of lay preaching and insist that worship leaders, irrespective of who they are, should never be prohibited from performing "official acts of the ministry." The truth is that this position is more reflective of an Anabaptist version of the Reformation than of the Lutheran and Calvinist one, and it represents too radical a democratization of the church. While it is true that the ~~Reformed tradition~~ has always rejected a clergy-laity distinction, in general it has also maintained the continued need for ordination or licensure of certain individuals in order to protect the pulpit. To put it differently, any hierarchy involved in this article is not an essential but a functional one.

The Reformation was largely driven by a rediscovery of the Scriptures, a humanist pursuit to recover the original meaning from the original languages and allow the Scriptures to speak to believers without dependence on the "priesthood" for its message of salvation. On this road, it is unavoidable that the pulpit must be guarded against uninformed preaching. Believers have the right to know and be assured that those who will enter the pulpit will have as thorough an education and training as possible. Thus, Article 53 merely echoes the sounds of Articles 6-8 where provisions are made to ensure that only those who are properly prepared will carry on the ministry of the Word.

Official Acts of Ministry

Aside from those given the right to preach in the worship services by reason of being ordained as ministers of the Word or ministry associates (Articles 10, 24), licensure to exhort is given to candidates for the ministry (Articles 6, 7), seminary students (Article 22), and gifted persons who do not intend to enter into the ministry (Article 43). These latter, however, "shall refrain from all official acts of ministry." The Supplement to Article 53 gives guidance to churches and individuals on these "official acts" as adopted by Synod 2001:

> 1) Certain acts of ministry—among them the preaching of the Word, the administration of the sacraments, the pronouncement of blessings for the people, the laying of hands on new leaders, and the reception and formal dismissal of members—are part of the ministry of Christ to his followers and are entrusted to the church and, within the church, to its ordained leaders, not to a specific office.
>
> 2) Therefore, no long-standing, organized congregation of Christians should be deprived of these liturgical acts simply because it cannot provide for the presence of an ordained minister or evangelist [ministry associate].
>
> 3) These acts of ministry symbolize and strengthen the relationships among the Lord, leaders, and the people of

God. Their use is a sacred trust given to leaders by the Lord for the purpose of strengthening the flock. Therefore the administration of these acts should continue to be regulated by the church.

Earlier, at Article 22, I shared some advice theological students receive at our seminary. It is equally relevant to all worship leaders who are not ordained nor preparing to be ordained as ministers or ministry associates.

Reading Sermons

When Article 53 refers to the "reading of a sermon," it has in mind a sermon that was crafted by a minister of the Word and read by an elder or other worship leader only after it has been approved by the consistory. The CRCNA makes many sermons available for this purpose on its website (www.crcna. org, "sermons"). These are acceptable in local churches because they were approved by the "Sermons for Reading Services Committee" of synod.

Our classis recently adopted the judgment "that elders are permitted to preach in their own congregations." Is this in accord with our Church Order?

As it stands, no. Elders may "read" an approved sermon when appointed to do so by the consistory, but they may not "preach." The CRCNA has never embraced what some call "lay preaching." Members and elders need licensure to exhort from the classis even if they wish to do so only in their home church.

I serve as the classical counselor for a church currently searching for a pastor. They are in dire need of guest preachers while the search continues. There are a fair number of ordained ministers available in our neighborhood. These are all known to deliver sound biblical sermons, but very few of them are familiar with the Reformed confessions. Our *Manual of CRC Government* seems to suggest that they must be committed to those confessions before they are allowed on our pulpits. Is that really the case? Are there any other regulations on this? Are councils free to decide these things on a person by person basis?

This is indeed the only direction we have in this regard. What you see in the *Manual* is a rephrasing of a decision of Synod 1904, which said (and I translate it as faithfully as I can): "A consistory may not allow ministers of other denominations to preach unless it has first assured itself that such persons are truly of Reformed persuasion."

A minister of an evangelical church may well be biblical in the preaching of the Word, but if and when asked to preach in a Christian Reformed setting, that minister should at least be aware of the Reformed Confessions on, say, infant baptism, so that the sermon does not needlessly offend the listeners by directly contradicting what the congregation officially holds. Ideally, synod said back then, the person should actually be committed to the Reformed confessions. Guarding the pulpit is our tradition because in preaching we shape the confessional stance of the church. I would hope that any visiting minister would at the very least be respectful of who we are in the CRCNA and be familiar enough with our creed so that the congregation is edified. And, yes, it is indeed the consistory (not, as you say, the council) that needs to make these judgments in each case without interference by a broader assembly. On the other hand, synod has spoken on this, and the consistory must be mindful of our covenant (see Article 29).

III. The Task and Activities of the Church

Article 54

> a. The proclamation of the Word shall be central to the worship of the church and shall be guided by the creeds and confessions.
>
> b. At one of the services each Lord's Day, the minister shall ordinarily preach the Word as summarized in the creeds and confessions of the church, especially the Heidelberg Catechism.

The proclamation of the Word of God is at the very heart of the church's life and central to its worship. It is through the regular heralding of Christ's saving work that the Holy Spirit produces faith in our hearts (Rom. 10:13-15), reconciles sinners to God (2 Cor. 5:18-21), and renews our lives in this world (Rom. 12:2). The "pure preaching of the gospel," says Article 29 of the Belgic Confession, is the first and foremost mark of the one true church.

Expository Preaching

Until just recently, this article was actually a little more specific about the nature of this proclamation. Ministers, it said for many decades, "shall officially explain and apply Holy Scripture." That may seem obvious, but it is clear to anyone who regularly attends worship services that sermons sometimes fail to comply with that directive. We have insisted on it being "official." That means it must be done by virtue of one's public office, with full accountability for how it is discharged. Sermons are not to be statements of one's private thoughts but messages of Scripture. Proclamation must be exercised in conformity with what the church asked and the minister promised at the time of ordination.

We have insisted on "expository" preaching, meaning that each and every sermon must "expose" or "lay open" the theme of the biblical text as addressed to its original audience and only in and through that to us today. The church is not looking for a moral lesson or a fascinating piece of religious discourse. It is not looking for just any story, uplifting as it may be. It is looking for the narrative of God's gracious revelation in Christ in a particular text of Scripture that will shape our lives just as it has for centuries among his people. There is a sign on every pulpit, real or imagined, that is directed at the preacher, giving voice to a congregational hunger: "Sir [or Ma'am], we would like to see Jesus" (John 12:21).

Centrality of Preaching

As indicated in the article, the sermon is central to worship in the Reformed tradition. Not the sacraments, not the prayers, not the hymns, and not the praise—all good and necessary things—but proclamation is at the center of what we do each and every Sunday. We need not be fanatic iconoclasts to prize and uphold this inheritance. We just need to insist on the Word's continued centrality. As the Heidelberg Catechism says, "the kingdom of heaven is opened by proclaiming and publicly declaring to all believers, each and every one, that, as often as they accept the gospel promise in true faith, God, because of what Christ has done, truly forgives all their sins" (Q&A 84).

Preaching Shaping Faith

Sermons not only declare the truth of God's Word. They also shape the believing response to that truth by the hearers. They are formative in how God's people confess and articulate their faith. Every sermon also teaches. Since the CRCNA is committed to the three Christian creeds and the three Reformed confessions, proclamation from its pulpits must be guided by those statements of faith—deliberately so. This does not mean that the text of Scripture is placed on the back burner by a slavish repetition of doctrinal

298

truth. On the contrary, the Bible is always the heart of the sermon. But the sermon is fleshed out in conformity to what we confess—sometimes subtly, sometimes explicitly, but always intentionally so.

We must remember that confessions are human documents: not God's Word, but human words in response to God's Word. We have procedures for revising them, editing them, something we definitely do not do with the Bible. The Reformation was not against human documents as such. The church has always responded with its creeds. The Reformation was about making sure that a religious tradition based on them is never elevated above the Word of God itself. A sermon shaped by the confessions is not truly a sermon if it is not alive with the God-breathed text of Scripture. The Word must always shape what we confess, not vice versa.

Nonetheless, there continue to be different traditions of confessing the faith. We may regret that development but we cannot deny it. This is why we choose to be Christian Reformed rather than Baptist, Methodist, or Episcopalian. Hopefully that choice is well-considered, not simply a reflection of where our parents had us baptized. Our ministers stand in that tradition, are trained in that tradition, and pledge to uphold that tradition. They do not follow it slavishly and often breathe new life into it, but they stay within community. A huge benefit for God's people is that in this way preachers are prevented from riding their hobbyhorses. The tradition helps to overcome their natural bias. If they are fascinated by the doctrine of predestination, they do not torture their congregations by slinging at them a series of twelve consecutive sermons on reprobation based on the Canons of Dort. On the other hand, if they dare not even so much as mention that doctrine, the confessions gently lead them at least occasionally to preach on Ephesians 1:4: "For he chose us in him before the creation of the world to be holy and blameless in his sight." They know, in other words, that they are bound to preach the whole counsel of God.

Confessional Preaching

The article makes specific mention of the Heidelberg Catechism. The CRCNA has done that from its beginning in conformity with the Synod of Dort (1618-19). That is because—in distinction from the Belgic Confession and the Canons of Dort—the catechism is intensely personal, practical, and pedagogically effective. Based on biblical truth, the catechism teaches the Apostles' Creed, the earliest of the Christian creeds, the Ten Commandments as the shape of the sanctified life, and the Lord's Prayer as the guide to a prayerful life. This article still expects every minister to "ordinarily preach the Word as summarized in the creeds and confessions of the church, especially the Heidelberg Catechism." This is to be done "at one of the services each Lord's Day," thus covering all fifty-two Lord's Days in one year.

A committee reporting to Synod 2010 recommended a new reading of Article 54 that would have eliminated these specific expectations. It did so, for one thing, because Synod 1973 "encourage[d] the use of the Belgic Confession and the Canons of Dort, as well as the Heidelberg Catechism, in preaching" (*Acts of Synod, 1973*, p. 65). For another, synods have repeatedly encouraged the use of the contemporary testimony "Our World Belongs to God" in worship. In addition, Synod 1995 began to allow for the possibility of only one worship service on any given Sunday. Put this all together, and it is clear that the practice of covering the catechism in one year—perhaps even two or three years—is literally impossible. Synod 2010, on the other hand, so valued the second service and the use of the Heidelberg Catechism that it refused entirely to eliminate these specific instructions for ministers of the Word (*Acts of Synod, 2010*, p. 905).

Are there any regulations about the length of sermons? Our pastor continues to try our patience.

You have my sympathy. I trust you've mentioned it to your pastor and to the council, not just to me. There are no specific rules about this in our Church Order. For your information and perhaps even amusement, let me cite for you two sixteenth century references to an issue for all times and places (freely translated):

> The ministers shall guard against excessively long sermons which presume on the memory of the listeners, discourage their enthusiasm, and, as it were, turn their stomachs, especially on those days where the people must be given sufficient time for handiwork and those on which there must be opportunity for prophecy. For these reasons, ministers should try to limit their address to one hour. The officebearers shall take care, however, that

the sermons during communion services are not extended to those hours during which the sacrament is to be administered, and thus reckon with the needs of the people, especially pregnant women and others in poor health (Convent of Wesel, 1568).

The ministers are admonished not to burden their audience with lengthy sermons and limit them to one hour as much as possible (Synod of Dordrecht, 1574).

In today's world, I have little hesitation in advising you and yours that a sermon of twenty minutes is probably plenty long. As an elder once said to me, "if you've been pumping that long and still haven't struck oil, perhaps it's best to call it a day."

What would be your definition of a good catechism sermon?

First and foremost, the sermon must be based on biblical text. Even if the Lord's Day is introduced as text and read before the message as a "summary of biblical truth," the sermon must contain explicit references to sources of that truth in Scripture. Some have even suggested that the text may never be the Lord's Day itself. That's a bit extreme, but the sentiment is sound. Never ever using the Lord's Day itself as "the text for the morning sermon" is also extreme. Preachers do well to choose a biblical text, quote the creed(s) in the sermon, and/or have the congregation respond in unison with the applicable part of the catechism. The catechism, after all, reflects the truths of God's Word.

Second, the sermon must truly communicate the Word of God to his people. It must not limit itself to being a doctrinal lecture or a teaching tool. I've heard that referred to as "dehydration"— draining away the personal and inspirational so clearly evident in the catechism's text. All sermons do some teaching, but good sermons do much more than teach.

Third, the sermon, like the ones that "reconstruct" the biblical text, must be thematic, not merely topical. The catechism is always asking how, say, Christ's resurrection benefits us (Q&A 45). It not only presents it as a doctrine but also delivers its goods. What the Pharisees and Sadducees taught about the resurrection, how modern theologians often deny that it is a historical fact, and how orthodox Christians will still cling to it as a real event is a topic. That our Lord's resurrection transforms us today in the very fiber of our being and implants hope of the coming kingdom in our hearts is a theme.

III. The Task and Activities of the Church

Article 55

> The sacraments shall be administered upon the authority of the consistory in the public worship service by a minister of the Word, a ministry associate, or, in the case of need, an ordained person who has received the approval of classis, with the use of the prescribed forms or adaptations of them that conform to synodical guidelines.

The sacraments, in the Reformed tradition, are two and two only: baptism and the Lord's Supper. According to the Heidelberg Catechism, they are "holy signs and seals." They were instituted by God himself to "make us understand more clearly the promise of the gospel" and have that promise sealed to us. Faith is produced in our hearts "by the preaching of the holy gospel," and the Holy Spirit "confirms" that faith "through our use of the holy sacraments" (Q&A 65). As the catechism goes on to say, the sacraments are all about assurance—the increasing conviction "that our entire salvation rests on Christ's one sacrifice for us on the cross" (Q&A 67). Similarly, the Belgic Confession speaks of the sacraments as "nourishing and sustaining our faith." "He has added these to the Word of the gospel to represent better to our external senses both what he enables us to understand by his Word and what he does inwardly in our hearts, confirming in us the salvation he imparts to us" (Belgic Confession, Article 33).

The sacraments are celebrated "in the public worship service" and there alone. The "public worship service" is the one held "upon the authority of the consistory." The consistory has invited the congregation to gather for the worship service, and it is in charge of what takes place within it. This means that in the Reformed tradition so-called "private administrations" of the sacraments are unacceptable. Royalty gathers with commoners, presidents with ordinary citizens, pastors with carpenters and lawyers and teachers, old with young, rich with poor, whites with blacks. Therein lies true communion: in God's eyes, all are in need of his salvation and, by grace through faith, united as his people. The diversity is as important as the unity. That's why baptism signifies God's promises to all who have been brought into fellowship with Christ. That's why bread and wine are not "served" at private weddings or youth outings at the beach, but only in official worship of the church.

When our Church Order says that "the sacraments shall be administered . . . by a minister of the Word, a ministry associate, or an ordained person" it speaks, as it often does, both descriptively and prescriptively. Usually it is the local pastor or a ministry associate or, in case of need, an elder designated by the classis, who serves communion. Elders and elders' assistants aid in the distribution of the elements. This practice expresses the close bond that normally exists between these pastoral leaders and their congregation. What the Church Order means to *prescribe* is that, apart from that one exception for "need," only ordained ministers of the Word and ministry associates may administer the Lord's Supper. The reason it does so is *not* to identify these persons as an elite group—"the clergy"—who must retain their power over the church at all cost. Such thinking would be foreign to people of Reformed persuasion. Rather, it does so to ensure that the sacraments will be intimately tied to the proclamation of the Word, without which they have no meaning. Ministers and ministry associates are the ones who preach, who bring God's promises in verbal form. They are therefore also the ones who baptize and serve communion, the "signs and seals" of those promises.

The liturgical forms appropriate for baptism and the Lord's Supper are found in the *Psalter Hymnal* and on the denomination's website. The synodical guidelines pertaining to any adaptation of these forms are found in the *Acts of Synod, 1994*, pp. 493-94 and in the *Manual of Christian Reformed Church Government* (2008 Revision), pp. 224-25, as well as on the CRCNA website.

Our church is a fair distance from the nearest CRC. Now that we have no minister, we struggle a great deal with pulpit supply, especially for communion Sundays. The local RCA pastor is willing to help us. Is a non-CRC minister permitted to serve the Lord's Supper in our church?

The Church Order nowhere limits the administration of the sacraments to ministers who are Christian Reformed. In the case you suggest it will even be done within the boundaries of our current ecumenical relationships: the CRCNA and the RCA are in full ecclesiastical fellowship. I see no reason why an RCA minister could not occasionally lead your congregation in celebrating the sacrament of communion.

Take careful note, also, of the latest addition to Article 55. Synod 2002 decided that "in the case of need, an ordained person who has received the approval of classis" may administer the Lord's Supper. The Supplement to the article indicates that this should be an elder. I advise you to designate an elder among you and get classical approval. This too will ease the pressure.

May unordained members serve communion? I mean, may they distribute the elements? Some in our church are insistent that only the minister and elders (and possibly the deacons) may be designated to serve the bread and wine to the congregation.

It is clear from Article 55 that the Lord's Supper must be administered "by a minister of the Word." Our polity, however, does not go on from there to prescribe the exact way in which the bread and wine must be distributed. In most churches the elders provide them to the people seated in their chairs or pews. But in some of our churches members come forward to form a circle and take the elements from the minister, passing them one to another with the words "the body of Christ for you" or a similar expression. In others, the ushers help in the distribution simply because of logistics—the congregation attaches no particular theological significance to their assisting. Still others use "elders' assistants" or "associate elders" or "pastoral workers" who have been commissioned but not ordained. In my judgment, it is best that the minister "administers" the Supper and that the "pastoral leadership" of the congregation be as visible as possible in the distribution of the elements.

If the sacraments are meant to confirm the (spoken) promise of the gospel and are only meaningful when they are closely tied to the preaching of the Word, why is it that we celebrate baptism before the sermon instead of after it?

A very good question indeed! Theologically you're right on. That's how I imagine adult baptisms should proceed. But, of course, we also have infant baptism, and the problem then, I suppose, is that the child destined to wail might interrupt the preacher. So you get them "done" before the sermon starts. Sometimes it's just not workable to put our good theology into practice. I did notice, while delving into ancient history, that the Convent of Wesel, 1568 (I.10), mentions this exact issue as an example of "indifferent matters" that are to be left unregulated and to the judgment of the local consistory.

You told us in class that sacraments are to be limited to the public worship service. So I followed your lead and refused to take the bread and the wine to the homes of those who are unable to attend. Now the elders are on my case. Help!

Thanks for valuing my teaching and following the order of the church. But life out there, as you're noticing, comes with its little nuances. I guess you didn't ask me about it that day, probably because it didn't even occur to you back then. Actually, I do happen to believe that elders and ministers are free to serve communion to the home-bound or to members in hospitals or rest homes. I don't view these as private celebrations of the sacrament but, rather, as extensions of official worship in the building.

Specifically, I have found it meaningful to have elders or elders' assistants serving such folk the bread and wine while playing tape recordings or DVDs of the service on a Sunday afternoon. That enhances the notion that these actually become "extensions." Then again, our elders sometimes do it in groups of three or four at hospitals or hospice facilities in a very simple ceremony along with prayer over one who is critically ill. This reminds me of James 5:14: "Is anyone among you sick? Let them call the elders of the church to pray over them and anoint them with oil in the name of the Lord." So I have a hard time saying that this violates the order of the church.

III. The Task and Activities of the Church

Article 56

The covenant of God shall be sealed to children of believers by holy baptism. The consistory shall see to it that baptism is requested and administered as soon as feasible.

Baptism: An Initiatory Sacrament of the Church

Baptism is an initiatory sacrament of the church because it is administered to a person just once in a lifetime to mark that person's entry into the visible church. While the denomination rejoices in "renewal moments" within a person's subsequent life of faith, it rejects rebaptism because that reduces or obliterates the force of the first. Baptism is the "sign and seal" that God in his mercy claims us as his own and promises to be God to us throughout our lives. That divine oath, proclaimed in God's Word, is for life. It must be taken for what it is even apart from baptism: an oath. Thus "godly parents ought not to doubt the election and salvation of their children whom God calls out of this life in infancy" prior to baptism (Canons of Dort, I.17). And if their children do live, are baptized, and mature, they as well as their children in turn ought never to doubt that God has chosen them in Christ "before the creation of the world to be

By being God, does that mean Savior is will?

307

holy and blameless in his sight" (Eph. 1:4). This Pauline reference, I believe, is more about a sanctified life than an eternal destiny, a doctrine for this life, not a clarifying peek into the "hidden . . . things of God" (Canons of Dort, I.12).

Baptism is the *sacrament* that marks a person's entry into the visible church. We use the word *visible* because ultimately we do not have the mind of God and are not able to know exactly who is recorded in what Revelation calls "the book of life." The church has always known that there are "unbelievers and hypocrites" (Q&A 84, Heidelberg Catechism) within it who may, in the end, despite our best efforts, not repent and be saved. It has also always known that there are those not within it whom God, in his mercy, will lead into his kingdom. That's why we are truly zealous to reach out to all with the gospel of Christ and his saving grace. We are assured of our "eternal and unchangeable election to salvation," as members of his church, "in due time, though by various stages and in differing measure." We notice within ourselves, "with spiritual joy and holy delight, the unmistakable fruits of election," namely, "a true faith in Christ, a childlike fear of God, a godly sorrow for [our] sins, a hunger and thirst for righteousness, and so on" (Canons of Dort, I.12). And as we affirm that, remembering our baptism, we are assured that we shall forever be in his presence.

Baptism is a sacrament *of the church*. We celebrate it as a community when it is administered to all who come into our fellowship. And as we celebrate it, it directs us once again to the root of our salvation: not that we chose him, but that he chose us (John 15:16; Eph. 1:13-14; Eph. 2:8-10). Baptism does nothing in and of itself. There is no automatic blessing or mysterious transformation. It is nothing more and nothing less than a sign and seal of God's gracious promise.

The Heart of Infant Baptism

It is not we who choose Christ but Christ who chooses us. Thus, when we ask "Should infants, too, be baptized?" the Heidelberg Catechism answers yes. "They, no less than adults, are promised the forgiveness of sin through Christ's blood and the Holy Spirit who produces faith." They are to "be received into the Christian church and . . . distinguished from the children of unbelievers" (Q&A 74). Indeed, nothing speaks of God's grace quite as profoundly as the water of baptism administered to an uncomprehending child. The sacraments of the church are not like our annual church picnics: events we choose to celebrate because it seems fitting, right, and even

308

edifying. They are God-ordained, as our creed says, "to seal his promises in us, to pledge his good will and grace toward us, and also to nourish and sustain our faith" (Belgic Confession, Article 33). So at Christ's command, the church gathers around the font with its newborns in its arms, not so much to present an individual, nor even so much to have that individual blessed, but to stand there as a community, prompted by this water of grace, to remember and proclaim that God chose us in Christ to be his people.

Private Baptism, Dedication, and Rebaptism

In the CRCNA, we baptize only in official worship services. We baptize infants of believing parents and do not accept dedication as a substitute. We baptize converts not previously baptized. We accept the baptism of anyone who comes from another Christian denomination if that baptism has been administered in the name of the triune God by someone authorized to do so. We oppose rebaptism of any kind, whether by reason of the so-called "second blessing of the Holy Spirit" or the experience of a prior baptism now considered less than meaningful to the recipient. We do these things in the conviction that this is God's will for us in Scripture.

In the real world, of course, things are never quite that simple. For instance, a hospital chaplain visits the maternity ward and is asked to baptize then and there a newborn child not expected to live. A mother asks the elders not to push her into baptizing her firstborn because her husband is opposed to infant baptism and it would cause too much tension in their marriage. She'd be grateful if they would let her dedicate her child instead. A recent immigrant from El Salvador thinks he was probably baptized by a priest as a child but craves rebaptism on the ground that, in his firm belief, the Roman Catholic Church is a false church. John, formerly very sober in his life of faith, recently went to an inspirational gathering at the Assembly of God congregation and returned triumphantly with the announcement that (a) he was rebaptized and (b) he now prays for a similar outpouring of the Spirit for his Calvinist brothers and sisters. In the CRCNA, how do we respond?

We are sensitive to requests for baptism of a newborn not expected to live, but we hold to baptism as a sacrament publicly celebrated in the midst of the congregation. The event is special not just for the person baptized but for every single worshiper in the pews. It is not first of all a family event. It is a family of God event. A hospital chaplain I spoke with recently feels so strongly about this that he cannot in good conscience baptize a baby outside of a worship service. He offers an alternative ceremony with appropriate lament, prayer, and gospel hope. If the parents insist on a baptism, they are informed that he would be happy to arrange for another chaplain in his group willing and able to come and do that on short notice.

We should be sensitive to those who ask for dedication instead of infant baptism. We must also ask, in all seriousness, whether they would not be greatly comforted by water that speaks of God's faithfulness and promises rather than resting in only half—the lesser half—that speaks of our believing approach to God. Openness toward dedication ceremonies sounds like a reasonable accommodation to those with differing views, but it robs the church of an opportunity to testify to and experience the comforting mysteries of God's sovereign grace. Besides, in a fundamental sense, baptism *is* dedication. But it is not "dedication" in the way people often apply that phrase to baptism. At baptism, parents do not so much dedicate their children to God. Rather, the parents acknowledge that God has done something for their children. When children are baptized, the parents and the church are dedicated—dedicated as instruments of God's love and grace so that these beloved children too might "grow in grace."

As an initiatory sacrament, baptism is deeply meaningful in and of itself, regardless of how we feel at the time. God is doing something inexpressibly wonderful in our life by claiming us as his own. Assurance of this is inevitably lessened when the possibility of rebaptism hangs in the air.

A confessing member recently requested infant baptism for her firstborn. Her husband is not a member of the church and shows no inclination toward becoming one. How must we handle this situation?

First, continue to work sensitively with this couple and gently and patiently try to disciple the husband into the body of Christ.

Second, you must baptize the child. The rules require only that one of the parents must be a confessing member, not both. However, this situation especially requires one or more sensitive pastoral visits. Make it a point to invite the father to support his wife in the vows she intends to make. In my experience such support is almost always there.

Finally, assuming that the husband is indeed supportive, try to include him in the ceremony by at least standing by the side of his wife at baptism and responding publicly and positively to a query whether he will support her in the promises she made. I would insist, however, that the wife present the child for baptism, even though her husband is at her side. A simple announcement in the bulletin that day that the father is not an adult confessing member at this time is about as far as I would want to go.

An unmarried teenager who has not yet made a profession of faith recently had a child out of wedlock. She has decided not to give the child up for adoption, and we have been very supportive in this decision. Now she requests infant baptism. The father of the child is out of the picture. Her parents are willing to "stand up" for her or with her. Given our pastoral stance, it now seems odd not to grant her request, but most in our council believe we have no choice: she's not a confessing member now.

If the child is not to be adopted by the teenager's parents, I side with the majority. At least one parent must be a confessing member and gain the right to present the child for baptism.

My advice is to lead the new mother, without undue pressure, to a profession of faith and postpone the child's baptism until that day. In the meantime, I believe it would be pastorally wise to introduce the newborn to the congregation, have the congregation make a temporary vow to be supportive, and pray together that the Lord might lead the young mother, now saddled with awesome responsibilities, to a strong and vibrant faith in him. The community looks forward to the day when she professes it and then has her child baptized.

May grandparents present a grandson for infant baptism when neither parent of that child is a professing member of the church? The parents have no intention of joining, have no objections to the baptism, but won't be attending.

I get this question a lot, so I suppose this phenomenon is fairly widespread. I can certainly understand the desire to have this grandson baptized. I can also fully understand the thought that covenantal theology ought to allow for this sort of thing, especially if one believes that the covenant line runs through the church as well as the (biological) family. The fact is that among those who uphold covenantal theology, this has been a long-debated issue that has surfaced on many occasions and is often described as the issue of the "halfway covenant." The debate goes all the way back through previous centuries. The theological problem is made more complex when the mother or father opposes the baptism or at least does not consent to it. In that case, the issue of legal custody arises. Historically the church has always respected the rules of civil society with respect to custody of children.

In line with churches of the Reformation throughout history, the CRCNA holds that children of believers ought to be baptized. Next, we hope, expect, and pray for a profession of faith of the baptized at an age of understanding so that the covenant line or believers' line is then visibly extended throughout the generations. We wrestle with why children fall away and always keep praying on their behalf that they will return. Nonetheless, and in tune with our expectations, we do not give non-confessing parents the right to present children for baptism. Fallibly, to be sure, we draw boundaries for the sake of the purity of the church.

Grandparents do not have the right to present grandchildren for baptism unless the child's parents are out of the picture entirely and they have actually received legal custody or, as sometimes happens, actually adopted the child. That's the current position of the CRCNA. I have seen some exceptions made to that position with which I do sympathize. In one case that comes to mind, the grandparents had unofficial yet very strong control so that they, in fact, were providing the chief nurturing influence. But going down the road of exceptions to our policy is nonetheless fraught with some difficulty, and I believe that exceptions should be made only for very compelling reasons. Here we need a great deal of wisdom and discernment. After all, our historic policy is also wrapped in much wisdom.

At the same time, we rejoice in a situation like yours where the parents have no objections and the grandparents are allowed, perhaps even encouraged, to bring the child into the life and ministry of the church. We must not forget, though, in our rejoicing, that as he gets older it will become more and more difficult for him because of the obvious contradiction in modeling between one generation and another.

How do we help? Here's one reason why it was so necessary for our churches to move toward the scenario where children ages seven to twelve are encouraged to make an "early" profession of faith—where, at their level of understanding, they express their love for the Lord and their desire to be nurtured within the Christian community. I hope that your congregation does this as a routine practice. This, I think, is the direction to go, namely, that the grandchild is enfolded in every possible way (with a presentation in worship short of baptism and then in church school) and steadily encouraged to make such an age-appropriate profession, whereupon baptism can take place. It would have to be the case, to be sure, that the parents of a minor in their custody do not object and provide that permission in writing. But it would be a powerful witness to the child's parents and would speak eloquently of a God whose covenantal promises are being fulfilled in our eyes even if, right now, a generation is seemingly skipped. The community continues to pray and support. When he is fourteen, his parents' lifestyle—if still the same—will look very tempting. Hopefully he'll resist and make an additional adult profession some four years down the road. What a thrilling thing that would be for you!

I realize I probably haven't convinced you at an emotional level. I've given you the long-held stance of the churches of the Reformation. I could reach back into theology textbooks of the seventeenth and eighteenth centuries. I could give you stories of children being baptized by the church just because three generations back their ancestors were members, and what happened to churches like that in the long run. But I'll leave it at this for now. Feel free to fire back.

A young couple in our church refuses to present their firstborn for baptism on the grounds that they cannot find direct biblical evidence for infant baptism. While they do not ridicule or militate against our practice, they would prefer not to engage in it themselves. How must we proceed?

Synod 1888 made it clear that a consistory may not accept anyone as a member of the church who denies and opposes infant baptism

(*Acts of Synod, 1888*, p. 19). This is consistent with our current provision that the covenant *shall* be sealed to children of believers. Nonetheless, Synod 1964 made it just as clear in the case of an appeal that consistories have a right to admit those to membership who (1) agree wholeheartedly with the Reformed religion except on the point of direct biblical evidence for the doctrine of infant baptism, (2) do not propagate views conflicting with our doctrinal position, and (3) are willing to be further instructed in it (*Acts of Synod, 1964*, p. 63). In other words, the persons in question did not "deny and oppose" infant baptism. I take it the latter is what you're facing.

If your consistory admitted this couple to confessing membership in that clear understanding and is continuing the process of discipleship, it probably should not insist on the baptism at this time. Such insistence may be counterproductive in the discipling process. Baptism must be administered "as soon as feasible." But neither may the tension be resolved by doing nothing at all. That would amount to a clear violation of the current provisions. Considering our recent "slippage" into a more generic evangelical position on this issue, I would encourage you to be quite serious about continuing discipleship, not only of this couple, but also of your officebearers and members in general. Hopefully they'll present their child fairly soon. But do remember: discipleship may sometimes have to lead to discipline. Don't shrink from that either if ultimately the parents refuse to present the child. (I don't mean excluding them, but perhaps pressing them to find a church fellowship with different practices.)

We have a request for baptism from parents who were once confessing members of our congregation but then moved to Georgia and joined a Wesleyan church. Now they have had a child and discovered that the church only dedicates infants. They would like to "visit" their former church and have their child baptized. Is that permitted?

At the time of their move to Georgia, these members had a choice referred to in Article 67 of the Church Order. They could have retained their membership in the church of their former residence, maintaining some contact from time to time, yet worship in a new community. In that case, you'd be in a great position to baptize their newborn because formally they would still be members of your church. They could also have had their certificates of membership sent to the nearest CRCNA. Same result. It could be done in your church or in that one. The provision of Article 67 is there precisely to protect them in their convictions about infant baptism even while they worship in a community with a contrary position on that score. The third choice, apparently, is the one they have made—to join the Wesleyan church as members.

If they did not know while making these decisions that the Wesleyan church does not baptize infants, there was a breakdown. They should have known. But at this point we can only deal with the fact that they voluntarily joined another church and thus attached themselves to creeds and standards that only permit the dedication of infants. My legal inclination is simply to observe that they cannot have their cake and eat it too.

From a pastoral point of view, however, I would present them with two options. One is to be really kind and ask the Wesleyan church council or board in written communication with you whether, considering their background and the late realization, they would have any objection to having these former members present their child for baptism. The other would be to fix the mistake and ask the parents as yet to transfer their membership back to your church or to the nearest CRCNA. If they choose not to exercise these options, then the request should simply be denied. It sounds harsh, but I believe quite strongly that we cannot have people shopping elsewhere for things that their church does not have in stock.

III. The Task and Activities of the Church

Article 57

Adults who have not been baptized shall receive holy baptism upon public profession of faith. The form for the Baptism of Adults shall be used for such public professions.

Adult baptism in the CRCNA is not rebaptism but first baptism.

Those who were baptized as infants and subsequently make a public profession of faith are not baptized a second time. Their admission to full-fledged confessing membership is the hoped-for and prayed-for result of God's faithfulness pledged in his Word and sealed to them in baptism when they were infants. Such admission is regulated in Article 59, not this one.

All adults who have not previously been baptized are given the sacramental sign upon the profession that God, by grace, has called them also into fellowship with Christ and his church. This includes those whose parents did not have them baptized as infants, for whatever reason, but now join the church of their own accord. It also includes those who have come to believe in Christ as Lord and Savior and join the church later in life by way of publicly making that good profession. It is first made to the consistory and then in the midst of the congregation.

Should adult baptism take place before or after the person's profession of faith?

Great question—similar to the question of why we baptize infants before the sermon instead of after the sermon. After all, the sacrament must gain its meaning from the Word proclaimed. If it must be before the sermon in the case of infants for practical reasons, such reasons don't exist when we are baptizing an adult. Similarly, I much prefer that the profession of faith come after the adult baptism. I'm aware that this preference directly contradicts the pattern suggested in our liturgical forms for the Baptism of Adults. There, the profession precedes the baptism. I would plead for an adaptation of that liturgical form (allowed in Article 52 if that adaptation "conforms to synodical guidelines") and, down the road perhaps, a newly approved form. Surely playing out the heart of Reformed baptismal theology in our worship meets those guidelines. And the person does make an "initial profession" to the consistory; that suffices to warrant the scheduling of the baptism and then, second, the public profession. As the hymn "My Lord, I Did Not Choose You" (*Psalter Hymnal* 496) puts it, "My Lord, I did not choose you, for that could never be;/ my heart would still refuse you, had you not chosen me./ You took the sin that stained me, you cleansed me, made me new;/ of old you have ordained me, that I should live in you."

I recently ran across this intriguing idea: in baptism, touching the person's head not only gets the water where we want it, but it is also a kind of laying on of hands, an ordination to the office of believer. Is that loading too much symbolism into the sacrament? Is it adding something to baptism that is not legitimately there?

Yes and yes. Our 1973 "guidelines" on ecclesiastical office and ordination do hold that the laying on of hands is a "symbolic rite" associated with Christ's call. But they add that it typically pertains to the appointment of the church's officebearers (elders, deacons, ministry associates, or ministers of the Word), not with a so-called "office of believer." That term confuses things.

What intrigues you, I suppose, is the idea that we ought also to have some symbolic rite which speaks of a believer's marching orders to go and serve the Lord. I don't think there's anything to prevent you from doing this, but I would advise you to associate it with public profession of faith instead, which, in the case of adult baptism, happens at the same time. My pastors refer to this experience as a "commissioning," a time to observe and celebrate not only that persons have come to faith but also that they're being set apart to use whatever gifts and resources they have for the upbuilding and mission of the church. At the time of this "commissioning" (after the profession), they lay hands on the believer's head to symbolize the mandate. Provided we continue to distinguish between this laying on of hands and that which is reserved for officebearing, I have no problems with it—indeed, I recommend it heartily.

As for the sacrament of baptism, I do wish you would just "tune in" to the water. That symbol is so rich and so full of meaning that cluttering it with others will definitely distract. In my view at least, the primary focus at baptism must be on God's incomprehensible grace, not the believer's calling and task.

What are your views on baptism by immersion?

Quite apart from architectural implications, the likes of which would send any building committee into orbit, I like it a whole lot. The symbolism of Romans 6:4 comes through so much more clearly than in mere sprinkling: dying ("drowning") and rising ("emerging from water") in Christ, the promised grace and power to die continually to the old self and the life of sin, to be raised by grace as a new self, day by day—this grace and power is precisely what baptism points to. As far as I know, this was also an ancient custom of the New Testament church. Reformed churches have never frowned on this alternative method. In fact, they have considered such matters "indifferent" because the precise method has "no firm foundation in the doctrine and example of the apostles" so that there is no reason "to tie the freedom of the churches down by any prescribed form" (Convent of Wesel, 1568).

Conversely, this is not to suggest that sprinkling is wholly inferior to immersion. The symbol of water as a cleansing agent is just as powerful. It is the mode the Heidelberg Catechism and the Belgic Confession refer to (especially in its Article 34). In any case, the substance is in God's promised Word, not the symbol itself. For that reason, when it comes to infants, I still prefer to sprinkle. I worry a whole lot about dunking them when they're that young. I'm much more comfortable doing that with teens and grownups.

III. The Task and Activities of the Church

Article 58

> The baptism of one who comes from another Christian denomination shall be held valid if it has been administered in the name of the triune God, by someone authorized by that denomination.

For a relatively small denomination, the position of the CRCNA on the validity of baptism is remarkably broad-minded. In it, the catholicity of the church of Christ is fully honored.

Augustine and the Donatists

What is stated in Article 58 clearly stands in the tradition of St. Augustine in his opposition to Donatism. The Donatists of the fourth and fifth centuries regarded themselves as the only pure church, one that was not tainted by, first, "betrayals of the faith" under Diocletian's persecution and, second, the current "cuddling up" to the Roman Empire, referred to as "the world." For that reason, as "untainted ones," they "refused to acknowledge baptisms performed in the catholic communion" and decided that any Catholics joining their group must be rebaptized. In response Augustine, the newly ordained Bishop of Hippo in North Africa, insisted that there is no such thing as an "untainted" or "pure" church. Rather the visible church is a "'mixed body' in which tares and wheat . . . grow together until the judgment." The holiness of that church does not depend on the "purity of the minister who baptized" but "simply on the gracious love of God himself." The "real and effective minister of the sacrament" is not "the human priest, the bishop or presbyter." It is Christ himself, working through the ministry of the human agent who is merely "a symbol and channel" (Williston Walker et al, *A History of the Christian Church*, 4th ed., 1985, pp. 201-02). Augustine did not write off the Donatists as heretics. Nor did he "repay in kind" on this issue. Instead he recognized the validity of their baptisms and worked tirelessly towards their reconciliation with the worldwide church (although without fruit).

In the wake of the sixteenth-century Reformation, both the Roman Catholic Church and the Protestant churches followed in the footsteps of Augustine on this issue. True, the Calvinist churches in the Netherlands did not spell it out in their official Church Orders. On the other hand, the Synod of Emden (1571) and those that followed did answer questions about the validity of baptism to this effect. In tune with that tradition, the CRCNA finally took the matter from obscurity into the light of day by placing the above provision of Article 58 in its revised Church Order of 1965.

In a Christian Denomination

Note that the baptism must have occurred in a "Christian denomination." That's where the lines are drawn: at the boundaries of the Christian church. The congregation must have been one that acknowledges Christ as Lord and Savior, has trinitarian beliefs, and administers the sacrament with water in accordance with New Testament teaching. Baptisms performed in sects or cults such as Jehovah's Witnesses or Unitarians are not deemed valid. Those that have taken place in the Roman Catholic Church, on the other hand, are valid.

This latter judgment does not sit well with some members of the CRCNA whose background includes a fairly recent break with Roman Catholicism in Central or South America. For them, the Augustinian and Calvinist position on this is a real stretch. They have so learned to condemn a church saddled with colonialist history, superstitions, and "unbiblical" teaching that they cannot find it in their heart to see any validity in baptisms there, including their own. They are faced, of course, with brothers and sisters whose break with Roman Catholicism occurred some 450 years

321

ago. The inevitable tension was palpable when the denomination debated Q&A 80 of the Heidelberg Catechism on the Mass and the Lord's Supper and chose, ultimately, to make its last three paragraphs (complete with the phrase "condemnable idolatry") "no longer confessionally binding" on its members (*Acts of Synod, 2006*, pp. 710-11). It was obvious in this debate that the validity of Roman Catholic baptism was, for many, a perfectly parallel issue. Nonetheless, the official stance of the CRCNA has not been revised.

An Authorized Agent

Note also that the baptism must have been administered by "someone authorized by that denomination." Those who baptize must be ordained or formally authorized to perform the sacrament on behalf of a recognized denomination or group of churches. Regular ordination makes good sense.

A lady in our congregation, several years ago, made profession of faith and was received into membership under my predecessor's ministry. She had grown up LDS (Mormon) and had been baptized by that group as a teenager. She was not baptized when she joined the CRC. Recently, she has asked the LDS church to remove her name from their membership records. They have notified her that to do so "cancels the effects of your baptism and confirmation and you will lose those blessings." Here are my questions:

1. Is LDS baptism trinitarian? I know that it is not in substance, but is it in form?
2. Should she have been baptized when she joined the CRC?
3. Is baptism appropriate now? Or is that "rebaptism"?

On the issue of validity of baptism, our Church Order insists on the group being a Christian denomination (Article 58). The Church of the Latter Day Saints is not, in form and in substance, no matter what the exact nature of their beliefs about the Trinity and their practices that issue forth from those beliefs. Hence we do not consider this person's baptism to be valid, and, as you suggest, she should have been baptized upon receiving membership. She cannot be said to be rebaptized when the first one is deemed to be invalid. The baptism you are now called upon to perform will give her all the assurance she may have lost in whole or in part when she read their threat about "losing the blessings."

It would help greatly if you would explain our regulation on the validity of baptism to the congregation prior to the baptism occurring because this is a very unusual case and because it will allay any fears on the part of anyone that we are now introducing rebaptism into our circles.

A person desiring to join our church showed me a document certifying that he was baptized soon after his birth in an intensive care unit by a Roman Catholic nurse who feared he was about to die. Is this baptism considered to be valid in our denomination?

Yes, Article 58 clearly takes that position. The fact is that the Roman Catholic Church authorizes nurses and other medical professionals to do this if they are truly acting in good faith. They are not ordained, it is true, but they do have formal authorization.

There was a time when churches would "conditionally baptize" such individuals. They would administer the baptism with the statement "If, in fact, you have not been baptized, or your previous baptism is not valid, I baptize you into the name of the Father . . ." In reflecting on that practice, I have come to the conclusion that I could not permit myself to do that. In this case, I would rather hold the baptism to be valid and rejoice with the person involved and the congregation that God keeps his promises to us. That's my take on it. I'll let you decide on yours.

III. The Task and Activities of the Church

Article 59

a. Members by baptism shall be admitted to the Lord's Supper upon a public profession of their faith in Christ with the use of a prescribed form. Before the profession of faith the consistory shall ensure that there be an appropriate examination concerning their motives, faith, and life. Their membership shall be designated as "confessing member." The names of those who are to be admitted to the Lord's Supper shall be announced to the congregation for approval at least one Sunday before the public profession of faith.

b. Confessing members who have reached the age of eighteen and who have made a commitment to the creeds of the Christian Reformed Church and the responsibilities of adult membership in the church shall be accorded the full rights and privileges of such membership.

c. Confessing members coming from other Christian Reformed congregations shall be admitted to communicant membership upon the presentation of certificates of membership attesting their soundness in doctrine and life.

d. Confessing members coming from churches in ecclesiastical fellowship shall be admitted to communicant membership upon presentation of certificates or statements of membership after the consistory has satisfied itself concerning the doctrine and conduct of the members. Persons coming from other denominations shall be admitted to communicant membership only after the consistory has examined them concerning doctrine and conduct. The consistory shall determine in each case whether to admit them directly or by public reaffirmation or profession of faith. Their names shall be announced to the congregation for approval.

In the CRCNA, children who have received the sacrament of infant baptism are not considered to be "non-members," "half-members," or "members-in-waiting." They are full members. We call them "baptized members." They have been incorporated into the body of Christ and, by way of their baptism, marked as members of the visible church. It is just that they have not yet been able to understand the church's creeds, let alone assent to them, and have not yet reached the age of maturity that would allow them to assume all the members' responsibilities. With the assistance of the nurturing ministry of the congregation they are led to make a public profession of faith and thus become "confessing" or "communicant" members.

Public Profession

Note that this *public* profession of faith is made before the church and the world (Matt. 10:32; 1 Tim. 6:12). It is done liturgically, meaning that it is done in the presence of the Lord and his people as we worship. That is why Article 59 is still classified under the subheading of "Worship Services." It is also why the first sentence uses the language of "admission to the Lord's Supper." "Communicant members" and "confessing members" are one and the same, and because they are one and the same, this commentator's personal preference for the reading of Article 59 was and remains:

a. Members by baptism shall be admitted to the Lord's Supper upon ***an age-appropriate*** public profession of their

325

faith in Christ with the use of a prescribed form. Before the profession of faith the consistory shall ensure that there *is* an appropriate examination concerning their motives, faith, and life. Their membership shall be designated as "*communicant* member." . . .

b. *Communicant* members who have reached the age of eighteen and who have made a commitment to the creeds of the Christian Reformed Church and the responsibilities of adult membership in the church shall be accorded the full rights and privileges of such membership. Their membership shall be designated as "*confessing* member."

Children at Communion

For some time the CRCNA has struggled with whether or not to permit the participation of children at the Lord's Supper and, if so, exactly how. Previously the matter was relatively simple and the Church Order fairly straightforward: there were "baptized members" and "confessing" or "communicant members." The transition from one to the other came at the time of "profession of faith" that (roughly) coincided with high school graduation, the beginning of adulthood. In other words, a person baptized as an infant was deemed to experience only one rite of passage in a lifetime of Christian pilgrimage. Once that rite of passage had occurred, the person was admitted to the table of the Lord.

That accepted understanding began to change when in 1984 Classis Rocky Mountain presented an overture requesting a synodical study of "covenant children partaking of the Lord's Supper." Synod obliged (*Acts of Synod, 1984*, p. 651). Initial reports of the study committee all agreed that the CRCNA should be moving in the direction of such early participation. At the same time, they differed on the precise way of admission to communion and how elders might then maintain their traditional role of oversight of those partaking (*Agenda for Synod, 1986*, pp. 346-70). Two years later, Synod 1988 did officially move towards children's participation, insisted on their making a public profession prior to it, and indicated that this profession of faith is "not necessarily an acceptance of adult responsibilities." That would occur "at age eighteen or as granted by the Articles of Incorporation" (*Acts of Synod, 1988*, pp. 558-60). Thus, the denomination was now considering two rites of passage: an earlier profession and assumption of member responsibilities at age eighteen.

A new committee appointed in 1991 to "clarify the requirement of public profession" approached Synod 1995 with a split decision on the basic principles involved. Half of this committee wanted to retain the requirement of profession of faith (suggesting "baptized members," "communicant members," and "corporate members" as the way to proceed). The other half argued that the "communal faith" of the church—not an individual profession—was sufficient to warrant the admission of baptized children, suggesting "baptized membership" and "corporate membership" as the two pertinent classifications, with all baptized members welcome at the table by virtue of their baptism (*Agenda for Synod, 1995*, pp. 265-303). In response, synod chose the former understanding but then specified that there be only "baptized members" and "confessing members" with no new category for those who accept adult responsibilities. This synod approved the current reading of Article 59, made arrangements for an "age-appropriate" liturgical form for early public profession, and asked congregations to "devise an appropriate means for securing a commitment to the creeds . . . and to the responsibilities of adult membership" upon reaching the age of eighteen (*Acts of Synod, 1995*, pp. 712-21, 762-63).

The confusion actually increased exponentially at Synods 2006 and 2007. Upon receiving a new overture to "study"—merely study—the possibility of admitting children by reason of their baptism alone, Synod 2006 made the unexpected and historic decision to "allow for the admission of all baptized members to the Lord's Supper on the basis of their full membership in the covenant community." It also directed the Board of Trustees to appoint a "task force" to implement this change (*Acts of Synod, 2006*, p. 730). With the approval of Synod 2007, this task force was named the "Faith Formation Committee." It was asked to engage churches in an ongoing dialogue, formulate proposals along the way, report to four synods (2008-2011) on an interim basis, and present a final report to Synod 2012. On the other hand, Synod 2007 took back the step taken a year earlier, refusing to "grant to congregations the freedom to admit all baptized members to the Lord's table" (*Acts of Synod, 2007*, pp. 653-57). The ongoing work of the Faith Formation Committee can be followed on the denominational website. In the meantime, the decisions of Synod 1995 on children at the table and its adopted reading of Article 59 remain in force.

Faith: Personal and Communal

Ever since 1995, the first sentence of Article 59a has the pronoun "their" before "faith in Christ." Persons are said to be making a "public profession of *their* faith" (*Acts of Synod, 1995*, p. 762). There is nothing necessarily wrong with that language. Surely such faith ought to be theirs, personally, deep within their hearts. But the strength of earlier versions that simply said "*a* public profession" or "*the* public profession of Christ" can easily be lost on us. The truth is that "*their* faith" is always also to be the church's faith, our corporate faith as it lives within the church as a whole and comes to expression in its creeds and confessions, the faith received and currently "entrusted to [our] care" (1 Tim. 6:20-21). The first goal of an "examination concerning their motives, faith, and life" may well be to hear and celebrate the expression of an individual's heartfelt faith. But the second goal, as important, is to test the individual expression to see if it truly matches the expression of our corporate faith. It is therefore a wonderful and "saving" corrective that Article 59a ends with "before *the* public profession of faith."

Announcements of Membership Status and Silent Approbation

The reason for announcements of public professions of faith to the congregation is to give all confessing members the opportunity to present possible objections to the consistory. Any such objections would have to be based on solid grounds of which the consistory had no knowledge. They are rare, as one would imagine, and if they are not forthcoming, the congregation has at least had the opportunity to give what is sometimes called its "silent approbation." It should be understood that the consistory makes the final judgment in any case, even if there are objections. Current members do not have veto power.

We were privileged to lead a thirty-four-year-old to Christ. It took two years of persistent discipling. We've asked our consistory to accept him as a member, but the elders refused. It seems that in our tradition converts must first master the Canons of Dort before we're willing to welcome them into our fellowship. How can this be?

Faith and intellect are not contradictory human functions. Faith begins with an expression as simple and straightforward as the Apostles' Creed. But then it seeks further understanding. Indeed, it is

---

forced to seek further understanding because the reality of different denominations with different confessions is bound to dawn upon a convert sooner or later. To be a member of a church requires a healthy agreement with the substance of the additional creeds and confessions.

On the other hand, such understanding and agreement always occur in a process, not as a bolt of lightning. We recognize this when dealing with our young people, prescribing as we do a lengthy process of church education and discipleship commensurate with their slow but steady development. It is my belief that such steady development must be celebrated on more than the two traditional occasions at the ends of the continuum, namely, baptism and profession of faith. What is true for young people is also true for those newly converted. Discipleship takes time.

My preference is for an intermediate "affirmation of baptism." A twelve-year-old and a thirty-four-year-old new to the Christian faith may well be far enough along to tell the church that they believe in Christ as their Lord and Savior, and do so even if they haven't yet encountered the teachings of the Canons of Dort. We should give them the opportunity to profess a simple faith (the heart of the matter) and welcome them to the communion table (though not to all privileges of full membership), provided they, for their part, make a commitment to become more fully acquainted with the church's expressions of faith, developed over many centuries, in order to make them their own. Then, when our creeds have been explained and grasped, at least in their substance, they could make a public profession of faith and assume all the privileges and responsibilities of confessing membership. Indeed, even this would still not constitute a "graduation" from the school of faith. It's just another rite of passage in the continually sharpening and deepening that faith seeks—a lifetime exercise. For the person you discipled, a heartfelt acceptance to the Canons of Dort can come into view at a later time.

A number of years ago we began admitting children to the Lord's Supper by way of an (earlier) profession of faith. The oldest of these will soon turn eighteen. If we understand the synodical decisions on this correctly, we should now be asking her to take on the full

responsibilities of church membership and express agreement to the creeds and confessions of the church. Is this to be done in public worship? We are confused.

As far as I can tell, you are correct in your understanding of synodical decisions. Synod 1995 made it quite clear that each congregation should "devise an appropriate means for securing a commitment to the creeds . . . and to the responsibilities of adult membership in the local congregation from confessing members who, having attained the age of eighteen, have not yet made such a commitment." Upon reflection, this statement does seem puzzling. It seems out of tune with our traditional denominational ethos. It wasn't that long ago that our synods would prescribe complete liturgies for all local congregations and insist on the exclusive use of approved liturgical forms. Adaptations weren't even allowed until 1994 and even now they must be consistent with denominational guidelines. How, then, do we explain this local "devising" of "appropriate means"?

The only answer that makes sense to me is that synod has deliberately refused to dictate that this rite of passage be observed in the worship setting. If you then ask what "appropriate means" it might have had in mind, let me suggest the following three possibilities, each of them likely to be preceded by a consistory interview:

- a bulletin announcement that, in the presence of the consistory, these persons have assented to the creeds and accepted all the responsibilities of church membership;

- a "public welcoming" during a worship service in the same way we welcome new members to our community, perhaps by standing and being recognized; or

- a full-fledged "worship event" where people reaffirm their faith in Christ, assent to the creeds and confessions, and accept full membership responsibilities.

In my judgment, this rite of passage is, indeed, very significant, and I would opt for the third alternative. One's confession is directed to the Lord of the church, not just to us and to the world. A now more informed public profession of faith and the solemn acceptance

330

of membership obligations belong in the midst of the covenant community at worship. A solemn liturgical event gives us a wonderful opportunity for their "commissioning" and, at the same time, a congregational pledge of prayerful support in the course of that person's pilgrimage.

Good professor, we have a retired minister of another denomination wanting to join our church as a member, but he wants dual membership! He needs to keep his membership in his own denomination because of pension and benefits, and so on, but he really wants to become a member here. What are we to do with his request?

Well, good colleague, in a perfect world we'd all have our membership in one local church and, by virtue of that, in the one and only universal Christian church. In the real world, however, our membership is in one local church with a specific denominational affiliation. You cannot be a member of two of these. You can only be a member of one. This person cannot have his cake and eat it too.

My advice to your consistory would be that you accept this person into your fellowship as an "associate member." You may define the rights and privileges of such membership as you wish, be it within certain limits. In my congregation, for example, one that worships on the campus of Calvin College and Calvin Theological Seminary, students may opt for associate membership. For us, that means they are not entitled to vote nor serve in office nor present children for baptism without the consent of their home church (doesn't happen often, obviously), but they are given appropriate pastoral care when needed, partake of the Lord's Supper, participate in adult education groups, and sometimes assist in the church's educational, diaconal, or missionary task. They are formally recognized in our church directory. There is a synodically approved precedent for this. Students at Calvin College and Seminary were permitted to place themselves in the temporary care of a local consistory, presenting a "Student Certificate" while retaining their membership in the home church (*Acts of Synod, 1953*, pp. 149-52).

I am confused about procedures regarding membership transfers, both in and out, and especially on what an "attestation" might be. Can you help?

In the case of a transfer to another congregation within the CRCNA, the consistory of the sending church sends records of the person's membership to the consistory of the receiving church and, along with that, also "attests" to that person's "soundness in doctrine and life" (Article 59c). The same holds true if the transfer is to a congregation within a denomination with which the CRCNA is in ecclesiastical fellowship (see Article 49). If the move is to another Christian denomination beyond that inner circle, the person is formally deemed to be resigning in order to join a congregation within that denomination and is given a "statement of membership" containing appropriate data (when baptized, when communicant, names of baptized children, and so on, but no "attestation"). The person presents this statement to the receiving church.

Transfers from another CRCNA congregation are handled by way of receipt of the membership record and accompanying attestation (Article 59c). These are usually accepted by the consistory during or after a brief introductory visit, and the names of those "directly admitted" are announced to the congregation. The same holds true, once again, if the transfer is from a congregation with which the CRCNA is in ecclesiastical fellowship. If the transfer is from another Christian church, the consistory decides on one of three options after an appropriate examination: direct admission, public reaffirmation (often done, for example, after a period of nominal or inactive membership in a church), or a profession of faith (Article 59d). The latter is done to indicate a commitment to Reformed confessions while testifying to a living faith in Christ.

I should add that it is possible some churches do not actually take up direct contact with the consistory of the receiving church but instead submit the membership record and/or the attestation via the members themselves. That, for example, is the practice of the Reformed Church in America and of the Protestant Church in the Netherlands, to name just two.

What do we do if a resignation is not just from our congregation alone but, God forbid, from the worldwide church as a whole?

This most often occurs while elders are disciplining a person for persistently "refusing to heed their admonition." What we used to do in such cases is refuse to acquiesce in the resignation. We would insist that a willful withdrawal from the body of Christ is, in and of itself, a grievous sin. If the person persisted, we would apply formal steps of discipline and eventually even exclude or excommunicate that person.

This may be theologically sound procedure, but it is definitely also illegal. For example, in 1989, an Oklahoma court, in the case of Guinn *v.* Church of Christ of Collinsville, declared that the church "had no right to discipline Marian Guinn after her withdrawal." It ruled that "just as freedom to worship is protected by the First Amendment, so also is the liberty to recede from one's religious allegiance." If we do anything of that nature, we risk lawsuits or "torts of outrage," as they are sometimes called. So now we acquiesce, announce it, solicit prayer, and send the person a final pastoral letter with an urgent plea to return to active membership in our congregation or, for that matter, any other congregation. It is our "final sermon." And that's our job—just to proclaim the Word.

May members of a lodge be admitted as members of the church?

No, they may not. The issue was cited as one reason for withdrawing from the RCA in 1857. The CRCNA still holds that "there is an irreconcilable conflict between the teachings and practices of the lodge and biblical Christianity, and that therefore simultaneous membership in the lodge and in the church of Jesus Christ is incompatible and contrary to Scripture" (*Acts of Synod, 1974*, p. 58).

Synod 1977 did recognize "the fact that some who take an oath or pledge in order to become members of a lodge do so without any conscious commitment to the religious positions which are basic to the lodge," but, in spite of that recognition, still insisted on a "formal termination" of lodge membership before admission to church membership, be it with the "compassionate and pastoral" assistance of the elders (*Acts of Synod, 1977*, pp. 104-05).

III. The Task and Activities of the Church

Article 60

The Lord's Supper shall be administered at least once every three months in a manner conducive to building up the body of Christ and in keeping with the teachings of God's Word.

The CRCNA makes provision for two—and only two—sacraments. As we have seen, baptism is the "initiatory" sacrament. In its administration, the congregation celebrates entries into the visible church. It is a family-of-God event in which believers are assured of the rich promises of his Word and focused once again on the root of their salvation. The Lord's Supper, on the other hand, is the "nourishing" sacrament. Christ "has ordained and instituted" it continually "to nourish and sustain those who are already born again and ingrafted into his family: his church" (Belgic Confession, Article 35). Like baptism, it is a sacrament *of the church*. It is celebrated "in the public worship service" (Article 55) and there alone. There are no private administrations.

The Signs of Bread and Wine

The Supper is celebrated in the New Testament church at the command of Christ: "Do this in remembrance of me" (Luke 22:19-20; 1 Cor. 11:23-25). Saved sinners are fed, nourished, and sustained. The believer, in company with all, experiences that "as surely as I see with my eyes the bread of the Lord broken for me and the cup given to me, so surely his body was offered and broken for me and his blood poured out for me on the cross." And as surely as the believer tastes "the bread and cup of the Lord . . . so surely he nourishes and refreshes my soul for eternal life with his crucified body and poured-out blood" (Q&A 75, Heidelberg Catechism). The bread and the wine are not changed into the actual body and blood of Christ, even though we call it the body and blood of Christ "in keeping with the nature and language of sacraments" (Q&A 78, Heidelberg Catechism). Even so, Christ, breaking bread and holding the cup, said to his disciples: "This *is* my body" and "This *is* my blood" (Matt. 26:26-28). As our confession states:

> we do not go wrong when we say that what is eaten is Christ's own natural body and what is drunk is his own blood—but the manner in which we eat it is not by the mouth but by the Spirit, through faith (Belgic Confession, Article 35).

Supervision of Attendance

Admission to the table of the Lord requires nothing more (and nothing less) than a truly repentant heart that trustingly looks to Christ for forgiveness, grace, and renewal of life (Q&A 81, Heidelberg Catechism). Our obedience to God's will, the "holiness" of the church we confess, to whatever extent it is present in our lives, is not our own accomplishment that buys us a ticket to the table. It is nothing but a gift of grace. Nor should a false humility keep us from sitting at the table. We need no spectacular measure of spiritual life, supposedly experienced only by a few, in order to participate in communion. The practice of avoiding the celebration for these reasons, not uncommon in the Reformed tradition, is in fact a regrettable decline of our Savior's gracious invitation, a disobedient response to his call to "do this." At the same time, a hypocritical pretense that we have arrived is unacceptable. Elders are to "exclude" those who are "unbelieving and ungodly" (Q&A 82, Heidelberg Catechism), meaning that they lack the required repentance and trust. This, especially, is why the CRCNA insists on supervision by elders of a local church.

Supervision of Administration

Further, the elders are to see to it that the Supper is administered "in a manner conducive to building up the body of Christ and in keeping with the teachings of God's Word." Such proper administration would include adequate preparation that speaks the words of Scripture, the use of actual bread and wine, liturgy that faithfully reflects the biblical record, and supervision that makes it clear that unbelievers are not invited to the table. Any other aspects of the mode or manner of taking communion are considered "indifferent," and subject to local custom or choice.

Frequency of Celebration

Finally, the article provides that this sacrament "shall be administered at least once every three months." Note especially the words *at least*, which make clear that this is a minimum requirement not meant to limit the frequency of celebration. As Synod 1971 put it, "the present wording not only allows for, but encourages, the churches to celebrate the supper more often than once every three months" (*Acts of Synod, 1971*, p. 131).

Early Christians "broke bread" daily (Acts 2:46), but already within the New Testament we find evidence of *weekly* celebration—on the Lord's Day, the day of Jesus' resurrection (Acts 20:7). This is the apostolic tradition, and it became the permanent pattern until the time of the Reformation.

The need to reeducate believers concerning communion, to free the sacrament of superstition and other unbiblical elements, and to restore the proclamation of the Word to its rightful position in the liturgy led Zwingli and other Reformers to advocate *quarterly* or *monthly* celebration. John Calvin fought to reinstate the apostolic tradition of weekly communion but failed to gain the approval of civil authorities who had control at that time. A persistent rationalism in the Netherlands fostered the notion that indoctrination was as important as the actual celebration of the Supper. Thus the sacrament came to be accompanied by lengthy liturgical forms and even "preparatory" and "applicatory" sermons—an affair spanning two or three weeks of worship. This lack of simplicity virtually guaranteed a practice that appears to be more Zwinglian than Calvinist, yet persists in most Reformed churches to this day.

Clearly, the *at least* in this article leaves room for a return to apostolic tradition. But the fact remains that "while the present rule *permits* the churches to be biblical, it *teaches* them otherwise" (Classis Hudson, Overture 1, *Acts of Synod, 1968*, p. 555). Since the Lord intends this food and drink to sustain us on our daily pilgrimage, perhaps our congregations should try gradually to increase the frequency of celebration, just as Synod 1971 intended.

What's your opinion—communion once a week, once a month, or four times a year? And why so?

I believe a once-a-month pattern with additional celebrations on Christian holidays (especially Good Friday, Easter, and Pentecost—not Christmas, please) is just about right. What is crucial is that the sacrament must receive its rightful place as further "sign and seal" of God's Word proclaimed. It should not outweigh the sermon. Ironically it tends to do just that when it is a special event occurring in our liturgy a mere four times a year.

How appropriate is it to postpone the celebration of communion? At the moment there is not a good spirit in our congregation. For one thing there are many rumors making the rounds; some involve the pastor and his conduct. It seems so hypocritical to me that we would gather around the table of the Lord as if there isn't a cloud in the sky. How strictly are we to interpret the requirement of the Church Order that we must celebrate communion at least four times a year?

I know how you feel. Once, in the frustration of dealing with some longstanding family feuds, not to mention my youthful ministerial enthusiasm, I made a very similar proposal to our council on a communion Sunday morning—on the spur of the moment. I felt that our celebration must be genuine—that it would be a sacrilege to carry on as if nothing were wrong within our fellowship. The elders agreed. But then, after the service, I was confronted by an older member, a widow, who posed a question that still haunts me to this day: "What right do you elders have to withhold this sacrament from me? It is the only time that I feel really close to both my Savior and my dear husband."

Yes, I believe that it is within the province of a council to postpone the celebration of communion scheduled for a certain date

---

if the circumstances of the congregation are such that it cannot be celebrated in a good and uplifting spirit. Such a postponement could have a shock effect and thus serve a disciplinary purpose. Be warned, however, based on my experience and further reflection, that it is not necessarily wise to withhold the means of grace from a congregation that now, perhaps more than ever, requires a large measure of grace for healing and reconciliation to take place. Will you stop preaching also, since it wouldn't be fitting to hear the Word in the pretense that all is well? To put it another way, no person and no congregation comes to the table of the Lord by reason of perfect righteousness or obedience. We come by reason of Christ's gracious invitation to all who, in their unrighteousness, are willing to confess it and firmly believe that it is all forgiven. We celebrate in spite of our failures, and we do so in order that the Spirit of God might lead us to greater sanctification.

Does the Church Order no longer specify how elders are to supervise attendance at the Lord's Supper? It seems to me that many of our churches have in fact gone to a system of open communion.

The Church Order never did specify precisely how this is to be done. The matter falls under what our current Article 60 calls "a manner conducive to building up the body of Christ and in keeping with the teachings of God's Word." While it is clear from Scripture and Church Order that communion is for those who believe in the Lord Jesus Christ as Savior and Lord and are members in good standing of a Christian church, it is purely our tradition that has governed the manner in which supervision is carried out. Christian Reformed practices I have experienced include the following:

- All visitors must report to the consistory prior to the worship service whenever the Lord's Supper is celebrated and assure the elders that they are eligible.

- All visitors are "screened" by a welcoming elder, their names recorded, then announced as visitors to the table, either to the consistory alone or to the entire congregation—if the latter, with or without names mentioned.

- All visitors are urged to sign a card that indicates in simple terms who is welcome to the table.

- During the worship service the minister reads the prescribed forms, which include warnings about "eating and drinking judgment to yourself" if you are not right with God or neighbor.

- During the worship service the minister announces who is invited (those who believe in Christ as Lord and Savior and typically take communion in their home church), and the consistory leaves it to any visitors in attendance to decide whether or not they will celebrate communion.

- No such announcements are made; it is all left to the discretion of those who attend.

The last, for all intents and purposes, is an "open communion" practice that should not be found among us. I prefer the second to last plus the elders' watchful eyes.

A fifty-five-year-old man, nominally Roman Catholic, recently divorced and now married to a longstanding member of our congregation, often comes with his wife to services and has indicated a desire to celebrate communion with us. Is this permissible?

The only criterion for deciding whether a visitor is welcome at the table is that he or she be a confessing member in good standing in a Christian church. If he can testify to that with integrity and you accept that testimony, he should be welcomed. By the way, I assume you have spoken to this man about joining your church. Is your community discipling him, especially considering the fact that you speak of him as a "nominal" Roman Catholic? Is a non-attending or rarely attending member of the Roman Catholic Church "in good standing"?

We should take careful note, also, that the opposite is not true. A Christian Reformed person should not feel welcome at the celebration of the mass in a Roman Catholic setting even if the local priest or worship leader invites that person. The truth is that the *official* position of the Roman Catholic Church is different from ours. It does not allow non-Roman Catholic Christians at the table of the Lord. So I do not partake, when I attend a mass, and refuse to do so as a matter of principle. I do wish that the Roman Catholic Church would change its stance.

III. The Task and Activities of the Church

Article 61

The public prayers in the worship service shall include adoration, confession, thanksgiving, supplication, and intercession.

Articles 61 and 62 on public prayers and offerings (respectively) are included as the last two regulations regarding "Worship Services." The congregation, after all, is "to hear God's Word, to receive the sacraments, to engage in praise and prayer, and to present gifts of gratitude" (Article 51a).

What is remarkable about this article is that it is truly minimal in its approach. It just spells out five dimensions that need to characterize the content of prayers spoken in the congregation's weekly worship.

Article 61 was entirely new in the Revised Church Order formally adopted in 1965 and appeared there without any precedent for it in the tradition. The study committee that introduced it acknowledged this fact but stated that "by common consent" congregational prayers are "such an important part in our worship services that it is well for the Church Order to indicate the chief elements of a normal congregational prayer" (*Acts of Synod, 1961*, p. 449).

The record is not clear exactly why the words "for all Christendom and all men" were added at the very end as a further comment on the nature of the "intercession" (*Acts of Synod, 1962*, p. 92). Perhaps it was meant to reflect the apostle Paul's instructions (e.g. Gal. 6:10; Eph. 6:18). The phrase was later changed to "for all Christendom and all humanity" (*Acts of Synod, 2007*, pp. 610-12) and then deleted entirely after a study committee characterized it as "archaic and problematic" (*Acts of Synod, 2010*, p. 905).

Is there any way to get our pastor to shorten the congregational prayer? He's much too sensitive to be approached about it, but my two middle-school kids just groan.

I hear you. It's not a healthy situation. It reminds me of the minister who typically used the prayer to announce in glorious detail exactly what the doctors did to his parishioners during their most recent surgeries. It took forever. He quit doing that only when Matilda fainted and, after the service, discovered it was his graphic description of George's procedure that did her in.

If the prayer is intolerably long, I suggest you speak to your elder about it and ask that it be raised as a concern at an opportune time during the next consistory meeting. Even sensitive ministers must be held accountable.

III. The Task and Activities of the Church

Article 62

> Offerings for benevolence shall be received regularly in the worship services. Offerings also shall be received for other ministries of the congregation and the joint ministries of the churches.

Alms and Offerings

The earliest of Reformed Church Orders going back to the sixteenth century held that deacons were "to collect alms and other contributions of charity" and "diligently to distribute the same" to the needy (English translation of Article 25, Church Order of 1914). In crafting a revised Church Order during the early 1960s, the study committee wanted to place this matter explicitly within the section on the "Task and Activities of the Church." Thus, having earlier referred to them as "gifts of gratitude" (Article 51), the Church Order of 1965 now also featured a new Article 62: "In the worship services Christian alms shall be received regularly" (*Acts of Synod, 1965*, p. 77). The intent is clear. Worship is not complete without the giving of alms, and alms are most appropriately given as we worship. That is probably also why the word *alms* was chosen. It signifies what is offered to the Lord in the service of worship even though it will be used to show mercy to others.

The intent in the language used was not changed when Synods 1987 and 1988 proposed and adopted the new wording presented above. The reference now is to "offerings for benevolence" and to their regular reception "in the worship services." I take that to mean, among other things, that something is lost when we present these offerings by having them automatically deducted from our checking account once a month.

Ministry Shares

The second sentence is an important addition. It was added to indicate that "our stewardship also includes other causes" and to clarify "for affiliating groups the way the CRC finances its ministries" (*Acts of Synod, 1987*, p. 623; *1988*, p. 553). The denomination employs a "ministry share" system whereby every member contributes toward classical and denominational agencies to carry on the church's varied ministries: home and world mission efforts, world relief, educational agencies, publication of materials, and the like. The huge advantage of this system of ministry shares (earlier referred to as "assessments" or "quotas") is that they are solicited without cost. Congregations allow their classis and synod to stipulate the amounts per annum, trusting that these assemblies will act responsibly in the exercise of regional and denominational stewardship. They then add what is required for "local needs" such as the minister's salary, local outreach, and the maintenance of a building in finalizing the annual budget. In this system, members do not receive constant solicitations like they do for any other charitable organization. The savings are immense.

In principle, this "ministry share" system flows out of the CRCNA's ecclesiology: its understanding of local congregations as one with the regional and (bi)national church. Members contribute toward the part-time worship leader's pay as well as campus ministries in the USA and Canada. They support outreach projects in their own church and community as well as contributing toward sending missionaries abroad. The exercise of stewardship, in other words, has worldwide dimensions, just as it did in New Testament times (2 Cor. 8, 9). Believers function as members of the church at home and of the "church universal."

There is a long history of debate on whether this is indeed the appropriate way to collect the contributions of God's people. Often, these debates centered on whether broader assemblies even have the right to "tax" the local church. The answer has been and remains that all the churches have covenanted together to be engaged in local, regional, (bi)national, and worldwide ministries. These churches have therefore allowed both classis and synod to make provision for and regulate those ministries that lie beyond their own jurisdiction (see Articles 73-77). The process accommodates orderly budgeting at every level of denominational life for the ministries essential to our calling.

Does the CRC have an official position on tithing?

As far as I know, the CRCNA has never taken an official position on tithing. My sense is that most churches promote good stewardship and seek to instill that in their parishioners. Sometimes "tithing texts" from Scripture serve a useful purpose in sermonizing on that topic. I am leery of those who smile or wink as they declare it to be an outdated Old Testament practice. Christ did not abolish the law, he fulfilled it. So tithing can still be a guide for us. Some can't meet it. Others may be called to exceed it.

My own congregation currently decides that an average contribution of 5 percent of our adjusted gross income is a "guideline" to which we commit ourselves for the general fund (including classical and denominational ministry shares) and a further 2 percent of that income for the local Christian education fund (to help those who can't afford the entire cost). Then there are our "mission commitments" to agencies with a special connection to our congregation, and these are adopted in amounts rather than percentages of our income. In addition, of course, there are our "alms," our "freely given" collections from week to week for various causes as determined by our deacons. Remember also that there are personal causes in the lives of each member/family that are also "counted" as contributions to the kingdom of God even if not given to the church as an institution, such as sponsoring a child with World Vision, and the like. I suspect that without resorting to a "tithing law," a fair number contribute much more than a tithe and that this tends to make up for those who aren't able to reach that level. It's called communal stewardship.

Some people who stood at the brink of not paying denominational ministry shares have been pushed over the edge by recent synodical

decisions. How must we respond, in council, when a member of the congregation informs us by letter that he will withhold all or a select amount of ministry shares?

Article 85 of the Church Order insists that "no church shall in any way lord it over another church." This emphasis is a precious part of our Reformed heritage. But it obviously refers to an abuse of authority, not to the rightful wielding of authority on the part of, say, the synod of the denomination as it carries out the work that churches have covenanted to do together. Such work includes classical and denominational missions and world relief, ministers' pension plans, educational and liturgical publications, and theological training for future ministers of the Word. Once the congregations have voluntarily bound themselves to the keeping of this covenant, revisions or changes in our practice can only come about by way of synodical decision.

At Synod 1990, the Dutton, Michigan, CRC (then still part of our denomination) argued by way of an overture that "the quota [later called "ministry share"] is only a recommended amount suggested as a guideline for giving and is not binding on the individual, church, or classis" (*Acts of Synod, 1990*, pp. 704-06). Every officebearer should read synod's response to this argument very carefully. Some statements follow:

> Quotas are not a compulsory payment to be made, but rather they are an amount agreed upon by the churches in covenant with one another. Synod 1972 stated, "The synod annually, *as the broadest official representative body of our denomination*, reviews all agency programs and approves budgets and quotas for these programs."

> Dutton CRC does not explain in what way its conscience is bound by synod with regard to quotas, particularly given the fact that synod is a representative body.

> 2 Corinthians 9:7 does not warrant a refusal to give what one has agreed to give (cf. 2 Corinthians 9:5).

Synod 1985 clearly outlined the route to take if conscience is burdened by actions or policies of agencies supported by quotas: "If there is an objection to the positions of a particular agency, such objections should be addressed to the agency involved and/or synod by way of the assemblies, rather than withholding denominational quotas" (*Acts of Synod, 1985*, p. 811).

If members sincerely believe that a synodical decision is contrary to the Word of God and/or the Reformed confessions, there are appropriate avenues for expressing such belief (see Articles 28-31). A statement to the council that ministry shares will be withheld is not an appropriate avenue.

We must understand that in our ecclesiastical covenant the entire congregation resolves that it will support our denominational efforts. If one member or family decides not to contribute, others must make up the difference in order to make good on the congregation's pledge. This is also true on the classical level. If one church decides not to contribute toward any or all causes, the other churches will be forced to make up the difference. Our covenanting together demands this in our chosen form of church government.

In other words, and to speak quite bluntly, if the practice of withholding ministry shares is undertaken in order to put pressure on a particular agency so that it might change its ways (a sort of lobbying tactic quite foreign to the Reformed tradition), people should realize that, in principle at least, the actual target turns out to be not the agency but fellow believers.

If I were a member of your council, I would argue for the following response to the member's request: to inform him or her that withholding ministry shares is an extreme measure that will put greater pressure on brothers and sisters of the same congregation and classis than on synodical agencies, and that the council is reluctant to grant such requests for reasons other than complete financial inability. I would also urge the member involved to follow the more appropriate and traditionally recognized avenue of appeal and/or protest according to synodical regulations.

III. The Task and Activities of the Church

Article 63

a. Each church shall minister to its youth—and to the youth in the community who participate—by nurturing their personal faith and trust in Jesus Christ as Savior and Lord, by preparing them to profess their faith publicly, and by equipping them to assume their Christian responsibilities in the church and in the world. This nurturing ministry shall include receiving them in love, praying for them, instructing them in the faith, and encouraging and sustaining them in the fellowship of believers.

b. Each church shall instruct the youth in the Scriptures and in the creeds and the confessions of the church, especially the Heidelberg Catechism. This instruction shall be supervised by the consistory.

The heading "Faith Nurture" that covers Articles 63 and 64 refers to the second "task and activity of the church." We are to share our commitment with future generations and all who enter the community. Article 63 focuses on "the youth," while Article 64 focuses on "adult education."

Nurturing Faith

In the early nineties, this heading replaced the one originally used in the Revised Church Order of 1965: "Catechetical Instruction." A similar adjustment was made to the article itself. From 1965 until 1993, this was the reading:

> Each church shall instruct its youth—and others who are interested—in the teaching of the Scriptures as formulated in the creeds of the church, in order to prepare them to profess their faith publicly and to assume their Christian responsibilities in the church and in the world.

Comparing this to the current reading above, we observe that the latter part of "preparing" for public profession and assumption of responsibilities has been retained. But the beginning of the article, like the heading, has seen significant change. Before 1993, the emphasis was on "instruction" and "teaching." Since that time, the church is said to have the task of "ministering," "nurturing," and "equipping." The words "instruct" and "instruction" are still there, in the second part of the article, but the focus has shifted from an understanding of doctrine to the act of believing itself (see *Acts of Synod, 1992*, p. 664). This recognizes the important truth that the educational task of the institutional church differs from, say, that of the school. While content of the creeds remains important, "especially the Heidelberg Catechism," the primary task of the church is to lay before youth the joys and challenges of living as citizens of the kingdom of God. It can never "give" or "induce" faith to its younger members and other "youth in the community." Only the Holy Spirit can do that. But the church can and must present Christ's claim on their life, proclaim the Scriptures to them in a more intimate educational setting, reveal the content of our faith as expressed in our creeds, and faithfully nurture whatever measure of faith the Spirit has graciously given them.

Given my previously discussed preference, it is a wonderful corrective that Article 63a ends with the words "instructing them in *the* faith" (italics mine). In the same way we once received it, we seek to pass on the church's faith to future generations.

Shaping the Identity of the Baptized

We must never underestimate the importance of shaping our children's and young people's identity for what it is at its root: that of baptized children of God. As we have seen, the water of baptism does nothing in and of itself, but it does speak loudly of God's promises to us and his subsequent claim on our lives. While family life and Christian day school education play an important role, our so-called "three-legged stool" must include an active church education program as well. For this reason, the CRCNA has traditionally been very strong in supporting a specific denominational agency (currently called Faith Alive Christian Resources) to provide our churches with sound curricula and helpful teaching aids. The aim is to help all baptized members live out their identity in a manner consistent with God-given entry into the visible church.

Agents of the Nurturing Task

There was a time when ministers of the Word were the only teachers in the church's educational program. In the CRCNA, that time is long gone. Although most ministers still have some teaching responsibilities, churches have tended to seek and train volunteers for this task or hire youth pastors or directors of church education who coordinate the efforts of a host of volunteers. Children's worship, Sunday school, vacation Bible school, boys' and girls' clubs, as well as weekly catechism classes all have their part in fulfilling the congregation's educational task. This may well be a healthy development. In this article, the Church Order does not specify exactly who must be involved in the faith nurture of the youth. It only insists that the "instruction shall be *supervised* by the consistory" (italics mine). It is a good reminder, however, that in Article 12 ministers of the Word are still mandated to "catechize the youth, and train members for Christian service" (Article 12).

My husband says I'm far too sensitive about this, but I think it's just awful that teachers and leaders in our church's education programs are rarely thought about, let alone encouraged and thanked for their mammoth responsibilities. Do you have a "read" on what our churches generally do to be a bit more considerate?

I'm going to leave your husband out of this. I hope you understand. But I agree that the attention paid to these people in your congregation is probably on the stingy side. It used to upset me greatly that the names of all leaders and helpers were printed in a church bulletin issued during the first week of September and that this constituted all that was ever revealed about them, let alone said to them in public. Consistories can do better than this.

I'm happy to say that in my congregation we have a formal commissioning of teachers, leaders, and children every fall, which takes place during the morning worship service. Among other things, the teachers indicate their allegiance to the church's creeds and confessions. That alone is a vast improvement of having them make no promises at all, don't you think? More to your point, teachers are publicly recognized, prayed for, and quite visible to all so they can continually be encouraged all season long. Children are publicly called upon to accept these folks as their mentors and teachers, and they too make a commitment to participate gladly and willingly. When summer is near, these same teachers and leaders and all the members of the Education Committee are asked to stand during morning worship and thanked for their indispensable service to our young people and to us all.

Do you have any ideas to improve attendance at catechism classes? It's getting really bad where I go to church.

I do. The idea that comes to mind is called an adult education program. We can *tell* our children to attend until we're blue in the face. It is so much more effective to *show* our children that all of us need instruction in the faith, to actually model that for them, perhaps even to join them on one evening a week or have a Sunday morning segment devoted to an educational program for all members, young and old.

III. The Task and Activities of the Church

Article 64

a. Each church shall minister to its adult members so as to increase their knowledge of the Lord Jesus, to nurture a mature faith in Christ, and to encourage and sustain them in the fellowship of believers.

b. Each church shall provide opportunities for continued instruction of adult members. This instruction shall be supervised by the consistory.

It seems odd and terribly inconsistent with a rich tradition of catechetical instruction, but it wasn't until the early 1990s that adult education was first mentioned in the Church Order of the CRCNA. An entirely new article regulating ministry to "adult members" was proposed by a "Committee to Study Youth and Young-Adult Ministry" in 1991 (*Acts of Synod, 1991*, pp. 737-44)—truly a stroke of genius—and formally adopted two years later (*Acts of Synod, 1993*, p. 578). For decades, if not centuries, the "public profession of faith" referred to in Article 59 appears to have functioned as a "graduation exercise." Adult education beyond that event seems to have been thought of as an optional luxury instead of what it truly is: a vital ingredient of a healthy Christian life.

Adult education need not be limited to a study of Scripture, creeds, and confessions. It is entirely possible that church members could truly benefit from, say, a communal exploration of our calling as citizens from a Christian perspective. We need to be delivered from simplistic approaches to the problems we face as a country, a state, a province, a city, a town. Spending time carefully weighing our responsibilities in this regard before the face of God is just one of the many ways adult education can be conceived.

Our church recently decided to shift all educational activities to a Wednesday evening. The main argument is that Sunday must remain dedicated to worship and not feature the clutter of additional Sunday school, adult education, catechism instruction, and so on. The trouble is that the church is now in competition with high school sports events, private piano instruction, and the like. It looks to me like we're losing that battle.

I actually have a great deal of sympathy for doing what your church has done. I have colleagues who used to bemoan the fact that the church could only carve one hour out of our busy weekly schedules— on a Sunday morning. But I also have colleagues who were upset that the church's commitment to an educational weeknight was largely ignored by day schools and other groups and thus fell into disrepair. In other words, the scheduling of these activities is so terribly dependent on the specific communities in which we live. That's probably why the Church Order leaves all of this to the judgment of the local consistory. But I will say this much: having entire families, young and old, come for instruction on one and the same weeknight is a powerful motivator for our children. They can see for themselves that adults are passionate about growing in their faith.

III. The Task and Activities of the Church

Article 65

> The officebearers of the church shall extend pastoral care to all members of the congregation and to others whenever possible. Home visitation and other methods, such as spiritual mentorship and personal contact, shall be used to encourage them to live by faith, restore those who err in doctrine or life, and comfort and assist those experiencing adversity.

The third "task" or "activity" of the church is that of "pastoral care." This heading covers the content of Articles 65 through 72—much more than what we usually understand these words to mean. It is not merely the professional counseling of client parishioners. The Church Order intends to cover all that is done to "encourage," "restore," "comfort and assist," and to raise issues relating to membership records, transfers, lapsing, as well as the church's role in marriages, funerals, and even Christian day school education. Pastoral care is the exercise of shepherding God's people in the entirety of their lives.

Agents of Pastoral Care

Although most of this points to the office of elder, all officebearers are to be involved in this exercise. Ministers, ministry associates, and deacons are to be engaged in it as well, each according to their particular office. Ministers, for example, have the proclamation of the Word of God as their central calling. As we read in a provision of the Convent of Wesel, 1568 (II.13), such proclamation is not only a public ministry from a pulpit but a private one to be exercised through the minister's meaningful presence in the lives of the believers. Deacons have the task of preparing God's people to live as obedient stewards of all they have received and as prophetic believers in a world full of greed and injustice. Their exercise of "pastoral care" involves what Article 25c designates as "words of biblical encouragement and testimony which assure the unity of word and deed."

Home Visitation

Home visitation or "family visiting," as it is sometimes called, is one of the methods used to encourage, restore, comfort, and assist (*Acts of Synod, 2010*, pp. 905-06). In the CRCNA, it has been understood to be a specific activity carried out by the elders of the church on a yearly basis. As it was often traditionally practiced, it became an outdated formality that even discouraged real spiritual conversation. Today, we see it as just one mode of shepherding, an important one, but still just one of a number of methods used to be "Christ's presence" in believers' lives. This is a welcome change.

The sixteenth century Reformers meant to deliver the medieval church from the notion that believers were there for the benefit of the clergy, not vice versa. John Calvin's indignation was not so much that there were, in fact, bishops, cardinals, and a pope. It was, rather, that these dignitaries were not functioning as true pastors: equipping the people "for works of service, so that the body of Christ may be built up until we all reach unity in the faith and in the knowledge of the Son of God and become mature, attaining to the whole measure of the fullness of Christ" (Eph. 4:12-13). They were shepherds who were feeding *on* their sheep (Jer. 23:1-4) instead of following the good Shepherd who feeds them (John 10:11-18). Elders who go on family visits must be aware that their task is not to measure the effectiveness of the church's ministry (though that might be broached briefly) but, rather, to build up, comfort, and encourage believers in their daily life before the Lord. Similarly, home visitation on the part of the minister can be an extension of proclamation of the Word and, for deacons, a way to encourage stewardship and a passion for justice and righteousness in our world.

Restoration of the Erring

"Restoring those who err in doctrine or life" is the other side of the same coin. It is patient and persistent pastoral care towards those who err in hope of true repentance and return to the ways of the Lord. It is possible—necessary, even—to view the entire fourth section of the Church Order (Articles 78-84) on "The Admonition and Discipline of the Church" as a further description of this difficult but vital task.

Comfort and Assistance

"Comforting and assisting those experiencing adversity" is an obvious part of shepherding. Precisely at the occasion of a serious illness or bereavement members truly experience what it means that their officebearers are Christ-representatives. People may not pay much attention to the meditation at a wedding, but they surely internalize the preacher's every word at a funeral. It is a marvelous privilege for ministers and elders to be "invited" into believers' lives especially at unique moments of joy, grief, and vulnerability.

Confidentiality

Finally, we note that all pastoral care must necessarily observe rules of confidentiality. A vow to that effect must be made at the time of all ordinations. While individual elders must sometimes share pertinent matters with other members of the consistory, these items should be kept to a minimum, and whatever is said at that meeting remains between four walls. Finally, there are civil laws that may compel officebearers to report certain things to appropriate authorities: fairly clear evidence of child abuse, for example, or knowledge that persons may be a serious threat to others or themselves. All other communications are privileged and must be "held inviolate" (*Acts of Synod, 1988*, p. 535). Not doing so ultimately makes true pastoral care impossible.

Is there a guide for home visitation?

I know of nothing official. I have seen some models: our seminary published one in a *CTS in Focus* segment (Fall, 1989), a document used by Covenant CRC of Edmonton, Alberta. Louis Tamminga has helpful material in a pamphlet called *So You've Been Asked To . . . Make Visits* (1999, 2008) and *The Elder's Handbook* (2009), both published by Faith Alive Christian Resources. I have come to believe that pastoral conversation is an art form, and congregations should always be looking for people who have that gift and are willing to develop it. Above all, remember the goal: people are to be comforted, restored, helped, and encouraged in their life of faith.

I am happily married, but I feel uncomfortable visiting a young widow in her home, even if I am joined by another elder. Is there no other way?

There surely is. If there are no women elders who can be asked to do this, I suggest you take your wife and this parishioner out for a lovely little dinner at a local restaurant or invite her to a small group meeting at your home with a few other well-chosen members of your district.

III. The Task and Activities of the Church

Article 66

a. Confessing members who move to another Christian Reformed church or to a church in ecclesiastical fellowship are entitled to a certificate, issued by the council, concerning their doctrine and life. When such certificates of membership are requested, they shall ordinarily be mailed to the church of their new residence.

b. Members by baptism who move to another Christian Reformed church or to a church in ecclesiastical fellowship shall upon proper request be granted a certificate of baptism, to which such notations as are necessary shall be attached. Such certificates shall ordinarily be mailed to the church of their new residence.

c. Ecclesiastical certificates shall be signed by the president and clerk of the council.

The certificate spoken of in this article has also been referred to as an "attestation." The council of one church attests to that of another that a person is active in the life of the church, sound in doctrine, and faithful in the Christian life. We might call it a "recommendation for membership" from one group of elders to another, or, for that matter, a request to take over the exercise of pastoral care.

In view of the fact that not all churches in the CRCNA accept "early professions" and permit children to participate in the Lord's Supper, councils are obliged to note for the receiving church whether "confessing members have assented to the creeds . . . and accepted the responsibilities of adult membership" (Supplement, Article 66a).

Certificates or attestations are sent to the receiving council only when that church is within the denomination or is in ecclesiastical fellowship with the CRCNA. If a member moves to a Christian church beyond those boundaries, the council does not attest to life and doctrine. In fact, it sends nothing to the receiving church at all. It considers the request to be a resignation of membership, one in which it acquiesces. It does that without much difficulty because the person is leaving a congregation, not the body of Christ in general. The council provides the transferring member with a "statement of membership" indicating only the facts: date of baptism, date of public profession, length of membership, and so on. The member, not the council, then presents that document to the receiving church.

It stands to reason that the consistory also makes appropriate announcements in case of transfers out, possible resignations as members, or declaration of lapsed membership. The announcement typically says that the consistory has approved the transfer, has declared the membership lapsed, or "acquiesced in" a resignation. If the resignation occurs in order for persons to become members in another Christian church, we consider it, like a transfer, to be a "happy" resignation and the announcement usually ends with best wishes within their new church home. If it occurs for more regrettable reasons, of course, it ends without such. Typically, consistories are not at liberty to reveal any more than the fact of acquiescence in the withdrawal.

May the certificate issued by one council and sent to another also include comments or "mild concerns" about these members that we might want to pass along?

As a rule, no, I don't think so. There is the matter of confidentiality. Breaking confidence by passing along comments of whatever kind quickly means people won't trust you with their stories. If, however, the members are currently under formal discipline, this should obviously

---

be noted. No details or explanation beyond the lack of repentance that led to the discipline must be given, unless the members have waived the confidentiality requirement in writing (see Supplement, Articles 78-84). The receiving elders can then deal with whatever these members themselves may wish to share.

As Article 66b says, appropriate "notations" may be necessary for members by baptism who have not made a public profession of faith. This might be an explanation as to why a fairly mature adult has not yet been admitted to communicant membership and what the elders have done to encourage it. It's the better part of wisdom to clear such a notation with the member involved, assuming we're dealing with a comprehending child or an adult.

We recently received the transfer papers of a husband and wife who were said to be "separated and in counseling to try and save their marriage." When we visited them, it became clear that the husband had already decided on pursuing the divorce. The wife has not abandoned the process and is still hopeful. Our elders decided to receive her as a member, but not the husband. We informed the "sending council" of our action and that council, in turn, wrote us and said that they had transferred both and would not agree to "take him back." Do they have the right to refuse?

Synod 1936 decided that "a member having requested his consistory to give him a testimony as to his membership remains a member of his church until his letter of membership has been accepted by the consistory of the church with which he desires to affiliate himself" (*Acts of Synod, 1936*, p. 51). I don't know of a more recent synodical decision. In other words, a consistory has the right to refuse acceptance of a person as member for good and necessary reasons. Such reasons must be clearly communicated to the consistory of the "sending" church. If there is disagreement it is possible, I suppose, to appeal to a broader assembly for resolution. In the meantime, however, that person is not a member of the "receiving" church.

The "sending" council does have other options. It could take appropriate disciplinary steps and continue to work with the husband as an "erring" member. It could even ask the council of the "receiving" church for assistance, especially when long distances are involved. If it believes that such discipline is not warranted (in spite of his most recent decision), it may acquiesce in a resignation, on paper or otherwise, and issue him a statement of membership to take to another church. If he is informed that he is still considered a member in good standing, yet does not attend and claims to be worshiping elsewhere, his membership could be declared lapsed as provided for in the Supplement to Article 67 of the Church Order.

III. The Task and Activities of the Church

Article 67

Members who move to localities where there is no Christian Reformed church and no church in ecclesiastical fellowship may, upon their request, either retain their membership in the church of their former residence, or have their certificates sent to the nearest Christian Reformed church.

Retaining Membership When Moving Away

This article was first adopted as a new feature in the revised Church Order of 1965. It is particularly relevant in our mobile society and should be carefully observed. As we noted with respect to a request for an infant baptism by a couple from Georgia (see commentary at Article 56), failure to clarify membership status when someone moves away can have unpleasant consequences. The article's intent is to respect a person's conviction about principles and practices unique to a Reformed denomination. A person baptized as an infant and now a confessing member moves to another place, for instance, chooses to attend an evangelical church, but resists formally joining it because said church insists on an adult baptism as a condition of

361

membership. The CRCNA allows that person to retain formal membership in one of its congregations. In doing so, it protects that person's right to deny the legitimacy of rebaptism.

Declaring Membership Lapsed

This article has also become a depository for rules regarding declaration of lapsed membership. These are found in the Supplement to Article 67. Declaring membership lapsed becomes an option for a consistory when, for a period of two years after departure, members have taken no actions to resolve the membership issue. This means that even after "serious attempts" on the part of the consistory, they are not requesting a transfer, are not exercising their right to retain CRCNA membership, and are not resigning. The consistory has the right to note this inaction, judge that a "meaningful church relationship is no longer possible," and declare the membership lapsed. This is not to be done in the case of temporary absence such as military service, university attendance, or non-permanent job relocation. The declaration is announced to the member and to the congregation.

Indeed, Synod 1976 went a giant step further by adding rules that deal with persons who have not moved away at all but have become "inactive" in their church. If members simply do not attend and do not support their congregation for as long as two years, the consistory may declare that their membership has lapsed. The "membership has become meaningless," and making this declaration is "simply an acknowledgment of an already existing rupture between the member and the congregation" (*Acts of Synod, 1976*, p. 25). But this may only be done if persons "claim to be still committed to the Christian faith," "claim to be worshiping elsewhere," and consistories "are not aware of any public sin requiring discipline." These conditions in the Supplement to the article are essential. If these persons are drifting away from the faith, not worshiping anywhere, or in any other way "straying" from an obedient Christian life, their home church consistories may well be the "last link" they have to the body of Christ. In that case, elders must do their very best to apply appropriate discipline for what is often referred to as their "neglecting the means of grace" in hope of repentance and return.

We are having a discussion at our church about how to define "inactive membership." I looked at the *Manual of CRC Government* and saw that Synod 1998 had something new to say about this. Can you point me in the right direction? What I'm remembering is a statement that inactive membership should not be indefinite in duration. Can you get back to me on this by Tuesday, 6 p.m.? Our elders meet that night.

What you're remembering is certainly the natural consequence of what was adopted in 1998. The agenda contained the following note: "Continued encouragement of inactive members and, if necessary, their final removal from membership should follow Church Order procedures" (*Agenda for Synod, 1998*, p. 215). The reference is to Article 67's Supplement on lapsed membership as well as Articles 78-81 on admonition and discipline.

Synod 1998 did not create a new category of membership. It adopted the designation of "inactive" as an adjective: inactive baptized membership or inactive confessing membership. It did so only in the context of reporting membership numbers that, among other things, determine a congregation's contribution to ministry shares. We need no longer report nonsupporting members and then expect active members to make up the difference. It's a statement about membership count and related financial matters. But here's the synod's intent: consistories are in no way relieved from the responsibility to address the pastoral issues involved with those who have become inactive. They must address the lack of attendance in one of two ways: faithfully "discipling" those who aren't worshiping anywhere or working toward a declaration of lapsed membership if they're worshiping at some other church.

Please explain the difference between "lapsing" and "erasure."

These two actions are similar in that they are both initiated by the consistory and have the same effect: the removal of members from the rolls of the local church. But that is where the similarity ends.

"Erasure" refers to a disciplinary procedure whereby a baptized member is excluded from the church of Christ (see Article 81a). The term is not found in our current Church Order, nor can it be found in any prior edition of it. It only appeared in questionnaires sent to clerks of CRCNA churches and in the denominational *Yearbook* from 1950, when we expanded statistical information, until 1987, after which time it became an unspecified category under the euphemistic rubric of "Reversions." The term was helpful in that it allowed a clear distinction between two different matters: disciplinary exclusion of confessing members (excommunication) and exclusion of members by baptism who have not made a profession of faith (erasure).

"Lapsing" refers to a nondisciplinary procedure whereby a member (baptized or confessing) is removed from the rolls of a particular congregation because "a meaningful church relationship is no longer possible." The person is not excluded from the church of Christ and the elders do not pass judgment on his or her relationship to the church universal. In fact, this procedure may not be used for a "covenant breaker" in need of restoration. It may be used only if the person "claims to be still committed to the Christian faith," "claims to be worshiping elsewhere," and is not involved in "any public sin requiring discipline." Such a situation arises because the person has found a spiritual home elsewhere and simply has not bothered to transfer papers or regularize membership status. Thus, the membership has lapsed and the consistories so declare. When elders use the "lapsing procedure" for persons who do not meet the three conditions, they wrongly abdicate their disciplinary responsibility—a disservice to the member involved as well as the church as a whole.

III. The Task and Activities of the Church

Article 68

Each church shall keep a complete record of all births, deaths, baptisms, professions of faith, receptions and releases of members, and excommunications and other terminations of membership.

This article speaks for itself. The church must be as meticulous in its record-keeping as any other organization in human society. Statistics gathered annually by the executive director of the CRCNA and printed in the denominational *Yearbook* are helpful for strategic planning, budgeting, and crucial data on how well we're doing, say, in outreach and church planting.

We have a baptized member who has requested her membership be transferred to a Roman Catholic parish. She is getting married there in October to one of its members, and it looks like she is committing to that community. What is the process for that?

This is not, technically speaking, a transfer because she is moving to a congregation outside of the CRCNA and even the wider circle of denominations in ecclesiastical fellowship with it (see Article 66).

We handle this as a member submitting a resignation in order to join, say, St. Paul Roman Catholic Church in Toronto. That is how it is announced to the congregation in the bulletin, typically with a statement wishing her well in her new church home. The member is given a "Statement of Membership" that has nothing more than the facts: has been a member of your church for X number of years and was baptized on this or that date, and so on. There is no "attestation" of sound doctrine and life in this case and the statement is given to the member, not sent to the church she will attend. The member is "released" and encouraged to remain active in the body of Christ.

The Church Order says that an announcement should be made to the congregation informing it of declarations of lapsed memberships (Article 67). Is there a similar requirement for a member who resigns? And must all this be printed in the weekly bulletin?

Yes, council is obligated to let the members of the congregation know of membership changes. This is usually done via the church bulletin, but it can also be done in other ways if that is necessary for purposes of confidentiality: a letter addressed to each and every professing member, an announcement and/or prayer at a worship service or at a congregational meeting. Just as Article 59 requires that the congregation is to be informed when council is admitting a new member, so the congregation should know about membership exit, even though the council has the final say in the decision-making process. I should add that the matter can't be done in a covert way anyhow. You can't spare people's pain over relatives leaving. People do notice changes in the directory. You must deal with their pain in some other way.

III. The Task and Activities of the Church

Article 69

a. Consistories shall instruct and admonish those under their spiritual care to marry only in the Lord.

b. Christian marriages should be solemnized with appropriate admonitions, promises, and prayers, as provided for in the official form. Marriages may be solemnized either in a worship service or in private gatherings of relatives and friends.

c. Ministers shall not solemnize marriages which would be in conflict with the Word of God.

Marrying Only in the Lord

The first and third sections of Article 69 have no precedent in any regulation of the Reformed churches prior to 1965. What regulation there was concerned just the solemnization of marriage, the wedding ceremony, addressed in the middle section of this article. From 1965 on, however, the Church Order significantly broadened that concern and to this day dictates the manner in which ministers and elders must exercise their pastoral care of the congregation as it relates to marriage. Specifically, it is said here, consistories are to "instruct and admonish those under their spiritual care to marry only in the Lord" and not to "solemnize marriages which would be in conflict with the Word of God."

There is a sense, of course, in which the concern of these two sections is fully justified. At a time in our culture when the very institution of marriage is threatened in so many ways, the church is surely called to proclaim relevant biblical teaching and bring it to bear on the lives of its members. At the heart of that teaching in Scripture is the institution of marriage by divine ordinance (Gen. 2:19-24; Eph. 5:21-33), its intended permanence (Matt. 19:3-9; 1 Cor. 7:10-11), and the required faithfulness of the partners to one another (Ex. 20:14; 1 Cor. 7:2).

What is problematic, however, is that this Church Order article severely limits the pastoral care expected of consistories to just the one issue of "marrying only in the Lord." True, it then speaks also of marriages that "would be in conflict with the Word of God," whatever that may be taken to mean, specifically, but there is no additional content given that would take it beyond that single concern.

Presumably, these references are based on Paul's first letter to the Corinthians, in which he reluctantly permitted widows to marry again, but then only if their intended "belong to the Lord" (1 Cor. 7:39). We must observe the context: how these women previously wrestled with becoming Christians while their husbands did not (1 Cor. 7:12-16). Should they divorce them? What if the husband leaves? It stands to reason that Paul would want them to avoid such wrestling if they were minded to marry again. So he tells them to "marry only in the Lord." But this does not touch on the heart of biblical teachings on marriage: its divine institution, intended permanence, and exclusivity in relationship. It is not helpful to go on and then associate this text—as is often done—with yet another in Paul's second letter to the Corinthians, namely, that Christians must not "be yoked together with unbelievers" (2 Cor. 6:14). There Paul is engaged in a general warning against idolatry. That may have some application to the issue of marriage partners, but Paul doesn't specifically mention it.

Biblical Teaching on Marriage

Regardless of how we interpret these passages, it is a mistake to apply only this biblical material to the pastoral care we must offer relative to marriage. The crispness of Article 69's assertions too easily leads to a legalistic bearing that fails to acknowledge the brokenness of our world and the healing balm of Scripture. The reader is therefore referred to a much broader summary of biblical teaching adopted by Synod 1980 that guides the shape of our pastoral care. This, we agreed back then, is what the church is called to do:

1. Emphasize the sovereign claim of God on all of life so that also in the marriage relationship the first consideration is to please God by doing his will.

2. Stress the God-willed permanence of marriage and counsel against violation of the marriage bond.

3. Proclaim that Christian marriage is a relationship in which the grace of God in Christ enables one to live within the unity God demands.

4. Teach that both partners in marriage fail in various ways to keep the covenant they make. Such failure is sin and such sin tends to separate those whom God has joined.

5. Teach that in Christ husbands and wives are called to be reconciled to each other. They are to confess their sins, forgive one another, make restitution, and again live faithfully to their vows to love, honor, and cherish.

6. Teach that we do not possess within ourselves the power to keep covenant. No one is able to keep the promise to be a husband or wife to the other and to love, honor, and cherish no matter what the circumstances of life or what the other does to us or fails to do. Only the powerful grace of God can make each able to keep covenant. Therefore, husband and wife must seek from God what they need in order to be faithful. The church must teach without ambiguity that God will give what each needs in order to keep covenant.

7. Teach that marriage is not an end in itself but finds its fulfillment and ultimate purpose in the family of God, and, therefore, that Christian marriage must pattern itself after the relationship of Christ and his church.

8. Promote a forgiving, sympathetic, and open church fellowship in which concern, compassion, and help can be freely offered and freely received.

9. Challenge the heresies of our day which destroy marriage, e.g., the heresies of selfism, individualism, and humanistic secularism.

Further, when a marriage is in crisis, the church must

1. Communicate hope to those who are losing hope.

2. Exercise a ministry of reconciliation.

3. Develop a corporate ministry of reconciliation.

4. Consider the purpose of discipline.

and, if the marriage ultimately does fail,

1. Continue to minister with special concern for those involved in this traumatic experience.

2. Speak with clarity where sinful conduct is overt and apparent.

3. Understand that marital breakdown and divorce requires pastoral attention which emphasizes repentance, forgiveness, and reconciliation.

4. Exercise formal discipline only when there is disdain for the biblical teachings and when unrepentance is beyond doubt.

5. Maintain within the life and work of the church a place of acceptance and appreciation for those who by divorce are living the single life so that they may experience the vital spiritual, moral, and social support they need (*Acts of Synod, 1980*, pp. 41, 481-83).

Solemnization of Marriage

The second section of Article 69 makes provision for the wedding ceremony. This may take place "either in a worship service or in private gatherings of relatives and friends." The former is rare in our day. It would mean that the council invites the entire congregation to worship and, thus, also to attend the ceremony. The latter is not meant to exclude fellow church members, but it permits full focus on the marriage in a somewhat smaller assembly of guests.

The one who solemnizes a marriage as an agent of the church must do so "with appropriate admonitions, promises, and prayers." While the *Psalter Hymnal* provides an official liturgical form, its use is not required. That is left entirely to the one who officiates. But biblical teaching, vows made before God, and petitions for God's help are mandatory. Ministers usually permit the bride and groom to help shape the wedding service.

We note the assumption of the Church Order, clearly spelled out in the third section of Article 69, that it is the ministers who do the solemnizing. It is indeed an assumption, not an explicit requirement. Civil laws typically speak of ordained ministers of religion receiving the state's authority to unite in marriage, but sometimes they speak more generally of religious leaders in the employ of a Christian denomination or other recognized religious group. In that case, ministry associates in the CRCNA might qualify. In general, those who solemnize marriages in Canada must have a license furnished by the province in which they reside. The Stated Clerk of the classis makes the arrangements. State laws in the United States are more ambiguous and differ from one state to another. Those asked to officiate must know the law of the particular state in which the wedding is held and, if ever in doubt, receive appropriate legal advice that clears the way.

Are ministers obliged to perform weddings whenever they are asked to do so?

No, surely not. Article 69c allows them to make a judgment. In my ministry, I have always consulted with the consistory and, in every case, insisted on receiving its blessing. The need for that was brought home to me when, early in my second charge, a woman called me out of the blue to ask if I would solemnize her marriage. When I inquired how she came upon my number, she said she'd been looking through the yellow pages, choosing the loveliest of church buildings, then calling the respective pastors. My church and I were the third on her list. When I asked when the event was to take place, she said: "Next Saturday." I could not hide my surprise and stuttered back that I was accustomed to providing premarital counseling sessions over a period of at least three months. She, in turn, replied that counseling was not necessary in her case. She had been married three times before. When, having gained some steam, I indicated quite sternly that she, in that case, would surely benefit from the counseling, even more, perhaps, than any "first-timers," she got angry, uttered a profanity ("exactly what this other bleep said too"), and then hung up, presumably to avoid further unpleasant advice. I assume her list had many further alternative locations.

More seriously, it has helped me to remember that there is always an alternative: a justice of the peace, a civil officer, can "do the job." In this respect, it was actually a welcome relief to be a minister in the Netherlands for a while. There every couple is obliged to go to city hall to be officially married before a civil magistrate. A subsequent solemnization in church by a minister of the Word is optional and requested only by those who are truly committed to the Lord and his people.

Ministers are authorized to function as agents of the state only as a matter of convenience. Their being an agent of the church must weigh more heavily.

I am working with a couple who desire to be married before God and his people but refuse to get a marriage license or allow any "state interference" in what they believe is a covenant between a husband and wife and their Lord. I'm not sure how to respond. Can there be a marriage before God without a legal document certifying that relationship? Is a minister an agent of the state or an agent of the church?

From the very beginning, Reformed churches have insisted on the state playing its legitimate role. After modern states finally began to do so in the latter part of the eighteenth century, these churches have continued to respect the state's interest and involvement in marriage and family. They have always acknowledged the mandate God gave to civil government (Matt. 22:15-22) to regulate, say, the legal protections afforded to those who are married "under the law." In North America, the ordained minister of the Word who solemnizes the marriage is an agent of both church and state. It is not an either-or situation.

It seems to me that the position of this couple is closer to an extreme Anabaptist attitude toward government than to what is clearly taught in Romans 13 and confessed in Article 36 of our Belgic Confession. Your solemnizing the marriage under these circumstances could itself result in some form of civil penalty applied to you for not complying with the law. Be sure, therefore, to get some legal advice on this issue as it plays out in your locale. The couple might be sobered by such a legal opinion. It might cause them to reflect on the legality of their own marriage down the road. If they don't face it now, they might be forced to face it with much greater pain involved when issues like legal custody of children or life insurance beneficiary statements come down the pike and they are found, in a court of law, to have never been legally married.

May an unordained person—in this case a theological student—perform a wedding ceremony? The Church Order does speak of "private gatherings" as a legitimate option. Most of us believe, therefore, that the "official acts of the ministry" of Article 53 are not involved in such cases.

I'm afraid I do not share your belief. Although Article 69 refers to "private gatherings," the intent is not to pronounce the wedding ceremony a "family affair" with only a symbolic role for the church. The intent, rather, is to say that a wedding may take place in a worship service, implying that all members of the congregation are expected to attend, or, alternatively, it may take place in a gathering where only those invited by the couple and their families are expected to attend. The Church Order is regulating ecclesiastical matters even when it uses the word "private."

You may be aware that all who solemnize marriages in the provinces of Canada must be licensed to do so. The one officiating must be a justice of the peace or an ordained minister or ministry associate who has received such licensure.

In the United States, the law varies by state. You should take careful note of the law that applies in your area, lest the couple awakens someday to discover that their marriage, though richly blessed, is not legal and never was. Most states do spell out the need for the one officiating to be a "member of the clergy." There are some, however, whose laws are less precise, requiring only, for example, that the person be a "recognized leader" of a church. In that case, it is conceivable that the public authorities do not require ordination. On the other hand, many such states do require that ecclesiastical law be consulted with respect to the definition of a "recognized leader." In the final analysis, I would have to say that our Church Order requires that those who solemnize marriages must be ordained.

In the meantime, of course, there is no law against the student taking part in the ceremony. The meditation, a prayer, a word of encouragement—all of these are fair game. But I would leave soliciting the marriage vows and declaring the couple husband and wife to an ordained officiant.

III. The Task and Activities of the Church

Article 70

Funerals and memorial services within the body of Christ should reflect the confidence of our faith and should be conducted accordingly. Such times provide opportunities to minister love, provide comfort, give instruction, and offer hope to the bereaved.

Early Reformed tradition had only one thing to say about the church's role on the occasion of a member's death: it must not have a role, and its funeral services are to be abolished. For more than a decade after Luther posted his 95 theses, citizens of the city of Strasbourg held no ceremonies of any kind, not in church and not at the grave. Without fanfare, families buried their dead on their own. We know this because the first synod, held in that city in 1533, adopted an early protest against the extremes of these new developments. Even Old Testament patriarchs and early Christians, it said, conducted burials with appropriate dignity and honor. Why should the Reformed do any less?

Church Orders developed in the sixteenth century did not pay heed to the Synod of Strasbourg. From the 1570s to 1940, the pertinent article in the tradition said only that "funeral services shall not be introduced." Synod

1940 of the CRCNA rephrased it with just a tiny reduction in negativity: "Funerals are not ecclesiastical but family affairs, and should be conducted accordingly" (*Acts of Synod, 1940*, p. 38). In the awareness that this reading too is far removed from current practices, Synod 2010 adopted the above version, thereby turning the negative into a positive at last (*Acts of Synod, 2010*, p. 907).

What accounts for this negativity is the Reformers' battle to rid the medieval Roman Catholic Church of customs and superstitions that, in effect, negated the gospel of unmerited grace. The priest spoke prayers over the body of the deceased to reduce time spent in purgatory. Meditations dwelled on the frailty of human flesh and the burden of our sin that leads to death. Village church bells tolled to remind all citizens to join in those prayers and, in the minds of many, to drive away the evil spirits. In some cases, funeral processions circled the cemetery three times to banish any remaining demons. There was no assurance of salvation, no real hope of the gospel in view, no testimony to the open grave of the firstborn of the dead. It was extreme, perhaps, but warranted "iconoclasm": these practices simply had to go in order to steer people back to the grace of Christ.

The new reading adopted in 2010 does not reject what the Reformers rightly sought to do in their reaction, nor does it alter the principle of the earlier article that funerals are family affairs. By using the term "body of Christ," the article points to the positive role of the Christian community (the church as organism). It does not advocate "official worship" or "ecclesiastical funerals" arranged for and determined by the local consistory. Those who lead memorial services and funeral rites must respect the wishes of the bereaved. They will offer assistance. But it is the family—not the institutional church—that has the "final say" in the events of the day. The leaders, however, may appropriately insist on opportunities for the body of Christ to display "the confidence of its faith" and to offer the bereaved its love, comfort, instruction, and hope.

My grandfather is dying. Will it be appropriate for an unordained person to conduct his funeral? We have a retired school principal in our congregation who knows almost everyone in town and is dearly loved. He was my grandfather's best friend. Since we are without a minister, we would like to ask him to provide the leadership. But is that permitted? Or must we ask a neighboring church's pastor who's new and definitely a stranger to most of us?

Thanks for checking with me in what must be a difficult time. When the time comes, by all means ask the principal friend. Funeral or memorial services are not official worship services of the church. They are occasions when families determine how things will go and then invite the rest of the Christian community to be there for them with the gospel's comfort and hope. So when "official" ceremonies are to be held at the funeral home, the church, the family's home, and/or the cemetery, the one who leads need not be ordained.

Does the CRCNA have an official position on cremation?

Not that I'm aware of. Church Order commentators Van Dellen and Monsma acknowledged that the Bible does not forbid the practice of cremation, yet clearly expressed their preference for burial. They based it on the practice of the early church and the testimony of Old and New Testament:

> The patriarchs were buried. God himself buried Moses. Lazarus rested in a grave. Our Lord Himself underwent burial, not burning. . . . On the other hand, many pagan peoples burned the bodies of their dead, and the only instances in which burning is prescribed by God for Israel is in the case of great sinners, as a special condemnation of such sinners on God's part (*The Revised Church Order Commentary* [1967], p. 271).

As far as I know, this preference for burial has never become official teaching.

Personally, I know of many God-fearing Christians who argue for cremation on ecological and other grounds. They are in no way motivated by pagan unbelief in the choice they've made. Since this is truly one of the "indifferent" matters, they have every right to make it. At the same time, I happen to agree with Van Dellen and Monsma that burial is more "expressive of the hope and expectation of the resurrection" (1 Cor. 15:42-44).

III. The Task and Activities of the Church

Article 71

> The council shall diligently encourage the members of the congregation to establish and maintain good Christian schools in which the biblical, Reformed vision of Christ's lordship over all creation is clearly taught. The council shall also urge parents to have their children educated in harmony with this vision according to the demands of the covenant.

The origin of this article can be traced to sixteenth century developments in the Netherlands. Early synods adopted the regulation that "everywhere consistories shall see to it that there are good schoolmasters, who shall not only instruct the children in reading, writing, languages and the liberal arts, but also in godliness and in the Catechism" (*Acts, Synod of Middelburg, 1581*, Article XII, freely translated). Note that the focus is on schoolmasters, not schools. Schools were controlled and supported by the government, a government that openly and publicly chose for a state religion—in this case, Protestantism. Separation of church and state was virtually unknown. Government and church leaders united in their ambition to establish popular education based on sound Christian doctrine. In this context it is important that consistories supervise the quality of schoolmasters and their teaching, not only as independent agencies concerned with people's life of faith, but also as arms of the state.

From Church Control to Parental Control

Given that history, it is understandable that the first Christian elementary schools established by Dutch immigrants in the state of Michigan were parochial schools owned and operated by Christian Reformed congregations. Early on, officebearers established and operated these schools directly. It was not until the last decade of the nineteenth century that the mood began to change. Due in part to Abraham Kuyper's notion of "sphere sovereignty," there was an increasing awareness of the need for separation of church, state, and civic life. Accordingly, the control and operation of these schools were transferred to societies for Christian education. A committee reporting to Synod 1912 suggested the following reading of this article of the Church Order:

> According to the demand of the covenant and Reformed doctrine, parents everywhere are obligated to establish and maintain Christian schools, and consistories are obligated to see to it that the education at these schools lives up to the demand of the covenant.

On the one hand there would then be an emphasis on parental control. On the other, there would be an insistence that consistories continue to supervise. Just two years later, however, synod dropped the latter and simply stated that

> consistories everywhere shall see to it that there are good Christian schools, where the parents have their children instructed according to the demands of the covenant.

"Seeing to it" refers to the promotion of the cause, not that consistories should do the establishing and controlling. In the version of Article 71 in force since 1965, this has become entirely clear.

Demands of the Covenant

It should be noted that the phrase "according to the demands of the covenant," appearing twice in the suggested reading of 1912, is not found in earlier Church Orders of the Reformed churches but appears to be wholly new and perhaps even unique to the CRCNA. The reference is almost certainly to the baptismal promises made by parents at the time of an infant baptism to the effect that they will not only train their children in the Christian faith but also, as the vow once read, "cause them to be instructed in the doctrine of salvation." This reference to doctrine has now shifted to adherence to a "Reformed vision of Christ's lordship over all creation" that should sway parents to send their children to a Christian school.

Principle and Application

As one finds in many evangelical circles today, so also in the CRCNA it was often a negative appraisal of the American or Canadian public school system that colored repeated pleas for a separate educational system. There have always been members, however, who, like their brothers and sisters in the Reformed Church in America, deliberately chose to send their children to a public school. Over the years, the tone of synodical regulation and discipline has become much milder. This is also true in the case of requirements for bearing office in the church. Those nominated and elected to office must favor Christian education, but whether or not they actually send their own children to Christian schools cannot in and of itself determine their eligibility. There is, to give just one example, the phenomenon of home schooling. When the Church Order now says "to have their children educated in harmony with this vision" we are no longer in the category of specifically having to send them to a particular school. The principle is clear, but its application is most often left to the judgment of parents, first of all, and then also to that of local councils, both well within their own realms of authority.

This is not to say that the CRCNA has weakened or drawn back from the principle involved. As recently as 2005, synod adopted a series of recommendations on Christian day schools, including one that left little ambiguity on that score:

> In view of the growing secularization of public schools, the Reformed tradition's long practice of good Christian education is an integral part of our Reformed kingdom witness and mission to our fellow citizens. This is one of our distinctive contributions to the growth of God's kingdom in North America (*Acts of Synod, 2005*, p. 770).

Must officebearers in the CRCNA send their children to Christian day schools?

This is a question that keeps nagging at many a local council in our denomination. It often rises to the surface when new elders and deacons are to be nominated and elected. So many have wonderful gifts to bring, it is said, but they're ruled out of the process without any deliberation simply because of the fact that their children attend a public school.

Article 71 of the Church Order insists that the council must "diligently encourage the members of the congregation to establish and maintain good Christian schools in which the biblical, Reformed vision of Christ's lordship over all creation is clearly taught," and "urge parents to have their children educated in harmony with this vision." It is hard to know how ministers, ministry associates, elders, and deacons who do not support Christian day school education can persuasively and with integrity "encourage" and "urge" members to do these things. So they must certainly embrace the vision. Its specific application is another matter.

A council on which I had the privilege to serve once nominated a person to be an elder who sent his son to public school. We could do this because the child had special needs that Christian schools could not supply. The elder shared the vision of Christ's lordship, but its application was for him no simple matter. He was even willing to bow to legalism, had we chosen to go down that road, but we insisted he could "encourage" and "urge" in good conscience.

What councils cannot do is to nominate people who simply don't share the vision and actually oppose all Christian day school education. That would lead to intolerable tensions. But so, in my experience, did the constant and insistent demand of a "prophetic preacher" I became acquainted with years ago. His sermons frequently insisted that his parishioners establish and maintain a separate Christian school when, in fact, that was totally and demonstrably beyond the resources of the community. When the pressures mounted, the lid finally blew off: an exasperated council went to the classis and requested release from his call. It would have been so much better, I believe, had this preacher focused instead on enriching his congregation's educational programs until such time as resources were sufficient. A significantly enhanced church education curriculum is exactly how the institutional church can still uphold the vision of Christ's lordship over all creation in such a situation.

My recommendation to councils is that they straightforwardly embrace the vision, do what they can in their context to see to its implementation, and studiously avoid the kind of legalism in application, one way or another, that can stifle our fellowship in Christ. As for those who don't share that vision, avoid nominating them as officebearers; instead, seek to disciple them into owning what we hold dear.

Does the CRCNA approve of homeschooling?

The study committee reporting to Synod 2005 recognized homeschooling as a viable option. It indicated that our denomination should "respect the choices these parents make to conduct schooling of the heart and mind at home, with themselves as the prime teachers." It did express reservations about possible unintended negative consequences of homeschooling such as isolation from the civic community, lack of socialization, and so on. And it also asked for respect in return: parents who choose this option should not oppose or even withhold support from a local Christian day school. But at the end of the day, the committee by no means renounced the practice (*Agenda for Synod, 2005*, pp. 415-16). As far as I can tell, subsequent decisions taken by Synod 2005 did not specifically mention homeschooling. We should probably interpret that silence to be an affirmation of what its committee had clearly placed before it for its consideration.

Does the CRCNA support Christian education beyond the high school level?

It most certainly does. The denomination has a long history of supporting Christian colleges and graduate schools including The King's University College (Edmonton, Alberta), Redeemer University College (Ancaster, Ontario), Institute for Christian Studies (Toronto, Ontario), Dordt College (Sioux Center, Iowa), Trinity Christian College (Palos Heights, Illinois), and Kuyper College (Grand Rapids,

Michigan). It also owns and operates Calvin College in Grand Rapids, Michigan. For the issue of denominational control of that college, see the following: *Acts of Synod, 1957*, pp. 39-46, 455-507; *1972*, pp. 59, 626; *1990*, pp. 682-86. In essence, synods have judged that privatization of the institution "may be possible in the future" but that for now it should remain as an agency of the CRCNA. For certain regions, ministry share contributions to Calvin College are reduced to accommodate the applicable area college.

III. The Task and Activities of the Church

Article 72

> The council shall promote and supervise groups within the congregation for the study of God's Word, for prayer, and for the enhancement of fellowship, discipleship, and service.

Article 72 does not intend to cover the church's educational programs. These were treated in Articles 63 and 64 under the heading "Faith Nurture." Here, under the heading "Pastoral Care," the Church Order is referring to voluntary groups within the congregation that gather for purposes of Bible study, prayer, fellowship, discipleship, and service. Prior to Synod 2010, these were referred to as "societies" to cover what in an earlier era were called Men's Societies, Women's Societies, Young People's Societies, and the like. All such groups are intended to nurture and build up the body of Christ. In recent years many congregations have developed small group programs that certainly meet this requirement. Whatever their shape and particular purpose, councils are to supervise them to ensure that their activities are consistent with the church's calling and edifying for those members who choose to participate.

Do you have any idea how Men and Women's Societies started?

In their *Church Order Commentary*, Van Dellen and Monsma suggest that their origin in the churches of the Netherlands involves those churches' own answer to the rise of private gatherings of believers in various homes. These conventicles, as they were sometimes called (and we translate literally), were prominent after the Secession of 1834 and served the useful purpose of building the participants' spiritual life and fellowship with God. On the other hand, according to these authors, they also had a propensity for pietism, for the "individualistic experiential side of Christianity" that tended to suppress the "objective truth as revealed in God's Word." Men's and Women's Societies were encouraged as a church-supervised alternative to these private gatherings.

How is it that we allow our local Young People's Societies, GEMS, and Cadets to be led by a nondenominational organization known, if I recall correctly, as Youth Unlimited?

The current name is Dynamic Youth Ministries, with divisions of Cadets, GEMS, and Youth Unlimited. These divisions are, indeed, parachurch organizations that provide services to our denomination's local groups or societies. Recent synods have characterized them as "denominationally related youth ministries," thereby openly acknowledging that they are not under synodical control. Accordingly, an annual list in the CRCNA *Yearbook* includes them as organizations recommended to our churches for one or more offerings per year.

Your question suggests that our denomination should have greater control of these organizations (as we once did when it was called "Young Calvinist Federation," if I remember correctly) and that we should take more responsibility for denominational services to local ministries. I assume that's where you're coming from.

In my research, I found that Synod 1991 saw fit to establish a standing Youth-Ministry Committee with a mandate, among other things, to supervise the work of youth ministry within the CRCNA and collaborate with Dynamic Youth Ministries as necessary (*Acts of Synod, 1991*, pp. 741-42). In addition, Synod 2002 asked each classis in the CRCNA to "seriously consider the appointment of a classical youth ministry consultant/coordinator to assist the member congregations of classis in their ministry to children, teens, and young adults (*Acts of Synod, 2002*, p. 545). I do not know how classes have responded, but we have certainly been conscious of the need to take these ministries seriously and support and supervise them as best we can.

You didn't tell me, but perhaps your concern was heightened by an action of Synod 2003 to dismiss said Youth-Ministry Committee with thanks for twelve years of work well done. Do take note that the very same synod formed a "Children's and Youth Ministry Council" and a "Children and Youth Advisory Committee" made up of various staff people that were to bring regular reports to the denomination's Board of Trustees (*Acts of Synod, 2003*, pp. 636-38).

In recent years the functions of these two groups have gradually been transitioned into the mandates of denominational staff. As far as I know, this has not been much of a controversial issue. I am informed that relationships between these staff persons and Dynamic Youth Ministries are healthy, complete with helpful consultation and cooperation. But I will grant you that the organizational vacuum at the denominational level created by Synod 2003 may well need to be addressed once again.

III. The Task and Activities of the Church

Article 73

The fourth "task" or "activity" of the church is that of "missions." In obedience to Christ's call (Matt. 28:16-20) and empowered by the outpouring of the Spirit (Acts 2), the well-equipped congregation calls all people it is able to reach into fellowship with its Lord and Savior.

Some people complain that this fourth task seems to be an afterthought. Others argue that the Church Order means to save the best for last, namely, that the congregation's worship, faith nurture, and pastoral care is really all about equipping it for outreach and evangelism. It is probably more helpful to understand the four-part "mission statement" of the third section of the Church Order as an ongoing circular activity, four tasks that are simultaneously pursued and equally significant. It is also critical to understand that the mission of the organized church is not identical to the "outreach" of the church as organism: light shines from lives lived to God's glory. But the hope for the church as institute is that through intentional evangelism those who do turn to Christ in fact join a congregation in worship, receive its nurturing and shepherding ministry, and, in turn, call others to Christ.

The Church Order assumes that all members of the congregation are called to be "witnesses for Christ in word and deed." Even as the Spirit is at work shaping our lives to be more fruitful in the coming of the kingdom of God (Eph. 3:14-19; Phil. 2:12-13), so he calls and empowers us to "go and make disciples of all nations . . . teaching them to obey everything I have commanded you" (Matt. 28:19-20). Second, Article 73 asks the church to send out its laborers to places of great need in God's world. Councils are asked to lead congregations in their support of "home and world missions by their interest, prayers, and gifts."

My impression is that the Christian Reformed Church is a "sleeping giant." It has so much to offer but is so little willing to share it with the rest of the world. What say you?

I'm not going to argue with you. If I remember correctly, the first church I served had an annual budget item of $8,000 for building maintenance and one for the Evangelism Committee amounting to the grand total of $500. There's something wrong with that picture. But I've learned that many do quite well in reaching out. It may not always be reflected in the "members added" statistic. I marvel at how much today's 263,000 members and their predecessors have done and are doing by God's grace in local evangelism projects, church planting, world missions and world relief. Check it out in the *Yearbook*. And yes, of course, we can and must do better. . . .

III. The Task and Activities of the Church

Article 74

a. Each church shall bring the gospel to unbelievers in its own community. This task shall be sponsored and governed by the council. This task may be executed, when conditions warrant, in cooperation with one or more neighboring churches.

b. Each church shall carry on a ministry of mercy. The deacons shall enable the needy under their care to make use of Christian institutions of mercy. They shall confer and cooperate with diaconates of neighboring churches when this is desirable for the proper performance of their task. They may also seek mutual understandings with agencies in their community which are caring for the needy, so that the gifts may be distributed properly.

We note that the CRCNA's missionary task, introduced in Article 73, is now spelled out in terms of the church's three dimensions: local, regional and (bi)national. Article 74 describes the responsibility of the congregation and the council, Article 75 that of the regional church and the classis, and Articles 76 and 77 that of the (bi)national church and the synod; the latter for work, respectively, at home and abroad. What especially merits our attention is that each of these four articles (74-77) gives equal weight to both word and deed, to "the ministry of the gospel" as well as "the ministry of mercy." This well-considered version of the "Missions" section was formally adopted in the late 1980s upon the recommendation of a study committee dealing with "the authority and functions of elders and deacons" (*Acts of Synod, 1987*, pp. 640-42; *1988*, pp. 553-54). In this way the coherence with Article 25 that describes the essence of these offices is abundantly clear.

When Article 74 speaks of "neighboring churches," is it referring to other churches of the CRCNA or, more broadly, of Christian churches in general?

The original focus, apparently, was on the former. In their commentary, Van Dellen and Monsma describe what the Church Order Revision Committee had in mind when this article was first adopted in 1965: "It stands to reason that, here and elsewhere, whenever the Church Order speaks of neighboring churches, the reference is to neighboring Christian Reformed churches." I seriously doubt, however, that it was this committee's intention to restrict cooperation in that fashion.

My guess is that it worked with the appropriate juridical assumption that the Church Order of a particular denomination can only regulate its own churches, not bind those in other church communions. So I harbor the hope that perhaps even back then, but certainly now, our urban congregations will feel free to cooperate, say, with the Lutheran church just down the road in their shared ministry to the inner city. That is certainly the thrust of the parallel diaconal section when it mentions "Christian institutions of mercy" as well as community agencies.

III. The Task and Activities of the Church

Article 75

a. The classes shall, whenever necessary, assist the churches in their local evangelistic programs. The classes themselves may perform this work of evangelism when it is beyond the scope and resources of the local churches. To administer these tasks, each classis shall have a classical home missions committee.

b. The classes shall, whenever necessary, assist the churches in their ministry of mercy. The classes themselves may perform this ministry when it is beyond the scope and resources of the local churches. To administer this task, each classis shall have a classical diaconal committee.

There is a twofold task for broader assemblies. They must provide resources for local churches in their missionary endeavors and, second, be engaged in that task themselves only when such work "is beyond the scope and resources of the local churches." Congregations may at times resent intrusion, but most experience classical and synodical guidance from people with much background and insight as a wonderful catalyst. Churches have much to learn from one another.

This is especially true in a rapidly changing culture where, if it is to be effective, one generation will have to reach out to an unbelieving world in totally different ways than their parents' generation ever dreamed of—apart, of course from the heart of it: bringing God's good news. At the same time, classis may itself run various programs with carefully chosen volunteers from member churches, start and supervise church plants, set up a food bank, or whatever else is just not happening by way of local initiative.

Is it appropriate for a classis to purchase and own property of any kind? Our Classical Home Missions Committee is recommending this for a brand-new suburb.

In general, only local churches own property. A classis, however, may certainly hold property on a temporary basis as a component of a church plant strategy. Presumably the plans of your CHMC are adopted by the assembly as a whole, and classis has the authority to determine classical ministry shares or make other arrangements for this project. Nonetheless, such plans typically provide at the outset that the deed will be transferred to what hopefully will become a vibrant organized congregation within the CRCNA. You might wish to direct people's attention to that if it is not yet explicitly on the table.

III. The Task and Activities of the Church

Article 76

a. Synod shall encourage and assist congregations and classes in their work of evangelism, and shall also carry on such home missions activities as are beyond their scope and resources. To administer these activities synod shall appoint a denominational home missions committee, whose work shall be governed by synodical regulations.

b. Synod shall encourage and assist congregations and classes in their ministry of mercy, and shall carry on such work as is beyond their scope and resources. Synod shall appoint a diaconal committee to administer the denominational ministry of mercy. The work of this committee shall be governed by synodical regulations.

What is true at the level of classis is also true at the level of synod: the broadest assembly must provide resources for the churches in their missionary endeavors and, second, be engaged in that task themselves only when such work "is beyond the scope and resources of the local churches."

Synod does the latter by appointing Boards of Home and World Missions as well as a Board of the Christian Reformed World Relief Committee.

At times, this assembly and its boards have leaned too far in the direction of doing things on their own; at other times, they have missed opportunities by relying too much on congregations and classes to do it all. It is a difficult tension that must be navigated. Serving as a catalyst for congregations brings the denomination's work of missions and mercy closer to the people. A group of volunteers sent by one local congregation to, say, Haiti for deeds of charity and words of hope inspires the entire church. On the other hand, doing mission work in, say, Nigeria or China requires skill and resources that go far beyond what any local church can handle.

What are the "synodical regulations" referred to in Articles 76 and 77, and where can I find them?

The Church Order's main reference here is to the so-called Mission Orders for Home and World Missions as these have been developed in our denominational history. Understanding the development is a science all its own. Synod typically entrusts the details to its Board of Trustees, but also insists on approving basic revisions in mandate. The days when the synod itself would designate specific "fields" like the Navajo territories in the United States or the country of Japan are definitely over. There's too much change and volatility in church and world. On the other hand, our spiritual ancestors have always warned us to be careful that assemblies don't give away the store to administrative boards and committees. If all members of the denomination are to experience ownership of the mission, the church's assemblies should continue to be at the helm.

III. The Task and Activities of the Church

Article 77

a. Synod shall encourage and assist the joint world mission work of the churches by regulating the manner in which this task is to be performed, providing for its support, and encouraging the congregations to call and support missionaries. To administer these activities, synod shall appoint a denominational world missions committee, whose work shall be governed by synodical regulations.

b. The denominational diaconal committee shall extend the ministry of mercy of the congregations and classes worldwide.

Article 77 ends the "Missions" section with the provision that the CRCNA must reach out far beyond its own setting to a world desperately in need of the gospel. There has always been some mission fervor in the denomination. On the other hand, it remains a curiosity that the current Articles 73-77 have little precedent in the Church Order prior to 1965. We hear of home missionaries being appointed as early as 1886. But the earliest provision for them did not appear in the Church Order until 1914. What was adopted that year as Article 51 now reads like a quaint statement as politically incorrect as one can get: "The missionary work of the church among the heathen and among the Jews is regulated by the Synod by means of its Form Mission." The last two words are an English translation of the Dutch *zendingsorde* that might better have been translated as "Mission Order." The statement itself, as well as the lack of precedent prior to 1965, is telling. One can only rejoice that the CRCNA has grown tremendously in its mandate to bring Christ's gospel to the world.

Do you think our missionaries to other lands should have to raise all or at least a certain percentage of their funding on their own?

No, I don't think so. I remain convinced of the genius of the denomination's ministry share system. It is so much more efficient and so wonderfully demonstrative of the character of a truly mission-minded denominational fellowship. These ministry shares, additional "general" contributions, and the "special" gifts of congregations that sponsor specific missionaries should account for 100 percent of the need. Proclaiming the gospel cross-culturally is difficult enough without having to be burdened with a fundraising chore.

Of course, a missionary on home leave may certainly mention the huge need on their own turf or that of others. It's a great "application" after the sermon or the "minute for missions." What I object to is that the very commissioning and the resultant missionaries' endeavors abroad are in whole or in part absolutely dependent on funds they have raised on their own.

Does the Church Order require that a missionary must be called and sent by the local church? Why couldn't synod do this directly?

Great question. I do not have sufficient time on my hands to communicate by email what our denomination wrestled with from 1896 to 1939. The controversy ran deep, including all manner of theological and ecclesiological debate. If you have time and inclination, you may wish to read about it in the fourth chapter of my dissertation, entitled *Equipping the Saints*. It's an interesting episode in our history. No, I do not have a free copy for you. The Hekman Library on Calvin's campus can lend you one.

The answer to your first question is yes. Synod (or the Board of World Missions on its behalf) "appoints the individual churches officially to extend missionary calls" (*Acts of Synod, 1939*, pp. 90, 191-95). These calls are extended only to those whom it is appointing (not those whom the congregations might choose). This respects synod's right to carry on the mission work that is beyond the scope and resources of the individual congregation(s), but also honors the principle that only a local congregation calls persons to an office (Article 4).

IV. The Admonition and Discipline of the Church

The first section of the Church Order dealt with the *who* of the institutional church: they are its leaders, given by Christ "to equip his people for works of service, so that the body of Christ may be built up until we all reach unity in the faith and in the knowledge of the Son of God and become mature, attaining to the whole measure of the fullness of Christ" (Eph. 4:12-13). The second section dealt with the *how* of the institutional church: officebearers do their work in mutual accountability and in recognition and pursuit of the unity of the body by way of the assemblies. The third section dealt with the *what* of the institutional church: worship, faith nurture, pastoral care, and missions.

This fourth section deals with the *what* of the institutional church when worship, faith nurture, and pastoral care do not have their desired effect.

It has often been debated whether there should even be a fourth section of the Church Order. Wouldn't it be healthier to include admonition and discipline in the tasks of proclamation and pastoral care? Would it not remove some of the "negative" thoughts about the disciplinary process if it didn't receive separate treatment? As we noted with respect to Article 65, isn't "restoring those who err" a matter of a patient and persistent pastoral approach?

That people reject "urgent appeals aimed at remorse and repentance" is a result we wish would not occur, but it does. When it does, it is important that the church has processes in place to deal with such hardness of heart. That officebearers would abuse their position of power and betray the trust placed in them for their own purposes is flagrantly at odds with what we associate with our godly leaders, but the fact is that it happens. And when it does, it is important that the church has processes in place to remove them from office and leadership positions. We cannot escape the fact that a redeemed church lives in a fallen world where the mysterious power of sin still infects the body of Christ.

IV. The Admonition and Discipline of the Church

Article 78

The purpose of admonition and discipline is to restore those who err to faithful obedience to God and full fellowship with the congregation, to maintain the holiness of the church, and thus to uphold God's honor.

The church must uphold boundaries. The purity of the church is at stake. When we confess it to be holy, we say that it was set apart from the world to be uniquely in Christ. That's the ideal. In reality, we also know that its behavior is not always in tune with the holiness that is the gift and calling of the church. Unpleasant as it may be, sometimes we must codify the unthinkable.

For many, the very terms *admonition* and *church discipline* have a negative tone. In part, that is because we live in an age of rampant individualism. People resent unwanted intrusion into their lives. But it is also because there are numerous examples of discipline gone sour—approaches by elders that appeared to be more punitive than restorative, more hypocritical than genuinely caring. It doesn't have to be that way.

It is revealing that by changing just one letter in the word *discipline* we have the word *discipling*. This is precisely what the fourth part of the Christian Reformed Church Order is all about: discipling people into the Christian faith and the Christian life. It is internal evangelism. The Scriptures repeatedly speak of the need for this. After all, "the Lord disciplines those he loves" (Heb. 12:6).

It is for this reason that the Heidelberg Catechism refers to church discipline as a key for opening and closing the kingdom of heaven (Lord's Day 31). Formal exclusion or excommunication is nothing but a final public and urgent sermon aimed at those who turn against Christ's claim on their lives. Church discipline is proclamation of the Word of God with restoration, not exclusion, as a final goal. But if the response is negative, church discipline is also the removal of pretense that allows the church to approach the erring believer—no longer as a brother or sister in Christ but as one who needs to be evangelized, discipled back into the community. An excommunicant reverts to being a focus of our outreach. Shunning does not have to mean complete disassociation. Rather, it can simply mean not counting those once among us as believers but then calling them to faith and new life in Christ.

A man in our congregation is under the first step of discipline. He is still attending, still involved, and still committed to our church. In our tradition there are only steps that continue to progress toward further sanctions. There aren't really any steps or guidelines for taking someone off discipline or how exactly to restore him. Obviously, we understand there must be signs of repentance, admission of guilt, changed behavior, and so on. But can you offer any advice about how to effectively restore someone?

Note: For an explanation of "steps of discipline" formerly required, please see Article 82.

I assume that this "first step" you've taken is to advise him not to take communion or, perhaps, to pray for him in public without revealing his name, or both. The fact that he is still attending is encouraging. Maybe the time has not yet come to pursue a "second step"—approaching the classis for permission to mention his name. Maybe there's already a hint of repentance. You seem to be suggesting this yourself and asking for appropriate "steps" of full restoration. Indeed, let's hope the desired repentance is soon quite evident.

The consistory is free to inform the person, given encouraging signs of repentance, that it is lifting the discipline and once again encouraging him to join the congregation at the celebration of the Lord's Supper, the place where we all testify that we are sinners—forgiven and free. There are no multiple steps toward restoration. It's fluid enough for consistory to do whatever seems right.

I hope that helps. If not, reply and I'll try again.

The man's behavior seems OK (he has not repeated his offensive action) but there is still a bit of an edge. For example, he recently asked somewhat cynically whether he'd been "spanked enough," but that is also a bit of his personality. His personality style is not one of humility but he is very egocentric to begin with. How do the elders know when enough is enough?

The elders must make that judgment; no one else can. It's a little like the interview with those who hope to do profession of faith. Can the elders really know what's in their hearts? Ultimately, elders have to accept what they say (with all the personality quirks they may display) as sincere and from the heart. If I were dealing with someone like this person, I'd probably err on the side of accepting changed behavior as a great start and not letting the discipline linger on and on. But I can't make that judgment. The elders must. Blessings!

We have recently engaged in "shunning." By that I mean that we have indicated to this person's immediate family, his closest friends, and the entire congregation that they must abandon all contact. Some people thought this was wrong but we stuck to our guns. Do you approve?

There are a number of Christian denominations that practice shunning and some that even insist on it as the only biblical way. I do not believe that the Scriptures insist on it as a specific instrument of discipline. To count someone "a pagan or a tax collector" (Matt. 18:17) may just mean that when we associate with the erring—as Jesus did!—we make it clear to them that we are no longer at the same table seeking Christ's sanctifying work in our lives. Things have truly changed and we are now together on different terms.

I once had an elder very upset with me because I led the consistory in a process to exclude his son from the fellowship. It was painful for him, I'm sure. But his son had clearly stated for three years running that he did not consider himself a Christian. It was not until I visited his son on two occasions after the exclusion, engaging in Christian apologetics and seeking to disciple him back, that we began to be on speaking terms again. I treated his son as a "pagan," yes, but by placing Christ's claim on his life once more. The excluded must be reached as much as those who never counted themselves as members of the church. Shunning, by definition, does not have that potential for outreach.

IV. The Admonition and Discipline of the Church

Article 79

> a. The members of the church are accountable to one another in their doctrine and life and have the responsibility to encourage and admonish one another in love.
>
> b. The consistory shall instruct and remind the members of the church of their responsibility and foster a spirit of love and openness within the fellowship so that erring members may be led to repentance and reconciliation.

Discipline in an Age of Individualism

The assertion of Article 79a is about as alien to our individualist culture as you can get. It comes with a notion of community that may have been prevalent in prior centuries but has long been abandoned. "A 1978 Gallup poll found that 80 percent of Americans agreed with the statement, 'An individual should arrive at his or her own religious beliefs independent of any churches or synagogues'" (Dean R. Hoge, *Converts, Dropouts, Returnees*, New York: Pilgrim Press, 1981, p. 167). The more traditional and realistic scenario, namely, that people come to their beliefs within a faith tradition and then either adopt it for themselves or depart from it, seems conveniently forgotten. So does the idea that a church might shape persons more than the other way around. In our society, individuals are self-reliant and sovereignly choose with whom they shall associate. They—no one else—decide who will be their friends on Facebook. Article 79, on the other hand, insists that members of the church belong to one another, live in community, and are mutually accountable "in doctrine and life." They are actually called to meddle in the lives of their sisters and brothers in Christ (Matt. 18:15-20).

In the Scriptures, the church is not a voluntary association of believers. That Israel should lose a major battle right after Jericho because one individual disobeyed the Lord is unacceptable in our culture, but instructive for his people today (Josh. 7). Paul warns that "a little yeast leavens the whole batch of dough" (1 Cor. 5:6) and reminds believers that it takes a community to lift an individual out of the doldrums of sin (2 Cor. 2:5-11). All Christians together must "see to it that no one falls short of the grace of God and that no bitter root grows up to cause trouble and defile many" (Heb. 12:15). In other words, self-discipline is a fruit of the Spirit and mutual discipline within the body a true gift of grace: "God disciplines us for our good, that we may share in his holiness" (Heb. 12:10). It is a "mark of the true church" that "it practices church discipline for correcting faults" (Belgic Confession, Article 29).

Preventive Discipline: Fostering Love and Openness

Article 79b is a gentle reminder that preventive discipline is a hundred times more effective than discipline formally applied. Perhaps that is why our Lord instructed us first to approach the one with a fault and have it out "just between the two of you." Only later are we to "tell it to the church" (Matt. 18:15-17).

It is the consistory's solemn obligation to "foster a spirit of love and openness within the fellowship." Elders must care. They must be willing to establish a meaningful bridge of contact that can be crossed when necessary. They must be willing to confront lovingly if that is called for. In the end, they must take steps clearly and specifically focused on leading those in their charge to "repentance and reconciliation." Keeping one another in the footsteps of Christ can be unpleasant but it alone can produce "a harvest of righteousness and peace for those who have been trained by it" (Heb. 12:11).

A spirit of love, caring, and openness rules out a vicious legalism that has Pharisees pointing fingers at the unholy. It also rules out an antinomian attitude toward the church that our society so often promotes: leaving people in a stubborn defiance of the claim of God is not acceptable. We must learn that no one is perfect but that all who are in Christ are to share the task of humbly seeking the renewal he provides in their own lives as well as the lives of others.

Give me a straight answer that's brief and clear: May a consistory ever ask a member to resign, especially in cases where he or she is simply not responsive to its admonitions and further pastoral actions are judged to be fruitless?

No.

Thanks for your delightfully short two-letter answer indicating that a consistory may never ask a member of the congregation to resign. Food for thought. Now let me turn it around and ask for an equally brief answer, if that is possible: May a member of the congregation ever submit a resignation, for example, to avoid formal discipline?

Yes, but only with a view to transferring to another church within the universal body of Christ (see Article 28, Belgic Confession). If it is done to withdraw from that universal body (as it usually is), it is essentially a matter of self-excommunication. Elders will then acquiesce in the resignation with deep regret, but never before the way of effective pastoral contact has been exhausted. Such formal action is announced to the congregation and becomes the occasion for appropriate prayer. That is because it is a very serious matter to ask for the severance of an arm from the body, the severance of a member from the church, the body of Christ.

You indicated in an earlier answer about members resigning that "elders will then acquiesce in the resignation with deep regret, but never before the way of effective pastoral contact has been exhausted." This statement needs to be clarified so as not to leave a consistory open to the kind of lawsuits filed throughout the country in connection with excommunication.

I agree. It is clear from the case of Guinn *v.* Church of Christ of Collinsville (57 U.S.L.W. 2462, Okla. Jan. 17, 1989) that just as "freedom of worship is protected by the First Amendment to the Constitution of the USA, so also is the liberty to recede from one's religious allegiance." In other words, people can resign and make an effective withdrawal and thereafter the church has no right to continue disciplinary proceedings. That's at the heart of lawsuits that allege "invasion of privacy" or "emotional distress."

But you will have noticed that I do not ask consistories to proceed with formal steps of discipline to the point of excommunication, nor do I ask them publicly to specify the sin involved or the particular admonitions that were given. These must remain confidential. What I mean is that elders have the sacred responsibility to point out to the person concerned that, according to the creed voluntarily assented to in his or her profession of faith, withdrawal of membership is a very serious matter indeed and must not be taken lightly. An urgent personal plea for reconsideration is legitimate when the member has agreed to "submit to [the church's] admonition and discipline" (Form for Public Profession of Faith).

If, nonetheless, the member resigns, the only formal move open to the elders is to acquiesce in the resignation with deep regret, and it is this formal move, and that alone, which is communicated to the congregation and prayed about. Specific details about the confidential pastoral and disciplinary process that preceded the resignation are inappropriate at this juncture, not only on legal but even on theological grounds. The public prayer, rather, should focus on how difficult it is for all God's people to remain open to the Spirit's leading.

IV. The Admonition and Discipline of the Church

Article 80

> The consistory shall exercise the authority which Christ has given to his church regarding sins of a public nature or those brought to its attention according to the rule of Matthew 18:15-17.

This is one of the few occasions when the Church Order resolutely applies a biblical text to the job description of ministers and elders. The Gospel of Matthew records Jesus' straightforward insistence on what the disciples are to do in the exercise of their authority. If the stubborn rejection of Christ's claims is public, they are to confront the person for the sake of the church and the integrity of its proclamation. Even if it is private and the lack of repentance is reported, they must investigate and, if necessary, proceed with similar confrontation.

Happily, the Church Order does not supply us with a catalog of private and public sins. To do that would only encourage legalism. On the other hand, the church must address all ethical and doctrinal deviation. It is not that such deviation itself sets the elders' formal disciplinary processes in motion. Rather, it triggers proclamation, a message to the individual that there's sin to address together with a direct appeal to repent. Only when such a message is plainly resisted or ignored does the need for formal steps arise. The primary goal is always a return to the fold, true reconciliation.

One of our congregation's ministry leaders who is not an officebearer was recently accused publicly of sexual molestation. We're not certain just what action ought to be taken.

Your concern must be shown to the alleged victim(s), the congregation, and the leader himself, in that order.

You, as an elder, do not indicate just how this tragic situation came to light. But it is clear to me that churches must provide a safe environment for those who are molested to report the occurrence of such evil acts. Responsibility to the victims includes reporting to civil authorities wherever the law requires it, especially in the case of minors. It also includes seeing to it that the matter is pursued in an appropriate manner within the congregation. Justice must be done.

Sins of a public nature require immediate action. There must not even be an appearance of wavering or inaction, which may suggest to the congregation that the council tolerates this sort of activity within its programs. While restoration of an errant member is one of the main purposes of admonition and discipline, so is maintaining the holiness of the church (Article 78). Members must be protected and councils must go to great lengths to ensure that this is done.

When a transgression comes to light, the lay leader must *immediately* be suspended from ministry activities without prejudice. A thorough investigation must follow. The congregation needs to know that the suspension without prejudice has been imposed and that an investigation has begun. This announcement can be made during the worship service, prior to a pastoral prayer, in which all involved are remembered before God. Personally, I would prefer that it be done at a special congregational meeting called for that purpose or, better yet, that all confessing members be notified by way of a sensitively written pastoral letter from the consistory. It is, after all, a public accusation that requires a public response. But the adjective *public* does not have to include nonmembers who happen to be visiting that morning.

It is for the benefit of the congregation but also of the leader involved that a thorough investigation is conducted and concluded as soon as possible. It is heartily recommended that the consistory receive help in this matter from outside the congregation. Most—if not all—classes in our denomination have formed Safe Church Teams that include professionals in the areas of law, social work, psychology, and the like. There are rules for procedure, and after hearing from both sides and any other witnesses, they owe the consistory a report and recommendations. Classical church visitors may also be called upon if that is deemed desirable. You should carefully consult denominational guidelines readily available from the CRCNA's Safe Church Ministry (www.crcna.org/safechurch).

In the end, however, the consistory must make the final determination with respect to the truth of the allegations and take appropriate actions. Sometimes this may have to await whatever public findings and consequences result from legal prosecution and/ or court rulings, including possible incarceration. The consistory has options: it may lift the suspension without prejudice, it may remove the "without prejudice" designation and continue the suspension for a time, it may permanently deny the person leadership roles, or it may proceed with formal discipline (Article 81).

Throughout the process, however, the consistory must not be in an exclusively judicial mode. It must find a way to "stand by" the accused and provide all the pastoral help and guidance he may need, regardless of whether or not he is guilty of the alleged offense. He may be an errant sheep, even a heinously errant sheep, but he remains within the flock until such time as he, God forbid, must be excluded from the fellowship—not just as a leader (and that may be necessary, usually on a permanent basis) but as a member of Christ's church.

IV. The Admonition and Discipline of the Church

Article 81

a. Members who have sinned in life or doctrine shall be faithfully discipled by the consistory and, if they persist in their sin, shall be excluded from membership in the church of Christ.

b. Members by baptism who have been excluded from membership in the church and who later repent of their sin shall be received again into its fellowship upon public profession of faith.

c. Confessing members who have been excluded from membership in the church shall be received again into its fellowship upon repentance of their sin.

d. The consistory shall inform the congregation and encourage its involvement in both the exclusion from and the readmission to membership.

When it comes to spelling out exactly what formal discipline consists of, the Church Order is, again, remarkably brief. It devotes just one article to the matter and omits much of what had been spelled out in much greater detail in earlier versions. This change from the specific to the general was made by Synod 1991 as it sought to give consistories greater freedom in exact modes of operation (*Acts of Synod, 1991*, pp. 715-23, 768-69). This was especially important as the CRCNA became increasingly diverse.

Steps of Discipline

One example of earlier processes no longer required is the so-called "steps of discipline" approach designed to up the ante of the church's proclamation. The consistory would first invoke silent censure (private advice not to partake of the sacrament). Then, in the face of further resistance to its admonitions, it would proceed with three steps: a public announcement and prayer in worship without the name, a public announcement and prayer in worship with the name, and then a public announcement in worship that an excommunication of the named person will take place at a certain time unless there is repentance. The classis would have to grant permission prior to the second step. The permission of the classis is still required, even after 1991. As the Supplement to Articles 78-81 indicates, classis monitors "whether proper procedure has been followed," assures that "adequate pastoral care has been extended," and determines that there is good cause "for proceeding with discipline." On the other hand, the "steps" are no longer required, and the consistory is free to use any announcements and liturgical forms it may consider appropriate.

Exclusion from Membership

Technically, exclusion from membership is what we used to refer to as an "erasure" or an "excommunication." The former is the exclusion of a member by baptism; the latter the exclusion of a confessing member.

The disciplinary exclusion of baptized members is applied only when such members have clearly come to the age of discretion. They have made all other basic life choices but have not responded positively to God's promises and his claim on their lives signified by their baptism. They have no desire to confess Christ as Lord and Savior and thus actively to join the church, which is his body, and to which, by baptism, they still belong. If after persistent prayer and pastoral admonition of such persons they do not respond positively, the elders ask for the prayers of the congregation, gain approval of the classis to proceed with the discipline and, ultimately (barring positive response, of course) reluctantly exclude them from membership in the church of Christ by way of announcement to them and to the congregation.

412

The disciplinary exclusion of adult confessing members is not only a biblical and confessional requirement but also an action voluntarily agreed to by a person making public profession of faith. In that profession, that person promises to submit to the admonition and discipline of the church. An excommunication is warranted only upon persistent refusal to heed that discipline. It is done reluctantly, with heavy hearts, and "God himself excludes them from the kingdom of Christ." The goal of excommunication remains that of reconciliation. "Such persons, when promising and demonstrating genuine reform, are received again as members of Christ and of his church" (Q&A 85, Heidelberg Catechism). It is the intention of the third section of this article to make this avenue to readmission utterly clear.

Congregational Involvement

Finally, the consistory is obliged to inform the congregation and "encourage its involvement in both the exclusion from and the readmission to membership." This merely underlines the countercultural biblical message that "the members of the church are accountable to one another" (Article 79). It also makes transparent that officebearers do not inflict disciplinary measures upon individuals with any personal malice but rather lead in a prayerful and patient process of discipline exercised by the church as a whole under their leadership.

What sorts of things qualify or signal the need for exclusion from membership? How serious must they be?

Only one thing signals the need for exclusion: lack of repentance. It doesn't matter what the particular nature of the sin or disobedience is. There is no one righteous, not even one, as Paul says (Rom. 3:9-20). We sin in many and varied ways. So we are never disciplined by reason of our sins alone, in and of themselves (if that were the case, we'd all be excluded), nor are we disciplined in degrees according to the severity of the sin. Rather, we are always and only disciplined by reason of our not wishing to repent, thereby rejecting the freely offered grace of Christ and his transforming work in our lives through the Holy Spirit. What qualifies us to gather around the table of the Lord (church membership) is not that we are perfected but

---

that we acknowledge our total dependence on our Savior and look to him alone to be perfected in a lifelong process of sanctification.

We're becoming increasingly frustrated in our attempts to apply church discipline to members who have become inactive. There's no point to it any more. It never has its desired effect. Instead, we're trying to adopt a more caring approach that is less confrontational. What are your thoughts?

Church discipline is almost always ineffective if it is not tightly wrapped in a caring, invitational, pastoral approach. This is especially true when it is applied to those who are inactive and neglect the means of grace. If those who have silently disappeared from the scene have not been told that they're missed, a warning of exclusion from membership tends only to drive them away. It is my belief that we must never focus on lack of attendance at worship services (that is but one indicator), but that the recipient must clearly hear from us our concerns about the deepest values in their lives and whether they reflect an ongoing walk with God. Only then can we proceed to discuss the necessity of nurturing our life of faith. In that sense, discipline is a lot like evangelism; it is outreach to those who are within. One always starts with an offer of salvation.

An old quip has an inactive member saying: "I have nothing against the Big Captain in the Sky; my beef is with his ground crew." We must avoid the often silent message that everything in the congregation is fine while we sternly wag our finger at the sinner among us. Some have been badly hurt in relationships with other believers. Others have become estranged from the particular way we go about worship. Still others struggle with beliefs badly explained to them. Approaching the inactive with an honest apology for all that the body may have done to hurt and estrange removes the pretense and creates new channels of communication. Some congregations have conducted formal surveys of the inactive, giving them every opportunity to explain what may have gone wrong. The message is, "Your views matter to us, and we will take notice." The responses often suggested new ways of reaching them or, at the very least, cleared the air so they could all get to more fundamental issues.

Transforming the confrontational into the invitational, however, cannot be our final answer. Our creeds commit us to the exercise of the keys of the kingdom. Our covenant commits us to the administration of church discipline. Sometimes, even after all the air is cleared, the fact remains that the inactive no longer display a genuine commitment to Christ. I know it's a parent's worst nightmare, and I find it hard to explain theologically, but in my ministry I've had to face the reality that some turn away in heart, not just in behavior. Here too the pretense must be removed. Exclusion may be indicated at some point. It will be the church's most urgent appeal at the end of a long road, a step reluctantly but decisively taken. In my view such cases must be limited to those where the recipients of our discipline stubbornly deny belief in Christ and deliberately reject him as Savior and Lord. Short of that, the time probably has not come.

I am deeply disturbed by the fact that our minister and elders publicly excommunicated a member during last Sunday's morning service. I know of at least two visitors who found this offensive and have decided that our church—if, indeed, any church at all—is not really for them. In addition, one of the member's relatives was so upset she's looking for another church to join. Is it really necessary to do this in the worship service?

I understand your feelings. I do hope and trust that the relative was notified beforehand in a pastoral manner. Elders have not always remembered this important dimension of discipline cases. I also hope and trust that the prayers uttered on this occasion included a repenting on the part of all members and some indication that the community may have borne some responsibility in things coming to a head in this way. I also hope that you had a long talk with these visitors. Are they aware this was a rare occasion? Do they now know why this was necessary? Did they catch that we weren't Pharisees with fingers pointed only to the sinner but also to ourselves?

I don't know of a specific rule that clearly obligates elders to excommunicate during a worship service. But this traditional practice is clearly implied by the fact that there are liturgical forms for that purpose. It also stands to reason when you consider that all *inclusion* into membership is formalized in a worship setting, deliberately before the face of God: baptism, profession of faith, reaffirmation of faith, and readmission.

I must confess that I have occasionally advised elders to announce disciplinary steps at congregational meetings. This was done, however, to prevent civil lawsuits involving "invasion of privacy." In some cases, this may be wise. However, I have never advised that an excommunication itself, should it be absolutely necessary, may also be withdrawn from the worship setting.

What has helped me in reflecting on these matters is to remember that discipline, at heart, is proclamation of the Word of God. Excommunication is one last powerful sermon: Repent and believe while it is still day! I hope we communicate that to the visitors who by circumstance go through the painful experience with us. They might even come to respect the fact that we take our beliefs seriously.

Does the Heidelberg Catechism in Q&A 85 actually mean that "whatever [we] bind on earth will be bound in heaven, and whatever [we] loose on earth will be loosed in heaven" (Matt. 18:18)? In other words, are we confident that when we exclude folks from membership in the church, "God himself excludes them from the kingdom of Christ"? By our action, these people spend eternity in hell?

I do not draw that conclusion. I think we administer discipline in recognition of our fallibility. We do it humbly. We do it sincerely. But in that sincerity, we are declaring an end to a person's membership in the visible church and thus proclaiming that this person is in danger of being out of fellowship with Christ and his people. This is indeed a stern but deadly serious message. On the other hand, we are not able to make final judgments about this person's membership in the invisible church, the church as only God can see it. We are not saying that this person's name is most definitely excluded from the "book of life" and destined for hell. There is some comfort in knowing that we do not make that final judgment—only God does. In the meantime, we proclaim the gospel of the one who is the "hound of heaven," relentlessly knocking at the doors of our hearts.

IV. The Admonition and Discipline of the Church

Article 82

All officebearers, in addition to being subject to general discipline, are subject to special discipline, which consists of suspension and deposition from office.

"General discipline" concerns the admonition and discipline of members; "special discipline" is that which additionally pertains to those who have been ordained. The former may lead to exclusion from membership; the latter may lead to suspension and deposition from office.

As the Supplement to Articles 82-84 indicates, "general discipline shall not be applied to an officebearer unless he/she has first been suspended from office." The reason, simply, is that ordination to an office is a step beyond confessing membership (Article 3), and this step beyond must first be reversed by suspension or deposition before "general discipline" of the member can occur.

Suspension is a *temporary* removal from office. The church withdraws from the officebearer concerned all authority to perform the tasks of a minister, ministry associate, elder, or deacon for a time. The suspension may be without prejudice. This occurs in instances where the matter at hand requires a thorough investigation that will result in a lifting of the suspension, a suspension with prejudice, or the further step of deposition.

Deposition is a *permanent* removal from office. It need not be preceded by suspension. This is left to the judgment of the "appropriate assembly." The church withdraws authority to perform official tasks for good. It is never without prejudice. Reinstatement is possible in some cases, not all, and then only under clearly prescribed conditions and circumstances (see Article 84).

There is a slightly higher bar for councils to depose ministers of the Word than to depose ministry associates, elders, and deacons. The deposition of a minister of the Word is "not effected without the approval of classis together with the concurring advice of the synodical deputies." We noted a similar higher bar for entry into that office (see Article 9); the same logic applies here. Councils may only suspend a minister and thereafter present their intent to depose to classis. On the other hand, council is free to suspend or depose a ministry associate, elder or deacon.

In all suspensions or depositions, however, the council must receive the "concurring judgment of the council of the nearest church in the same classis." If that council does not concur, the original council must withdraw its original intent or "present the case to classis" (Supplement, Articles 82-84). Thus, the council is held accountable to the broader church in all matters of special discipline. A council of the nearest church and/or the classis must be convinced that the discipline imposed is not wanton or arbitrary but well-founded and necessary for the wellbeing of the congregation and for the church at large.

Synod 1998 adopted some very important guidelines that pertain to special discipline of ministers of the Word. The Supplement to Articles 82-84 advises councils to consult the *Acts of Synod, 1998* (pp. 396-99) if they are called upon to proceed with suspension or deposition.

If we read the Supplement to Articles 82-84 correctly, the council must be involved in the suspension/deposition of an officebearer: the deacons as well as the minister and elders. Is that true? The articles themselves say nothing about that. Some of us believe that discipline is always to be the territory of the consistory, not the council.

Synod 1990 approved a number of changes designed to ensure that the right terminology is being used deliberately and consistently in our Church Order. What was then known as Article 91 on the suspension and deposition of elders and deacons was knowingly changed to read "council" rather than "consistory." The consistory wields "general discipline," but it is the council—all the ordained in that church—that must wield "special discipline." The deacons are to be included. This regulation remains the same even though it is now found only in the terminology of the Supplement to Articles 82-84: the Supplement is a binding synodical decision.

The Supplement to Articles 82-84 indicates that the suspension of a minister of the Word requires the concurring judgment of the council of the nearest church in the same classis. Is this concurrence limited to matters of procedure, or must the neighboring council also form a judgment of substance—for instance, that abuse of office did in fact occur and that it warrants suspension? There seems to be some confusion about this among us.

The provision you indicate makes no such distinction. Whenever a concurring judgment of any kind is mentioned in the Church Order, the substance side of your distinction is almost always included. Safe to say, I think, that this judgment should not be limited to procedural matters alone.

The reason for the necessity of the concurring judgment in this instance is the prevention of wanton or arbitrary suspension. In the spirit of true accountability, the neighboring council should be satisfied that the suspension is being applied for the right reasons and with due cause.

This is why a delegation of the council of the neighboring church should be invited to join such a council in its deliberations from the very beginning of and throughout a disciplinary process.

A retired minister whose credentials are held by our council has committed an offense and is unrepentant. We believe he should be suspended and/or deposed. But he is retired. How do we proceed?

There are two schools of thought on this matter. You might say that one reflects a more "Presbyterian" approach and the other a more

"Continental Reformed" approach. The first interprets Article 18 of the Church Order to mean that the retired minister is still in office and that all the rules of "special discipline" found in Articles 82-84 and their Supplements apply. The other interprets the words "shall retain the title of minister of the Word and the authority, conferred by the church, to perform official acts of ministry" to mean that these persons are no longer in office (they retired from it) and that the only remedy is to deprive them of that title and authority. The problem with the first view (argued eloquently by Van Dellen and Monsma in their *Revised Church Order Commentary*) is that our Church Order in no other place recognizes "inactive officebearers." There is no such thing in Christian Reformed polity, for example, as an inactive elder. An office is never merely a "position"—it is an appointment to certain tasks in the midst of the congregation. Thus, the retention of title and granting of authority simply indicates a continuing accountability in whatever tasks the retired minister still chooses to take on.

If you agree with me that the second interpretation is the one to be preferred, I would suggest that you proceed along lines analogous to those suggested in Articles 82-84 and their Supplements, but that instead of "suspension" or "deposition" you use the phrase "removal of the title of a minister of the Word and of authority to perform official acts of ministry." To rise above any confusion injected by differing interpretations of those who love to dabble in church political theory and to be absolutely clear, you might just indicate in proposals to your classis and in announcements to be made that the action to be taken with respect to the retired minister is the equivalent of suspension and/or deposition from office, whichever is appropriate in your case. That way the difference between Presbyterian and Reformed is not elevated to status of major significance.

IV. The Admonition and Discipline of the Church

Article 83

> Special discipline shall be applied to officebearers if they violate the Form of Subscription, are guilty of neglect or abuse of office, or in any way seriously deviate from sound doctrine and godly conduct.

Special discipline, like general discipline, is focused on both doctrinal and ethical deviation. When officebearers no longer honor their commitment to subscribe to the church's creed in whole or in any part and persist in that error, the council has no option but to suspend or depose. Similarly, when they are guilty of neglect of office or abuse of office, the council must impose the requisite discipline, sometimes even if the person is truly sorry for what has occurred.

There is a solemn obligation to act. Leadership comes with heavy responsibilities. It is possible, from time to time, to allow a member to express reservations about our confessions. On the other hand, when the ordained do this the result is intolerable confusion. The congregation has a right to expect that its leaders will carry out their responsibilities in tune with the beliefs and commitments of the denomination it belongs to. Leaders must also manifest "godly conduct." Neglect of office is not acceptable. Abuse of office is not acceptable, especially when it is the kind of abuse that causes serious harm to parishioners.

In this connection, we note that synods of the CRCNA have adopted "procedures and guidelines for handling abuse allegations against a church leader." These guidelines were first adopted in 1997 upon the recommendation of the denomination's Safe Church Ministry (then known as the Office of Abuse Prevention), updated in 2005 and again in 2010 (*Acts of Synod, 1997*, pp. 674-85; *2005*, pp. 776-77; *2010*, p. 870). The most recent version can always be found at the denominational website: www.crcna.org/safechurch.

Is it not possible for an officebearer to express some reservation about a small part of the creed without immediately being suspended or deposed?

Yes, it is, but only when the officebearer has submitted a formal "confessional-difficulty gravamen" (see Supplement to Article 5). The council then decides whether to tolerate the reservation. If the council is unable to make that judgment, it may submit the matter to the classis and it, in turn, may do the same to the following synod. A judgment by one or more assemblies that the difficulty can't be tolerated must be taken seriously by the officebearer. An appeal, of course, is always an option. If, upon appeal, the church persists and he or she truly cannot in good conscience conform, a resignation is typically offered. If, on the other hand, the officebearer persists, deposition may have to follow.

I understand that if an elder insists on deviating from parts of our creed, and deposition is thus required, the council will need the concurring judgment of the council of the nearest church. But what happens if a large number of officebearers (more than half of the council) are guilty of such deviation, persist in it, and thus all need to be deposed? How does that take place? It's not likely that the council will impose this upon itself, is it?

Deposition from office is indeed the action of a local council. So if there's one person to be deposed, the council deposes. If there are more, the council deposes the minority—not as a group but one at a time as individuals.

If there's a majority to be deposed, you're quite right, the council would most assuredly fail to do so, or to go to the neighboring congregation or classis to request permission. The minority of council could ask for it, of course, and send an appeal from the decision of the council as a whole not to do so to the classis, but classis would likely be reluctant to sustain such an appeal.

Nonetheless, there have been rare occasions where classis has deposed an entire council or a majority of a council (not as a group, but naming the individuals). Synod 1982, in response to an appeal, declared that "it is indeed proper according to Reformed Church polity for either classis or synod to intervene in the affairs of a local congregation, if the welfare of that congregation is at stake." Relatively recent actions of this kind are those of Classis Huron toward the council of Goderich in 1980 and of Classis Lake Erie towards the Washington, Pennsylvania, council in 1991. Both involved the conduct of ministers and of councils that, in majority, continued to back them.

Less recent instances occurred in 1924 in Grand Rapids with respect to the "common grace" controversy and in 1921 in Sioux Center with respect to the appointment of certain Sunday school teachers. Even further back, we note a situation involving a dispute about a custodian in Zeeland in 1864 where Classis West Michigan came in and "dissolved" the entire council (a euphemism for deposition) and arranged for a new election. The same action was taken to address a controversy surrounding Gysbert Haan in Grand Rapids in 1861. In these early stages of CRCNA history, there seemed to be little caution expressed about such intervention on the part of a broader assembly. It was especially the influence of Abraham Kuyper's church political theories (a more "Congregationalist" approach) that produced the necessary caution in the twentieth century and beyond.

If this interests you, may I suggest that you read all about these matters in Chapter 7 of my dissertation, entitled *Equipping the Saints*? Or would that be terribly immodest on my part?

Our minister was recently confronted with what we believe to be sexual abuse. He has asked that we allow him to resign in order to transfer to another denomination. Must we grant such a request?

No, you must deny his request. We may never shrug from our responsibility to impose special discipline or avoid it by passing him on without comment to another church fellowship. You've probably seen the kind of damage that has done, if not in our own denomination, then certainly in others. Sexual abuse of parishioners is a horrible betrayal of trust. Not to decisively label it as a serious violation of God's will and act accordingly is to distort the gospel, making unbelievers even more upset about what they perceive to be the church's flagrant hypocrisy.

IV. The Admonition and Discipline of the Church

Article 84

> Persons who have been suspended or deposed from office may be reinstated if they give sufficient evidence of repentance and if the church judges that they are able to serve effectively. Requests for reinstatement to office by those deposed for acts of sexual abuse or sexual misconduct shall be dealt with according to guidelines adopted by synod.

Reinstatement to office after suspension is typically referred to as a "lifting" of the suspension. The term *reinstatement* applies more readily to one who has previously been deposed.

As with all general discipline, it is manifestly clear that there must be sufficient evidence of repentance before special discipline can be withdrawn or "reversed." We might even go further and insist that there must be complete reconciliation as well as repentance. A person might come to an inner sense of complete repentance, and be quite sincere in the belief that he or she is contrite before the Lord and has now been forgiven. But reconciliation involves others, specific individuals who were harmed or a community of fellow believers that was dishonored. Furthermore, repentance is something that is evidenced and tested over time, with the understanding that the emotional experience of repentance is followed by the hard work of changing behavior. This is true in matters of "general discipline" but even more so in matters pertaining to reinstatement to office.

We can be more specific on this point of "reconciliation." If a person wishes to be reinstated, the church must make a judgment not only about repentance but also about whether that person is "able to serve effectively." Older language in our Church Order spoke of this as "being able to serve without the handicap of one's past sin." It is within the prerogative of an assembly to deny reinstatement to a truly contrite and repentant person. One can rejoice in that repentance, of course, but the real issue is whether this person can ever truly be a leader again, be a recognized Christ-representative, and be this without compromising the implicit role of model to the Christian community.

Ever since 2004, the CRCNA has insisted that acts of sexual abuse or sexual misconduct are so serious that important guidelines now apply to requests for reinstatement. These are found in the Supplement to Article 84. Reinstatement will be denied if such misconduct was against a minor, against more than one victim in a single church or community, in more than one community or church, or together with other related ungodly conduct such as pornography, voyeuristic behavior, and the like. In addition, a minister will not be reinstated in any other cases of sexual misconduct beyond these categories unless the church has received legal counsel and the advice of a licensed psychologist regarding possible re-offense.

The suspension of an officebearer requires the concurrence of a neighboring congregation (Supplement, Articles 82-84). Does the lifting of the suspension or, for that matter, the reinstatement to office likewise require the concurrence of a neighboring church?

In the case of ministers of the Word, a reinstatement after *deposition* requires approval of classis and synodical deputies. Any concurrence of the council of the neighboring church is then not a separate matter because that council also belongs to the classis, and its delegates have a vote.

A lifting of *suspension* of any officebearer does not require the concurrence of a neighboring church. The only thing the Supplement to these articles says about this is that it is "the prerogative of the assembly which imposed the suspension," the local council. Consulting with the neighboring church might be a matter of wisdom but it is not required.

In the case of ministry associates, elders, or deacons, a reinstatement after deposition is similar to a lifting of a suspension. It can be done by the council acting entirely on its own. It is best accomplished by way of a process of nomination, selection, and re-ordination.

Is it possible for a divorced person to serve or continue to serve as a minister of the Word?

The question you pose obviously arises out of life experience filled with much pain. You should know that I was touched by your letter. It is very compelling. I wish everyone could read the three-page narrative you sent me and taste just a bit of your situation back then and today. But I promised you I'd keep it all in confidence. So I will. As you also suggested, the question you end with is asked by many others and requires a public response even if it is on a less personal basis. I'll give it a shot.

Our Church Order says that only those persons who "meet the biblical requirements" are eligible for office. Passages like 1 Timothy 3 and Titus 1 teach that, among other things, an "overseer" must "be above reproach," "have a good reputation with outsiders," and be "self-controlled, upright, holy and disciplined." These and other passages are read every time officebearers are ordained. They are familiar to us. The challenge, of course, is for our councils and broader assemblies to apply them in specific cases of ministers who experience divorce or wish to be remarried.

Are there clear rules for applying them? The Church Order offers no *specific* guidance here. The section on suspension and deposition, for example, uses the language of "deviation from godly conduct." In addition, most synodical regulations and guidelines on divorce and remarriage address membership. Officebearing is not in view. The one has to do with the other, of course, but they are not the same. More can be expected of our ministers. This leaves us with little to go on except precedent, case law.

Research in this area is very difficult. Most information is kept in confidential minutes of our assemblies. I do have personal knowledge of recent stories: stories of divorcees ordained to the office, of ministers being suspended or deposed, of those who applied for reinstatement—some allowed and some denied reentry. Based on those anecdotes alone, I can say yes, it is possible today for a divorced or remarried person to serve in the office. It happens. Everything depends on the circumstances and the spiritual condition of the one involved.

For a very long time, I simply *assumed* what case law might have been before I arrived on the scene, namely, that our denomination absolutely did not permit divorced persons to serve in office, period. Challenged by your letter, I finally did the little research that *can* be done in public records. The result was a huge surprise to me.

I was not surprised by the stand taken by Synod 1894: divorce is permitted for the "innocent party" only in cases of adultery or desertion by an unbelieving partner. And when this assembly was asked whether a minister petitioning for a divorce for a different reason could stay on, it said: "Of course not!" The surprise came in the story that unfolded during the next six years, probably involving the same minister. Even though synod had warned against it, he was officially divorced. In response, synod insisted that he seek from the court an annulment of the divorce decree and attempt reconciliation. As might be expected, the court responded by saying that there was no such thing as an annulment of a divorce and that only a remarriage to the divorced spouse could accomplish the purpose. When the minister next convinced Synod 1900 that he had made numerous attempts but that his former wife was totally unresponsive to his pleas, the assembly actually made the judgment that the church may "carry him in love in his present position." Even then, apparently, it was possible, and it happened.

A study committee reporting in 1980 wrote that the church must consider "the multiplicity of personal factors which surround particular cases. . . ." Factors such as "repentance for personal failure in the breakdown of the previous marriage," "forgiveness of others," "understanding of the divinely intended permanence of marriage," and "a renewed dependence on the grace of God for the success of the remarriage" must be weighed very carefully. This is said about members in general. When it comes to reinstatement to ministry, of course, there is the additional consideration of whether the person involved is "able to serve effectively" (Church Order, Article 84) or, as we used to say with greater clarity, "could then serve without being hindered in his work by the handicap of his past sin" and whether "his restoration would be to the glory of God and for the true welfare of the church" (e.g., Church Order, 1983, Article 94).

You can see the need for our Lord to grant our assemblies sharp and true spiritual discernment in the midst of brokenness, pain, and a great deal of unmerited grace.

Conclusion

Article 85

No church shall in any way lord it over another church, and no officebearer shall lord it over another officebearer.

This first of two concluding articles in the Church Order of the CRCNA is reminiscent of the second sentence of Article 2: "These offices differ from each other only in mandate and task, not in dignity and honor." As we saw earlier with respect to that article, Reformed church government acknowledges this parity of all offices. There is to be no essential hierarchy. Since Christ is Lord of all and our *only* Lord, officebearers must refrain from "lording it over" others.

Article 85 is also reminiscent of Article 27. As we noted there, Reformed church government does not hold to an *absolute* autonomy or independence of local congregations. Instead, it acknowledges a "relative autonomy," the right to reasonable space within denominational fellowship, but not without an obligation also to strive for the collective rights and interests of all. Together the churches have sought and continue to seek "the unity of the Spirit through the bond of peace" (Eph. 4:3). Thus, all congregations, regardless of size, have equal voice and equal responsibility at broader or governing assemblies (Articles 39, 45). These assemblies, however, are vehicles of denominational cooperation, not ruling bodies with sovereign sway over all things local. Since Christ is Lord of all and our *only* Lord, "no church shall in any way lord it over another."

> **I thought that the original "anti-hierarchical" provisions of the Church Orders of the sixteenth century Reformation referred to ministers not lording it over other ministers and elders and deacons not lording it over other elders and deacons. How is it that our current Article 85 does not faithfully follow that reading?**
>
> You're right. The earlier provisions read as follows:
>
> > Equality shall be maintained among the ministers of the Word with respect to the duties of their office and in all other matters as far as possible, according to the judgment of the consistory and, if necessary, of the classis. Likewise equality shall be maintained among the elders and deacons.
> >
> > There shall be no lordship in God's church, whether of one church over another church, of one minister over other ministers, or of one elder or deacon over other elders or deacons.
>
> In both cases there is room for the interpretation that the principle of "equality" applies only *within* the office of minister of the Word and also only *within* the offices of elder and deacon, not to all officebearers. These articles reflect the idea of a *functional* hierarchy whereby the ministry of the Word is considered to be more significant to the life of the church than the services of elders and deacons. On the other hand, notions of *essential* hierarchy are clearly inconsistent with the Reformed tradition. So Synod 1965 felt perfectly free to end all ambiguity in earlier formulations by adopting the current statement that clearly acknowledges a parity of all offices.
>
> I remain curious as to why you raise the issue. If you're a historian I forgive you. If, on the other hand, you're a minister on a "power play"

looking to rule the roost among the elders and deacons the Lord has placed in your path, I do more than forgive you: I admonish you to be humble and bow before collective judgment.

Conclusion

Article 86

> This Church Order, having been adopted by common consent, shall be faithfully observed, and any revision thereof shall be made only by synod.

Words such as these are a feature of every federal government's constitution. Without them, participating states or provinces can revise whatever stands in their way and the society as a whole will quickly crumble into anarchy. This is true of every civil organization. There's such a thing as due process. This is equally true for the church, especially so when we confess that it is "to be governed according to the spiritual order that our Lord has taught us in his Word" (Belgic Confession, Article 30).

If member churches of the CRCNA can defy the plain intent of the church's constitution, the denomination quickly breaks up into a collection of independent groups that become a law unto themselves. The result is a stifling congregationalism or, even worse, a crippling form of ecclesiastical anarchy that plays havoc on those we are called to serve. As we have seen with respect to Article 1, well-founded order and sound leadership inspired by God's Word allows Christ truly to be "the only head of the church" and "the only universal bishop" of our souls (Belgic Confession, Article 31).

It unites us to one another, a gift of grace Christ prayed for (John 17). Biblically based order does not place roadblocks on our way through history. It thoroughly enhances the mission our Lord has given us.

Just as it ought to be, especially in the churches of the Reformation, revision of the Church Order is entirely possible. It is even necessary. The CRCNA, like all other denominations, is on a pilgrimage. It moves through different times, places, and circumstances. Yet as it does, it must continue to test all of its specific polity against the general rules drawn from the Word— the Word that abides unchanged. Our congregations have agreed to do that only at our broadest assembly, the synod that represents us all. Should any person, council, or classis have a better way to travel, that person or assembly is bound to share this wisdom with us all so that we all can benefit.

Our classis recently decided to adopt the Belhar Confession as one of our creeds along with the current six creeds and confessions. I don't think classis has the authority to do this. What can we do about it?

You're right, classis doesn't. Article 47 is eminently clear when it says that "the task of synod includes the adoption of creeds. . . ." The broadest assembly also regulates the content of the "Form of Subscription" that includes a precise listing of creeds and confessions every officebearer must assent to at appropriate occasions (see Article 5).

So here's what you need to do. You must send your congregation's delegates to the next meeting and have them insist that all other delegates (without exception) write a hundred times in their notepads: "The adoption of creeds is the task of synod alone." After that, and only then, have them consider the written protest you will place on the agenda in advance. If they persist in their naive or willful disobedience (I will not judge which adjective fits best) and formally reject your protest, you will have to appeal to synod. In a day when synods often feel ignored, I'm sure the assembly receiving your appeal will be more than delighted to use the clear language of Article 47 and descend upon your classis with appropriate indignation.

I'm copying this response to some of my students for their benefit. Hope you don't mind!

I think I know which classis did this. . . .

Shhh! It doesn't matter. Someone's already started fixing it.

Index

Note: Numbers in parentheses refer to Church Order articles. Principal article(s) are listed first, then, after the semicolon, secondary references in other articles.